ABOUT THE AUTHOR

Dr Sarah Edelman is a clinical psychologist, author and trainer. In addition to her clinical work, Sarah conducts training programs for psychologists, industry and the public. In the past she worked at the University of Technology Sydney as a researcher and lecturer. She has published articles in professional and mainstream journals and is a regular guest on ABC radio.

CHANGE *YOUR* THINKING
WITH CBT

OVERCOME STRESS, COMBAT ANXIETY AND IMPROVE YOUR LIFE

Dr Sarah Edelman

Vermilion
LONDON

17 19 20 18

Vermilion, an imprint of Ebury Publishing,
20 Vauxhall Bridge Road,
London SW1V 2SA

Vermilion is part of the Penguin Random House group of companies
whose addresses can be found at global.penguinrandomhouse.com

Penguin
Random House
UK

This edition published in the United Kingdom by Vermilion in 2018
First published in the United Kingdom by Vermilion in 2006

www.penguin.co.uk

A CIP catalogue record for this book is available from the British Library

ISBN 9780091906955

Printed and bound in Great Britain by Clays Ltd, St Ives PLC

Penguin Random House is committed to a sustainable future for our business, our readers
and our planet. This book is made from Forest Stewardship Council® certified paper.

The information in this book has been compiled by way of general guidance in relation
to the specific subjects addressed, but it is not a substitute and not to be relied on for
medical, healthcare, pharmaceutical or other professional advice on specific circumstances and in specific locations. Please consult your GP before changing, stopping or
starting any medical treatment. So far as the author is aware the information given is
correct and up to date as at March 2018. Practice, laws and regulations all change, and
the reader should obtain up to date professional advice on any such issue. The author
and the publishers disclaim, as far as the law allows, any liability arising directly or
indirectly from the use or misuse of the information contained in this book.

Contents

I think these difficult times
have helped me to understand better than before
how infinitely rich and beautiful life is in every way
and that so many things one goes around worrying about
are of no importance whatsoever.

KAREN BLIXEN

Introduction

The greatest discovery of my generation is that a human being can alter his life by altering his attitudes of mind.

WILLIAM JAMES (1842–1910)

Have you ever found yourself ruminating over some issue for hours or days, and later realised that it wasn't really important after all? Or maybe you have experienced a time when you were feeling upset about a particular issue, and then you talked it over with a friend. They said some things that you hadn't thought about, and when you took their ideas on board you felt much better? Talking to your friend showed you another way of thinking about your situation, and when you started to think differently, your feelings changed.

Every day we experience situations that demonstrate the simple principle—the way we think determines the way we feel. Things go wrong; people act selfishly; disappointments happen. Whether or not we get upset by them and the degree of distress we feel depends largely on our thinking. Sometimes we can make ourselves feel very miserable, even when our life circumstances are really not that bad, by thinking in a negative, self-defeating way. While we may blame people or life events for our unhappiness, it is actually our perceptions that create our suffering.

This is good news because while we may not be able to change people or our life circumstances, we can change the way we think about them. And if we can learn to think in a healthy balanced way, we can stop upsetting ourselves unnecessarily.

Changing the way we think about things changes the way we feel. This simple concept is a key principle of cognitive behaviour therapy (CBT for short)—an approach that is used in psychological therapy and stress management programs all over the world. (The word 'cognitive' refers to thought processes. Therefore a cognitive therapy is one that helps us to change aspects of our thinking.)

Since the 1970s, CBT has emerged as the most common form of psychological therapy used by mental-health practitioners. This is because studies conducted around the world have shown CBT to be helpful in the management of a wide range of psychological problems, including anxiety, depression, panic attacks, sleep problems, phobias, relationship difficulties, shyness, eating disorders, anger, drug and alcohol abuse, sexual dysfunction, post-traumatic stress disorder, chronic pain, health problems, bipolar disorder and social phobia. While different components of the CBT approach are used for treating different problems, the focus is always on changing cognitions and behaviours.

CBT has been described as a 'living therapy' because it continues to evolve over time. The techniques that make up current CBT treatments have been evaluated at research institutions around the world and their results have been compared to waitlist control groups, other psychological treatments, sham treatments and placebo pills. The findings of these studies are continually being published in psychology journals and presented at conferences. Through this process new treatments are developed, and earlier treatments are modified and improved. Psychologists then update the techniques that they use, based on the findings of the most recent research.

While CBT was originally developed for the treatment of particular disorders, it is now widely used by people wanting to reduce stress and improve their quality of life. CBT strategies are helpful in the management of daily life stressors—from minor hassles to major psychological challenges. Because the principles of CBT are easy to learn, the approach is highly suitable for use as a self-help tool.

In recent years, mindfulness-based techniques have been added to treatments widely used by psychologists. Based on ancient Buddhist practices, mindfulness has been popularised in the West, prompted by the pioneering work of Professor of Medicine Emeritus at the University of Massachusetts, Jon Kabat-Zinn. A large body of research is currently under way examining the effects of mindfulness practices for various psychological conditions. Emerging evidence suggests that mindfulness techniques may augment treatment outcomes when combined with CBT strategies. For this reason a chapter on mindfulness has been added to this edition of *Change Your Thinking*.

This book describes how to apply the principles of CBT to potentially stressful events that arise in our daily life. Readers will learn to recognise some of their own thinking patterns that create unnecessary distress, and they will discover strategies to help modify these. This may involve taking certain actions, as well as challenging some of the thoughts and beliefs that contribute to unhappiness.

Although this book is designed for self-help, it is not a substitute for psychological therapy. If you suffer from a particular psychological problem or disorder (e.g. depression, obsessive compulsive disorder, eating disorder, bipolar disorder, etc.), it is important to receive treatment from a qualified mental-health professional. While *Change Your Thinking* may help to reinforce some of the information provided during treatment, it does not cover specific disorders in detail. Books that describe CBT approaches to managing specific psychological problems are listed in the Recommended Reading section at the end of this book.

ONE

Cognitive Behaviour Therapy (CBT)

We are what we think.
All that we are arises with our thoughts.
With our thoughts we make the world.

BUDDHA

SOME HISTORY

In the first half of the 20th century, Sigmund Freud's theories of the mind and his approach to psychological therapy dominated Western psychiatry. Freud believed that all psychological problems are driven by repressed unconscious longings from early childhood, and his therapeutic approach, called 'psychoanalysis', involved daily sessions, sometimes for many years, exploring the depths of his patients' unconscious minds. The goal of psychoanalytic therapy was to enable patients to gain insight into the source of their unhappiness, and through this process free themselves from repressed desires, and the resulting psychological distress.

In the 1950s, other psychotherapeutic approaches started to emerge. Among these were some derived directly from Freud's theories (including 'psychodynamic', 'existential' and 'humanistic' psychotherapies), and others that took a very different approach. The most significant of these was later to become known as Cognitive Behaviour Therapy (CBT).

The two most influential figures in the development of CBT were psychologist Albert Ellis and psychiatrist Aaron Beck. Both started their careers as Freudian therapists and both ultimately became disillusioned with psychoanalysis. **Albert Ellis** criticised the painstakingly slow exploration of childhood experiences that was central to psychoanalysis, as well as many of Freud's underlying theories. In the early 1960s, Ellis started to focus on the role of thoughts and beliefs in creating psychological distress. He argued that individuals upset themselves by thinking irrationally, and that psychological problems can be resolved by teaching people to think in a more rational, balanced way. He developed a therapy that encouraged patients to focus on what was happening in their lives and challenge some of the irrational thoughts and underlying beliefs that were contributing to their distress. Ellis's style of therapy was initially called 'Rational Therapy' and subsequently changed to 'Rational Emotive Therapy' (RET), to reflect that the aim of therapy was to apply rational thinking to change emotional responses. In the 1990s, the name was changed to Rational Emotive Behaviour Therapy (REBT), to acknowledge that behavioural strategies play an important role in this approach.

Aaron Beck made his initial contribution to the development of CBT in the area of depression. He observed that depressed individuals have faulty or distorted thinking patterns. These stem from what he called **schemas**—core beliefs developed in childhood in response to early life events, which bias the way we subsequently perceive our experiences. Beck described schemas as 'templates' we unconsciously use to determine the meanings we give to our experiences. Schemas like 'I am inferior', 'people can't be trusted', 'I will be abandoned' or 'the world is dangerous' influence the content of people's thoughts in day-to-day situations, and therefore contribute to distress and psychological problems. Like Ellis, Beck maintained that the aim of therapy should be to help individuals recognise and change faulty thinking and self-defeating behaviours, using a variety of cognitive and behavioural strategies.

While Ellis used the term 'irrational' to describe thoughts and beliefs that give rise to emotional distress, others have used words like 'negative', 'maladaptive', 'unhelpful', 'unrealistic', 'faulty' and 'self-defeating'. The various terms are used interchangeably throughout this book to convey the idea of thoughts, beliefs and perceptions that make us feel bad or behave in self-defeating ways. While there are differences in some of the techniques and terminology used by various schools of CBT, the underlying aim is to help individuals alleviate distress by modifying unhelpful cognitions and behaviours. CBT treatments for particular problems have been repeatedly revised and updated since the time when Ellis and Beck first started describing their ideas. As research continues to uncover new findings, more effective treatments continue to evolve.

CBT STRATEGIES

CBT strategies comprise the following:

Cognitive strategies: learning to recognise the negative thinking habits that create distress, and using various techniques to develop more reasonable ways of thinking.

Behavioural strategies: undertaking various behaviours that help us to change the way we think and feel. These include behavioural experiments, repeated exposure to feared situations, practising deep relaxation and breathing techniques, problem solving, goal setting, using assertive communication, utilising social support and activity scheduling.

In recent years a third component has been added to many CBT treatments:

Mindfulness strategies: bringing one's full attention to present-moment experiences with an attitude of openness and curiosity. This may include awareness of one's breath, thoughts, emotions or body sensations as they arise. Through meditation and mindful attention during daily life experiences, thoughts come to be seen as objects of the mind rather than 'reality' or 'truth' (see Chapter 12 on Mindfulness).

COGNITIONS

Our **cognitions** are mental processes including the thoughts, beliefs and attitudes that we operate with on a daily basis. Some of our cognitions are conscious, or may be brought to conscious awareness through brief reflection. Other cognitions are unconscious, and may require more specific processing in order to be brought to awareness. Still others will always remain unconscious.

While they are related, our thoughts and beliefs are not the same thing. **Thoughts** are transient and often conscious. It has been estimated that the average person has between 4,000 and 7,000 thoughts each day. Most of the time we are not aware that we are thinking; however, if we are to stop and observe our current thoughts we can usually identify their presence. Our thoughts influence the way we feel and behave.

Beliefs are reasonably stable and usually unconscious assumptions that we make about ourselves, others and the world. Although we can sometimes consciously think about our beliefs and even challenge their validity, we don't do this most of the time. Our beliefs influence the contents of our thoughts, as well as our emotions and behaviours.

> *Bob narrowly avoids a car accident when another motorist fails to give way to him. As he gestures angrily at the other driver, Bob thinks to himself, 'Stupid idiot!'*

Bob's thoughts are easy to identify—'Stupid idiot!' But what about the beliefs that gave rise to them? Like many people, Bob believes that *others should always do the right thing*—and, in particular, *they should obey the road laws*. In fact, it was this belief, and not the other person's poor driving, that made Bob feel angry. If Bob only held a preference that people should obey the road laws rather than a belief that they *must always* do so, Bob would have responded with brief irritation rather than anger. Similarly, if you believe that people must always do the right thing, chances are you are going to get upset on occasions when they don't.

EMOTIONS

We all know what it feels like to be happy, sad, fearful, angry, disgusted or surprised, but what exactly are emotions? They are actually difficult to define. In general terms, emotions can be described as the way we **feel** in our mind and body in response to events that occur. They originate from a **trigger**, which may be:

➤ an *external event* (e.g. noise from next door; a comment from a friend) or
➤ an *internal event* such as a *body sensation* (e.g. tightness in the chest, surge of heat) or a *thought* (e.g. 'I said a silly thing', 'I will be alone all day', 'I did a great job').

The resulting emotions include a combination of cognitive appraisals and physiological responses.

Cognitive appraisal (the way we think about things) is based on the meaning that we give to the event. So, for instance, if your friend has not returned your call, you may feel angry ('She only calls when she needs something'), worried ('I hope she's OK'), indifferent ('She's so busy; I'll need to call her again') or hurt ('She doesn't care about me'). Our appraisals can be brought to consciousness quite readily; however, sometimes it may be difficult to identify what we are perceiving at the time (for instance, when you feel upset, scared or annoyed but don't know why).

Physiological response (e.g. increased heart rate; tightness in tummy muscles or chest; feelings of heat, arousal, heaviness, etc.)—as emotions always involve physical sensations, to get in touch with emotions, people are often encouraged to 'notice what's happening in your body'.

EMOTIONS MOTIVATE BEHAVIOURS

Emotions evolved as signals to motivate behaviours and help us to survive. By feeling pleasant (e.g. happiness, love, excitement) or unpleasant (e.g. anxiety, guilt, hurt, despair), they direct our attention to issues we perceive to be significant, and motivate us to respond by *doing* something. As we want to experience pleasant emotions and avoid unpleasant ones, both types of emotion play a role in motivation, although the desire to avoid unpleasant emotions is the stronger motivator.

Unpleasant emotions alert us to issues that need our attention, and motivate us to address them. Doing so helps us to achieve things that contribute to our wellbeing.

For example:

➤ Kirstin's anxiety motivates her to work on her essay over the weekend.
➤ Neil's anger motivates him to communicate assertively with his supervisor.
➤ Corrine's loneliness motivates her to join a singles group.
➤ Sid's guilt motivates him to turn off the TV and take his children to the park.

Sometimes, however, we respond to unpleasant emotions by trying to numb them, rather than addressing the issue they are alerting us to. Our actions may provide short-term relief but do not address the original problem and, consequently, the unpleasant emotions continue to dog us.

For example:

➤ Cheryl procrastinates doing her tax because she finds it boring.
➤ Laura avoids medical appointments because of anxiety about her health.
➤ Leonie numbs anger and fear by playing on poker machines.
➤ Chris avoids social situations because they make him feel sad and inadequate.
➤ Jim responds to feelings of guilt by drinking to excess.

Pleasant emotions are sometimes the 'carrot' that motivates us to make sacrifices in the 'now'. Behaviours such as working long hours, cleaning the house, going to the gym or putting in a long day with the kids are often done in the knowledge that rewards (feeling good) will come later. Pleasant emotions, such as joy, personal satisfaction, feelings of security or self-worth are the long-term rewards that motivate us to put our current desires on hold. However, as with unpleasant emotions, their pursuit can also motivate us to engage in self-defeating behaviours. This may happen when we pursue short-term rewards at the expense of longer-term benefits, such as living beyond our means, partying too hard or pursuing an exciting romance that we know is going to end in tears.

COGNITIONS AFFECT EMOTIONS

Our cognitive appraisals—the ways we think about the things happening in our lives—determine our emotions. Some examples are demonstrated below:

COGNITION	EMOTION
Something bad might happen.	anxiety
They did a bad thing and they shouldn't be able to get away with it.	anger
I did a bad thing, and I deserve to be punished.	guilt
Things are going really well for me.	contentment
I have lost something that I value.	sadness
The world is a bad place, I am a worthless person, and the future is hopeless.	depression
I did an immoral thing and people think badly of me.	shame
Things are not going the way that they should.	frustration
Something good is going to happen.	excitement
That is repulsive.	disgust
I am inferior to others.	inadequacy
I am a bad person.	self-loathing
That's not what I expected.	surprise
S/he does things to deliberately hurt me.	contempt

EMOTIONS AFFECT COGNITIONS

Not only do our cognitions influence our emotions, but our emotions also influence our cognitions. Indeed, the 'content' of our thoughts and the meanings we give to current events is shaped by the emotions we are experiencing at the time. So, for example, when we feel angry, many of our thoughts focus on perceived injustice and desire for revenge. When we feel depressed we interpret events in a negative way, often perceiving failure, hopelessness and rejection where it does not exist. When we feel anxious we focus on threats, and start to perceive dangers in situations we would normally view as harmless.

BEHAVIOURS

Behaviours include the way we respond in specific situations, as well as our regular habits and routines. Our cognitions play a central role in influencing our behaviours. Below are some examples:

COGNITION	BEHAVIOURS
I must be loved and approved of by everyone.	Excessively try to please others; avoid assertive behaviour.
I must do things perfectly.	Procrastinate; perform slowly and inefficiently.
Making mistakes is an opportunity to learn—it's not a catastrophe.	Willing to try again—several times, if necessary—to reach goals.
People should do what I believe is right.	Unfriendly or hostile towards those who do not meet expectations.
I am likeable and worthwhile. People respond positively towards me.	Willing to reach out to people, initiate friendships and take social risks.
My life should be easy—I shouldn't do things that are difficult or not enjoyable.	Avoid activities that are challenging or unpleasant, even if they are for the best.
I am incompetent.	Avoid trying to learn new things.
I must have someone stronger than myself whom I can rely on; I can't cope on my own.	Stay in unhealthy, loveless or destructive relationships; tolerate abusive treatment.
I can get anything I want if I'm willing to work hard towards it.	Willing to spend time and effort in working towards goals.
If I want something, I must have it immediately.	Engage in addictive behaviour, such as drinking alcohol, smoking, taking drugs, poor diet, etc.
Everyone is trying their best. No one deserves to be judged or condemned.	Get on well with most people.
I am flawed; I am not OK.	Self-monitoring in social interactions; avoid eye contact; avoid taking social risks.

BEHAVIOURS AFFECT EMOTIONS AND COGNITIONS

While our emotions affect our behaviours, the reverse is also true—our behaviours influence our emotions. This happens in two ways. Firstly, certain behaviours have a direct mood-enhancing effect. Secondly, some behaviours affect our cognitions, which in turn influence the way we feel.

THE DIRECT MOOD-ENHANCING EFFECT OF BEHAVIOUR

We have all experienced situations where changing our behaviour made a difference to the way we feel. Perhaps at a time when you were feeling down, you made a decision to telephone a friend, and doing so made you feel better. Or perhaps you did some physical exercise, played some music or became absorbed in an interesting project. Actions such as these can lift our spirits because they are inherently pleasurable, and distract us from negative thoughts. Doing things that give us a sense of achievement or purpose is also spirit-lifting. For this reason cleaning out a cupboard, painting a room, writing a letter or finishing an outstanding job can make us feel good.

THE INDIRECT EFFECT OF BEHAVIOUR ON THE WAY WE FEEL— VIA COGNITIONS

Many of our behaviours serve to reinforce existing cognitions. For instance, avoiding social contact with other people can reinforce the belief that we are not OK, or that people don't like us. This in turn may lead to feelings of loneliness, depression or poor self-esteem. Behaving unassertively much of the time may reinforce the belief that it's not acceptable to ask for what we want. The behaviour reinforces our feelings of inadequacy. Choosing to avoid situations that we fear reinforces the belief that those situations are highly threatening. As a result, we feel anxious whenever we need to confront those situations. Trying to do things perfectly all the time reinforces the belief that everything we do must be perfect. As a consequence, we become anxious or immobilised in situations where we may not be able to do a perfect job.

Conversely, changing some of our behaviours can help us to think differently about our situation, and feel better as a result. For instance, initiating social contact may help to challenge the belief that we are incapable of making friends, and our new cognition—'I can make friends when I make the effort'—may cause us to feel better about ourselves. Confronting some of the things we fear—the dreaded social function, the speech or that unpleasant phone call—can lead us to stop perceiving those situations as highly threatening, and our revised cognitions—'I can handle it; it's not so bad'—help to reduce our anxiety in those situations. Completing some tasks less than perfectly can help us to recognise that things don't have to be perfect, and this revised belief frees us from unnecessary anxiety. Communicating assertively in order to resolve a conflict can make us realise that we are capable of solving certain problems, and to feel happier as a result. Doing certain things that we keep putting off (e.g. doing your tax return, having the in-laws for dinner, painting the bedroom) can help us to recognise that they are not so bad after all, and so reduces our guilt and frustration, and increases our confidence. And, believe it or not, being nice to someone we dislike can enable us to perceive them more positively and feel more comfortable in their presence. All of these behaviours can help us to feel better through their influence on our cognitions (see also Chapter 3).

Cognitions, emotions and behaviours interact with and influence each other. Understanding the interrelationship is helpful because it reminds us that making a positive change in one of these areas will have a positive effect on the others. The strategies described in the following chapters provide ways in which such changes can be made.

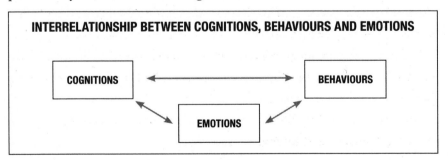

WHY DO WE THINK THE WAY WE DO?

As cognitions play such an important role in the way we feel and behave, the question arises: 'Why do I think this way?' And why is it that some people think in a healthy, balanced way most of the time, while others have negative, biased and self-defeating perceptions much of the time?

The answer lies in the various influences that have shaped our thinking over the course of our lives. Most important of these are:

➤ early infancy—the bonds that were formed with our parents during our infancy, based on their love, availability and responsiveness to our needs;

➤ childhood experiences—the messages we received from our parents, as well as significant others (e.g. grandparents, siblings, teachers, school friends, etc.) during childhood and adolescence; and

➤ temperament—aspects of our personality that are innate (i.e. biologically determined).

Events that occur early in our lives influence the way we subsequently think and feel. Individuals who were fortunate enough to have loving, emotionally attuned, sensible parents are more likely to develop the capacity for dealing with stress or adversity, compared to those who were not. At the other end, those who experienced neglect, trauma or abuse during childhood are more likely to suffer emotional difficulties later in life. However, while early life experiences play an important role, even those who had good parenting may develop psychological problems because temperament (see below) also influences the way we think and feel. Conversely, some individuals who suffered adversity in childhood manage to develop a healthy psychological outlook in adulthood due to their inherently resilient nature.

In addition to early life experiences, other factors at various stages of life also influence our thinking. These include:

➤ key relationships throughout our lives, including our partners, friends, family members and work colleagues;

➤ significant experiences, including achievements, losses, failures, successes and rejections;

> ➤ the accumulated messages we receive from the popular culture via social media, TV, billboards, magazines, newspapers and cinema; and

> ➤ the knowledge and information we acquire through various sources, including the internet, reading, courses and educational institutions.

THE ROLE OF TEMPERAMENT

While there is no gene for negative thinking, biological factors influence the way we respond to situations, and the meanings we give to them. Our **temperament** is the biologically determined component of our personality.

Aspects of temperament are often visible in early childhood, sometimes as early as just a few months of age. Some people are born with a nervous system that is very sensitive to change or threats, and are therefore particularly prone to experiencing upsetting emotions like anxiety, depression and anger. Some have a highly anxious temperament and therefore perceive lots of neutral events as threatening ('Why is that van driving in this street?'; 'Why is my right cheek so red?'). Others have a melancholic temperament, and are therefore more likely to perceive themselves and their experiences in a negative way ('I have achieved very little today'; 'I have failed yet again'). Some are introverted by nature, and may therefore be particularly shy or sensitive in social situations. They may, for instance, perceive rejection or disapproval in response to neutral social situations ('Why did they sit over there, and not next to me?'; 'He just looked away—he is obviously bored with me'; 'She laughs when speaking to my colleagues, but not when she speaks to me'). And some people have an irritable temperament, which makes them more likely to overreact or get angry in situations that might not bother others.

Although biology can influence our psychological disposition, this does not mean that negative feelings are unavoidable. People who have a biological disposition towards cardiovascular disease do not necessarily end up having a heart attack or stroke. However, they need to work harder than others at maintaining a healthy diet, getting regular exercise and reducing cholesterol levels. Similarly, those with a temperament that increases their likelihood of experiencing upsetting emotions need to work harder at managing their cognitions and responses compared to those with a resilient temperament. CBT strategies can help us develop greater cognitive flexibility, and therefore increase our resilience. Doing so will reduce the frequency and intensity of upsetting emotions, and enable us to recover faster in situations where we do get upset.

MESSAGES FROM SOCIETY

Many of the messages we receive from popular culture contribute to unhappiness by influencing our beliefs. Communications via social media, TV, movies, billboards and magazines promote the importance of things like:

➤   having wealth and material possessions;
➤   popularity—having lots of friends;
➤   career success—having a high-status, well-paid job;
➤   being young and attractive; and
➤   having happy, harmonious family relationships.

People buy into these messages to different degrees. Many believe that to be successful they must have a highly paid job and own expensive consumer items, or that they must be slim and youthful in appearance or have lots of friends. The more strongly we hold our beliefs, the more likely we are to feel unhappy when our life circumstances don't live up to them. For example, if you believe that you must have happy, harmonious family relationships, but in reality your family relationships are dysfunctional, the belief that things must not be this way makes you feel miserable or inadequate. While there is no problem with preferring to have happy family relationships, beauty, friends, achievements or material wealth, believing that things *must* be a certain way is guaranteed to create unhappiness.

CBT IS NOT JUST 'POSITIVE THINKING'

If you are a reader of popular psychology and self-help books, you have probably come across books that suggest positive thinking can be achieved by repeating certain affirming statements over and over again. Typical statements include:

> ➤ I am prosperous and I am a winner.
> ➤ Every day, in every way, I'm getting better and better.
> ➤ My world is full of abundance.
> ➤ Things are working out to my highest good.
> ➤ I love myself and I approve of myself.
> ➤ The universe lovingly takes care of me.

Many people use statements like these in an attempt to think more positively, but do they really work? The answer is: it depends on whether or not you believe them. Affirmations can help to reinforce things we already know, but ignore. For instance, reminding ourselves of our strengths, achievements and the people who love us may improve our perspective at times. However, reciting statements that we don't believe will not magically imprint them on our unconscious mind. In CBT the emphasis is on realistic, balanced thinking, not wishful thinking.

APPROPRIATE VERSUS INAPPROPRIATE EMOTIONS

The aim of CBT is not to eliminate all unpleasant emotions, but to respond to situations appropriately. There are some situations in which it is reasonable and appropriate to feel sad, regretful, angry or disappointed. If we lose something that we value, it is appropriate to feel sad. If we fail to achieve a particular goal, it is appropriate to feel disappointed. If we do something that we subsequently discover has been hurtful to another person, it is appropriate to feel regret. If someone else does something we consider to be unfair, it is appropriate to feel annoyed. Psychologically healthy responses produce emotions that are appropriate, given the circumstances. Accordingly, we experience regret rather than crippling guilt, disappointment rather than devastation, concern rather than overwhelming anxiety, sadness rather than depression, annoyance rather than explosive anger.

As we saw earlier, upsetting emotions have benefits when they motivate us to *act* in order to improve our situation. For instance, unpleasant emotions may motivate us to apologise, communicate, arrive early, complain to the manager, focus on a task, make amends for hurting someone or get a second opinion.

Even emotions like grief are appropriate at times. The death of a loved one, the loss of one's home, the diagnosis of a serious illness or the loss of a long-held dream is likely to generate grief for most people. The pain of a significant loss can sometimes last for years, and although time eventually heals or at least lessens the pain, the scar often remains. Unfortunately, there is no easy way to shortcut grief. However, even in grief, negative thinking can generate additional unnecessary suffering.

> *Gabriel is grieving for the loss of his wife, who died of cancer two years ago. While his grief is an appropriate response to the loss of his wife, his guilt and anger are not. By blaming himself for not having been a better husband, and blaming the doctors who were unable to save her, Gabriel creates additional distress that serves no useful purpose. His anger and guilt only intensify his pain and prolong his torment.*

THE ABC MODEL

Most of us presume that it is the things that happen to us that make us feel the way we do. So, for instance, when we feel angry, anxious, frustrated or depressed we tend to blame other people or our life circumstances. However, as Ellis pointed out, events and people do not make us feel good or bad—they just provide a stimulus. It is actually our cognitions that determine how we feel.

To illustrate this, Ellis devised the ABC model, where:

A stands for 'activating event'—the situation that triggers our response.
B stands for 'beliefs'—our cognitions about the situation.
C stands for 'consequences'—emotions (including physical sensations) and behaviours.

While we tend to blame 'A' (the activating event) for 'C' (the consequences), it is actually 'B' (our beliefs) that make us feel the way we do. Let's look at a simple example:

> Imagine that you are running late for an appointment, and you are feeling anxious.
>
> A   activating event—running late for an appointment
> C   consequences—physical tension, anxiety, fretting, reckless driving

You are feeling tense and anxious and driving recklessly (C) not because you are running late (A), but because of your beliefs (B) about punctuality and the consequences of running late. Your beliefs might include things like, 'I must always be punctual'; 'People won't like me if I arrive late'; 'People should approve of me' and 'The consequences are likely to be dire'.

INTRODUCING D: DISPUTE

Ellis used the term **dispute** to describe the process of challenging the way we think about situations. Once we identify the thoughts and beliefs that make us feel bad, our next step is to dispute them. For instance, in the above example we might tell ourselves, 'My past experiences have taught me that even when I'm running late, I usually still get there on time or just a little late. I prefer to be punctual, and I usually am, but if I am late on this occasion, it's unlikely to have dire consequences.'

Disputing is a key component of CBT. Learning to change rigid, inflexible cognitions enables us to avoid or release emotions that cause unnecessary distress. In the above example, it might result in our feeling concerned rather than overwhelmingly anxious. It may also cause us to modify our behaviour; for instance, not driving recklessly.

IN SUMMARY

➤ Cognitive behaviour therapy (CBT) is based on the tenet that cognitions—our thoughts, beliefs and attitudes—determine the way we feel and behave.

➤ Cognitions, behaviours and emotions interact with and influence each other. Making changes in one of these areas usually results in changes in the others.

➤ Unpleasant emotions (such as anger, anxiety, sadness, resentment, guilt) can sometimes be helpful if they motivate us to do things that benefit us in the longer term. However frequent upsetting emotions often reflect a negative cognitive style, which gives rise to pointless distress.

➤ Various factors contribute to the way we think and feel, including our early history, temperament and environment.

➤ The aim of CBT is not to eliminate all upsetting emotions, but to develop reasonable, balanced cognitions and respond appropriately to life's challenges.

TWO

Recognising faulty thinking

If you're pretty crazy then you're in good company because the human race as a whole is out of its goddam head … Now the problem is to admit this about yourself, and then to do something about it.

ALBERT ELLIS

If we brought together the happiest people in the world, what do you think they would have in common? Lots of money? Good looks? Career success? Fame and admiration from others? Wrong! The happiest people are those with the most flexible attitudes. Of all the people you consider to be genuinely happy (most of us can count them on one hand), are any of them rigid, demanding or uncompromising? Do they get upset when things don't go their way?

A key characteristic of happy people is their ability to adapt to life circumstances—a trait called **cognitive flexibility**. This doesn't mean that they are weak or apathetic—in fact they are often keen to work towards the things that they care about. But they are also willing to accept that some things are beyond their control. Much of the distress that we experience in our daily lives stems from rigid, inflexible thinking.

IRRATIONAL BELIEFS

Albert Ellis observed that most people by their very nature are inclined to think in ways that are irrational and self-defeating. He noted that some people are particularly predisposed towards upsetting emotions because they habitually think in self-defeating ways. According to Ellis, our thinking is irrational if it goes against our basic desire for happiness and long life. So, if holding a particular belief makes you experience inappropriate anger, frustration, anxiety, depression or feelings of worthlessness, or if it thwarts your ability to experience good health and long life, then by Ellis's definition the belief is irrational. This includes beliefs that cause us to engage in self-defeating behaviours such as procrastination, social avoidance, aggression and neglecting our physical health. Ellis described many irrational beliefs that contribute to unhappiness and psychological distress, including the common irrational beliefs listed below.

COMMON IRRATIONAL BELIEFS	CONSEQUENCES
I must be loved and approved of by everyone.	anxiety, unassertive behaviour, depression, poor self-esteem
I must be competent, adequate and achieving in every respect.	anxiety, self-downing, depression, frustration, shame, procrastination
The world should be a fair place and I should always be treated fairly.	anger, resentment, frustration, depression
People should have the same values and beliefs as me, and they should do things the way I would do them.	anger, resentment, poor relationships
Certain people are bad, and they should be blamed or punished for their misdeeds.	anger, resentment, hatred, depression
When I do something badly, I am a bad person, a failure, an idiot.	poor self-esteem, frustration, depression
The world should provide me with what I need. Life should be comfortable. I shouldn't have to suffer or be inconvenienced.	frustration, depression, despair
It is awful when things don't go the way that I would like.	frustration, anger, depression
It's easier to avoid problems than to confront and deal with them.	procrastination, unresolved problems, relationship difficulties
Human unhappiness is caused by life circumstances, and it's impossible to be happy when things are not going well for me.	helplessness, hopelessness, failure to take responsibility, despair

COMMON IRRATIONAL BELIEFS	CONSEQUENCES
If there is a chance that something bad might happen, I should dwell on it now.	anxiety, ongoing worry
There is a correct solution to every problem, and it's awful if I can't find it.	indecision, procrastination, anxiety

While these are some common irrational beliefs, there are literally hundreds of others that could be added to the list. Throughout this book we will look at other beliefs that contribute to upsetting emotions.

TYRANNY OF THE SHOULDS

When we believe that things 'should' or 'must' be a certain way, rather than simply having a preference, we make ourselves vulnerable to distress. Ellis called this lack of flexibility 'demandingness' because we instinctively demand that things should be a certain way. In 1939 American psychiatrist Karen Horney used the term **tyranny of the shoulds** to describe this notion. 'Shoulds' are the rules or beliefs that we hold about what is necessary in our world. Some of our shoulds focus on expectations of ourselves, while others focus on how people ought to behave and how the world should be. While not everyone has a rigid thinking style, most people have at least some shoulds that give rise to unpleasant emotions at times.

Many of the following shoulds get people into trouble. Can you identify any that affect you?

- ❏ I should always do a perfect job.
- ❏ I should never make mistakes.
- ❏ I should always be productive in the use of my time.
- ❏ My life should be easy and hassle-free.
- ❏ I should always be treated fairly.
- ❏ I should always be in control over events in my life.
- ❏ Other people should always do the 'right' thing.
- ❏ Other people should like and approve of me.
- ❏ I should be slim, youthful and attractive.
- ❏ I should be competent and effective in everything that I do.

- ❏ I should be doing and achieving more than I am.
- ❏ I should always be totally independent.
- ❏ I should always be positive, bright and cheerful.
- ❏ I should be married or in a committed relationship.
- ❏ I should have a harmonious, loving, supportive family.
- ❏ I should be a perfect parent.
- ❏ I should be sexy and have a high libido.
- ❏ I should be working.
- ❏ I should have a high-status job.
- ❏ I should be making lots of money.
- ❏ I should be witty, interesting and fun to be with.
- ❏ I should be like other people.
- ❏ I should have lots of friends.
- ❏ I should be as smart as the cleverest people I know.
- ❏ I should always say 'yes' to requests from others.
- ❏ I should never be afraid or insecure.

Holding these beliefs can make us feel bad because our life experiences do not always match them. For example, the belief that 'Everybody must like and approve of me' creates problems when we say or do something that might elicit disapproval from others. We may not be as youthful or slim as we would like to be, and we may not have a highly paid job or a happy marriage. We may not be as smart, witty or interesting as we would like. From time to time we make mistakes, people disapprove of us, our performance falters, hassles present themselves and friends let us down. The more strongly we believe that it must not be this way, the more distress we experience.

It is not so much the content, but rather the rigidity of our beliefs, that makes us unhappy. Beliefs are not a problem when they are held as preferences. We will not upset ourselves if we merely desire career success, good relationships, independence or a comfortable life, as long as we recognise that things don't have to be this way. It is also perfectly reasonable to prefer people to like us, to want them to do what we believe is right and to treat us fairly, as long as we are flexible enough to accept that it won't always happen. Life constantly challenges us to be flexible. When things don't work out the way we would like, we can make ourselves miserable by demanding that it should not be this way, or we can adjust and move on by choosing to think in a more flexible way.

A note of caution—some people put too much emphasis on spoken words rather than their underlying meaning. Simply eliminating the use of the word 'should' or 'must' from your vocabulary does not make you a flexible thinker. It is not the words we use, but the things we believe that matter. Being flexible requires us to adapt our cognitions—not just our vocabulary.

AWFULISING

Ellis coined the term **awfulising** to describe the common tendency to exaggerate the negative aspects of our life situations. Awfulising (also often referred to as 'catastrophic thinking' or 'catastrophising') causes us to experience undesirable or unpleasant situations as more aversive than they need to be. As a result, we create distress that is disproportionate to our life circumstances, whether we are facing minor hassles or serious problems. Largely inconsequential events such as being kept waiting, having to spend time with someone we don't like, looking silly in front of others or forgetting an appointment can feel catastrophic when our thinking is maladaptive. Even more serious problems such as losing a job or having a car accident will give rise to mild, moderate or severe distress depending on our cognitive style.

Shoulds and awfulising go hand in hand, as both reflect cognitive rigidity. We get upset when things don't go our way because we assume that the consequences will be catastrophic. For example:

➤ I must do it perfectly—it's terrible to make mistakes.
➤ People must like and respect me—it's awful to be disapproved of.
➤ I must find a partner—it's awful to be single.
➤ I should be slim—it's dreadful to be overweight.

By developing cognitive flexibility we learn not to awfulise. This helps us to cope when hassles invariably occur.

MONITOR YOUR THINKING

Our thoughts are like an inner voice, reflecting our perceptions of what is happening in our world. Most of the time we are not conscious of our thoughts—they just go on in the background of our mind. However, if we pay attention, we can often identify some of their contents.

Many of our thoughts are neutral in content—they generate very little emotion: 'I'd better let the cat in'; 'I need to return that phone call'; 'I must remember to pick up that parcel'; 'Do these shoes match this top?' Some of our thoughts generate more salient, pleasant emotions: 'I did a really great job'; 'Hallie took her first steps today'; 'This is going to be a lot of fun!'; 'That dog is gorgeous'; 'They're such nice people—I think they liked me'. Other thoughts generate unpleasant, upsetting emotions: 'What an idiot I am! I really screwed up badly'; 'I hate doing this! What a bore!'; 'They are going to think I'm stupid'; 'He's late yet again. How typical!'. Thoughts that are negative or biased typically give rise to unpleasant emotions. However, as our thinking happens largely without our awareness, we rarely notice our thoughts, unless we take the time to observe them.

Tuning in to our thoughts helps us to identify those that are rigid, irrational or biased. Sometimes just recognising that our thoughts are unreasonable enables us to see things differently. At other times we need to challenge them more vigorously using a thought monitoring form. In either case, it is helpful to monitor our thinking, particularly in situations where we are feeling bad.

> *Sally made arrangements to go out with her girlfriend on Saturday night, but her friend cancelled at the last minute. Now it's too late for Sally to make alternative arrangements. Sally feels miserable. She thinks to herself, 'Everyone else is going out and having a good time, but I've got nowhere to go. It's so depressing.'*

While it is reasonable for Sally to feel disappointed at the last minute cancellation, is it necessary for her to feel despondent? Whether Sally feels indifferent, disappointed, annoyed, furious or devastated will depend on her cognitions. Sally feels bad because she believes:

➤ Everybody goes out and has a good time on Saturday nights.
➤ If I don't go, I am missing out.
➤ I should always go out on Saturday nights. It's awful to have to stay at home.

To change the way she feels Sally needs to become aware of her cognitions and challenge the rigidity of her thinking. For instance, she may tell herself: 'I prefer to go out on the weekends and I usually do. Many people go out on Saturday night but not everyone does. I was not guaranteed to have a fabulous time even if I did go out with my friend. Now that I am not going out I can watch a movie and play computer games. It's disappointing to stay home tonight, but it's not the end of the world.'

> *Rosanne arranged to go overseas with her boyfriend some time ago, but in the last two months she contracted glandular fever and has been very unwell. Now, a week prior to the departure date, she lacks the strength or desire to travel. Rosanne feels anxious and guilty because she doesn't want to disappoint her boyfriend. She thinks to herself, 'This is a very bad thing for me to do—he will be terribly disappointed.'*

While it is reasonable for Rosanne to feel sorry for not being able to stick to her arrangement, is it necessary for her to feel guilty and anxious? Rosanne's beliefs include:

➤ Once I make an arrangement I should always stick to it, no matter what.
➤ I should always put other people's needs first. I should never do anything that might disappoint others.
➤ Disappointing someone else makes me a bad person.

In order to perceive her situation in a more reasonable way, Rosanne will need to develop some cognitive flexibility. This will involve challenging some of her shoulds (e.g. 'I prefer to be reliable and I usually am, however sometimes that's not possible'). Of course, this is not to say that her boyfriend's feelings are not important. Going out of our way for people that we care about is a normal part of human relationships. However, sometimes things don't work out, and in spite of our best intentions we are not able to meet our commitments. Open and honest communication as well as flexible thinking will enable Rosanne to manage her emotions more effectively as well as maintain healthy relationships.

> *Jonathan has just completed his final year of high school. He has worked very hard all year, and has had his heart set on studying law at university. Upon receiving his results, Jonathan discovers that his grades were not high enough to get into law. Jonathan feels depressed. He thinks to himself, 'I have worked so hard all year—all that sacrifice for nothing! What a waste of a year! My future is ruined.'*

It is reasonable for Jonathan to feel disappointed at missing out on something he dearly wanted. It is appropriate for him to feel sad for a period of time, as he comes to terms with his disappointment and contemplates his future. However, the magnitude of Jonathan's despair is influenced by his beliefs, which include:

➤ I must always succeed in the goals that I set for myself.
➤ If I don't do law, my future is ruined.
➤ The consequences of this situation are catastrophic.
➤ Life should be fair—if I work hard towards something then I should always get it.

CONSCIOUS AND UNCONSCIOUS THOUGHTS

Although we can often identify our thoughts simply by observing them, sometimes it is not that easy. For instance, when Lara switches on the computer to start working on her essay she can feel her anxiety rising, but she is not aware of having any thoughts at all. Similarly, when Brian gets ready to head home from work on Friday afternoon, he can feel his mood plummet, although he is not aware of any particular thoughts. And when Ginni goes to see a psychologist for the first time she is feeling anxious, even though she is not consciously thinking anything much. While our thoughts are not always conscious, we can usually identify the emotions that they give rise to (anxiety, sadness, guilt, embarrassment, worry, anger). These emotions provide clues regarding the content of our thoughts.

> Whenever you have difficulty identifying your thoughts, try this exercise:
> Close your eyes and ask yourself 'What's going on for me right now?'
> Take two minutes to observe your inner world—feelings, body sensations, images and thoughts. Very often, thoughts that are at the 'back of the mind' (just below consciousness) will become apparent.

When Lara stopped to observe what was going on in her mind she discovered: 'So much work to do, and so little time!' Brian realised that his thoughts were on the theme: 'The weekend is here, and there is nothing for me to look forward to', while Ginni was thinking, 'This psychologist may not be able to help me and I may never recover.'

Have you ever walked into a room of strangers and felt your anxiety rise? What might be the thoughts (conscious or unconscious) that create anxiety in that situation?

DISCOVERING FAULTY THINKING

In Aaron Beck's book *Cognitive Therapy of Depression*, he describes some common examples of faulty thinking (reasoning errors) that contribute to emotional distress. These are particularly prevalent when people are depressed, however even when not depressed, most people make reasoning errors at times. The following are some of the most common examples of faulty thinking identified by Beck and other researchers.

BLACK-AND-WHITE THINKING

This is the tendency to see things in a polarised way, without recognising the middle ground. For instance, you may evaluate people or situations as good or bad, positive or negative, successes or failures. It is the inability to see that most situations fall somewhere in-between that makes this type of thinking unreasonable.

Black-and-white thinking is particularly common among people with perfectionist traits. In the example above, when Jonathan tells himself, 'Not getting into law means that I've ruined my future', he displayed black-and-white thinking. By assuming that anything other than his first preference is totally unacceptable, Jonathan ignores the fact that he has many other options that may also lead to favourable outcomes.

Ian had been working on a report for months, and after having finally submitted it, he discovered an error in one of the sections. Although the error does not have significant consequences, Ian is devastated. 'I really stuffed up that report,' he despondently thinks to himself. Ian's thinking is black-and-white because he assumes that 'unless it is a hundred per cent perfect, it's a disaster'. The inability to see the middle ground— that overall, it is a good report—causes Ian unnecessary distress and prevents him from appreciating his achievement.

*

Sasha has two categories for her acquaintances—good and bad. Whenever someone does something that she disapproves of, Sasha adds them to her 'bad' list and writes them off. As time goes by, the number of people on her 'bad' list grows. Sasha ignores the fact that everyone has both positive and negative traits, and that it is possible to like and accept people even when they sometimes do things that displease us. Sasha's black-and-white thinking causes her to feel unnecessary resentment, and limits her ability to make friends and enjoy social relationships.

OVERGENERALISING

When we overgeneralise, we draw negative conclusions about ourselves, other people and life situations, on the basis of limited evidence. Sometimes, just one experience is all it takes for us to start thinking in terms such as 'always', 'never', and 'everybody'. For instance, 'Whenever things start to look up, something bad always happens'; 'Every time I try to communicate I get nowhere'; 'I always screw up'; 'I haven't achieved anything worthwhile in the last ten years'; 'I'm a failure in my work and in my relationships'.

When Hannah's son was in high school, she worried that he might start using drugs, and this in fact did occur. Since that time Hannah started to believe that her worries are justified. 'My fears get realised,' she tells her friend. 'When I worry about things, I'm usually right.' Closer scrutiny reveals that this is a major overgeneralisation. Although her earlier worry was justified, over 99 per cent of the things she worries about do not occur.

*

Heather has had three long-term relationships in the past ten years, each of which eventually ended. After the third break-up, Heather concluded, 'I'm not capable of having a relationship. I can't trust men—they're all the same.' Thinking this way made her feel depressed. While it is appropriate for Heather to examine some of the problems that existed in her previous relationships and to try to learn from her experiences, overgeneralising about her ability to have meaningful relationships is simplistic. It would be more helpful for Heather to acknowledge that not all her past relationships resulted in rejection (she had terminated some of the relationships), and not all of the men she had known were untrustworthy.

*

Since her marriage broke up two years ago, Desire stopped communicating with most of her married friends. Her withdrawal began after someone had confided to her that one of her girlfriends thought that Desire was flirting with her husband. After initially feeling incensed, Desire concluded, 'Now that I am single, I am a threat

to my female friends—they think I'm going to steal their husbands.'
This overgeneralisation motivated Desire to give up on several
friendships, which subsequently contributed to loneliness.

PERSONALISING

When we personalise, we feel responsible for things that are not our fault, or we incorrectly assume that other people's responses are directed at us.

Maggie felt responsible because one of the guests at her dinner party
was quiet all evening and did not appear to have a good time. In
spite of her best efforts to include him, he did not join in much of the
conversation, and Maggie felt that this was somehow her fault.

*

Rochelle feels offended by a work colleague who rarely says 'hello'
when he passes her in the office. It hasn't occurred to Rochelle that her
colleague has severe social anxiety, and his behaviour reflects his own
timidity, rather than any bad feelings towards her.

*

Glenda's mother has been depressed ever since her husband died
more than a year ago. Glenda feels guilty every time she speaks to her
because she feels responsible for her mother's unhappiness. Although
she is already doing everything she can to support her mother, Glenda
nevertheless perceives that it is somehow her responsibility to resolve
her mother's grief.

*

Kylie's husband has a low libido, and Kylie takes it personally.
'He obviously finds me unattractive,' she thinks to herself. In fact,
her husband's libido has dropped because of biological factors,

including the natural effects of ageing and blood pressure medication. In addition, Kylie's sensitivity to this issue causes her husband to experience performance anxiety, which dampens his libido even further.

The challenge not to personalise is even greater when someone behaves rudely towards us.

Frank felt offended when his boss spoke to him in an abrasive manner over some minor issue. Although initially he took it personally, Frank subsequently realised that his boss was under a huge amount of stress, and that his angry outburst reflected his own vulnerable state. As a result, Frank continued to be loyal and supportive of his boss—a response that was later acknowledged and appreciated.

It is easy to feel indignant and trade insults with or 'write off' someone who is rude; it is harder to understand them. Recognising that the behaviour of others largely reflects their own personality and state of mind, and choosing not to take offence at their behaviour requires insight and cognitive flexibility. However, doing so generates enormous benefits, including healthy relationships in the long term.

FILTERING

Negative beliefs about ourselves, other people and the world can bias the way we perceive many of our experiences. For instance, we may find ourselves focusing on just the negative elements of a situation, while ignoring all other relevant information. Our mind is quickly alerted to events that confirm our own prejudices, insecurities and fears, while we filter out information that does not support those cognitions. So, if you are anxious by nature, you focus on evidence that the world is unsafe, while ignoring information that is inconsistent with this view. If you have poor self-esteem, you notice any events that suggest that you are incompetent or disliked, while ignoring evidence that you are competent and valued. And if you believe that the world is hostile and uncaring, you will notice information that confirms this view, but filter out any evidence that people are kind.

Lana is a sales representative for a large pharmaceutical company. Although she is bright, energetic and competent, Lana's poor self-esteem causes her to ignore her strengths and successes, but focus on her perceived weaknesses. For instance when she was recently told that her sales figures were the highest in the state, she put this down to good luck. However, when Lana occasionally makes a mistake or completes a task less than perfectly she feels incompetent and ruminates about it for days.

*

Rita recently gave her first radio interview, and was subsequently told by the producer that it went well, particularly for a debut performance. Instead of being pleased with the positive feedback, Rita felt upset. In her mind the comment focused on her inexperience, and implied that she was not good enough. By selectively focusing on 'debut performance' while ignoring the other feedback, Rita interpreted the comment as a criticism rather than a compliment.

*

Silvio gave a presentation to his work colleagues, which went very well; however, he was disappointed to receive two slightly critical evaluations among the 40 positive ones. He keeps thinking about these two evaluations, and no longer feels happy with his presentation.

JUMPING TO NEGATIVE CONCLUSIONS

Many of us are inclined to draw negative conclusions in all sorts of situations, in spite of limited evidence to support them. We may assume the worst when things go wrong or interpret other people's comments or motives in the most negative light.

George notices feelings of tightness in the chest whenever he is under stress. Although he has been repeatedly reassured by numerous medical tests that he does not have a heart condition, his immediate thought is, 'There is something wrong with my heart.'

*

Nicki has not heard from her work colleague Linda for nearly two weeks. As they usually speak quite frequently, Nicki assumes that Linda must be angry with her because she intends to apply for a position that Linda is also interested in. The more she thinks about it, the more annoyed she becomes. Nicki remains angry for several days, until Linda finally calls her and explains that her daughter has been in hospital.

*

For her Honours thesis Rochelle is doing a project that involves surveying a large number of single mothers. She has sent two emails describing the nature of her research to a website for single mothers, hoping that they might be willing to inform suitable participants about her research. After receiving no reply, Rochelle concludes that they are obviously hostile to researchers and don't want to help. She later discovers the website is run by volunteers, and is often unattended for days or weeks.

MIND READING

This is a specific type of jumping to conclusions, based on the assumption that we know what other people are thinking. We assume negative evaluation by others, without any evidence that this is the case.

Simone had been unusually quiet during a catch-up with her old friend Les. In the course of the evening, Les observed that she seemed quiet and asked whether she was OK. Simone interpreted this comment to mean that Les was bored with her company. She concluded that unless she is bright and chirpy, Les is not interested in spending time with her. Les, on the other hand, perceived Simone to be very distant that evening, and presumed that she must be feeling angry towards him. As he couldn't work out what he had done wrong, Les thought that she was judging him unfairly. As both engaged in mind reading, the two friends did not speak to each other again for almost a year.

As so often happens when we mind-read, not only do we feel bad, but we also behave in self-defeating ways.

Len would very much like to have a girlfriend, but is horrified at his friend's suggestion to try internet dating. 'What if someone I know sees my profile on the website? They'll think I'm desperate!' he tells his friend. In addition, Len hates going to parties or social events because he assumes that people are looking at him and judging him harshly. As is typical in these situations, no one actually notices Len or gives him any thought at all. However, Len's belief that people are judging him leads to self-defeating behaviours—he avoids opportunities that might enable him to get what he wants.

*

Prue has a tendency to blush, which would not be a problem except for the fact that she assumes that other people notice and think there is something wrong with her. Prue's worrying that people notice her blushing, and her concern that they think she is strange, feeds her anxiety and, ironically, keeps her blushing.

Mind reading and perceived negative evaluation by others is a major contributor to social anxiety and social phobia. We often assume that people are thinking about us and judging us harshly when, in reality, most people (outside of our immediate family and friendship group) do not notice or give us much thought at all. We are just not that important in other people's minds, in the same way that they don't figure very much in ours.

You would care very little what people think of you
if you realised how little they do.

BLAMING

From time to time things go wrong in our lives, people let us down and unforeseen mishaps occur. While some people can readily accept disappointments and human foibles, others are drawn to blaming and condemning people for their faults. Blaming is usually overly simplistic as it fails to acknowledge the numerous factors that contribute to outcomes, over and above the people we hold responsible. It also wastes our energy on feelings of anger, bitterness and resentment, and prevents healing from taking place.

Mary has felt stuck in an unhappy marriage for the past 25 years, and has spent much of her adult life blaming her husband for her unhappiness. Unfortunately, blaming has not helped Mary resolve the problems within the marriage, but has made her bitter and unhappy. As Mary has chosen to remain in the marriage, she would benefit from accepting that her husband is not perfect, communicating to encourage him to change some of the behaviours she dislikes and focusing on positive aspects of the marriage.

*

Two years after his sacking Harold continues to blame the company he worked at for six years for terminating his employment. Although the circumstances were complex, Harold blames management for holding a grudge against him, and for not appreciating his years of loyal service. While it is appropriate for Harold to go through a period of anger or grief, his need to keep blaming and ruminating is counter-productive. It does not change his situation, but robs Harold of peace of mind. It is only when Harold starts to accept the events of the past, and begins making plans for the future, that he starts to feel better.

> Acceptance doesn't mean endorsement or saying that things are good.
> It means accepting bad reality and accepting that limited change is likely in
> the world right now.
>
> **ALBERT ELLIS**

LABELLING

Everyone is fallible. We all make mistakes or do silly things at times and there are some things that we are just not good at. Sometimes we behave inappropriately, make stupid comments, do things that have a negative impact on others, perform badly in our work, ignore symptoms of failing health, make unsound financial decisions or fail to achieve the things that we want.

The way that we think about our mistakes or perceived flaws reflects our degree of cognitive flexibility. Sometimes it is rational and appropriate to tell ourselves, 'That was a silly thing to do—I need to be more careful', or 'I'm not very motivated when it comes to cleaning the house', or 'My memory is not as good as it used to be'. Thoughts such as these do not create problems because even though they acknowledge mistakes or perceived weaknesses, they are *specific* rather than *global*.

In contrast, when we label ourselves as an idiot, a failure, ugly, no good, stupid, lazy, a loser or incompetent, we make global generalisations about ourselves on the basis of specific behaviours or experiences. As a result, we diminish our self-esteem and create upsetting emotions such as shame, self-loathing and feelings of inadequacy. Labelling is the ultimate overgeneralisation because it ignores the fact that people are a complex mixture of characteristics and behaviours, and we cannot be defined by just one or even a few of these.

While some individuals are inclined to label themselves, others tend to label other people: 'That guy is a jerk'; 'My boss is a moron'; 'My sister-in-law is a bitch'; or 'That politician is a sleaze-bag'. Labelling others is just as unreasonable as labelling ourselves, since we sum up an entire person on the basis of particular behaviours or characteristics. Labelling others is also self-defeating because it fuels resentment, wastes our energy and makes it harder to get on with people. This does not mean that we should never judge people's actions. As with our own behaviours, it is totally reasonable to think that a person's behaviour was unreasonable, unfair, unethical or silly. However, it is important to distinguish the person's actions from the person as a whole.

Vince had an unpleasant exchange with his sister-in-law over a family matter, and he now perceives her as the enemy. Labelling her in this way produces a number of negative consequences, including stress for his wife, tension between families and social awkwardness whenever their paths cross. It also deprives his children of the opportunity to develop relationships with their cousins and to enjoy the benefits of an extended family.

*

Christine spent six months working in a law firm with very poor work practices and an uncaring culture. Inadequate training and lack of access to advice caused Christine to slip up in some of her cases, and consequently she received negative appraisals from her supervisor. When Christine finally left the firm, she perceived herself as incompetent and a failure. Labelling herself in this way further undermined her confidence, which in turn made it difficult for her to find another job.

Whenever things don't work out, it is always useful to appraise the situation and objectively reflect on the reasons. Identifying factors that contributed to our negative experiences instead of labelling ourself as a failure gives us the opportunity to learn from those experiences without diminishing our self-esteem (see also Chapter 7).

PREDICTING CATASTROPHE

Some people habitually focus on negative possibilities—failure, rejection, loss, pain or catastrophe. Self-talk about imminent disasters is typically expressed as 'what if?' For instance, 'What if I lose my job, and can't pay my bills?'; 'What if I make a fool of myself in front of all those people?'; 'What if I get sick and can't do what I promised?'; 'What if I don't know anyone and have no one to talk to?'; 'What if I can't find somewhere to park the car?' By focusing on the possibility that things might go wrong, we make ourselves anxious in the present, and lose our ability to engage fully with the things happening around us.

> *Brenda is a self-employed interior designer. When some of her clients are slow to pay their bills, Brenda immediately assumes that they are going to default, and starts to imagine the worst-case scenario. Although nearly all of her clients pay their bills in the end, Brenda is quick to visualise scenes of conflict, litigation and threats. This creates anxiety, which distracts Brenda from her current projects.*

*

> *Jan became worried after she had told one of her work colleagues about her diagnosis of breast cancer. Although Jan asked her colleague not to tell anyone, she continues to worry that others will find out. When lying awake at night, Jan thinks to herself, 'What if she tells someone, and then everyone finds out, and then it will get back to management, and they'll decide that I'm a bad risk. They will think less of me … It might affect the way I am perceived by others …'*

*

> *Trevor gets twitching in his muscles from time to time, but he is terrified to go to the doctor as he fears it could be a serious neurological disease.*

The truth is that the world is full of uncertainty. The things that Brenda, Jan and Trevor worry about could conceivably happen, although their likelihood is small. By overestimating the probability of bad outcomes, they create worry and anxiety, and deprive themselves of ease of being.

The challenge is to learn to live with uncertainty, particularly in situations beyond our control. This means acknowledging that bad things can happen (although most of the time they don't), and recognising that even if they should happen we will cope with them when we need to.

COMPARING

Many people appraise their status, success and personal worth by comparing themselves with others. The comparisons may be limited to members of their own peer group—friends, family, people their own age or those they went to school with. Or they may be made with a broader group, including the rich and famous—media personalities, business moguls and politicians. Comparing can make us feel inadequate, as invariably there are people who do better than us in any given area.

Mia felt excited when she got dressed up for the staff Christmas party. However, on her arrival she became despondent. As she saw how attractive some of the other women looked, she suddenly felt unattractive. To add insult to injury, one of her colleagues had lost ten kilograms and looked fantastic!

*

Raymond can't help feeling resentful when he reads about the mounting wealth of one of the country's top entrepreneurs. It feels like someone is rubbing his nose in it, saying, 'You just haven't cut it!'

*

After listening to adoring speeches about members of the groom's family, Sol leaves his friend's wedding feeling utterly devastated. 'This is what a family should be like,' he thinks to himself. 'Mine is so dysfunctional!'

*

Marty was diagnosed with cancer four years ago, and is distraught to hear that a famous movie star has recently died of the disease. Suddenly she is terrified about her own mortality.

JUST WORLD FALLACY

The expectation that things should be fair is a common human response. In an ideal world that would be the case—however, we don't live in an ideal world. The reality is that many things in life are not fair, and the belief that they should be leaves us feeling angry and resentful.

Rupert has just been told that with the coming restructure, he will need to relocate, and that another staff member will be moving into his office. Rupert feels incensed by the injustice of this decision. He has worked hard since he has been in this position—why should he have to move?

*

Ramona feels resentful that her brother frequently receives money and favours from her elderly parents, while he contributes very little. Although Ramona has voiced her objections on several occasions, her parents reason that her brother has difficulty looking after himself, and needs support, while Ramona is competent and makes a good living.

*

Someone dug up and stole two beautiful new orchids that Stella just planted in her garden. Stella is furious.

While it is reasonable to feel angry when something is unfair, ongoing resentment makes our lives miserable. Sometimes we need to accept that life is unfair, and focus on things that are within our control.

There are some things that we can control, and others that we can't. Our job is to work out which is which.

HINDSIGHT VISION

When we look back on the actions that we have taken in the past, we might observe some that led to negative consequences. We may tell ourselves that we should have known at the time that our decision was wrong, and if we had done things differently, we would be much happier now. This type of 'hindsight vision' has sometimes been referred to as 'shoulda, coulda, woulda' as we retrospectively reflect on all the things we should or could have done differently.

Hindsight vision is irrational because whatever we do, we are always operating with limited knowledge and awareness. The decisions we make at any time are always constrained by limited knowledge at the time. We don't know the consequences of our actions ahead of time because we are not fortune tellers. So, insisting that we should have done things differently does not make sense.

Secondly, we are assuming that a different decision would have resulted in a better outcome. But how do we know? We can never know the consequences of taking an alternative route because we didn't go there. Many actions have unforeseen consequences, so we have no way of knowing whether different choices would have resulted in better outcomes.

Andy feels regret that he chose to study law, as his job is very stressful. He is sure he would have been happier if he had become a writer, which was always his passion. Now he frequently reproaches himself for not following his instincts. 'Why didn't I do what I wanted?' he often thinks to himself. 'I would have been much happier now.'

*

Selena catches herself thinking about what life would have been like if she had not married Stephan. 'I had so many men to choose from, why did I pick him?' she often wonders. Although they have been married for 30 years and now it is too late to leave, Selena can't help ruminating about the idea that she could have had a better life.

*

Mordy frequently has difficulty deciding what to order from the menu. No matter what he orders, he usually regrets his choice. 'I should have ordered the fish instead of the steak,' he thinks to himself as he is halfway through his meal.

EXERCISE 2.1

For each of the following examples:

a   identify the faulty thinking pattern that creates distress (e.g. black-and-white thinking, personalising, predicting catastrophe),

b   identify any shoulds or inflexible beliefs. (Sample solutions are given at the back of the book.)

1   Jo's daughter had a turbulent marriage, which ended acrimoniously. Jo can't help thinking that if she had been a better mother, her daughter would have made better choices, and would have been happier now.

2   In the course of a social evening Helen made a stupid comment. She immediately realised that it sounded dumb, and regretted having said it. Helen's main memory of that night was her stupid remark, which spoiled the evening for her.

3   Kay is a lively and interesting person; however, she often feels inadequate because, unlike her friends, she left school early and did not go to university.

4   Pauline works for a large corporation that is currently undergoing a restructure. This makes her feel extremely anxious because she assumes that she will be retrenched, and that she won't be able to find another job.

5   Thomas looks back at his life and all he can see is a series of failures and rejections.

6   Peter is a musician and in his recent performance he felt that he just couldn't engage the audience. He thinks of the concert as having been a complete disaster.

7   A teacher has described Jarrod's nine-year-old son as 'easily distracted' and 'not working to capacity'. Jarrod is plagued by visions of his son growing up aimless, unemployed and living off his parents for the rest of his life.

8   Greta ruminates over her decision not to have children, made 20 years ago. She believes that she would have been much happier if she had had a family, but now it is too late.

9 Con gets very sweaty when he is socially anxious, particularly in unfamiliar social situations. The sweating adds further to his anxiety because he is sure that people notice it, and must be thinking there is something wrong with him.

10 Bill has made two attempts at starting a business, but it did not work out. Now Bill perceives himself as a failure. He believes that he has never achieved anything worthwhile.

11 Fred felt depressed after his friend told him that he has just purchased a great investment property. There is no way that Fred could afford to buy an investment property.

12 Sally does not have any respect for one of her work colleagues, whom she regards as an idiot. As far as Sally is concerned, nothing that he says has merit, and everything he does is stupid.

13 Terry invited some friends for a birthday get-together. When two friends declined due to pre-existing arrangements, Terry felt hurt. 'They obviously don't want to come,' he thinks to himself.

14 Nina and Brian went through some difficult times during their marriage. While their relationship improved substantially after they attended some counselling sessions, they still have occasional arguments. Whenever this happens, Nina immediately assumes that the marriage is not going to work, and the counselling has been a waste of time.

15 After working for four years as a financial manager in a large company, Nola had a falling out with her supervisor and left in upsetting circumstances. Now her confidence is eroded and Nola has serious doubts about her own ability to do a good job.

16 Rodney has had a headache for three days. He worries that he has a brain tumour.

17 Melanie feels guilty at not doing the housework, and becomes angry when her husband starts cleaning the house. She assumes that he is trying to humiliate her.

18 After a protracted battle with the local council, Jason lost in his final bid to prevent the neighbours from building an extra storey on their house. Jason is furious.

19 Tony has huge regrets about spending the past 20 years travelling. Upon his return, now in his mid-40s, he finds that most of his friends have settled down with children and stable jobs, while he has neither. 'I should have done things differently,' he keeps thinking to himself.

20 Tamara has been a bit absent-minded lately. Today she misplaced her reading glasses and her keys, and last week she lost a referral letter from her doctor. Despondently she tells herself, 'I seem to be forgetting everything these days. Nothing sticks in my brain.'

21 Lovena believes that if she visualises a parking spot when she is driving, a spot will appear at her destination. Her belief is reinforced whenever she promptly finds a spot, but she ignores or forgets occasions when she drives around for extensive periods until she locates a spot.

22 At a group dinner, Annabel notices that her friend is very quiet, and assumes he must be hating the company. He is in fact feeling very unwell, having contracted a stomach bug recently.

23 Des feels ongoing resentment over what he believes to have been an unreasonable division of assets when he divorced his wife.

24 After being advised to work through an online self-help program for depression, Rogerio thinks to himself, 'This might work for other people but it will not work for me.'

IN SUMMARY

➤ Upsetting emotions such as anger, frustration, guilt, anxiety and depression are often caused and perpetuated by beliefs that are negative, biased or unreasonable. These beliefs are often held as rigid rules or 'shoulds', within our mind.

➤ Negative beliefs can cause us to feel bad, and to behave in ways that are self-defeating.

➤ Most people have certain patterns of thinking that contribute to unnecessary distress. These are often referred to as 'faulty thinking' or 'reasoning errors', and include awfulising, black-and-white thinking, overgeneralising, personalising, filtering, jumping to negative conclusions, mind reading, blaming, predicting catastrophe, comparing, just world fallacy and hindsight vision.

➤ To develop more psychologically healthy ways of thinking, it is useful to identify our own thinking patterns that contribute to unpleasant emotions or self-defeating behaviours.

THREE

Disputing negative cognitions

... personal happiness is possible, even in an unhappy world. Now, you
won't be *as* happy in an unhappy world as in a better one. I don't think
there's much doubt about that, but you can still choose to be pretty damned
happy, even in a poor environment. That's possible. And fighting irrationality
and trying to be happy in a nutty world has great advantages in itself. It's
challenging. It's interesting. It's rewarding. It's self-helping ... Your very
determination to work at it can keep you reasonably happy.

ALBERT ELLIS, 'RATIONAL LIVING IN AN IRRATIONAL WORLD' TALK, 1974

Awareness of our thoughts is helpful. The habit of noticing and labelling
unreasonable thinking (e.g. 'I'm personalising again', 'I'm mind-reading' or
'I just jumped to another negative conclusion') can help us to see things in a
more reasonable light. In addition, learning to dispute negative cognitions and
identify a more balanced perspective can help us to develop a more healthy
cognitive style. Let's now take a look at some specific disputing techniques.

LOGICAL DISPUTING

Upsetting emotions are often caused by thinking that is inflexible, unrealistic
or irrational. One way to counter this type of thinking is to use logical
disputing. This involves challenging the rigidity of our thinking (that is, our
assumption that things *must* be a certain way) and identifying a more balanced
perspective. Here are some examples of logical disputing statements that can
be used to challenge the common irrational beliefs described in Chapter 2.

BELIEFS	LOGICAL DISPUTING STATEMENTS
I must be loved and approved of by everyone.	I prefer people to like me but it's unrealistic to expect everyone to like me. I can cope even if some people don't like me, in the same way that others can cope if I don't like them.
I must be competent, adequate and achieving in every respect.	I am competent in some things and not in other things. While I can work on improving my skills, there is no reason why I must be competent in every area.
The world should be fair and I should always be treated fairly.	I prefer things to be fair, but I acknowledge that the world is full of injustice. Lots of things aren't fair, and chances are that at times I'm going to experience some injustice.
People should have the same values and beliefs as me, and they should do things the way I would do them.	People have the right to different values and beliefs from mine, and will sometimes say or do things that I don't like. It would be nice if others always did what I believe is right, but there is no reason why they must.
Certain people are bad, and they should be condemned for their actions.	People sometimes behave unfairly or inconsiderately. I can criticise poor behaviours, but I don't have to damn or condemn them as people.
When I do something badly, I am a bad person, a failure, an idiot.	Like everyone else, I sometimes make mistakes or do silly things, but that doesn't make me a failure or a bad person. I have done millions of things over the course of my life, and labelling myself on the basis of just some of my behaviours is unreasonable and self-defeating.
The world should provide me with what I need. Life should be comfortable. I shouldn't have to suffer or be inconvenienced.	It's nice when things go well for me, and much of the time they do. But there is no reason why things must always go smoothly. Hassles are a normal part of life.
It is awful when things don't go the way that I would like.	It is disappointing and inconvenient when things don't go the way that I would like, but it is very rarely awful or catastrophic.
It's easier to avoid problems than confront and deal with them.	Avoiding my problems may be easier in the short term, but not in the long term. It is often helpful to move outside of my comfort zone to confront problems and try to solve them.
Human unhappiness is caused by life circumstances. It is impossible to be happy when some things are not going well for me.	It is possible to feel good, even when some things are not going well for me. My life comprises many different areas, and I can enjoy some aspects of my life, even when facing major challenges in other areas.

BELIEFS	LOGICAL DISPUTING STATEMENTS
If there is a chance that something bad might happen, I should dwell on it now.	Dwelling on situations that I can't control doesn't change their outcomes, but creates anxiety. Rather than speculating on what may or may not happen, I can choose to deal with problems when they actually arise.
There is a correct solution to every problem and I should be able to work it out.	Most problems do not have one correct solution, but many possible solutions. Our decisions can only be based on the information that is available to us at the time, and often there is no obvious choice.

WRITE IT DOWN

Throughout this book we will see lots of examples of how negative or faulty thinking can be logically disputed. Some cognitions are easier to dispute than others, and those that are less ingrained can often be challenged mentally. However, most thoughts and beliefs are more effectively challenged in writing. Identifying the cognitions that contribute to distress, writing them down, and then writing statements that challenge those cognitions can help to transform vague notions into clear concepts. Writing also adds an extra level of processing, and so reinforces new perspectives. Re-reading those statements helps to consolidate learning. A written record of rational statements can also serve as a useful guide for future reference.

USING THOUGHT-MONITORING FORMS

A thought-monitoring form is a useful tool for reflecting on and clarifying cognitions. Different types of thought-monitoring forms have been devised, varying in design and complexity. The thought-monitoring form that I recommend provides space for identifying and disputing beliefs as well as thoughts. It also provides space for recording positive actions, and so also encourages the use of problem solving.

POSITIVE ACTIONS

Although it is not always possible to solve a problem, it is important to consider possible solutions. Sometimes we can do things to resolve the problem or lessen its severity. At other times the best that we can do is change the way we think about our circumstances. And sometimes we can do a bit of both. This is what the highly celebrated Serenity Prayer is all about:

God give me the serenity to accept the things that I cannot change,
the courage to change the things that I can
and the wisdom to know the difference.

Here are some examples of how thought-monitoring forms can be used to challenge negative cognitions:

During the course of a busy week, Elisabeth discovered that her wallet was missing. The realisation triggered anxiety and despair. 'This is disastrous!' she told herself. 'I had so many valuables in that wallet!' That night Elisabeth went to bed in a state of great distress. The following day she decided to take control over the situation. This meant problem solving, as well as challenging some of the catastrophic thoughts that were fuelling her emotional distress. She filled in her form as follows:

SITUATION	Discovered my wallet was missing. It had my credit cards, driver's licence, money and other valuables.
FEELINGS	Panic. Despair. Heart palpitations, tightness in the chest, knot in my stomach.
THOUGHTS	This is a complete disaster! I have lost everything.
	This mess is going to go on and on. I can't cope with this.
BELIEFS	The situation is disastrous—it will never be resolved.
	Things should always go smoothly. I can't cope when things go wrong.
THINKING ERRORS	Awfulising, predicting catastrophe, shoulds
DISPUTE	This is very inconvenient and will require lots of problem solving, but it is not a disaster.
	Hassles are an unavoidable part of life.
	I need to focus on solutions. I can get through this one step at a time.
POSITIVE ACTIONS	Start problem solving. Report missing wallet to police. Contact banks regarding my credit cards. Make alternative arrangements for monthly repayments. Write a 'To Do' list and follow up on each step.

THOUGHT-MONITORING FORM

SITUATION **FEELINGS**	
THOUGHTS **BELIEFS**	
THINKING ERRORS	❏ Shoulds ❏ Awfulising ❏ Black-and-white thinking ❏ Overgeneralising ❏ Personalising ❏ Filtering ❏ Just world fallacy ❏ Jumping to negative conclusions ❏ Mind reading ❏ Blaming ❏ Labelling ❏ Predicting catastrophe ❏ Comparing ❏ Hindsight vision
DISPUTE Alternative, more balanced view? What would I tell a friend who was in this situation?	
POSITIVE ACTIONS	

When reflecting on her situation Elisabeth realised that she had two problems: the first was the missing wallet, with all the inconvenience associated with chasing up banks, insurance companies and other organisations. The second problem was the panic, arousal, frustration and despair that resulted from Elisabeth's catastrophic cognitions ('This is a complete disaster!' etc.). The latter caused her suffering. Elisabeth realised that if she could manage her emotional response, she would have the inconvenience of her situation to deal with, without the additional burden of her distress. By challenging her thoughts Elisabeth was able to reduce the emotional distress that had become a second part of the problem. This made it easier for her to focus on problem solving.

Sonia separated from her husband Don a year ago, after he started a relationship with another woman. Sonia feels anxious every time she thinks she might see Don at social functions or when he comes to pick up the children on weekends. Sonia decides to challenge some of the unhelpful cognitions that cause her to feel so vulnerable. She writes the following notes on her thought-monitoring form:

SITUATION	Going to Christine's party. Don and his new woman are likely to be there.
FEELINGS	Anxious. Butterflies in my tummy. Can't relax.
THOUGHTS	I will look tense—people will see how uncomfortable I am. They'll feel sorry for me, and Don will think I'm pathetic.
BELIEFS	I must show everyone that I'm coping well. If I look uncomfortable people will judge me.
THINKING ERRORS	Predicting catastrophe, mind reading, shoulds
DISPUTE	Although I feel uncomfortable, it's not that obvious to others. Most people don't notice and don't care. Even if some people do notice that I look uncomfortable, it's not that surprising. I have a right to feel uncomfortable in these circumstances. Most people have been very supportive. What Don thinks doesn't matter any more. He is no longer part of my life.
POSITIVE ACTIONS	Call Erica and ask if she and Joe can pick me up on the way, so that I don't have to go there on my own. Tell them that I might need their support at the party, just in case I'm feeling fragile.

Steven's aged father in the UK had written to him asking Steven to come for a visit. Steven has had financial problems and was unable to go. Shortly afterwards his father died, and Steven feels very guilty for not having gone to see him.

SITUATION	Re-read Dad's last letter to me. Cried.
FEELINGS	Very guilty and sad. Feel heavy, lethargic.
THOUGHTS	Oh God, why didn't I just go and see him when he asked me? It would have made him happy. I'm such a rotten person.
BELIEFS	If a family member asks me to do something I should always do it. I should always put other people's needs before my own. I should be able to foresee all possible contingencies and act accordingly.
THINKING ERRORS	Shoulds, blaming, hindsight vision
DISPUTE	In retrospect, I can see that it would have been good for me to have gone to see him, but I didn't know that at the time. I was acting with the limited awareness that I had at the time. I try to be available to family members whenever I can, but I can't always meet everyone's needs. It's OK to take my own needs into account at times. That doesn't make me a bad person. I had a good relationship with my father, and not seeing him before he died doesn't change that.
POSITIVE ACTIONS	Write down all the things that I would have liked to have said to my father before he died. Talk to Sandra about it.

Pete is the General Manager of a successful marketing company. Recently sales have been down and Pete is angry at the lack of commitment and poor attitude of some of the sales staff. He writes the following notes in his thought-monitoring form:

SITUATION	Sales were down for the third quarter in a row.
FEELINGS	Angry and frustrated. Tension in all my muscles. Tight stomach.
THOUGHTS	That team is bone lazy—the lot of them. They waste a lot of time and put very little effort into their work. They just don't care.
BELIEFS	Everyone should have the same work ethic as me. They should all be as motivated as I am.

THINKING ERRORS	Labelling, overgeneralisation, shoulds
DISPUTE	I wish they were more diligent, but it's unrealistic to expect everyone to have my standards. At times I expect too much of others. It's up to me to come up with strategies to increase their motivation.
POSITIVE ACTIONS	Conduct a thorough review to identify the reasons for reduced sales, and look at ways in which we can motivate the sales team.

EXERCISE 3.1: PRACTISE LOGICAL DISPUTING

For each of the following examples, write down some logical disputing statements that could be used to challenge the negative thoughts and beliefs, and suggest some positive actions that could be taken. (Sample solutions are at the end of the book.)

THE NEGLECTED BIRTHDAY

SITUATION	Husband didn't make a fuss about me on my birthday.
FEELINGS	Hurt, angry, hot, tense.
THOUGHTS	He doesn't care about me.
BELIEFS	Birthdays are important. If he loved me, he would have made a fuss.
THINKING ERRORS	Jumping to negative conclusions, overgeneralising, shoulds, black-and-white thinking
DISPUTE	
POSITIVE ACTIONS	

THE FRUSTRATED PUBLIC SERVANT

SITUATION	I was meant to finish that report today, but spent much of the day with low priority tasks.
FEELINGS	Frustrated, anxious and angry at myself. Heart racing, tightness in chest.
THOUGHTS	I'm so hopeless! I have wasted the entire day and achieved nothing.
BELIEFS	I should always use my time productively. The consequences are likely to be dire.
THINKING ERRORS	Labelling, black-and-white thinking, shoulds, predicting catastrophe

DISPUTE

POSITIVE ACTIONS

THE FORGOTTEN BREAKFAST ARRANGEMENT

SITUATION	I made an arrangement to go out for breakfast with a friend, but slept in and forgot all about it. By the time I remembered she had gone out.
FEELINGS	Guilty and anxious. Body feels tense. Knot in stomach.
THOUGHTS	She must be angry at me. She probably thinks less of me now. This could ruin our friendship.
BELIEFS	I should always be reliable. It's terrible to let people down. The consequences of this situation are likely to be dire.
THINKING ERRORS	Jumping to negative conclusions, shoulds, predicting catastrophe

DISPUTE

POSITIVE ACTIONS

DE-CATASTROPHISE

The terms 'awfulising' and 'catastrophising' describe the human tendency to exaggerate the negative consequences of our situations (see page 30). Exaggerating the badness means that we experience our situation as if it were truly catastrophic, even though in most cases it is only undesirable or unpleasant. In fact, any negative situation can be experienced as a disaster if we think about it in that way. Awfulising about life situations can make us feel intensely anxious, frustrated, guilty, embarrassed, depressed or resentful.

This is not to say that nothing can be catastrophic or awful. There are some things that are very bad: contracting a very painful, degenerative, incurable disease; being the victim of a brutal attack; the death of a loved one or becoming severely disabled as a result of an accident. On an 'awfulness' scale of 0 to 100, these things could be rated as somewhere between 80 and 100.

However, most of the things that go wrong in our lives are really not that bad. Most people acknowledge that the vast majority of the things that upset them fall somewhere between 0 and 20 on an 'awfulness' scale. Even though events like making a stupid comment to someone we like, missing a flight or losing a contract may feel like a major catastrophe at the time, in the total scheme of things, the consequences are usually not that bad. The trouble is that when we awfulise, we experience situations as though they really are totally awful—around 100 on the awfulness scale.

AM I AWFULISING?

Here are some simple questions that can help you to put things into perspective:

➤ Have I felt this way before? Have I been wrong before?
➤ Will this matter in five years' time?
➤ On an awfulness scale of 0 to 100, how bad is this?
➤ [Think of someone you know who is a very positive person.] How would they perceive this situation?
➤ Is this within my control? What can I do about it?
➤ Is there anything good about this situation? What can I be grateful for?

➤ What can I learn from this experience?

➤ What is the worst that can happen? Best that can happen? Most likely to happen?

SOCRATIC QUESTIONING

Some negative thoughts are reasonably easy to challenge, and simply recognising that our thinking is unrealistic can help us to feel better. In other situations it is helpful to question the validity of our thoughts. *Socratic questioning* comes from the Greek philosopher Socrates, who made a habit of asking provocative questions to challenge people's assumptions about the world. The aim of Socratic questioning is to hold our thoughts up to logical scrutiny, identify any evidence that discredits them and come up with a more reasonable perspective.

Many different types of Socratic questions can be asked, depending on the situation. Below are some general questions that can be applied in many situations. Because these questions involve looking at objective evidence instead of relying on gut feelings, they are sometimes referred to as 'reality testing'. These questions are particularly useful when we jump to negative conclusions or make unreasonable assumptions.

REALITY TESTING

1 What are facts?
2 What are my subjective perceptions?
3 What evidence supports my perceptions?
4 What evidence contradicts my perceptions?
5 Am I making any thinking errors?
6 How else can I perceive this situation?

Rodney experienced an upsetting incident over a morning tea celebration at work. Having heard that one of his colleagues was leaving, Rodney volunteered to go out and buy some cream cakes for the occasion. By the time that Rodney had returned with the cakes the celebration was almost over. Apparently no one had bothered to wait for him, even though he had gone out of his way to contribute. Rodney feels hurt and humiliated.

You can probably sympathise with Rodney, in these circumstances, however does he really need to take it so badly? Depending on Rodney's history and cognitive style, the event has the potential to cause him anything from huge personal insult to a brief irritation. Rodney decides to evaluate his immediate response by using Socratic questioning:

1 What are facts?
Work colleagues didn't wait for me to start morning tea when I went out to buy the cakes.

2 What are my subjective perceptions?
They are treating me with contempt. I have been humiliated. If they respected me they would have waited for me.

3 What evidence supports my perceptions?
They started morning tea without me.

4 What evidence contradicts my perceptions?
Most of staff are usually friendly towards me. When I walked in with the cakes a few people said that they should have waited for me.

5 Am I making any thinking errors?
I am jumping to negative conclusions, personalising and awfulising. I'm interpreting this in a negative way—that it's deliberate and personal.

6 How else can I perceive this situation?
Most people at work are busy with their own stuff, and they don't always think about others. They didn't wait for me because they didn't think about it—not because they don't like me. People do take my needs into account some of the time, but not always. It wasn't personal and it wasn't a big deal.

Jill has had a long-standing disagreement with her neighbours over the removal of a large tree that affects both properties. This evening when Jill came home from work she noticed that her dog Jessie had not eaten his dinner—an unusual event, as Jessie normally has a healthy appetite. Jill immediately went into a panic. She thought that the neighbours had poisoned Jessie and that they are trying to get back at her for not cooperating with them over the tree.

After some catastrophising, Jill decided to use Socratic questioning to challenge her perceptions:

1 What are facts?
Jessie didn't eat his dinner this evening.

2 What are my subjective perceptions?
Jessie has been poisoned by the neighbours.

3 What evidence supports my perceptions?
Jessie didn't eat his dinner—he normally has a good appetite.

4 What evidence contradicts my perceptions?
Jessie is not showing any other signs of being seriously ill, which would probably be the case if he had been poisoned. I have had some disagreements with the neighbours in the past, but they have never been malicious or vindictive towards me.

5 Am I making any thinking errors?
I am jumping to negative conclusions.

6 How else can I perceive this situation?
There are many possible reasons why Jessie did not eat his dinner—I have no evidence that he has been poisoned, or that this has anything to do with the neighbours.

Elsa's husband has been working long hours, and when he comes home he is often tired and uncommunicative. Elsa feels hurt and rejected. 'He doesn't love me any more,' she thinks to herself. 'If he cared he'd want to spend more time with me, and he'd want to talk to me when he arrived home.'

Elsa decides to challenge her cognitions by using Socratic questioning:

1 What are facts?
Bill is working long hours. He is often uncommunicative when he comes home from work.

2 What are my subjective perceptions?
Bill doesn't love me.

3 What evidence supports my perceptions?

Bill doesn't say much when he comes home from work, and he has not shown any desire to cut down his work hours.

4 What evidence contradicts my perceptions?

Bill is still affectionate to me at times. When I get upset over things he shows his concern and says things to try to make me feel better. On weekends when he's relaxed he's more communicative.

5 Am I making any thinking errors?

I am personalising and jumping to negative conclusions.

6 How else can I perceive this situation?

Bill works long hours because his work is very important to him, and he is trying to create a successful business. He is often quiet when he comes home because he is exhausted. I have no evidence that his feelings towards me have changed. However, I can communicate more, and tell him how I feel. Perhaps we can negotiate a more balanced arrangement with his work hours.

BEHAVIOURAL DISPUTING

While using logical disputing on a regular basis can help us to develop cognitive flexibility, there are some situations where this type of disputing is difficult. For instance, we may be able to see that our thinking is irrational, but on a 'gut' level it feels true. This is where behavioural disputing can be helpful.

The way we behave often serves to reinforce our existing cognitions, including those that are unrealistic or self-defeating (see page 9). For instance, when we behave coldly or rudely towards someone that we dislike, we reinforce the belief that they are a bad person and deserve our contempt. When we avoid confronting an unpleasant task, we reinforce the belief that it is a loathsome task. When we behave unassertively with our friends, we reinforce the belief that we are not as good as them. When we avoid doing things that involve the possibility of failure, we reinforce the belief that failure would be unbearable. By behaving in these ways, our cognitions remain unchallenged and are often strengthened over time.

While our behaviours can serve to reinforce unhelpful cognitions, they can also be used to dispute them. Behaving in a way that is inconsistent with certain cognitions can help us to discover that those cognitions are incorrect. This process is called **behavioural disputing** because we challenge our cognitions using behaviours. It is also often referred to as **behavioural experiments** because by changing our behaviour we create the opportunity to discover the consequences. The aim of the experiment is to find out whether or not our assumptions are correct. If the negative outcomes that we had expected come to pass, we can use logical disputing to de-catastrophise, look at the reasons for the outcome and if appropriate, plan further behavioural experiments using different strategies. If, on the other hand, the negative outcomes we had expected do not eventuate, we come to realise that our perceptions are wrong. Behavioural disputing is one of the most powerful ways of challenging negative beliefs because we learn experientially.

> Words may help you to understand something.
> Experience allows you to know.
> **NEALE DONALD WALSCH, *CONVERSATIONS WITH GOD***

Fred works as a supervisor in a government department, and stays back for hours each evening to complete his outstanding work. Fred is reluctant to delegate to members of his team because he believes that they might not do a good job. Consequently, he is often overloaded with work, and arrives home late each evening. Fred recognises that he is a perfectionist, and has a very strong need for control. His beliefs include: 'If I delegate tasks to others they may not do a good job, and it may reflect badly on me.'

Fred can challenge his beliefs logically, by disputing the view that only he is capable of doing the tasks to an acceptable standard. He may use Socratic questioning to objectively examine the evidence for and against his thinking. In addition, Fred can do a behavioural experiment: he can delegate some of the work to his team members and observe the outcome. If Fred discovers that most of the delegated work is done to an acceptable standard, he will have good evidence disputing his belief that only he can do the job properly. If, on the other hand, the work is not done adequately, Fred will need to spend some time training members of his team and communicating more clearly what he expects from them. Delegating again after his team have been properly trained will help Fred discover that many of the jobs he is currently doing can be effectively done by others.

> *On two occasions over the past year Ruth's car was hit from behind while she was stationary at traffic lights. On one of those occasions she suffered severe whiplash. Now Ruth is afraid to drive, as she believes that if she does, she will have another accident.*

Ruth can challenge her beliefs logically, by realistically rating the probability of having another accident, and acknowledging that it is very low. She can also remind herself that she had been driving for nearly 20 years and, until last year, has had just a couple of very minor accidents.

However, the most powerful and effective challenge to Ruth's catastrophic cognitions will come from behavioural disputing. Ruth's behavioural task will involve getting into her car (initially taking a supportive friend with her) and driving around for short distances. As she discovers experientially that no negative consequences arise, her next step will be to drive alone and gradually increase the distance that she drives. As her confidence increases, she chooses to drive on busier roads. The discovery that nothing terrible happens provides a direct challenge to Ruth's catastrophic thinking, and enables her to regain confidence over time.

Behavioural disputing is a particularly useful tool for challenging irrational fears, as directly confronting the things we fear helps us to perceive on a deeper level that they are not dangerous after all (see also pages 148, 153 and 156).

> *Neil never communicates his true feelings because he wants to be perceived as masculine and strong. He believes that talking about feelings is 'girls' stuff'. Recently Neil went through a personal crisis that culminated in the break-up of his marriage. Although he feels depressed*

and lonely, Neil is reluctant to seek counselling as he believes that talking about his problems is a sign of weakness. He also believes that he is a bad person, and that if he was to be totally honest, a counsellor would judge him harshly.

Neil can challenge his beliefs logically, by reminding himself that being depressed is a good reason to see a counsellor, and that this does not mean that he is weak or defective. He can also use Socratic questioning to examine the evidence that supports and contradicts the idea that he is a bad person, and to help him recognise that he is irrationally labelling himself.

In addition, Neil could challenge his beliefs through behavioural disputing. Neil's behavioural experiment involves arranging to see a counsellor and, in spite of his anxiety, talking honestly about his feelings and experiences. This experiment helps Neil to discover that revealing his history and difficulties to an appropriate person does not lead to negative consequences, and it actually helps him to feel better.

Jerry hates social events. The strain of trying to make conversation with people he doesn't know makes him feel anxious, and Jerry fears that he may end up standing alone all night. As a result Jerry deliberately avoids parties and most other social functions. By staying away, Jerry escapes the discomfort of feeling self-conscious and awkward. However, avoiding these situations also reinforces Jerry's perception that social situations are high risk, and that he would not be able to cope.

Jerry can use logical disputing to challenge his belief that it would be awful if he ended up standing by himself at social functions, and acknowledge that although it may be boring, no catastrophic consequences are likely to occur. He may also use Socratic questioning to examine the evidence for his perception that he never enjoys himself at parties.

In addition, Jerry can challenge his beliefs via a behavioural experiment. This will involve taking the opportunity to attend social functions, starting with some easy, low-threat social events, and eventually going to some that feel more challenging. Exposing himself gradually in this way enables Jerry to discover that he can usually engage with someone when he makes the effort, and even on those rare occasions where he doesn't say much, the consequences are not disastrous.

EXERCISE 3.2: PRACTISE BEHAVIOURAL DISPUTING

Suggest behavioural experiments that can be used to test the unhelpful cognitions in each of the following situations. (Sample solutions are at the back of the book.)

1   If I speak up in front of the class I will make a fool of myself—they will laugh at me.
2   I just can't take that flight—I'll have a panic attack and collapse or go mad.
3   I should always say what people want to hear, because otherwise they won't like me.
4   There is a wrong and right decision, and I have to be one hundred per cent sure of the right decision before I make a move.
5   If I try to talk to people at that conference, they might not respond, and I will look like an idiot!
6   That essay needs to be perfect. I can't submit work that is less than perfect.
7   Exercise is important, but I'd need to get up an hour earlier to fit it in. It's too difficult to get up early.
8   It's awful to be alone. It's better to be with anyone, than to be by myself.

GOAL-FOCUSED THINKING

So far we have looked at disputing our cognitions **logically**, by directly challenging the unhelpful aspects of our thinking, and **behaviourally**, by taking actions that challenge unrealistic cognitions. A third method of disputing is **goal-focused thinking**. This involves recognising the self-defeating nature of our cognitions—reflecting that our current perceptions prevent us from achieving the things we want. Goal-focused thinking is sometimes referred to as 'persuasive disputing' because we persuade ourselves to release unhelpful cognitions through acknowledging their negative impact. It is a **motivational strategy** designed to encourage us to stop thinking in a self-defeating way.

In goal-focused thinking we remind ourselves to stay focused on the 'big picture'—our underlying goals. As we acknowledge the negative consequences of thinking the way we do, we become motivated to release unhelpful thinking. The following key question helps us to do this:

> Does thinking or behaving this way help me to feel good or to
> achieve my goals?

When faced with upsetting emotions we can ask this particular question, or we can tailor our question to address our specific situation. For instance:

➤ Does telling myself that my work has to be perfect help me to get things finished on time?

➤ Does staying angry with my partner help us to be happy and to have a good relationship?

➤ Does focusing on the injustice of this situation enable me to feel good and get on with my life?

➤ Does demanding that others should have the same values that I do help me to get on with people?

➤ Does telling myself that I am a bad person for making that mistake help me to have good self-esteem?

➤ Does worrying about the way I look tonight help me to relax and enjoy the evening?

Goal-focused thinking can be used in many situations, but it is particularly useful when we feel angry, resentful or frustrated.

Cynthia and her husband have gone away for a holiday to a beach resort with their friends John and Nancy. After two days, Cynthia starts to feel annoyed by some of the things that John and Nancy are doing. For a start, they are not making an equal contribution to buying the daily provisions. Secondly, Nancy spends ages in the bathroom, and John seems to be a lot more selfish than Cynthia had realised. As time goes on, John and Nancy seem to become more and more irritating. By day six, even the way they breathe is annoying!

The problem for Cynthia is that thinking this way is making her feel bad, and is ruining her holiday. Cynthia decides to challenge her response using goal-focused thinking, focusing on the self-defeating nature of her cognitions: **'Does thinking this way help me to feel good or to achieve my goals?'**

I've come here to have a good time, but I'm feeling resentful and annoyed much of the time. Getting irritated by their behaviour is only punishing me—I'm ruining my own holiday! I can choose to let go of these feelings by accepting our differences, and not worrying about petty things.

In addition Cynthia can challenge her beliefs using logical disputing:

They don't contribute as much as we do, but the amount of money involved is trifling, and they're not doing it on purpose. Most of the things that are annoying me are trivial. They are basically well-meaning, although they do things differently to us. It's really not such a big deal.

*

Karen has had a falling out with a fitness instructor at her gym. Now, she can't stand him. Every time she sees him, the word 'jerk' comes instantly to her mind. Whenever she hears him talking to others, she mutters 'halfwit' under her breath. The problem for Karen is that thinking this way is self-defeating, because her resentment affects her mood when at the gym.

As Karen comes to realise that her attitude is self-defeating, she uses goal-focused thinking to motivate herself to change her response: **'Does thinking this way help me to feel good or to achieve my goals?'**

> *Focusing on his faults makes me bitter and wastes my energy. It also makes coming to the gym less enjoyable. As I'm here almost every day, I want to feel comfortable, and not worry about him. It's in my own interests to stop criticising him and just focus on getting fit!*

In addition, Karen challenges her beliefs using logical disputing:

> *He's not someone I would choose to spend time with, but he's not a terrible person. He behaves in accordance with his own values and beliefs, and he has the right to be who he is. I don't have to like him, but I don't have to hate him or focus on his flaws.*

*

> *Linda has agreed to go out to a restaurant with a group of friends. The woman who organised the function has extravagant tastes, and one look at the menu reveals that Linda is in for an expensive evening. Linda feels angry that whenever her friend selects a restaurant, it is always expensive.*

Now, Linda can spend the rest of her evening fretting about the prices and her friend's thoughtlessness. Alternatively, she can choose to use goal-focused thinking: **'Does thinking this way help me to feel good or to achieve my goals?'**

> *I'm here now. Focusing on the prices is not going to make the meal any cheaper—it's just going to ruin the evening for me. I choose to let this go now, and just have a good time.*

In addition, Linda challenges her beliefs using logical disputing:

> *Even though it will be an expensive meal, in the end it will not make a significant difference to my overall budget. I can choose to worry about it or choose to forget it, but it won't change the situation. Next time my friend wants to arrange a meal I am going to suggest the restaurant, or at least reserve veto rights if she comes up with another one like this.*

EXERCISE 3.3: PRACTISE GOAL-FOCUSED THINKING

Suggest goal-focused thinking for the people in each of the following situations. (Sample solutions are at the back of the book.)

1 Kim is looking forward to her 40th birthday party, but her mum has insisted on attending. Kim doesn't want her mum to be there, and believes that her presence will spoil the evening. She feels angry and resentful.
2 Sandra is angry with her partner because he made so little effort to converse with her parents when they went there for lunch. To pay him back, he is in for some cold-shoulder treatment over the next few days.
3 Richard agreed to go to the movies with his girlfriend, even though he had a lot of studying to do before his approaching exam. Throughout the film Richard feels anxious and annoyed as he thinks to himself that he should not have come. He has so much work to do—he should have been more assertive.
4 Cindy has noticed that one of her work colleagues has a very poor work ethic, and spends much of her time on personal telephone calls. Although she chooses not to say anything to her, Cindy feels infuriated every time her colleague gets on the phone.

IN SUMMARY

➤ **Logical disputing** involves identifying the irrational aspects of our thinking, labelling their faulty aspects and coming up with more realistic and balanced ways of perceiving our situations.

➤ Writing down negative cognitions and the disputing statements that challenge them helps to reinforce more reasonable ways of thinking. A thought-monitoring form is a useful aid in this process.

➤ Cognitions can also be challenged via **Socratic questioning**. This involves putting our thoughts under logical scrutiny by asking specific challenging questions.

➤ Some negative assumptions and beliefs are better challenged using **behavioural disputing**. This involves changing our behaviours and observing the outcomes. This method is particularly powerful because we often learn experientially that our thinking is incorrect.

➤ **Goal-focused thinking** is a motivational strategy to encourage us to change our perceptions. It involves focusing on the self-defeating nature of our current cognitions—recognising that they do not help us to feel good or achieve the things we want.

FOUR

Overcoming frustration

We must learn to suffer what we cannot evade;
our life, like the harmony of the world, is composed, of contrary things—
of discords as well as of different tones,
sweet and harsh, sharp and flat, soft and loud.
If a musician liked only some of them, what could he sing?

MICHEL DE MONTAIGNE, *OF EXPERIENCE*

Frustration is a feeling we experience when we don't get our needs met, or when some obstacle impedes our ability to achieve a goal. People typically feel frustrated when confronted with problems that cannot be easily resolved; however, some people manage life's frustrations better than others. Some people have low frustration tolerance—LFT for short—which means they get frustrated very easily. Albert Ellis first described the notion of LFT in the 1960s. Ellis sometimes referred to it as 'can't standitis' because people with LFT frequently complain that they *can't stand* this or that. Consequently, they upset themselves excessively in situations where they don't get what they want.

Learning to deal with frustration is a normal part of human development. Babies and young children have LFT, because they have not yet developed the maturity for tolerating frustration. As we get older, we learn to delay our desire for immediate gratification, and to accept that hassles and frustrations happen without becoming excessively distressed by them.

However, even in adulthood, many people don't cope well with frustration. This may be partly because of biological factors, such as an irritable temperament, which makes them prone to overreacting in response to common annoyances. An irritable temperament may be genetically determined, or may develop in response to highly stressful experiences in early childhood such as inconsistent messages; physical or emotional abuse; chaotic, disorganised environments or unpredictable parental behaviour. These experiences result in high levels of physical *arousability* later in life. This means that our body becomes over-sensitised and produces high levels of adrenaline in response to minor stressors. Consequently we become tense and physically aroused very easily.

In addition, our environment and culture also influences the way we respond to frustrating events. Ellis observed that people living in modern Western countries often become frustrated easily because they are so used to getting their needs met much of the time. Advances in modern technology and increased affluence over the past half-century have had a huge effect on our lives. Modern medicine has enabled us to avoid or control many of the deadly diseases that afflicted our ancestors and still affect people living in poorer countries today. Many unpleasant conditions—including headaches, nausea, indigestion, constipation, anxiety, itching, insomnia and even impotence—can be relieved by swallowing a pill. Internal plumbing in our homes has enabled us to maintain good hygiene with a minimum of effort, and avoid facing the elements when we go to the toilet at night. Modern appliances enable us to stay warm in winter and cool in summer. Boredom can be assuaged with the press of a button, and hunger can be alleviated by going to the fridge. Detailed information about any subject can be accessed in a matter of seconds. The internet and digital technologies have revolutionised our lives in ways that previous generations could not have dreamed. All of these developments are for the good—they have made our lives easier, and more comfortable and interesting than ever before. However, there is a downside.

Because we expect our lives to be easy, many of us have not learned to accept the difficult, frustrating or unpleasant situations that are an unavoidable part of life. We become overly upset when things go wrong or when we are confronted with hassles or inconveniences. We awfulise and complain, and we become physically aroused. Consequently, in addition to the original problem, we create a second one—upsetting emotions, such as anger, resentment or despair that come from the belief that **it must not be so**.

> *Harry is having a bad day. He left home at 6 am to go to the gym, only to find that the doors were still locked. Apparently there was a mix-up with the keys, and one of the fitness instructors has had to go home to get a spare set. Harry is fuming. 'What a waste of my time! I could have slept in,' he thinks to himself. After his abridged workout, Harry battles peak-hour traffic, and by the time he gets to work he is feeling particularly irritable. To add to his annoyance, Harry is told that his secretary has called in sick. 'Great!' Just when he thought that things couldn't get any worse, Harry is informed that the computer network is down and it will take several hours to restore. 'That's all I need!' he yells, as his blood pressure rises and his agitation grows.*

Harry's business partner, Ian, is dealing with similar problems but, unlike Harry, Ian keeps his cool. When things go wrong, Ian stays calm and focuses on finding solutions. Although he doesn't enjoy hassles, Ian does not awfulise when they happen or demand that they should not arise. Ian thinks differently to Harry, and is therefore able to deal with problems without making himself overly upset about them.

While Harry blames his troubles on other people, the traffic, technology and bad luck, his biggest problem is his thinking. No one enjoys it when things go wrong, especially when several things go wrong at once. The reality is, however, that hassles are an unavoidable part of life. The challenge is to accept this simple truth, while seeking solutions whenever possible.

Whether we are dealing with a computer virus, a car that won't start, a child who won't cooperate, employees who call in sick or people who think differently from ourselves, it is sensible to look for solutions whenever possible. However, in situations where there is nothing that we can do, our best strategy is to *practise acceptance*, instead of 'demanding' that problems should not exist. Ironically, the expectation that things should not go wrong creates additional distress when they inevitably do.

> When hassles arise,
> demanding that they should not exist
> only makes us feel worse.

PATTERNS OF THINKING THAT GENERATE LFT

Low frustration tolerance is associated with rigid, inflexible thinking. We internally demand that things should go our way (shoulds) and believe that unless they do, the situation is intolerable (black-and-white thinking). We add to our distress by exaggerating the negative consequences of those situations (awfulising).

> ➤ *Patricia feels depressed at having to stay home to work on her thesis while her friends are going out and having a good time.*
> ➤ *Hugh believes that only one political party can solve the country's problems and he becomes angry and despondent when it fails to win the election.*
> ➤ *Miriam is miserable because the renovations on her house are taking much longer than expected and the chaos feels intolerable.*
> ➤ *In his job Nick has to deal with members of the public, whom he considers demanding, difficult and stupid. Consequently he hates going to work each day.*
> ➤ *Bob walks out of the bank after having stood in the queue for 20 minutes. He is furious at the slow service, and at the fact that he will need to go back on a second occasion.*

While each of the above situations is potentially frustrating, the degree of frustration and other unpleasant emotions we experience in response to them will depend on our ability to adapt to situations over which we have no control. LFT contributes additional distress.

COMMON BELIEFS UNDERLYING LFT
> ➤ My life should proceed smoothly, without hassles.
> ➤ People should think and behave the way I think is right.

➤ It is awful to have to do things I don't enjoy.

➤ I shouldn't have to put up with poor behaviour by others.

➤ Because I don't like certain things, I shouldn't have to experience them.

RESPONDING TO LFT

Stan is setting off to work on Monday morning. As he opens the garage door he discovers that someone has parked their car over his driveway. 'Damn it!' he thinks to himself. 'This is such a pain in the neck! Why can't people do the right thing?' Stan feels frustrated and angry.

It is reasonable for Stan to feel upset when he discovers this unexpected hassle, and some short-term cussing is a normal human response. The question is, what should he do after that? A psychologically healthy response is to **look for solutions**. These might include actions such as:

➤ Sit in the car and toot the horn for few minutes to see if the owner of the other car surfaces.

➤ Knock on the doors of neighbours to ask if they know who owns the car.

➤ Leave a note on the windscreen of the car, asking the owner to move it.

➤ Call the police and ask for their assistance.

➤ Call the supervisor at work to tell her what happened. Let her know that I will be late for work this morning, as I will be travelling to work by train and bus.

Once he has taken these actions, Stan stops to reflect on his own emotional response. He recognises that some of his **beliefs** include:

➤ People should always do the right thing.

➤ My life should proceed smoothly and without hassles.

➤ It's awful when things go wrong.

➤ The consequences are likely to be disastrous.

At this point Stan starts to challenge his beliefs with **disputing statements** such as:

➤ I wish people always did the right thing, but that is not realistic.

➤ Hassles are a normal part of life. Things go wrong for everybody at times.

➤ This is inconvenient, but it's not a disaster. On the 'awfulness' scale it only rates five per cent. It's not going to matter in five years' time.

➤ What's the worst thing that can happen?—I'll have to catch public transport to work today.

➤ I can ruminate about the problem, but I prefer to focus on solutions.

As it happened, the police contacted the owner of the car in the late afternoon, and it was finally shifted that evening. While the whole episode was a nuisance, Stan realised that it was not a disaster. However, he would have experienced it as a disaster if he had continued to awfulise and demand that it should not have happened.

By choosing to remain goal-focused, Stan was able to avoid becoming overwhelmed by upsetting emotions. On the following weekend Stan painted a big 'No Parking' sign on the door of his garage. While he realised that the sign would not guarantee the situation would never happen again, Stan felt good for having taken action to reduce the likelihood.

Robert bought tickets for himself and his girlfriend, Alicia, to see one of his favourite entertainers in concert. The time printed on the ticket was 7 pm. Although this seemed early, Robert assumed that it must be an early show. However, when they arrived at the venue at 6.45, the door was locked and there was a sign outside stating that some tickets had been printed with an incorrect starting time. In fact, the supporting act was due to commence at 8 pm, while the main act was due to start at 9.15. As it began to dawn on him that they had arrived two-and-a-half hours early, Robert became frustrated and angry. He would have liked to demand his money back, but there was no one to speak to—the box office was closed. Alicia was in the same situation as Robert but she was not too worried about the wait. Her only concern was Robert's angry reaction.

So here are two people in exactly the same situation—one feeling very angry and frustrated, while the other is unfazed. Why do they respond so differently? Who is right?

It's all about cognitions. As Robert has rigid, inflexible beliefs about how things should be, he creates distress, not only in this situation but in many others as well. Let's take a look at the cognitions that cause Robert to feel this way:

THOUGHTS

- ➤ They've screwed up! How outrageous!
- ➤ Over two hours until the main act—what a waste of time! I could have done lots of other things instead of hanging around here!

BELIEFS

- ➤ People should be efficient and reliable. It's terrible when they're not. Mistakes like this shouldn't happen.
- ➤ All my time should be spent productively. I should never waste time.
- ➤ It's bad to have time on my hands with nothing planned.

As Robert noticed Alicia's calm response, he started to question his own response. 'Perhaps I am overreacting?' he thought to himself. Robert decided to challenge some of the cognitions that were making him feel distressed:

DISPUTING STATEMENTS

➤ I prefer to use my time productively and most of the time I do, but it's OK to have unplanned periods at times.

➤ We can find other things to do until the main act comes on.

➤ It is good for me to challenge my need for constant time efficiency.

➤ This is a hassle, but it's not a disaster.

As Robert reflected on new ways of thinking about his situation, he started to relax. He talked to Alicia about how they could use the extra time that was now available to them, and they decided to do the following things:

POSITIVE ACTIONS

➤ Walk down to the cinema centre to see if there are any films that we would like to see.

➤ If there are no suitable films, go down to a café for a focaccia and coffee.

➤ If we still have time left over, go and watch the supporting act.

When he looked back on the situation, Robert realised that he could have spoiled a perfectly good evening by his negative attitude—whingeing, complaining and making a fuss. While he could have demanded a refund when the box office opened, this would have been like cutting off his nose to spite his face, as both he and Alicia wanted to see the show. By catching himself in the process, and making a conscious decision to relax, Robert prevented himself from ruining the evening.

SIMPLE DISPUTING STATEMENTS TO MANAGE FRUSTRATION

➤ Hassles are a normal part of life.

➤ Where is it written that things should always go smoothly?

➤ I can't prevent hassles, but I can choose not to upset myself when they arise.

➤ Will this matter in five years' time? Don't sweat the small stuff.

USING A THOUGHT-MONITORING FORM

While logical disputing can be done 'in our head', it is usually more effective when done in writing. This is particularly the case when we are learning to develop cognitive flexibility. Recording our thoughts and the underlying beliefs that support them highlights the unreasonable aspects of our thinking, and makes it easier to come up with more adaptive perceptions. Using this process on a regular basis enables us to learn to be more flexible in our thinking over time.

> *Leanne agreed to her boss's request to stay back at work to finish a project. When she returned home that evening, Leanne discovered that her dog, Fred, had escaped through a broken plank in the backyard fence. After ringing around anxiously, Leanne discovered that Fred had been picked up by the pound, and it would cost her $200 to retrieve him. Anxiety turned into frustration. It seemed so unfair—she was doing them a good turn at work, and now she was inconvenienced and out of pocket.*

SITUATION	After agreeing to work late, I came home to discover that Fred had escaped and had been picked up by the pound. It will cost me $200 to get him back.
FEELINGS	Angry, frustrated, tense.
THOUGHTS	How unfair! I was doing them a good turn, and now it has cost me. I should have said 'no', and it wouldn't have happened.
BELIEFS	Things should be fair—generous actions should be rewarded, not punished. The situation has turned out really badly.
THINKING ERRORS	Just world fallacy, awfulising, hindsight vision
DISPUTE	There is no law that says that good actions are always rewarded. Bad things can happen even when you're doing something good. Things go wrong for everybody at times. Frustrations are a normal part of life. Although it seems like a lot of money, Fred is safe and that is worth more than $200. The fine is disappointing but, in the end, it's not going to make a difference to my financial situation.
POSITIVE ACTIONS	Pay the $200 and collect Fred from the pound. Ring up a handyman and arrange to get the fence repaired as soon as possible.

POSITIVE ACTIONS

In some situations, it is not enough to simply challenge our cognitions—we need to **take action** to problem solve as well. In fact, some situations cry out for action.

> *Nina frequently feels frustrated because her two young sons often make a mess in various rooms of the house, and take no responsibility for tidying up. As a result, Nina is frequently cleaning up after them. Her husband, Tim, does little to help her.*

Nina fills out her thought-monitoring form as follows:

SITUATION	The boys are constantly making a mess, and I have to clean up after them all the time. Tim doesn't help. I came home late yesterday and the place was a pigsty.
FEELINGS	Frustrated, angry, heat surges.
THOUGHTS	I can't stand this mess! Why can't they take some responsibility for cleaning up after themselves? Why does it always fall to me to clean up after them?
BELIEFS	They should be more responsible. They should take an interest in keeping the house clean. Tim should be more supportive of my concerns.
THINKING ERRORS	Shoulds, just world fallacy
DISPUTE	I wish that they were more responsible and helpful, but they are behaving like normal boys of their age. If I want them to help, I need to use some strategies to motivate them. Tim doesn't clean much, but he does other things that I don't do. I'd like him to help more with the housework, so I need to talk to him about it.
POSITIVE ACTIONS	Have a long talk to Tim—tell him how I'm feeling, and what I'd like from him and the boys. Have a family meeting. Talk to the boys about what I expect from them. Implement an incentive scheme—make their pocket money conditional on their cleaning up their rooms, and not leaving their things around the house. Deduct pocket money for each time they leave a mess.

In this example, taking action is an important part of the solution. While Nina can reduce her frustration by reminding herself that her children's behaviour is normal, and that her husband helps her in other ways, it is also important for her to communicate with her husband and children, and negotiate possible solutions such as rewards for good behaviour and punishments for reneging on their agreement. Good communication can help us to solve many problems and reduce the likelihood of others arising in the future.

EXERCISE 4.1

1   Tick any of the following situations where you have experienced LFT:
   ❑ being stuck in traffic
   ❑ your children 'mucking about'
   ❑ wanting something that you can't have
   ❑ having to do a boring or difficult task
   ❑ dealing with someone who thinks differently to yourself
   ❑ dealing with someone who does things slowly
   ❑ physical limitations brought on by ageing or a health problem
   ❑ mistakes you have made
   ❑ your partner not wanting the same things you do
   ❑ poor service
   ❑ waiting in a slow-moving queue
   ❑ errors in bills that have been sent to you
   ❑ attempting to get through on a call to a large bureaucratic institution.
2   In each instance how did LFT affect the way you felt?
3   Assuming that you cannot change the situations themselves, how would you *like to think and feel* when you are in each of these situations?

'BUT I DON'T WANT TO LET IT GO!'

Although it is reasonable to assume that we always want to feel good and avoid feeling bad, this is not always true (our mind is complex!). In some situations we instinctively want to hold on to our current emotions, even unpleasant ones, because at a deeper level they feel protective. In the above example, Nina may notice some resistance to disputing her thoughts because it feels like releasing her anger will have negative consequences. Perhaps releasing those feelings will mean that nothing will change? Staying angry is Nina's way of trying to ensure that her concerns are not ignored.

Beliefs about our own thoughts and emotions are referred to as **metacognitive beliefs**, a concept first described in relation to CBT by British psychologist Adrian Wells. These beliefs are usually held on an unconscious level, but can often be brought to consciousness through reflection. These beliefs can motivate us to engage in unhelpful cognitive processes such as worry, rumination and ongoing self-criticism, and hold on to unpleasant emotions such as anger, anxiety, frustration, hopelessness and guilt, because at some level they feel protective. (In fact, it is true that unpleasant emotions sometimes do have benefits, although the costs of *ongoing emotional distress* outweigh any possible benefits.) For example, Nina's metacognitive beliefs include, 'Staying angry gives me power. If I release my anger things will not change.' Seeing the downsides of staying angry and using other strategies to get her needs met (such as effective communication, problem solving, providing rewards and punishments for her children and following up on their agreement) is likely to result in far better outcomes than holding on to her anger.

LFT AND PROCRASTINATION

Low frustration tolerance (LFT) creates unnecessary distress because we become overly upset when confronted with situations that don't meet our needs. LFT also has another disadvantage—it often gives rise to procrastination and self-defeating behaviours. Finding it difficult to endure situations we do not enjoy, we put things off and sometimes avoid doing them altogether. This can be a problem because achieving many of the things that are important and worthwhile requires us to tolerate some discomfort along the way. Confronting someone about an unresolved issue, leaving an unsatisfactory job, doing regular exercise, making a potentially unpleasant telephone call, completing a course, improving our diet or initiating contact with a new acquaintance—all require a willingness to step outside our comfort zone. It feels unpleasant in the short term. This explains why so many people remain stuck in abusive relationships, unhealthy lifestyles, lonely lives and soul-destroying jobs.

The path of least resistance is appealing because it's easy—we just keep avoiding. However, we miss opportunities to improve our circumstances and gain control over distressing aspects of our lives.

> LFT then becomes short-range hedonism: indulging in immediate self-gratifying, in spite of its future consequences.
>
> **ALBERT ELLIS**

Susan has been in an unhappy marriage for the past six years. She frequently complains that her husband is mean-spirited, miserly, controlling and hard to live with. Although she would love to leave, Susan has never seriously contemplated doing so or even standing up to her husband. Some people ask why an intelligent and attractive woman like Susan would remain married to someone she detests. Susan's desire to avoid the transient distress of ending her marriage outweighs her determination to improve her life in the longer term. She chooses familiar suffering in preference to the uncertainty of change.

Initiating change involves the possibility of pain—fear, upheaval and loneliness. Sometimes it seems easier to let things be than to risk the emotional distress that comes with change. However avoiding short-term pain may come at the cost of long-term benefits, and may cause us to remain stuck in unhappy situations.

> A full life is a life full of pain.
> But the only alternative is not to live fully or not to live at all.
>
> **M. SCOTT PECK, *THE ROAD LESS TRAVELED***

Of course this doesn't mean that people who are in unhappy relationships should always leave their partner. Sometimes there are good reasons for staying in a less-than-perfect relationship. However, whatever we choose to do, we increase our chances of being happy when our choices are based on rational, considered judgements rather than inertia or LFT.

EXERCISE 4.2

1 Describe a situation where you have been putting off doing something that you need to do.

2 To what degree does LFT contribute to your procrastination in this situation? _____%

3 What would you need to believe to feel motivated to act? (For example: 'It's not really so difficult; it will get easier once I get started'; 'It's OK to do things that I don't enjoy as the rewards are worth it' and so on. See also Chapter 9.)

BEHAVIOURAL DISPUTING FOR LFT

In addition to logical disputing, we can modify our cognitions by using behavioural disputing—taking actions that enable us to discover that our assumptions are incorrect (see page 60). A good behavioural experiment for challenging LFT is to choose to do things that move us outside our comfort zone. Exposing ourselves to situations that are difficult or unpleasant enables us to realise that they are really not so awful, and we *can* stand it after all. Ironically, once we stop trying to run away from discomfort, we discover that the object we are running away from is really not that bad. As we increase our tolerance for frustration, we get more things done, and situations that would normally upset us no longer matter.

> Doing things we don't enjoy enables us to discover that they are not so bad after all. The idea of doing them is often worse than the act of doing them.

Betty used to get frustrated every time she had to attend dinners and social functions with certain members of her extended family. She considered them to be ignorant peasants, and hated having to spend time with them. Consequently, every family get-together was an ordeal. Sometimes she made up excuses to get out of attending, much to the annoyance of her husband and mother-in-law. Sometimes she came along begrudgingly but made no effort to converse. Finally, Betty decided to try to change her attitude. Her first decision was to stop making excuses, and attend all the family dinners she was invited to. When she attended she deliberately chose to participate in the conversation, even with people she disliked. Instead of ignoring or judging them, Betty listened to what they had to say, and tried to acknowledge their right to their point of view. Although her own views were quite different, Betty came to accept that they are entitled to their perspective, and that she could talk to them without judging them. What used to be a major chore became painless because Betty changed her behaviour as well as her attitude.

> Look for the fun and enjoyment—not merely the pain and problems—of doing difficult things that are in your best interest.
>
> **ALBERT ELLIS**

Ken gets frustrated whenever he perceives that he is wasting time. The belief that he should always use his time productively causes him to become angry whenever he is stuck in traffic, has to wait in a queue or when the service is slow. Sometimes he becomes so agitated that he makes a scene and behaves obnoxiously. Under advice from his psychologist, Ken decides to do some behavioural disputing to challenge his LFT. He starts by driving his car at a slower speed and avoiding constant lane changes and pushing in on other drivers. In the supermarket, he allows people who have just a few items to get in front of him, and twice a day he takes a few minutes to do a mindfulness-of-the-breath exercise. By deliberately slowing down Ken learns that even when things take extra time, the consequences are insignificant. They just take a little longer—that's all.

*

Greg's lifestyle has become increasingly sedentary since he stopped playing football ten years ago. Now in his mid–40s, Greg recognises that he is unfit and overweight. His doctor has advised Greg to modify his diet and do some exercise every day, but this doesn't sound easy. Greg enjoys junk food and has little time for exercise. He'd like to make those changes, but why does it have to be so hard?

In order to make positive changes to his life, Greg needs to accept a degree of frustration and discomfort. As a first step, he makes a commitment to get out of bed at six o'clock each morning (even those cold winter mornings when he'd much prefer to stay in bed) and do a brisk half-hour walk. In addition, he commits to limiting junk food to weekends. This will mean buying a sandwich or roll for lunch and snacking on fruit or nuts instead of chocolate bars. There is no doubt that sticking to his commitment is going to be difficult, as it will involve giving up some of the things he enjoys. Learning to accept some discomfort will help Greg to increase his tolerance for frustration and ultimately make it easier for him to maintain a healthy lifestyle.

When people ask me how to do something, I remind them that they already know how; they are really asking, 'What's the easy way?'
On planet Earth, 'easy' is hard to find. Any accomplishment requires effort, courage, and will ...

DAN MILLMAN, *NO ORDINARY MOMENTS*

IT SHOULD NOT HAVE HAPPENED!

One style of thinking that frequently causes frustration and self-downing, is the belief that something that happened should not have happened. Sometimes we make this assumption about other people's behaviours ('He shouldn't have done that'), but more often we think it in relation to our own ('I shouldn't have done that'). The more rigidly we believe that we should or should not have done what we did, the more upset we become. Although it is useful to learn from our actions and try to avoid making the same mistakes again, telling ourselves that we should not have done what we did is both pointless and irrational.

'I should be able to envisage all possible problems and prevent them from happening.'

All events are causally determined—this is a basic scientific principle that applies to human behaviour as well as to the laws of nature. Everything that happens in the universe occurs because the circumstances that prevail at the time cause it to happen. Whether a volcano erupts or a leaf falls from a tree or your computer crashes, it happens because all the factors that were necessary for those events to occur were present at that time. This same principle also applies to human behaviour. Everything we say and do, including those things that turn out to have negative consequences, happen because all of the factors that were necessary for them to occur were present at that time. We could not have behaved differently, given all of the factors that prevailed, including our limited knowledge and awareness at that point in time, and if all of those circumstances recurred, we would do the very same thing.

In retrospect, we can see the consequences of our actions and recognise that it may have been better to have done some things differently. After the event, we can learn from the experience (new knowledge and awareness) and try not to repeat our mistakes. However, as we did not have that knowledge and awareness at the time, blaming ourselves for our past actions is both irrational and self-defeating.

It is so. It cannot be otherwise.

ZEN SAYING

Here is a personal example:

After severe hailstorms in Sydney some years ago, the roof of our house was badly damaged. As many houses in the area had also experienced hail damage, roofers were scarce, and it took several weeks before I *finally found a company that agreed to do the work within the next month. The company insisted that I pay a deposit of ten per cent before they started the job. As our insurance company had provided us with a cheque for the full amount quoted, I simply passed this on to the roofing company. In the three months that followed, no work was done, and our roof continued to leak. My telephone inquiries were often ignored or rebuffed, and sometimes I couldn't get through to anyone at all. Finally, the news came—the company was in receivership with debts of over $2 million. The money would not be refunded, and no, the work would not be done. 'Sorry ... bad luck.'*

In looking back on what happened, it's easy to see that paying the full amount upfront was a mistake. Once the money had been paid, the company had no incentive to make our job a priority. If I had paid ten per cent rather than the full amount, perhaps the job would have been done, or at worst, I would have lost only ten per cent. In retrospect, it is easy to be self-damning, frustrated, angry and perhaps even depressed. I can blame the company for being so unethical and blame myself for being so stupid. I can tell myself over and over again that I was an idiot, and that I should never have done what I did (a good example of *hindsight vision*). But is it logical to say that I shouldn't have done what I did?

When I handed over payment for the full amount, I was acting with the awareness that was available to me at that time. (Actually, it did momentarily occur to me that paying upfront might be risky, but I chose to go ahead because my overriding assumption was that things would be OK.) If I had had greater awareness that something might go wrong, I would have done things differently. So it is not logical for me to now tell myself that I should not have done what I did. Given my awareness and thought processes at the time, I could not have done things any other way—that's causally determined reality.

Demanding that things that happened should not have happened is as rational as shouting at the sky on a cloudy day, demanding that the sun should be shining.

BUT I SHOULD FEEL BAD—IT'S MY FAULT!

As we saw earlier, sometimes we want to hold on to upsetting emotions, because doing so feels protective. So, for instance, we may find it hard to forgive ourselves when we have made a mistake, because we believe we need to suffer in order to learn from the experience. On an unconscious or semiconscious level, the belief 'If I make a mistake I *should* feel terrible; if I forgive myself I will do it again', can keep us self-critical and guilt-ridden for weeks, months or more.

So, is it really necessary to suffer interminably in order to learn from our mistakes? For instance, in my own example (where I paid upfront for the roof repair), should I have suffered for weeks or months before forgiving myself? Was I letting myself off the hook too easily by reminding myself that I can't change what has already happened, and making a commitment to do things differently next time a similar situation arises? Would it have been helpful to keep blaming myself for weeks, raging at the roofing company and remaining angry or getting depressed? Would doing so get my roof repaired, or serve any purpose at all?

It is reasonable to feel upset when we make a mistake, but ongoing flagellation has few benefits. We stand to benefit much more by acknowledging our mistake, and thinking about what we have learned from the experience and what we will do next time a similar situation arises.

Paul has recently injured his back after moving a heavy pot plant in the backyard. Paul feels particularly frustrated because he had declined a friend's offer to lend a hand. 'Why didn't I get him to help me?' he thinks to himself. 'What an idiot I am!' Now Paul has two problems—the first is his bad back; the second is his frustration. After a couple of days ruminating over his mistake, Paul decides to challenge his upsetting cognitions using a thought-monitoring form.

SITUATION	Injured my back while shifting heavy pot plant.
FEELINGS	Frustrated and angry at myself.
THOUGHTS	I should have accepted Bert's offer for help. I should have been more careful. What an idiot I am! This could be a permanent injury.
BELIEFS	I should be aware of all possible problems and prevent them from happening. I should never make mistakes.
THINKING ERRORS	Shoulds, hindsight vision, blaming
DISPUTE	It's easy to be wise in retrospect—not always so easy at the time. Everyone makes mistakes at times, and so do I. Blaming myself won't change things and will only make me feel bad. I can learn from this experience and be more careful next time.
POSITIVE ACTIONS	From now on, ask for help if I need to lift anything heavy. Make an appointment to see a physiotherapist.

REMEMBER

➤ We all make mistakes.

➤ It's easy to see our errors in retrospect, but not so easy at the time.

➤ Ongoing rumination and excessive self-blame does not change the reality of what has occurred.

➤ We can reflect on our mistakes and learn lessons without making ourselves suffer extensively.

EXERCISE 4.3

1 Describe a situation where you have treated yourself harshly for making a mistake.

2 Was it rational for you to give yourself a hard time? (Hint: think about causally determined realities.)

3 Was it helpful in any way? How?

4 Describe a more positive way to view this situation if it should arise again in the future.

IN SUMMARY

➤ Many people experience frustration when obstacles prevent them from getting what they want.

➤ Some people have very low frustration tolerance (LFT), and therefore become emotionally distressed very easily.

➤ LFT contributes to procrastination and self-defeating behaviours. For instance, we may choose to satisfy our immediate desires rather than looking after our best interests in the longer term.

➤ When frustrations arise in our lives, it is always helpful to focus on problem solving as a first step.

➤ To increase our tolerance for frustration, it is helpful to challenge the beliefs that underpin LFT. This can be done by using logical or behavioural disputing.

➤ Sometimes we feel reluctant to release self-criticism or upsetting emotions because at some level they feel protective. Beliefs about the benefits of those thought processes or feelings can make us reluctant to change the way we think or feel.

FIVE

Managing anger

The reason to forgive is for our own sake. For our own health. Because beyond that point needed for healing, if we hold on to our anger, we stop growing and our souls begin to shrivel.

M. SCOTT PECK, *FURTHER ALONG THE ROAD LESS TRAVELED*

Anger is our response to the perception that something is bad or unfair. Our sense of injustice is accompanied by a perception of threat—feeling offended, wronged or endangered. Most often, anger is directed at other people; however, sometimes we may feel angry at ourselves, or an entity such as an organisation, a government, a system or even the world.

> *Emma was not in her office when Katie came in looking for her. Katie stopped and took a peek at Emma's payslip, which was lying on the desk. Looking at the statement filled her with rage. Although Emma and Katie do similar work, it turned out that Emma gets paid almost $10,000 more annually. Katie was furious. Without thinking about the consequences she walked straight into her boss's office and demanded a pay rise.*

Anger affects the way we behave. When we feel angry we may withdraw, lose our temper, act on impulse, become aggressive or say things we later regret. Intense or prolonged anger drains our energy, impairs our concentration and interferes with our ability to be happy and to have good relationships. The episodes of pointless rumination that accompany long-term anger can distract our attention and create unhappiness for years or even decades.

APPROPRIATE VERSUS INAPPROPRIATE ANGER

Sometimes it is appropriate to feel angry and an occasional burst of anger is not usually a problem. For instance, it may be reasonable to feel angry when we discover that a fellow employee is getting more money for doing the same job, or when someone has unfairly accused us of something we didn't do, or when we discover that someone has lied to us. However, the frequency, intensity and duration of our anger, as well as the associated behaviours may be unreasonable.

> *Nicky's husband, Bill, criticised her in front of their dinner guests, so it was reasonable for Nicky to feel angry. It was also appropriate for her to talk to Bill about his behaviour after the guests had gone, and to explain why it had upset her. However, if Nicky gets so mad that she hurls abuse, smashes the crockery and sends the dinner guests packing, her anger is inappropriate and unhealthy. Apart from upsetting herself, regular bursts of anger are likely to damage Nicky's relationships and reduce the number of friends who are willing to risk dinner invitations.*

THE FIGHT-OR-FLIGHT RESPONSE

Think back to a time where you were involved in a hostile confrontation with another person. If you were tuned into what was happening inside your body, you may have noticed that your heart was beating harder and faster than usual, your face had become flushed and you were feeling hot. You may also have noticed that your breathing was faster than normal and that your muscles had tensed up. These and other changes are part of a primitive biological response to perceived threat. It is called the **fight-or-flight response** because for our stone-age ancestors confronting dangerous situations (usually a predator or an enemy), it provided the extra reserves of energy needed to either fight or run away.

During the fight-or-flight response, a number of physical changes mobilise reserves of energy, enabling them to be rapidly available. In response to the perception of threat, our brain sends an electrical impulse to the adrenal glands (at the top of our kidneys), which release the hormone adrenaline. This causes a number of changes, including:

➤ nostrils and air passages in the lungs expanding to enable us to take in more air quickly.

➤ breathing becoming more rapid, enabling more oxygen to enter the bloodstream.

➤ heart beating harder and faster and our blood pressure rising. This enables the oxygen that has entered the bloodstream via the lungs to be rapidly delivered to the muscles where it is needed for energy.

➤ liver releasing glucose to provide an additional quick source of fuel.

➤ digestion and other bodily processes that are not immediately essential slowing down or stopping.

➤ blood being diverted to the muscles, which tense up in preparation for action (fight or fleeing).

➤ our mind becoming focused on the source of threat, and other information being ignored.

Together these changes optimise our chances of survival during times of danger. Although we still respond in the same way as did our stone-age ancestors, in most situations today the extra reserves of energy created by the fight-or-flight response are not necessary, as we are not confronting real physical danger. In fact, the effects are often counterproductive because they create unpleasant physical symptoms and impair our ability to think clearly and function well.

BENEFITS OF ANGER

Although there are many disadvantages associated with getting angry, sometimes anger has benefits.

ENERGY AND MOTIVATION

The high level of arousal generated by the fight-or-flight response can give us the courage to confront someone or do something positive to solve a problem. For instance, anger might spur you to confront an inconsiderate neighbour; challenge someone who has spread a nasty rumour; talk to your partner about an unresolved issue; write a letter to the editor about some injustice; arrange to talk to your Member of Parliament; donate money to a just cause or complain to the manager about poor service. Anger can be a particularly useful motivator for people who are not normally assertive. Spurring us to action can help us to solve a problem and therefore get our needs met.

POWER

Getting angry can also give us power, as once we get mad we can be scary to others. Most people hate being on the receiving end of someone else's wrath and will go out of their way to avoid it. This means that we can sometimes intimidate people into giving us what we want. In hospitals, restaurants, hotels, department stores and airports, angry, demanding people frequently get more immediate attention and better service than those who are passive and patient. In families and in workplaces, people who are prone to anger often have others walking on eggshells, doing what they can to avoid conflict. While this might make them feel powerful, there are of course lots of disadvantages in using anger this way.

DISADVANTAGES OF ANGER

A short occasional period of anger is not usually a problem, as long as it is proportionate to the situation, and does not result in aggressive, unreasonable behaviour. On the other hand, frequent, intense or prolonged anger can have detrimental effects on many aspects of our lives, including our ability to stay focused on current tasks, have good relationships, feel relaxed and happy and achieve the things that we want. Anger affects our thoughts, body and behaviours.

THOUGHTS

Anger interferes with our ability to think clearly and rationally. It steals our attention away from the things that matter, and directs it towards perceived violations, injustices and people's misdemeanours. Anger is sustained and escalated through **rumination**—a reprocessing of thoughts about what might or should have been, playing themselves out over and over again; for example: 'And then he said … and I said … and he said … I should have told him … How dare he! … I should have said …' These ruminations sustain or intensify our anger, leading to more angry thoughts and even more anger. The vicious cycle can keep us stuck in futile cogitations that keep us distracted and aroused for long periods of time.

BODY

Anger produces physical arousal. If we are experiencing only a brief episode of anger, our body state returns to normal in a short period of time. However, frequent or persistent anger keeps us in a chronic state of tension and arousal, which puts additional stress on the adrenal glands and other body systems. These changes can cause sustained elevation in blood pressure, resulting in increased risk of hypertension and, according to some studies, cardiovascular disease.

BEHAVIOURS

Anger spurs people to behave aggressively. We may argue, attack, abuse, hit, blame or withdraw. Unless we are in a situation that involves genuine physical danger (in which case being prepared to attack could be useful), this type of behaviour is usually unhelpful, and creates more problems than it solves. Anger may also provoke impulsive behaviours and cause us to exercise poor judgement. In some cases it can lead to violence, destruction of property and abuse of alcohol or drugs.

While an occasional episode of anger may enable us to intimidate others, it is rarely a good way of getting our needs met. As aggressive behaviour alienates people, we lose goodwill in the longer term. At best, angry outbursts make people wary of us; at worst, they create enemies.

Angry responses create tensions within our existing relationships and may hurt the very people we care about. Sometimes we say or do things we will later regret. Within families, the power imbalance created by frequent angry outbursts often leads to alienation, poor communication and breakdown of relationships. Individuals who are easily moved to anger are often lonely—people don't want the stress, so they keep away.

Some people express their anger through passive aggression. Their aim is to punish or hurt the other person through subtle strategies such as silence or withdrawal. They may choose to ignore the other person, physically distance themselves or respond to attempts at conversation with monosyllabic answers. While passive-aggressive behaviour can indeed make life unpleasant for the other person, it is counterproductive in the longer term. If our aim is to have healthy relationships, passive aggression is not the way to achieve that.

Finally, anger limits opportunities for negotiation and problem solving. Angry exchanges put people on the defensive and create a tense, uneasy atmosphere that is not conducive to good communication. As our focus turns to threat, we lose sight of the argument. We are far more likely to resolve disagreements and maintain healthy relationships when our anger is kept under control. It also makes it easier to communicate assertively rather than aggressively, and therefore get our needs met more often (see Chapter 10).

ACUTE VERSUS LONG-TERM ANGER

People experience different types of anger. Some are prone to acute anger— short and sharp angry explosions. They may fly into a rage in seconds, but the storm passes quickly and within 20 minutes most of their anger has dissipated. While these angry outbursts are brief, they can do a lot of damage. During episodes of acute anger, drivers commit road rage; supervisors alienate their staff; spouses abuse their partners; parents hit their children and friendships are destroyed. On the other hand, some people are prone to long-term anger or **resentment**. Here, anger is a constant presence for weeks, months or years, distracting attention, draining energy and impairing one's ability to focus, feel good and be happy.

THE EFFECTS OF STRESS

Stress in other areas of our lives can shorten our fuse and make us more prone to angry outbursts. Physical tension and arousal put us into a state of 'preparedness' where our body is ready for action, so that even a minor annoyance can trigger a major response. For instance, if you are under a lot of pressure at work, you are more likely to get mad over minor annoyances that would not normally upset you. People in long-term stressful situations (e.g. unemployment, financial hardship or turbulent relationships) are more likely to experience angry outbursts, as their constant state of preparedness makes them 'ready to fire' in response to minor provocations. Even aspects of the surrounding environment such as noise, overcrowding or heat can increase the likelihood of angry reactions.

THE VULNERABILITY FACTOR

Anger is associated with perceived threat. Although on a conscious level we are fuming at some perceived injustice, our anger also helps to override feelings of fear, hurt or vulnerability. By becoming angry, we override emotions that make us feel vulnerable with those that make us feel strong.

Tony felt threatened when his girlfriend told him that their relationship was over, and asked him to move out of their apartment. He responded with an angry, abusive tirade against her. Tony's anger displaced his initial feelings of hurt and rejection.

*

Bert felt intense anger towards his wife's medical specialist after he informed the couple that her cancer had spread. Bert's anger helped to displace the fear that gripped him as he contemplated a new, frightening reality.

*

Sophie feels hurt and rejected by a work colleague who has shown no interest in her, in spite of her regular attempts to flirt with him. Her initial feelings of hurt subsequently transformed to anger. This helped to override the pain of rejection, and made her feel less vulnerable.

EXERCISE 5.1

1 Think of a situation in which you have felt very angry.
2 What aspects of the situation did you consider to be bad or unfair?
3 Can you identify any fear, hurt or vulnerability that contributed to your anger?

DISPLACED ANGER

Sometimes we may find ourselves venting our spleen at some poor innocent person. Displaced anger happens when we have no one to blame or when we are unable to express our anger at the appropriate person. For instance, Fred cannot vent his anger at his demanding boss, so he shouts abuse at other drivers on his way home, snaps at his wife, yells at his children and kicks the dog. A child who feels angry and helpless about the domestic violence at home may pick fights with weaker students at school or abuse his teachers. Bert felt angry with his wife's medical specialist— even though he knew he was not to blame for his wife's cancer—because there was just no one else to blame. Displaced anger is irrational and unfair because we direct it at people who are not responsible for our pain.

THE ANGER-PRONE PERSONALITY

Some people have a personality style that makes them prone to anger. This may be due to various factors—biological, psychological and developmental. In some cases, the disposition towards anger is the result of a rigid cognitive style and a low tolerance for frustration. This style of thinking makes the individual prone to getting upset whenever things go wrong (see page 74). For example, some people are prone to angry outbursts because they perceive others as untrustworthy, and so they frequently misinterpret people's behaviours as offensive and personal.

Highly stressful or traumatic events in early life can also influence the way we perceive the world, including how we interpret other people's motives. For example, a woman who was sexually abused as a child may perceive people as exploitative and untrustworthy. A man who was often verbally abused by his domineering father may feel hostility towards people in positions of authority.

People who have a self-focused personality style are also often prone to anger. Their inability to see life events from the perspective of others causes them to perceive injustice in situations where they don't get their needs met. Empathy—the ability to see things from the perspective of others—helps to curtail anger.

A predisposition towards anger and aggression can be also biologically determined. For instance, some people have an irritable temperament as part of their biological make-up, which makes them prone to arousal and angry outbursts. In some cases, people with abnormally high levels of particular hormones (prolactin in women, testosterone in men) show high levels of hostility and aggression.

Faulty regulation of neurotransmitters—the chemical messengers in the brain (in particular, serotonin and dopamine)—can also increase one's disposition to anger and aggression. The expression of these chemicals is influenced by genes, and it is sometimes the combination of genetic disposition plus negative early life experiences, that switch on the lifelong disposition to anger. Experiences of emotional or physical abuse, trauma, chaos or ongoing stress and uncertainty in childhood can influence gene expression (a process described in the new scientific field of **epigenetics**) and sensitise the nervous system to become permanently over-reactive. This makes the individual prone to vigilance and frequent physical arousal, so that even minor events provoke rapid threat responses. For this reason, they may flare up in response to small provocations, or what may seem like no reason at all.

Individuals with high susceptibility to anger usually need to work hard to keep their anger in check, or face the unpalatable consequences—interpersonal conflicts, loneliness, frequent emotional distress and, possibly, health problems. Understanding anger, learning management skills and practising them on a regular basis can help to reduce the frequency and intensity of angry outbursts.

TOO LITTLE ANGER

Some people rarely express anger. This may reflect a flexible cognitive style or, alternatively, the suppression of anger. When we suppress anger we put on a brave face, while below the surface we are seething with resentment. Suppressed anger often leads to passive-aggressive behaviours—we make subtle carping, negative comments or try to undermine the person, while pretending not to be angry. People suppress anger because they don't feel empowered or don't know how to express it appropriately, or because they believe that it is wrong to feel that way. The problem with suppressed anger is that we continue to hurt inside, and create barriers from others.

In contrast, some people very rarely feel angry; they require a very high level of provocation to experience any anger. While this makes them easy to live with, there can be a downside. As anger motivates us to confront or stand up for ourselves, people who rarely experience anger may behave unassertively much of the time. If we have no expectations of a fair deal from others, we may be willing to endure poor treatment without protest. I have occasionally seen people who tolerate abusive or unreasonable behaviours (often from a spouse or family member) without complaint. The absence of anger, perhaps stemming from a lack of sense of entitlement or fear of conflict, means that they are not motivated to stand up for themselves or set boundaries for acceptable behaviour. In cases like these, some anger would be healthy and useful.

HOLD IT IN OR LET IT OUT?

There is a commonly held theory that it is better to let your anger out than to hold it in. The theory presupposes that an explosive response—yelling and screaming for instance—is a healthy way of releasing anger. Some of the psychotherapies popularised in earlier times (e.g. Janov's 'Primal

Scream' therapy) were designed to encourage people to release their anger through screaming. Even today, some therapists encourage angry clients to 'let it out rather than hold it in'.

It is true that physical activity can provide a good outlet for releasing pent-up anger or frustration. Hitting a punching bag, digging in the garden, going for a run or doing any form of physical exercise can provide short-term relief. If you are experiencing just a brief episode of anger, that may be all you need.

While exercise can help us to let off steam, shouting at somebody is rarely helpful. Shouting often provokes others to shout back, which usually escalates tension. Many people report feeling angrier after a fiery exchange, because aggression causes anger to grow. Shouting is also often hurtful to the people we care about, and this can leave us feeling guilty and remorseful afterwards.

> Some people seem to think that if they shout loud enough, then other people will do what they want … This might produce compliance, but it does not produce real cooperation or problem-solving … Dealing effectively with difficult situations requires composure.
>
> **RAYMOND W NOVACO, 'WHAT REALLY WORKS FOR ANGER MANAGEMENT', SELFHELPMAGAZINE.COM.**

EXERCISE 5.2

1 Think of a time when you shouted at someone because you felt angry.
2 Did shouting make you feel better or worse? Did you feel guilty or regretful later?
3 How did shouting affect your relationship with the other person? Would it have been better to have communicated assertively rather than aggressively?

STRATEGIES FOR MANAGING ANGER

When it comes to anger management, strategies that can be used to deal with sudden anger outbursts are different to those that are appropriate for managing long-term anger and resentment. This is because the brain processes involved in each case are different. In order to understand how this works, it is useful to know a little about the physiological processes involved.

ANATOMY OF ANGER

At the front part of our brain is a large outer section called the **prefrontal cortex.** This area is responsible for thinking, judging, reasoning, evaluating, decision-making, planning and organising. It is sometimes referred to as the 'executive' part of the brain. Lower and deeper inside our brain is a section called the limbic system, which comprises a group of structures that together function as the brain's emotional centre. The limbic system is the more primitive part of the brain that, among other things, controls biological drives and responses. One of its structures is the **amygdala**, a small, almond-shaped mass on either side of the brain. The amygdala plays an important role in emotions and motivation, particularly those related to survival. In a separate area near the centre of the brain (just above the brainstem) is another structure called the **thalamus**. This structure is the 'gateway' for information coming from our senses, and it usually directs impulses generated by our sensory neurons to appropriate areas of the prefrontal cortex.

Under normal circumstances, as we receive information from the outside world via our five senses, our prefrontal cortex evaluates this information and gives it meaning. During normal functioning, the prefrontal cortex can modulate emotional impulses that are generated in the amygdala. However, if something particularly stressful or threatening is perceived, the thalamus (which acts as a 'relay station' directing information into appropriate parts of the brain) bypasses the prefrontal cortex altogether, and sends the information directly to the amygdala. If the incoming information triggers enough emotional charge, the amygdala creates a state of alarm that dominates current mental processes. This state is sometimes referred to as 'hot' emotion.

During this state the prefrontal cortex is overridden, and we are therefore unable to think logically or use sound judgement. Psychologist and author of the book *Emotional Intelligence* Daniel Goleman, coined the term 'amygdala hijack' to describe the overwhelming and disproportionate emotional response triggered in this process. During the 'hijack' we may say or do things that we will later regret. For most people it takes up to 20 minutes before information starts flowing to the prefrontal cortex (that is, for us to start thinking rationally again). During this time, a lot of damage can be done.

PREVENTING AN ANGRY EXPLOSION

People who are prone to angry outbursts know only too well the downside of uncontrolled anger—lost friendships, problems at work, broken marriages and social alienation, to name just a few. It is therefore important to have a strategy in place, ready to go as soon as the anger 'fuse' has been lit.

A key requirement for defusing acute anger is being able to recognise the warning signs. As our amygdala sounds the alarm we experience strong physical sensations: tension, heat, pounding heart and trembling. Our brain is 'on the warpath' and we feel ready to fight. Being vigilant to these sensations helps us to recognise that we are currently 'at risk', and alerts us of the need to intervene. The following steps can help to defuse an amygdala hijack.

DEFUSING AN AMYGDALA HIJACK

1 **Label and observe:** As soon as you notice the physical symptoms that signal the start of acute anger, mentally label the experience 'amygdala hijack'. Turn your attention inwards and observe what is happening inside your body. You may even visualise your amygdala pulsating and firing, sending 'high alert' signals to every part of your body. The very act of labelling and observing your internal state moves your attention from threat-focused information (the object of your anger) to your own cognitive processes. Sometimes this can reduce reactivity and enable parts of the prefrontal cortex to re-engage.

2 **Breathe:** Take in a few slow, deep breaths. This helps to lower physical arousal, distract from threat-focused thoughts and also re-engages the prefrontal cortex.

3 **Leave:** Physically remove yourself from the situation. Depending on the circumstances, you may go outside, go for a walk or go home. In a work environment or situation where leaving is not possible, walk away

for just a few minutes by going to the bathroom or to another room and take some more breaths. Doing so will keep you out of harm's way during the height of the 'hijack' period when the urge to attack dominates.

4 **Exercise:** If possible do some exercise: walk, run up and down the fire escape stairs, clean the house, hit a pillow or do workout at the gym.

AFTER THE HIJACK—WHEN EMOTIONS ARE STILL HOT

Although the peak of our anger may last for only a short time, it is not unusual to continue feeling angry for hours or days afterwards. Anger can be self-perpetuating because when we feel angry, our mind produces ruminations that fuel the emotion. Feelings of anger are accompanied by recurring thoughts or images of the 'culprit' and their particular transgressions. Typically the thoughts pop into our mind repeatedly, sometimes dozens of times an hour. Ruminations about the culprit's various misdemeanours, the types of punishment we would like to dispatch and how sorry and powerless they would feel as a result fill our mind.

Most people acknowledge that in this state they feel drawn to their ruminations—imagining that we are despatching punishment feels good. However, ultimately they leave us feeling unsatisfied, as we also know the 'culprit' is not really being punished. In addition, our ruminations take up a huge amount of mental space, distracting us from other things and keeping us in an intimate relationship with the very person we detest. As though it's not enough that we feel hurt by their actions, we allow them to lodge inside our brain and continue to harass us.

MINDFULNESS

When emotions are 'hot', logical disputing is extremely difficult as our amygdala dominates our responses. We may even feel a 'tug of war' between the prefrontal cortex (the thinking part of our brain) and our amygdala (primitive emotional response), as attempts to think rationally are overridden by primitive emotion. In these situations it may be helpful to use our mind in a different way.

Periods of intense unpleasant emotion (like anger, fear, frustration, guilt or impatience) can provide a good opportunity to practise mindfulness.

During this process our aim is to be present with current experience, observing with curiosity and without judgement (see Chapter 12).

To engage mindfully during an episode of anger turn your attention inwards and notice what is happening for you in this moment. Observe how your thoughts dart around, focusing on themes related to injustice, betrayal and revenge, and how some thoughts keep returning. Notice the physical sensations in your body, including changes in muscle tension, breathing and heart rate. You may observe the desire to lash out and punish—if so, observe the impulse with curiosity.

Mindful attention to our thoughts, emotions, body sensations and behaviours helps us to step back and observe our inner experiences with curiosity and without judgement. We can become more aware of our ruminations, noticing each time they enter our mind. The practice of observing our own responses can produce a subtle shift in cognitive processes, which reduces our emotional temperature.

Watching thoughts pop into our mind, labelling them (e.g. 'That's my angry ruminations again'), and acknowledging that they are just thoughts can help to change the way we relate to them. While it does not necessarily switch off angry ruminations, it produces a space from which to observe them. In the book *The Mindful Way Through Depression*, the authors Mark Williams, John Teasdale, Zindel Segal and Jon Kabat-Zinn describe the process of observing recurrent thoughts as being like watching a tape running in the mind. The tape 'will continue to be an inconvenience until the "batteries" run down and it ceases of its own accord'. By mindfully observing our ruminations without engaging with them or elaborating on their contents, we create a space from which their 'batteries' can run down. Although mindfulness is not intended as a quick fix for upsetting emotions, many people report reduced intensity of emotion when they step back and observe it.

STAY GOAL-FOCUSED

Once the intense heat of anger has started to subside and the prefrontal cortex is engaged again, it becomes possible to begin thinking logically. Goal-focused thinking (see page 64) can be a useful tool for putting things into perspective. Ask yourself, 'What are my goals here?' There are usually very good reasons to work on releasing anger. For example:

➤ To get on with people.
➤ To have happy, well-adjusted children.
➤ To have a good relationship with my partner.
➤ To be successful in my career.
➤ To avoid unnecessary stress.
➤ To enjoy the evening.
➤ To look after my health.

Whatever goals are relevant at the time, ask yourself whether getting angry helps you to achieve those goals. When you look at the big picture, in most cases holding on to anger is self-defeating.

MORE TIME OUT

For most people, leaving the scene for even a few minutes will defuse a potentially explosive response. However, in situations where the desire to lash out continues, it may be necessary to take some additional time out. Depending on the circumstances, you might go for a walk, listen to music, do some gardening or make some unrelated telephone calls. Taking additional time out provides an opportunity to calm down, focus on your main goals and, if necessary, plan some possible solutions. It also reduces the likelihood of saying or doing things you may later regret.

If you are prone to angry outbursts, it is a good idea to plan your time-out activity. Once you recognise your anger surfacing, tell yourself 'I need time out', and move to the activity that you have prepared. This increases your ability to stay in control.

Rena goes into the bedroom and closes the door after failing to reason with her screaming two-year-old. Although Rena doesn't like to leave her daughter for long, taking some time out prevents Rena from losing her temper and smacking or yelling at her child.

*

Elizabeth goes into the garden for a little while when her mother, who suffers from dementia, becomes too demanding and unreasonable. This gives Elizabeth a chance to calm down and remind herself that her mother can't help being the way she is.

*

Following an unpleasant confrontation with his boss, Rick calls his accountant, picks up the dry-cleaning and pays his gas bill. Although Rick needs to go back and speak to his boss, taking time out to focus on mundane issues gives him the space to regain his composure and put things back in perspective.

*

When Roy becomes angry at his teenage son's unreasonable behaviour, he goes into the lounge room and listens to his favourite opera. The time out gives him a chance to calm down and prevents him from yelling and therefore inflaming the situation.

REDUCE PHYSICAL AROUSAL

Anger triggers a state of heightened arousal that prepares our body for action. When we reduce our level of arousal, our anger also recedes and ruminations often diminish. For this reason, strategies that lower our arousal, such as physical exercise, slow breathing and deep relaxation can also reduce feelings of anger.

Some people are susceptible to becoming physically aroused very readily, and may therefore benefit from the regular practice of arousal modulation techniques. They may also benefit from avoiding high caffeine drinks, and getting adequate sleep each night (sleep deprivation makes us irritable). Drinking excessive amounts of alcohol can also increase the likelihood of an aggressive outburst because of its disinhibiting effects.

EXERCISE

Physical exercise helps to expend the surge of energy generated by the fight-or-flight response and improves our mood. After exercising, our level of arousal drops substantially and our body starts to relax. Vigorous exercise also stimulates the release of endorphins—our body's natural opiates—which increase our sense of wellbeing. For this reason, exercise is an excellent anger management tool. While the most frequently recommended types of exercise are aerobic (brisk walking, jogging, cycling, swimming or working out in the gym), any sort of vigorous activity, including weightlifting, hitting a punching bag or even sexual activity can help to reduce anger levels. Perhaps less enjoyable but equally effective is vigorous housework—mopping the floor, washing the windows, vacuuming the house or digging in the garden.

DIAPHRAGMATIC BREATHING

For thousands of years, the breath has been used in practices such as yoga and meditation for reducing physical arousal and inducing a state of inner calm. Slow breathing into the lower lungs is a useful strategy for lowering arousal when we feel angry or anxious. Repeating calming words, such as 'relax' or 'letting go' each time we breathe out can help to deepen our level of relaxation (see page 185).

DEEP RELAXATION

Deep relaxation is a physical state in which all of our major muscle groups are extremely relaxed. As it is difficult to practise deep relaxation during a highly aroused state, the technique is not suitable during acute anger (physical exercise, rhythmic breathing or mindful awareness are more appropriate at that stage). However, deep relaxation is a good maintenance tool which, when practised daily, helps to lower baseline arousal, and so reduces the predisposition towards rapid angry outbursts.

DEALING WITH SUSTAINED ANGER

Unlike acute anger which peaks and recedes fairly quickly, sustained anger requires a longer-term approach. The remainder of this chapter deals with strategies for managing anger that does not disappear within a few hours or days.

PROBLEM SOLVE

Whenever we perceive that some injustice has occurred, it is sensible to think about actions we can take to address it. Sometimes there is nothing we can do, and our only option is to accept the situation, using the various cognitive strategies described in this chapter. At other times we can resolve the situation—partially or completely—through problem solving. Whether or not we succeed, knowing that we gave it our best shot provides some consolation. If, in spite of our best efforts, we do not manage to change things, it helps to know that we tried and that there is nothing more we can do.

Whenever you find yourself feeling angry about a particular situation, look for aspects that might be within your control. Remember the key question: **'What is the best action I can take to resolve this problem?'**

Rochelle feels angry because she received a fine after parking in a spot that was poorly marked. She really couldn't tell that it was a 'no parking' zone.

*

Eva lent her friend a book that was precious to her. Upon enquiring about the book six months later, her friend denied ever having borrowed it.

*

Karen feels angry at her partner, Tony, because he doesn't contribute to the housework.

*

Rowan has paid a substantial sum of money to have his bathroom renovated, and is angry at the shoddy workmanship.

In each of these examples, the individuals feel angry because someone has done something that they regard to be bad or unfair. In each case, there are actions that they could take in an effort to resolve the injustice. Rochelle might write to the relevant authorities to explain that the parking area was poorly marked, and send a photograph of the spot to support her case. Eva might communicate assertively with her friend, tell her that the book was precious to her and ask her to make a special effort to look for it. Karen might talk to Tony about their current domestic situation to let him know that she is unhappy about doing most of the housework, and to ask him to contribute. Rowan should call the tradesman and politely but assertively explain the specific problems that need to be remedied. He might also consider taking further steps, such as lodging a complaint with the appropriate consumer body or consulting a solicitor. In many cases, taking constructive action helps to resolve the problem, partially or completely.

SOMETIMES IT IS BETTER TO LET IT GO

Sometimes we find ourselves in situations that are clearly unfair, but there is nothing we can do to change them. Or, we may recognise that our chances of achieving a just solution are small, while the cost of pursuing it is likely to be high. Fighting an unwinnable battle may not be worth the time, effort, energy, stress or financial cost involved. When we weigh up our chances of success against the likely cost of failure, we might make a rational decision to let it go. In situations like these, our best option may be to practise acceptance. The acceptance affirmation below can be particularly helpful when we find ourselves in situations that we do not like, but cannot change.

ACCEPTANCE.

THIS IS HOW IT IS.

NOT HOW IT

—Was

—Might have been

—Should have been.

NOT HOW I

—Wanted it to be

—Hoped it would be

—Planned it would be.

I ACCEPT THAT THIS IS HOW IT IS.

Now I get on with my life

in a positive way.

AUTHOR UNKNOWN

EXERCISE 5.3

1   Think of a situation that you currently feel angry about.

2   Is there anything that you can do to remedy the situation?

3   What do you need to accept in relation to this situation?

Antonio works as a carpenter on building sites for a large company. He is an excellent tradesman—conscientious, hardworking and ethical, and some people describe him as a perfectionist. He takes pride in his work and always gives 100 per cent in everything that he does. Unfortunately few of his fellow workers share his attitudes. The majority are laidback, and some are indifferent, sloppy and careless. Antonio finds their attitudes infuriating. Although he has complained to his supervisor on a few occasions, no one seems to care. Antonio's anger towards his fellow employees causes him to hate the job and makes him irritable and unhappy. He has recently started getting headaches that seem to be stress-related. Although Antonio is looking for another job, he knows that this will not fix the problem, as part of the problem is his own expectations. Antonio fills in the thought–monitoring form below:

SITUATION	Tradesmen work slowly, talk a lot and do sloppy work. I told the boss, but he hasn't done anything about it.
FEELINGS	Anger, frustration, physical tension, headaches.
THOUGHTS	They are hopeless! They don't give a damn.
BELIEFS	Everyone should have a responsible attitude and work hard. They should have the same work ethic as I do.
THINKING ERRORS	Labelling, shoulds, black-and-white thinking
DISPUTE	I wish they had a better attitude, but unfortunately they don't. Not everyone has to have the same attitude as me. Things still get done, even though it takes longer than it could. It is a boring job, so perhaps that's why they look for distractions. The boss is not concerned, so I don't need to make this my problem.
POSITIVE ACTIONS	If problems arise, let the boss know, but don't take responsibility for what others are doing. Stay focused on my own work.

In addition to challenging his cognitions, Antonio uses **goal-focused thinking** to motivate himself to relax: **Does thinking or behaving this way help me to feel good, or to achieve my goals?**

My goals are to do a good job, enjoy my work, feel relaxed and be healthy. Every time I get angry I distract myself from my own work, I feel bad and I become physically tense. This is not good for my health or happiness. I don't have to do this—I can choose not to worry about what other people are doing.

Antonio starts to distinguish events that are within his control from those that are not. He works on letting go of things he cannot change, like the attitudes and behaviours of his fellow workers, and he starts taking responsibility only for things that he can control—such as his own work. In addition, whenever Antonio notices that he is caught up in angry ruminations he reminds himself: 'I am doing it again!' and he switches his attention to the task he is working on. Antonio now acknowledges that although his work situation is not ideal, it is really not so bad.

GIVE YOURSELF SOME 'STEWING TIME'

When dealing with a significant injustice, we initially need some time to process our thoughts. At the onset of anger, give yourself permission to 'stew' for a while. During this period it is helpful to exercise, talk about it or even write a letter. As long as you don't say or do things you will later regret, it is OK to experience anger for a few hours or days.

TALK ABOUT IT

The very process of talking about things that upset us can help us to feel better. This is particularly the case if our listener is empathic. Sometimes all we need to defuse the situation is to be heard and validated by a caring individual.

While talking to a third party can be helpful, sometimes it is best to speak directly to the person we feel angry with. Describing how we feel can help us to release accumulated anger and resentment. However, it is usually not helpful to have things out during the acute stage of anger, when the likelihood of a hostile confrontation is high.

WRITE A LETTER OR EMAIL

Sometimes it is difficult to directly confront the person we feel angry with because the issue is too upsetting and we don't feel confident that we will remain calm and express ourselves well. High levels of arousal can make it difficult to communicate coherently, and can lead us to prattle or sound aggressive. For this reason, writing is sometimes a better option. Taking the time to compose our thoughts enables us to say exactly what we want, without the pressure of more intense emotions that may accompany face-to-face encounters. While sending the letter or email helps the other person to understand our position, sometimes it is the process of writing that matters, and the letter can be discarded or deleted after it has been written.

CHANGING YOUR THINKING

When we feel angry, attention is focused on the wrongdoing of others. We blame and condemn: 'S/he makes me so mad!' The truth is other people do not make us angry—they merely provide a stimulus. Like all emotions, anger is fuelled by cognitions. People's actions are often unreasonable, but whether or not we get mad, and how mad we become, depends on our own thoughts and beliefs. For this reason, situations that fill some people with rage (e.g. a friend who is chronically late, sloppy service or inconsiderate drivers) do not raise even an eyebrow for others—it's all about the meanings we give to things.

METACOGNITIVE BELIEFS ABOUT ANGER

In Chapter 4 we saw that metacognitive beliefs—our beliefs about our own thinking processes and emotions—can make us resistant to changing the way we feel (see page 82). It is as though a part of us wants to hold on to unhelpful emotions because at some level they feel protective. This is particularly the case in relation to anger.

Anger typically releases a torrent of rumination about things we perceive to be bad and the person/s we hold responsible. We repeatedly return to their perceived misdemeanours and ponder what we should have said or done at the time; how unfair it was; how the person should suffer for their sins; what we will say if we ever get the chance and what we would like to do in the meantime to make them pay. Although we can rationally see that this wastes our time and energy, there is a part of us that does not want to stop. Our anger feels appropriate. We may feel reluctant to release angry thoughts because it feels like this would be letting the culprit off the hook. Our beliefs about the benefits of our anger keep us trapped in a holding pattern of futile rumination.

As long as a part of us wants to remain angry, this undermines our motivation to let it go. Recognising and challenging the beliefs that maintain the urge to engage in angry ruminations, helps to remove a key obstacle to releasing anger. Below are some examples of how we can challenge positive beliefs about anger.

POSITIVE BELIEFS ABOUT ANGER	ALTERNATIVE, REALISTIC VIEWS
Staying angry gives me power—letting go means surrendering my power.	Staying angry gives me no power at all. Anger distracts my attention, wastes my energy and keeps me thinking about the very person I resent. This takes away my power.
My anger punishes the other person.	My anger has no effect on the other person—it only affects me.
Releasing my anger provides a victory for 'them'—it means that they win and I lose.	Releasing my anger makes no difference to them, as they are not affected by what is on my mind. It would be a victory for me, because I am the one who is disempowered by my anger.
My anger keeps the other person at a distance—they cannot harm me.	My anger keeps me intimately connected to that person because they are on my mind much of the time. I can choose to keep my distance without being angry.

Anger is like drinking poison and hoping that the other person will die.

CARRIE FISHER

Since her boyfriend, Jim, broke off their relationship three months ago, Cindy has been seething. From Cindy's point of view, Jim's callous behaviour is not worthy of forgiveness. 'Why should I be the one who has to work on releasing my anger when he's been such a bastard? I should be angry!'

The question is, Cindy, who is suffering?

While it is totally reasonable for Cindy to feel angry in the initial period after the break-up, staying angry for weeks or months is painful and self-defeating. Anger does not hurt the other person—it hurts us! Even if we are able to make the other person uncomfortable by snubbing them, bitching about them or being overtly hostile, chances are we are suffering alongside them. Why do it to ourselves?

THE COST/BENEFIT ANALYSIS

A cost/benefit analysis of anger provides powerful evidence of the counterproductive effects of staying angry, and can motivate us to work on letting it go. By writing a list of all the benefits and costs of staying angry, we can see more clearly how pointless and self-defeating it really is.

Let's take a look at Cindy's cost/benefit analysis of staying angry at Jim:

BENEFITS	COSTS
• It feels right—I think I should be angry. • It gives me and my friends something to talk about.	• It's on my mind—it distracts me at work and stops me from thinking about other more worthwhile things. • It upsets me—I get all churned up in the stomach when I think about it. • It stops me from getting a good night's sleep—I lie awake thinking about it. • It makes me feel bad whenever I have to see him or any of his friends. • It makes me hard to live with. I'm irritable and cranky with Mum. • It's such a waste of my time and energy.

After weighing up the pros and cons, Cindy recognises that the costs of staying angry far outweigh the benefits. This makes her feel more committed to doing whatever it takes to release her anger.

> For every minute you remain angry,
> you give up sixty seconds of peace of mind.
> **RALPH WALDO EMERSON**

GOAL-FOCUSED THINKING

Anger is counterproductive because it usually prevents us from getting the things we want. These things might include having a good relationship with our partner; being respected by our colleagues; getting on with our children; enjoying a night out or simply feeling happy and relaxed. Because anger makes us feel bad and can impair our relationships, it is not in our interests to feel this way.

Goal-focused thinking (see page 64) can be a useful motivator to work towards changing our thinking. Like the cost/benefit analysis, this type of disputing focuses on the self-defeating nature of our thinking. Remember the key question: **Does thinking this way help me to feel good or to achieve my goals?**

> *Derrick frequently gets angry at his two teenage sons because he believes they spend little time on study and too much time on the computer and watching TV. He feels irritable with them a lot of the time and frequently loses his temper. As a result there is tension in the house, and the boys often avoid or ignore him. Derrick recognises that what he is doing is not working, but does he really have to change his attitude?*

Derrick decides to use goal-focused thinking to motivate himself to change his own responses: **Does thinking this way help me to feel good or to achieve my goals?**

> *My goals are to have a close family—to have good relationships with Val and the boys. Getting angry when I think they're wasting time doesn't change their behaviour—it only makes them feel bad and pushes them away. Demanding that they should behave more responsibly doesn't change their behaviour, and it creates distance between us. I've told them what I think several times—now I need to let it go and allow them to take responsibility for their own actions.*

*

> *Jenny feels angry because her partner wants to see his children from a previous marriage on the weekends, while Jenny would prefer him to spend the time with her.*

She decides to use goal-focused thinking to change her attitude: **Does thinking this way help me to feel good or to achieve my goals?**

> *My goal is to have a happy, loving relationship with Steven, yet I get angry and give him a hard time whenever he spends weekends*

with his children. We often fight about it, and he gets upset and then I withdraw. My anger is making it difficult for us to communicate or to negotiate compromises. It leads to fights and jeopardises our relationship. It's in my own best interests to stop making a fuss and learn to accept this.

*

While Sam and Sally were preparing to go out for the evening with their friends, Sam made a comment that caused Sally to see red. 'That's it!' Sally thinks to herself. 'I'm really cheesed off now!'

Although Sally is tempted to stay angry and withdrawn for the rest of the evening, she recognises that this is going to spoil things for everyone. Sally asks herself: **Does thinking this way help me to feel good or to achieve my goals?**

'We're going to a nice restaurant with people I like—I want to have a good time! Why spoil it by getting angry over that comment? It's not worth it!' Sally decides to stop focusing on the comment and have a good time instead.

*

Danielle's mother-in-law frequently makes nasty comments about people, and is often negative and mean-spirited. Her life philosophy seems to be, 'If you can't say something bad about a person, then don't say anything at all.' Danielle can't stand her and feels resentful whenever the family have to see her. Danielle feels totally justified in feeling this way because her mother-in-law is so obnoxious.

Danielle decides to use goal-focused thinking to motivate herself to respond differently: **Does thinking this way help me to feel good or to achieve my goals?**

My goal is to be happy and not get hassled. Feeling angry and resentful every time we have to see her only makes me feel bad, and it upsets Larry. I don't want to waste my energy stressing over this issue. I'd rather accept her and be pleasant on the occasions I need to see her.

Watch the cost-benefit ratio of dealing with difficult people and situations. Hating them, running away from them, refusing to cope with them may be easier in the short-run—but not in the long-run.

ALBERT ELLIS, *FEELING BETTER, GETTING BETTER, STAYING BETTER*

IDENTIFY AND CHALLENGE ANGER-PRODUCING COGNITIONS

Once we are motivated to work on releasing our anger, our next step is challenging the rigid cognitions that perpetuate it. Anger-prone thinking manifests in **shoulds**—rigid, inflexible beliefs about how other people ought to behave, and how the world should be, such as:

- ➤ My friends should be supportive.
- ➤ My son should study hard for his exams.
- ➤ My husband should communicate well.
- ➤ My wife should want the same things that I do.
- ➤ My work colleagues should be conscientious.
- ➤ My boss should be fair.
- ➤ The trains should run on time.
- ➤ Shoppers should return their trolleys to the supermarket.
- ➤ Pet owners should clean up after their pets.
- ➤ Neighbours should keep their music down.

Holding these beliefs in a rigid way makes us prone to anger. Of course, this is not to say that we should have no expectations of others or that we should accept unreasonable behaviour without challenging it. At times it is important to take a stand and do what we can to resolve an injustice.

However, it is also important to be flexible and accept that in the real world, people will not always do what we think they should.

COMMON BELIEFS THAT CREATE ANGER

> ➤ People should always do the right thing (or what I believe is right).
> ➤ The world should be fair, and people should always behave ethically and decently.
> ➤ I should always be treated fairly.
> ➤ I shouldn't be inconvenienced or put out as a result of other people's failings.
> ➤ If people do the wrong thing, they are horrible and deserve to suffer for their sins.

JUST WORLD FALLACY

The common theme in all of these beliefs is the expectation of justice. We expect the world to be fair, and that we should always be treated fairly. This belief develops from an early age. Children are quick to point out injustices they perceive in their own lives—'She's getting more cordial than me!'; 'That's not fair!'; 'How come he's allowed to stay up till 8 pm and I'm not?'.

The problem with this expectation is that it doesn't match with what happens in the real world. Throughout history, tyrants and despots have prospered. Even today, people live in countries governed by oppressive and corrupt regimes and suffer the injustices, deprivation and hardships meted out by these governments. Others live in affluent democratic countries and enjoy personal freedom and a very comfortable existence. Within our own society, children born to poor families have fewer life opportunities than those born to wealthy families, and people on low incomes have poorer health and higher death rates from all causes than those who are well-off. Look in any large workplace and you will find talented, hardworking employees who are poorly rewarded (and sometimes discarded), while others in senior, well-paid positions may lack competence and dedication. Callous individuals are often not held to account for bullying or intimidation of fellow workers. Individuals blessed with good looks, sporting prowess or the ability to make people laugh receive special treatment and privileges that are not available to the rest of us. Injustices exist within every society, every family, and every workplace. Even the very system created to uphold justice in our country is inherently unfair (try taking someone to court without a big bag of money to pay your legal bills). Perhaps we should be taught from early in life that many things are simply not fair.

> The truth is lots of things aren't fair.
> And often there's nothing that we can do about it.

Of course, that doesn't mean that we should passively accept unfair, unethical or bad behaviour without taking a stand. If there is something that we can do to resolve injustice, it is important to act. Sometimes we can make a difference.

But not every injustice can be undone. Sometimes we need to accept that we live in an imperfect world, full of imperfect people and situations. A psychologically healthy approach is to take action to solve problems whenever we can, while accepting that there are many things we cannot change.

LOGICAL DISPUTING STATEMENTS FOR RELEASING ANGER

➤ People are motivated by their own values and beliefs, which reflect their own history, experiences and temperament. So they won't always share my values and beliefs.

➤ It would be great if the world was always fair, but it's not. If I can't change the situation, expecting that it shouldn't be that way will not make it better.

➤ Injustice happens to everyone at times. It is an unavoidable part of life.

➤ I have been on the privileged end of global injustice for much of my life.

➤ Choosing to accept situations that I can't change is a strength, not a weakness.

Matt recently had a car accident that was clearly the other driver's fault. Because the driver acknowledged responsibility at the time, Matt didn't bother to get a witness—he assumed that there would be no problem. Two weeks later, a statement came from the other driver's insurance company, claiming that Matt had caused the accident. The other driver had blatantly lied about the circumstances of the accident. Matt is furious; now he will have to claim on his own insurance, and that will mean paying the excess and losing his no-claim bonus. After stewing for several days Matt decides to use a thought-monitoring form to challenge his thinking.

SITUATION	Car accident was the other driver's fault, but he lied about the circumstances. Now I have to claim on my own insurance, at my expense.
FEELINGS	Angry, tension in the chest
THOUGHTS	What a rotten thing to do! How can people be so dishonest? That guy is a jerk.
BELIEFS	People should be honest and behave ethically. The world should be fair. I should always be treated fairly.
THINKING ERRORS	Just world fallacy, awfulising
DISPUTE	Some people behave dishonestly and there's nothing I can do about it. People like that exist and occasionally our paths will cross. Thankfully, I don't encounter it very often. Ruminating about the injustice will not change anything. When there is nothing I can do about it, I can accept that without making things worse for myself by demanding that it should not happen.
POSITIVE ACTIONS	Write a letter to the insurance company explaining what happened. Learn from the experience—if it ever happens again, get a witness, even if the other person acknowledges liability.

FAULTY THINKING

People who are prone to anger very often have a black-and-white view of the world, and fail to see the shades of grey. They have rigid beliefs about how others should behave, and are quick to judge those who do not conform to their rules. A perceived misdemeanour produces negative appraisals of the entire person: 'jerk', 'fool', 'idiot' or 'moron'. Labelling others as defective and worthless is unrealistic and self-defeating. Psychologically healthy adaptation means not hating anyone, even though there are some people we are less fond of than others.

Siobhan hates her ex-husband with a passion. 'He's such a jerk,' she tells anyone who will listen. Siobhan feels outraged whenever she hears that any of her friends continue to see him socially. 'Either they are with me or against me,' she thinks to herself, 'and those who continue to see him are against me—I don't want anything to do with them.' Siobhan's black-and-white thinking in relation to her ex-husband, as well as the people who continue to socialise with him, fuels her anger and alienates her friends. It also causes her to behave in an irrational, self-defeating way (because she loses friends who continue to see him) and ultimately adds to her unhappiness. Although Siobhan blames others for her unhappiness, the key to releasing her anger lies in challenging the black-and-white nature of her thinking.

*

Fiona has been put on notice by the school principal following complaints about her teaching from some of her students. The principal has asked her to address some of their concerns, including lateness, lack of preparation and a failure to hand back essays. Fiona is outraged. 'They are carrying out a vendetta against me,' she tells her friends. 'Just because a couple of hopeless students have complained, I'm being victimised!'

Fiona sees the situation in black-and-white terms ('I'm right, they're wrong'; 'I'm good, they're bad'), and does not consider that the issues they have raised might have some validity. This is self-defeating not only because it creates unnecessary anger, but also because it prevents her from responding appropriately to their complaints. Fiona is therefore not motivated to look at possible weaknesses in her teaching or to take the necessary steps to improve it.

INJUSTICE MAY BE SUBJECTIVE

In the above example, Fiona's students thought her teaching left a lot to be desired, while from Fiona's point of view, her teaching was completely adequate, and the complaints were unjustified. This example demonstrates how the concepts of right or wrong can be highly subjective. While there are undoubtedly some situations that are unfair by any reasonable measure, many others fall into that vast area of grey. In spite of our own beliefs about good and bad, right and wrong, fair and unfair, there is no universal standard of justice that applies to every situation. Injustice is often in the eye of the beholder:

When Leon was passed over for a promotion to a new position at work, he was furious. 'That's not fair,' he thought to himself. 'I have worked hard for twelve years—I deserve a promotion!' From management's point of view, Leon is a 'plodder'—his work is reasonable but not outstanding. They decided to give the position to a newer employee because he showed greater ability and promise. What is fair from management's point of view appears blatantly unfair from Leon's perspective.

*

Ryan is outraged because in his parents' will, they are leaving a greater proportion of their estate to his younger brother, Tom. 'That's not fair,' Ryan thinks to himself, 'we should get an even 50/50 split.' From his parents' point of view, Ryan has an excellent career and is well-off, while Tom is financially insecure. They chose to leave extra money to Tom because his needs are greater. From Ryan's point of view, the fact that he has a good job and financial security is testament to his many years of hard work—why should he be disadvantaged for that?

Justice is often subjective.
What seems fair by one person is not always fair to another.

The lesson to be learned here is that although we may be strongly attached to our point of view, it is not necessarily 'truth'. It is merely one of many possible ways of seeing our situation.

When Maxine received a call from an old acquaintance asking if she could stay with her for six weeks while completing a summer school program, Maxine agreed. It didn't work out too well. Her friend took several liberties, including helping herself to food without replacing it, making long-distance calls and occupying the bathroom during the morning rush. Her friend never offered to contribute financially, and did not leave even a token of appreciation at the end of her stay.

Maxine filled out a thought-monitoring form to help her deal with her anger:

SITUATION	Vera stayed for six weeks. She took various liberties, showed no appreciation and didn't even buy me a gift at the end.
FEELINGS	Furious
THOUGHTS	I have been taken advantage of. She took constantly but gave nothing, and showed no appreciation. If I were in her position I would have been much more considerate.
BELIEFS	Good deeds should be appreciated. People should do the 'right thing'. She should have been grateful and showed appreciation.
THINKING ERRORS	Just world fallacy, shoulds, awfulising
DISPUTE	I would have behaved differently in her situation, but she is not me. People like Vera exist, and from time to time they enter my life, albeit briefly. She behaved poorly but, in the end, it did not result in great cost to me. The issue is her lack of gratitude, rather than the financial cost, and I can live with that. I do not need to deal with her again, and I do not have to upset myself by holding on to this anger.
POSITIVE ACTIONS	Observe the thoughts that pop into my mind, label them as 'rumination', and then switch my attention to what is happening in the present moment. If she ever asks to stay again, say no.

PERSONALISING

When someone acts unfairly, rudely or aggressively towards us, we usually take offence because we perceive their behaviour as a personal attack. However, it's not always personal. Other people's behaviour reflects their own personality, life experiences, beliefs and communication style—often, it is not about us at all.

Sometimes we may even discover that other people feel the same way towards them, and this is a source of relief. When we discover that others also dislike that unpleasant supervisor at work or that crabby neighbour or the difficult sister-in-law, it reassures us that the problem is them, not us.

Nathan's 'buttons are pressed' whenever people treat him in an offhand way. When he is driving and another driver fails to give way to him, Nathan feels violated and gets angry. When a waiter speaks to him in a haughty tone, Nathan feels put down and wants to hit them. When the taxi he tries to hail fails to stop for him, Nathan takes it as a personal rejection and sees red. When his friend does not return his telephone call, Nathan feels snubbed. When the intransigent bureaucrat is unwilling to bend the rules, Nathan feels that he is being personally slighted. And when his boss, who is consistently unpleasant to everyone, makes a curt remark, Nathan takes it personally.

*

Sonia always hated the man who lived next door. His manner was often unpleasant and he sometimes made unreasonable complaints about the behaviour of the young people sharing Sonia's house. She was therefore shocked and horrified to hear that he had taken his own life. This event led Sonia to realise that his behaviour was not personal. It became apparent that this man was suffering from his own demons, and what had appeared to be rude behaviour directed at her actually reflected his own unhappy state of mind.

At times people behave rudely, selfishly or obnoxiously, but it's not always about us. When we observe this in others it is instructive to ask ourselves, 'What does this behaviour tell me about this person?'

> The hateful, the intolerant, the angry, the obnoxious —
> you do not need to wish them to go to hell.
> They are already there.

Bev's mother is highly anxious, and frequently criticises Bev's driving when she is taking her places. Bev finds this infuriating, especially when she is doing her mum a favour.

SITUATION	Drove Mum around to various appointments. She complained about my driving on the way.
FEELINGS	Angry; felt like strangling her!
THOUGHTS	She is ungrateful! She doesn't even appreciate that I'm doing her a favour. She's so neurotic!
BELIEFS	She should be calm, positive and reasonable. People should be grateful for generous acts, and not complain.
THINKING ERRORS	Shoulds, just world fallacy, personalising
DISPUTE	I wish that she was more easygoing, but that's not her nature. She's always been anxious, and that's why she behaves that way. Her behaviour reflects who she is—I don't have to take it personally. I don't like the way she behaves, but I can accept that that is her nature.
POSITIVE ACTIONS	Talk to Mum calmly. Explain to her that it upsets me when she criticises my driving. Ask her to try to relax—remind her that we always arrive in one piece. (Don't expect miracles—accept that she's not likely to change.)

EMPATHY

It's easy to feel resentment towards people who say or do things we don't like. It is much harder to understand them—their thoughts, their motives, their insecurities or their pain. Perhaps at some stage in the past you have experienced a situation where you initially disliked someone, but then you developed some empathy towards them? When you see a person's vulnerabilities and understand how things are from their perspective, anger disappears and empathy takes its place.

It is useful to remember that we are all trying to live, using whatever resources are available to us. Our resources include our cognitive style, our problem-solving skills, our social support, our innate sense of security and self-worth and our ability to communicate and get on with people. The resources available to each of us are determined by two factors:

➤ our life experiences, and
➤ our biology (including hundreds of chemicals and structures that determine our temperament, reactivity to stress, intelligence, energy levels, physical strength, memory and many other processes).

Some people have been blessed on both counts; consequently they are well-equipped to deal with life's challenges. They think adaptively and have good communication skills, a sense of humour, healthy self-esteem and lots of friends. They are generous and good-natured because they feel secure and have a positive view of themselves and the world.

Others have been dealt a meagre hand. They have few resources to call on and they habitually respond to situations in dysfunctional ways. They may come across as rude, negative or arrogant, and they may lack the self-awareness to even realise it. Behaviours that appear to be unreasonable, selfish, stupid, neurotic, boorish or obnoxious often reflect the person's limited resources with which to respond to life's challenges. They may not know how to respond differently.

It is of course possible for people to change the way they think by consciously reflecting on their own responses, listening to feedback from others, learning from life experiences, disputing their negative thoughts and reading self-help books. However, before getting to this point they need to be aware that their thinking is dysfunctional, and they need to feel motivated to work on changing it.

Understanding how it is for other people, and why they behave as they do does not mean that we like their behaviour—in fact, we may loathe it.

However it helps us not to take it personally. Empathy produces benefits for us as well as them.

> Forgiveness is not an occasional act;
> it is a permanent attitude.
>
> **MARTIN LUTHER KING JR, 'LOVING YOUR ENEMIES' SPEECH, 1957**

BEHAVIOURAL DISPUTING

If you are feeling resentful towards someone (perhaps a work colleague, a neighbour or a family member), here is a behavioural experiment for you to try: be nice to them (not obsequious—just nice). If you don't see this person very often, try sending them a card or friendly email. This can be a difficult task as it goes against the grain. That is the challenge. Changing our behaviour towards a perceived adversary alters interpersonal dynamics, and often changes our emotional reactions. A 'laying down of arms' releases tension and not infrequently reduces feelings of animosity. As we release resentment, we free ourselves to focus on other more worthwhile things.

'But what if the experiment goes horribly wrong?' you ask. 'What if I am nice to them, and they are nasty back to me? Why give them a victory?' While in most cases, people respond positively to a peace offering, even if this doesn't happen, what has been lost? We can enjoy the moral high ground knowing that we behaved with civility, regardless of their response. After all, we don't need to let other people determine how we should behave.

Behavioural disputing can be one of the most powerful techniques for releasing anger or resentment. Many people who do this exercise are surprised at its effects, as it can bring years of bitterness and wasted energy to an end, freeing us to focus on more useful pursuits. If you find it hard to work up enthusiasm for this exercise, start with a cost/benefit analysis of holding on to hostilities. Does it really serve your interests?

COMMUNICATION

When faced with a situation we perceive to be unfair, it is often helpful to communicate. The appropriate action may be to write a letter, speak to the manager, lodge a claim, make some phone calls or rally others for support.

Good communication skills are an invaluable tool for solving problems, redressing injustices and getting on with people. Communicating with others when we feel angry can help us in two ways.

Firstly, when you tell someone they have done something that is a problem to you, they may choose to change their behaviour. Sometimes people are simply not aware of how their actions affect us, and telling them how we feel may prompt them to do things differently. For instance, if you feel angry because a friend is frequently late, telling her how this affects you may encourage her to be more punctual in the future. If you feel angry because a work colleague does not carry out some of his responsibilities, and this impacts on your job, then talking to him about this in a non-threatening way may motivate him to lift his game. If you feel angry because your partner put you down in front of other people, telling them that their behaviour upset you may encourage them to be more sensitive and tactful in the future.

Secondly, the very process of communicating can sometimes make us feel better. Telling someone that we feel angry or upset over something they have done can enable us to release our anger. This is particularly the case if we speak directly to the person we feel angry with. If we are able to communicate in a calm, non-threatening manner, they may even **validate** our concern— that is, express understanding for how we feel. Sometimes they may acknowledge that they did the wrong thing or apologise for their behaviour. While this does not always happen, in situations where it does, it is like salve to our wound. Most people are able to forgive transgressions by others, when mistakes are acknowledged and apologies are given.

> *Helen has finally plucked up the courage to tell her friend Emily that she feels hurt and angry that Emily failed to support her during her hour of need, when her marriage was ending. Emily feels sorry and ashamed, and acknowledges to Helen that she had behaved poorly. While her past action cannot be undone, her expression of remorse enables Helen to let go of her resentment, and consequently, their friendship endures.*

Although it is usually appropriate to speak to the person who we perceive as the transgressor, sometimes we may need to talk to a third party who has the power to intervene. This is particularly the case when our initial approach does not achieve results. For instance, you might end up speaking to the school principal about the unsatisfactory behaviour of a teacher, or to the manager about the poor service at the store, or to the foreman about the attitude of some of your fellow tradesmen.

Sometimes communication is best done in writing. This is necessary when we need to make a formal complaint, or when face-to-face communication feels too difficult. Taking time to compose our thoughts enables us to provide clear messages. Whether spoken or in writing, messages conveyed calmly and rationally are always preferable to confrontational statements. They increase our likelihood of resolving problems and help us to maintain positive relationships in the longer term (see also Chapter 10).

EXERCISE 5.4

For each of the following situations describe:
- actions that you could take that might help to resolve your anger
- the beliefs that contribute to your anger
- disputing statements that you could use to reduce your anger. (Sample solutions are at the back of the book.)

1 Someone you considered to be a friend was not available to help you when you needed them.
2 Your partner has behaved rudely in a social situation.
3 A friend is constantly late. You have made a lunch arrangement with her and have been kept waiting for over an hour.
4 Someone keeps putting their garbage in your paper recycling bin when you leave it out for collection.
5 You have told someone something in confidence, and now you have discovered that they have told others about it.
6 You are extremely inconvenienced by some ridiculous bureaucratic procedure imposed by a particular government organisation.
7 You are kept waiting in a telephone queue for half an hour each time you try to call a particular telecommunications company.
8 You have been substantially overcharged by a tradesman.
9 The company you work for has a ruthlessly exploitative policy towards its employees.
10 Someone is rude to you for no reason.

IN SUMMARY

➤ Anger is created by the perception that something is bad or unfair, and is accompanied by feelings of threat or vulnerability. While it can sometimes motivate us to behave assertively or solve a problem, anger has many negative consequences.

➤ Acute, explosive anger is potentially harmful because it generates behaviours that hurt us (as well as other people) in the longer term. Sustained anger also drains energy, makes us unhappy and can adversely affect our health. Different strategies are appropriate for dealing with acute versus long-term anger.

➤ The desire to stay angry is maintained by beliefs about its benefits, including the belief that it gives us power, or that releasing anger would provide a win for the other person. Paradoxically, the opposite is true. Recognising the self-defeating effects of staying angry can increase our motivation to let it go.

➤ Cognitive strategies that can help to release anger including a cost/benefit analysis, goal-focused thinking, thought monitoring and disputing, mindfulness, empathy and challenging beliefs about the benefits of staying angry.

➤ Behavioural strategies include arousal reduction techniques (such as physical exercise and deep relaxation), problem solving and utilising effective communication strategies. In addition, behavioural disputing—choosing to be nice towards someone we feel angry at—can also have positive effects.

SIX

Coping with anxiety

The mind is in its own place, and in itself
Can make a heaven of hell, and a hell of heaven
JOHN MILTON, *PARADISE LOST*

Anxiety is that feeling of apprehension and dread that comes with the perception that something bad might happen. It is accompanied by physical symptoms, such as increases in our heartbeat, breathing rate and muscle tension; tightness in the chest and sweating. While everyone feels anxious from time to time, some people experience frequent anxiety that affects their ability to do things, enjoy life and feel safe in the world. Problems related to anxiety are the most common reasons why people seek help from mental health practitioners (such as counsellors, psychiatrists and psychologists). Both men and women suffer from anxiety; however, women are twice as likely to be affected by anxiety and its disorders.

Anxiety is created by a perception of threat—a sense that something bad is going to happen. Normally it is a temporary state that passes once the threat has gone. Running late for an appointment, having to confront someone about an unpleasant issue or having to give a speech are situations that often trigger anxiety. The feeling may last for a few minutes, a few days, several weeks or, in some cases, months or more. For instance, when you see the flashing light of a police car in your rear-view mirror, you might experience a short burst of anxiety; once the car passes, you relax and feel immediate relief. Anxiety about needing to confront someone may last several days or weeks (the longer you put it off, the longer it lasts), and anxiety about your finances or your child's illness may last for many months. Usually however, once our perceived threat passes, so too does the anxiety.

The word 'anxiety' is often used interchangeably with 'fear', but it is not quite the same thing. 'Fear' is a reaction to perceived immediate physical danger, such as being cornered by a vicious dog, going on a scary carnival ride or walking in a dark alleyway in an unsafe area. Anxiety is a response to perceived future threat, such as having to give a speech, needing to make an unpleasant phone call or anticipating a painful medical procedure.

COMMON THREATS

We become anxious when we perceive that something we value is threatened. The most common threats are to our:

➤ physical safety—such as when we are walking alone at night or when awaiting the results of a pathology report;

➤ material wellbeing—such as when we are faced with a large debt, risk of redundancy or when starting up a new business;

➤ self-esteem—such as when we have made a significant error at work, or when we struggle to do things that others find easy;

➤ social safety—such as when we think that someone disapproves of us, or we are going to a social function where we won't know anyone; and

➤ psychological wellbeing—such as when we start to feel depressed or overwhelmed by anxiety (anxiety or depression can themselves become sources of threat).

EVOLUTIONARY BENEFITS

Evolution favours anxiety—historically our anxious ancestors had a survival advantage. Over the thousands of years in which our species evolved, anxiety heightened our ability to detect threats in the environment and optimised the likelihood of escaping danger. For our stone-age ancestors, the fight-or-flight response produced the extra reserves of energy needed to run away or stay and fight. Even today, there are some situations where the fight-or-flight response can be useful. For instance, if you are being chased by a bull in a paddock or running away from a brawl, the surge in energy triggered by the fight-or-flight response will enable you to run further and faster than usual.

The world we live in has changed dramatically since when our ancestors were roaming the savannah, and most of the situations we find threatening have also changed. Today we perceive threats in relation to emotional rather than physical safety: deadlines, demanding customers, financial pressures, exam stress, demands at home and at work, and unpleasant confrontations. Although these situations don't present a threat to our survival, our body still responds as though our life is at stake.

Unfortunately getting highly aroused and ready for action in these situations has few benefits. In fact, the physical changes caused by frequent arousal can lead to problems such as tension headaches, chest pains, an upset stomach, twitches, agitation, exhaustion and panic attacks.

Stephen is a talented young design consultant who has been running his own business for nearly ten years. Although the business is thriving, Stephen feels anxious much of the time. When he is busy, he worries that he may not be able to keep up with the demand for work. When he is not so busy, he worries that he may not be able to continue generating work. Stephen also worries about his ability to meet deadlines, satisfy client expectations, compete with new large design companies and retain the current premises. While Stephen is regarded as one of the top designers in the field, his anxiety makes it difficult for him to enjoy his success or feel optimistic about the future.

PREDISPOSITION TO ANXIETY

Like Stephen, many people are predisposed to anxiety. We call this **high trait anxiety,** because the disposition is part of one's personality. People with this trait are more likely to perceive neutral or low-threat situations as dangerous, and typically overestimate the likelihood that bad things will happen (e.g. 'My child might have an accident'; 'I might miss the plane'; 'They might think badly of me'). This can be a major obstacle to personal wellbeing, as it impairs our ability to relax, focus on what we are doing and enjoy the moment.

Studies that compared anxiety levels between identical and non-identical twins have found that the predisposition to anxiety is influenced by both genes and early childhood experiences (about 50 per cent each). Predisposing childhood experiences include parents who were critical, punitive or unpredictable, or who communicated an overly dangerous view of the world. It might also include exposure to poverty, violence, insecurity or an unstable home environment. In addition, biological factors can give rise to an anxious temperament.

While having an anxious disposition increases the likelihood of becoming anxious, it does not mean that we are destined to suffer anxiety for the rest of our lives. However, we need to put more effort into keeping our anxiety in check compared to those who are low on trait anxiety.

WE GET ANXIOUS ABOUT DIFFERENT THINGS

While there are certain situations that most people experience as threatening (such as having to give a speech and being diagnosed with a serious illness), we also differ in many areas. For instance, some people get particularly anxious when there is a chance that someone may disapprove of them, but they are far less concerned about their physical safety. Others get anxious about their financial security but do not get overly concerned about disapproval from others. Some people become particularly anxious about threats to their physical health, but do not worry too much about their performance at work. The specific issues that press our 'anxiety buttons' are influenced by our early history, which affects the meanings we give to life events.

ANXIETY DISORDERS

While anxiety can be a normal response to threatening situations, if it interferes with our lives and our ability to function, it may be classed as an anxiety disorder. The symptoms of anxiety disorders and their effects on our lives are more pervasive and debilitating than normal state anxiety, and may last for months or years.

Studies estimate that each year 14 per cent of the Australian population are affected by an anxiety disorder. These include generalised anxiety disorder, social phobia, panic disorder, agoraphobia, obsessive compulsive disorder, post-traumatic stress disorder and specific phobias (such as fear of flying, enclosed spaces and spiders). Anxiety disorders can interfere with our ability to do things like keep a job, catch a plane, drive a car, leave the house, have friends, enjoy normal relationships or feel safe in the world. People who have anxiety disorders may also suffer from other problems such as depression or insomnia.

Because anxiety disorders are more disabling than normal anxiety, they are difficult to control through self-help alone. If you have an anxiety disorder, it is important to seek help from a mental-health professional who has expertise in treating anxiety disorders. Specific CBT treatments have been developed for each of the anxiety disorders, and as they continue to be evaluated and further refined, their outcomes continue to improve.

This chapter provides information on managing anxiety and some of it will be useful for dealing with anxiety disorders. However, like all self-help material, it is not a complete treatment for specific anxiety disorders, and professional treatment is highly recommended.

EFFECTS OF ANXIETY

Anxiety affects our thoughts, body sensations and behaviours.

THOUGHTS

While our thinking style influences our disposition to anxiety, the reverse is also true—anxiety influences the content of our thoughts. When we are in an anxious state, our thinking becomes more threat focused and our mind keeps scanning for possible danger. We overestimate the likelihood that bad things will happen, and mentally exaggerate their consequences if they should occur.

Because anxiety narrows our attention to threat, it limits our ability to concentrate on other issues. For instance, if you feel anxious about talking to people at a party, you might find it hard to hear what they have to say because part of your attention is focused on how you are coming across. Many anxious individuals worry about their memory and ability to concentrate, as paying attention to perceived dangers limits the mental resources available for focusing on other issues.

BODY

As we saw earlier, anxiety triggers physical arousal. People who are high on trait anxiety experience **somatic** symptoms (i.e. physical symptoms produced by psychological factors). The most common of these are heart palpitations, tremors, tightness in the chest, sleep disturbances, headaches, nausea, dizziness and fatigue. Also very common are numbness, tingling, twitching or 'electrical' sensations, loss of appetite, diarrhoea, vomiting, digestive disturbances, light-headedness, missed heart beats, itchy or crawly skin, muscle stiffness, tightness in throat or difficulty swallowing, heat surges, pain or tightness in the scalp and feelings of unreality.

As these symptoms are unpleasant and hard to explain, many anxious individuals worry that there is something wrong with their health. Focusing on our physical sensations may give rise to further anxiety, and a self-perpetuating cycle is established: anxiety produces somatic symptoms, the symptoms are perceived as dangerous and this perception produces further anxiety, which produces further somatic symptoms. It is not uncommon for anxious individuals to end up in hospital emergency departments because of benign physical symptoms related to anxiety or panic attacks.

BEHAVIOUR

While all emotions influence our behaviours, anxiety is arguably the most powerful motivator of all. It can mobilise us to do things that protect and sustain us. It can also give rise to behaviours that seriously limit the quality of our lives.

MOTIVATION AND PERFORMANCE

A moderate degree of anxiety can sometimes can be helpful. In sport for instance, the anxiety that comes prior to competition can increase motivation and push players to excel. Pre-exam anxiety can motivate students to study hard and perform well on the day, and public speaking anxiety can motivate us to prepare thoroughly and give a brilliant performance. Moderate levels of anxiety in response to a demanding job can keep us motivated and focused.

While a degree of anxiety can improve performance, severe anxiety impairs it. High anxiety at work can lead to diminished concentration, errors, reduced productivity and burnout; in competitive sport, it impedes play; the stage actor who is terrified on opening night may forget his lines; and intense anxiety during an exam can lead to mental blanks and errors.

AVOIDANCE

Avoidance behaviours are common characteristics of anxiety and anxiety-related disorders. When we perceive things to be unsafe, we try to avoid them. For instance, if we have social anxiety, we avoid social situations where we might be expected to talk to people. If we have health-related anxiety, we might put off having medical tests for fear that it might lead to the discovery of a health problem. If we have anxiety about the possibility of panic attacks, we are likely to avoid public places and situations (e.g. shopping centres, public transport, tunnels) from which escape would be difficult. If we are anxious about the way others perceive us, we are likely to avoid expressing our opinions, communicating assertively or making unpleasant telephone calls. If we are terrified of failure, we are likely to avoid situations where failure might occur, such as job interviews, challenging work or higher education.

Avoidance enables us to evade the discomfort that accompanies anxiety, and so makes us feel better in the short term. However, it is counterproductive because it reinforces beliefs that the world is unsafe, and so maintains anxiety in the longer term. Not confronting our fears means that we never learn to overcome them. Avoidance can also impose major limitations to our lives. People who allow their anxiety to rule their behaviours often end up with limited and uninteresting lives.

> Life shrinks or expands in proportion to one's courage.
> **ANAÏS NIN**

Some people try to avoid anxiety by numbing themselves through eating, abusing alcohol, smoking, taking benzodiazepines or illicit drugs, or gambling. Because these often do provide temporary relief, we feel drawn to use them again and again. The trouble with these 'remedies' is that they do not work in the longer term, and often create more problems than they solve. In fact, anxiety is a common precursor to addictive habits and other self-defeating behaviours.

SAFETY BEHAVIOURS

Looking for ways to protect ourselves is a normal response to situations of danger. For instance, if we should notice the smell of smoke while at the cinema, we are likely to make for the nearest exit. This is a normal and appropriate response that can protect us from harm. However, if you are high on trait anxiety, you overestimate the likelihood of danger, and consequently you are frequently doing things to protect yourself from harm. These **safety behaviours** (strategies aimed at minimising risk of harm) can be mental strategies (such as reviewing a recent conversation for signs of disapproval), or specific actions (such as making repeated medical appointments to rule out the possibility of illness). Other common safety behaviours include:

➤ Having someone go with you in order to avoid facing the situation alone;

➤ Making regular phone calls to loved ones to ensure that they are safe;

➤ Checking the internet for possible causes of current symptoms;

➤ Over-preparing and mentally rehearsing things;

➤ Trying to do things perfectly in order to gain approval or avoid criticism;

➤ Sitting next to the exit so that you can make a quick escape;

➤ Taking vitamin pills and having unproven therapies in order to protect your health;

➤ Carrying bottled water and sipping frequently;

➤ Avoiding situations that are associated with anxiety;

➤ Monitoring and checking things; and

➤ Planning solutions to imagined problems.

Although safety behaviours are intended to reduce the risk of harm, they rarely achieve this, and usually they create more problems than they solve. Safety behaviours maintain anxiety because they prevent us from learning that our fears are unjustified. When bad things don't eventuate, we unconsciously attribute this to our safety behaviours instead of recognising that bad things rarely happen anyway.

In order to release or reduce our anxiety, we need to identify and relinquish safety behaviours. This can be done in small steps so that we can get used to the new behaviour without feeling overwhelmed. By gradually dropping our safety behaviours and therefore facing our fears we discover that our world is safe after all. Most things turn out OK without our intervention and, more importantly, even on the rare occasions when things don't go our way, we learn that we are able to cope.

EXERCISE 6.1

Keep a diary of the safety behaviours that you use in order to keep yourself safe (including the things you avoid). Keep adding to these as you notice other behaviours.

What have been the consequences of these behaviours? Have they really protected you or your loved ones from harm?

Write a list of all the downsides of these behaviours.

HABITS OF THINKING THAT PERPETUATE ANXIETY

Anxiety stems from the perception of threat. Identifying the thought patterns and behaviours that maintain our anxiety, and learning to modify these can help us to reduce threat perceptions. The following are common habits of thinking that maintain our anxiety.

WORRY

Worry is a series of thoughts about bad things that could happen. It is normal and adaptive to worry occasionally, as the process can help us to find solutions to problems that arise. However, many people worry far beyond the point where it provides an advantage. When we feel anxious or depressed we worry more than usual, as our emotions influence the content of our thoughts. Worry is a common feature of all anxiety disorders; however, the issues we worry about are influenced by the specific disorder. For instance, people with social phobia worry about social situations; people with health anxiety worry about illness; people with panic disorder worry about the possibility of further panic attacks and people with phobias worry about having to confront the object of their fears.

Persistent worry about a variety of issues is a key feature of **generalised anxiety disorder** (GAD), which affects five to seven per cent of Australians at some stage in their lives. People with GAD are more likely to interpret ambiguous events in a catastrophic way (e.g. 'Why didn't my boss smile at me? She must be annoyed with me'; 'My husband is late from work—maybe he has had an accident?') and they frequently engage in speculative worrying. For instance: 'What if I lose my job?'; 'What if I fall over?'; 'What if I make a fool of myself?'; 'What if I get sick and can't work any more?'; 'What if I can't find a parking spot?'; 'How will I cope if my partner dies?'.

> *While standing outside at a party one evening, Gina noticed some blood on her finger and, assuming it to be her own, instinctively licked it. This was not a problem until she discovered that the blood actually belonged to a young man who was standing on the veranda above her, who had cut himself with a bottle opener. The realisation that she had licked someone else's blood sent Gina into a tailspin, as she immediately thought that it could be HIV-contaminated, and that she would therefore get AIDS. Although there was no evidence that the blood was contaminated (or that licking someone's blood is likely to cause AIDS), Gina's tendency to focus on threats, and to grossly overestimate the likelihood that bad things will happen, caused her to panic.*

METACOGNITIVE BELIEFS ABOUT WORRY

In Chapter 5 we saw how metacognitive beliefs about anger can motivate us to hold on to it. Similarly, metacognitive beliefs about worry can motivate us to persist with worrying. People who are prone to worry often describe feeling compelled to focus on their fears, and being uncomfortable with the idea of giving it up. This is because worrying feels beneficial. Many people have positive beliefs about worry; for example, 'Worrying gives me control'; 'Worrying helps me to find solutions'; 'Worrying prevents bad things from happening' and 'Worrying prepares me for the worst'.

Most of these beliefs are held just below consciousness; however, they can often be brought to awareness through reflection. While positive beliefs about worrying are largely irrational, on a gut level they feel true and we rarely stop to scrutinise them. As long as we believe that worry protects us or provides benefits, we will be reluctant to release the habit. For this reason, it is helpful to identify and then challenge irrational beliefs about the benefits of worrying. Below are some examples of how this can be done.

POSITIVE BELIEFS ABOUT WORRY	ALTERNATIVE, REALISTIC VIEWS
Worrying can prevent bad things from happening.	Worrying makes no difference to the things that happen. Unless I am doing something to solve a problem, the process of worrying has no effect on life events.
Worrying helps me to prepare for future threats.	It is impossible to prepare for every negative contingency. Being too focused on possible threats causes me to plan for unnecessary contingencies, and may cause me to ignore other more immediate needs. It can therefore produce other problems, as well as wasting my time and energy.
Worrying helps me to find solutions.	Problems can be solved without worrying. People who do not worry are just as effective (or more effective) at solving problems as those who do. Worrying does not 'add value'.
Worrying prepares me for the worst. If it should happen, I will be emotionally prepared.	Worrying beforehand will not protect me emotionally if bad things should happen—it just produces anxiety for no benefit. Why suffer 'just in case'? If things should go wrong I will cope with them when I need to. Worrying in advance provides no additional protection.

POSITIVE BELIEFS ABOUT WORRY	ALTERNATIVE, REALISTIC VIEWS
Worrying gives me control.	Worrying does not give me control. Unless I am problem-solving or taking some positive action, worrying makes no difference to outcomes.
Worrying motivates me to do things.	I can achieve the things I need by setting goals and following through with action. I don't need to worry in order to get things done.

Why destroy your present happiness by a distant misery,
which may never come at all?
For every substantial grief has twenty shadows,
and most of the shadows are of your own making.
SYDNEY SMITH

Greg hates going to the dentist and he has not had a dental check-up in the past fifteen years. Finally, under threat of divorce from his wife, Greg reluctantly agreed to go. As soon as he made the appointment, he started worrying and imagining how awful he would feel if he needed to get fillings. On the dreaded day, as he sat in the waiting room contemplating his fate, Greg's anxiety was intense. Indeed, the dental examination confirmed his worst fears— two cavities that needed filling. Now, while Greg did experience some discomfort during the procedure, the worst of it lasted for only six minutes—sixty seconds for the injections and five minutes of drilling. Ironically, the anxiety that Greg experienced beforehand lasted for weeks, and was far more distressing than the brief period of dental work.

*

My own experience of planning a trip to Melbourne in winter illustrates the same principle. A mid-year break seemed like a good opportunity to visit my family, so I booked a flight to Melbourne for a short stay. The weather in Melbourne can be cold at the best of times but in the middle of winter it is usually bleak. As I feel the cold more than most people, I spent two weeks prior to the trip anticipating and dreading the winter chill. As it turned out, Melbourne's weather was no problem at all—I was either rugged up or indoors most of the time, and I enjoyed the opportunity to catch up with family and friends. The trip itself was enjoyable, while the previous two weeks of negative anticipation were a pain! I put this experience down to a timely reminder that the bulk of our misery comes from negative anticipation rather than the event itself.

EXCESSIVE NEED FOR APPROVAL

Wanting to be liked is a normal part of being human. Our desire for acceptance is hardwired. For our stone-age ancestors, being accepted provided safety within the tribe, while to be cast out meant death. Things have changed, and in modern society we can survive perfectly well without universal love and acceptance. However, some of us still crave it—it is as though our very lives depends on it.

Those of us who are high on trait anxiety often have an excessive desire for approval. This makes us overly sensitive to the messages we receive from others—both verbal and non-verbal. For instance, we might feel anxious if someone seems more distant than usual, and we are more likely to misinterpret neutral comments or gestures as signs of disapproval or rejection. We might also become self-conscious about our own behaviours and how we are coming across to others. Thus we tend to worry about things we say or do, and about how others might perceive them.

If we have low self-esteem, this strengthens our desire for approval because we perceive ourselves to be at high risk of rejection. So we look for validation from others as a way of reassuring ourselves that this will not occur. We might look for signs of approval, such as body language and comments, and sometimes try too hard to make people like us. We may also be reluctant to take social risks or to respond assertively within our relationships for fear of generating disapproval. We dread situations that involve a possibility of conflict and will sometimes go to great lengths to avoid them.

While having his house renovated, Rick noticed some faults with the workmanship in the kitchen and bathroom. When he spoke to his builder, Rick received reassurance that his concerns would be addressed; however, the job has now been completed and most of the faults remain. Rick knows that he should talk to his builder again and insist that the problems be addressed, but the thought of a possible confrontation makes Rick feel anxious. As he hates to 'cause trouble' or get people offside, Rick chooses to say nothing and rationalises that the faults are not really such a big deal.

Rick's behaviour is typical of people who have an excessive need for approval. The anxiety generated by the possibility of conflict gives rise to unassertive behaviour. We ignore our own long-term interests for the sake of keeping the peace.

BEHAVIOURAL DISPUTING

As with all beliefs, the excessive need for approval and fear of rejection is reflected in the way we behave. For instance, we might typically try to please or impress people by agreeing with them; not clearly stating what we think or want; being excessively generous or trying too hard to be likeable. In the above example, Rick avoided telling his builder what he really thought of his workmanship because he feared the possibility of disapproval.

For those who worry too much about what others might think of them, behavioural disputing is a great way to confront this concern. Changing our behaviour enables us to test the assumption that catastrophic consequences will follow if we do things that others might disapprove of. This approach is embodied in '**shame-attacking exercises**', originally described by CBT pioneer Albert Ellis. Shame-attacking involves deliberately doing things that might elicit negative appraisal.

In a now famous personal anecdote, Ellis described his experience of confronting his own fear of rejection by asking out over 100 women who he approached on a park bench. According to Ellis: 'I realised that throughout this exercise no one vomited, no one called a cop and I didn't die. The process of trying new behaviours and understanding what happened in the real world instead of in my imagination led me to overcome my fear of speaking to women.' (From an interview with Claire Warga, reported in *Psychology Today*, 1988.)

Other shame-attacking exercises that have been suggested by advocates of this method include:

➤ Get into an elevator and stand facing your fellow travellers instead of the door.

➤ Sing to yourself while standing at a crowded location.

➤ Wear attention-grabbing clothes, such as a t-shirt with an outrageous logo, a loud tie or a funny hat.

➤ Go into a DVD rental store and loudly ask where you can find their pornographic section.

➤ Walk up to someone in the street and tell (rather than ask) them the time.

➤ Sit on a bus or train and call out the stations every time it pulls into a stop.

In CBT group programs for social anxiety, it is often the shame-attacking exercises that participants report to be the most important learning experiences. Said one participant: 'I could never have believed that dancing a conga line in the main street of Sydney could be so liberating. Most people didn't even look at us, and those that did didn't seem to care. It really brought home to me the fact that so much of my worry about what others think of me is just inside my own head.'

Exercises such as these enable us to learn that even if we do look silly or draw attention to ourselves, people rarely notice or care and, even if some do think we are strange, there are rarely any significant consequences.

While the exercises listed above may be too 'crazy' for some people, any action that involves reducing approval-seeking behaviour qualifies as a shame-attacking exercise. More conventional exercises include using assertive communication in situations where we would normally say nothing, or being honest and open about things that we would normally feel embarrassed to admit. If you usually avoid expressing your opinion for fear of disapproval, then challenge yourself by speaking up when the opportunity arises. Say what you think rather than what you believe others want to hear, and observe whether negative consequences ensue. If you frequently agree with others in order to win their approval, then practise expressing your disagreement when you genuinely disagree. If you often use excessive generosity to win other people's affection, then consciously curb this behaviour—or better still, ask them to do *you* a favour. Be on the lookout for opportunities to spontaneously perform shame-attacking exercises. Whenever you find yourself thinking, 'I can't do that—I would look bad', use this as your cue to rise to the challenge.

Behavioural disputing is anxiety-provoking, as the new behaviour is inconsistent with our strongly held beliefs. However, by repeatedly confronting our fears we learn experientially that our assumptions are incorrect. People are rarely as judgemental as we assume, and even when some do disapprove, we are able to cope far better than we had thought.

EXERCISE 6.2

If you have an excessive need for approval, write down some things that you sometimes do to win approval from others. Conduct some behavioural experiments that involve dropping these behaviours over the next few weeks. What are the consequences of changing your behaviours? Did it result in rejection or disapproval? Are there many negative consequences? Are there any positive consequences?

PERFECTIONISM

Like most human traits, a perfectionistic personality may develop in response to a biological disposition and/or early life experiences. Parents who have very high expectations of their children; who are frequently critical of their children; whose affection is contingent on their children's achievements; and who display perfectionist behaviours themselves are more likely to give rise to children with perfectionist traits. Adults who were very gifted and capable in childhood are also more likely to have perfectionist traits because of the high expectations that were set for them by teachers, families and their peers. In addition, individuals with high trait anxiety are often drawn to perfectionist behaviours because it creates the illusion of control.

We strive for perfection because it makes our world seem less random, and therefore safer. The behaviour also sustains our desire for approval, as we believe that doing things perfectly will elevate our standing in the eyes of others. It may feel like excelling in what we do will make us popular and respected.

While having high standards can have its benefits, the belief that things must be done perfectly is anxiety-producing, because of the ongoing possibility that we will not live up to our expectations. Perfectionist attitudes often cause procrastination, as the fear of falling short makes it hard to get started. It also makes us inefficient, as our inability to say 'That's good enough' causes us to spend too much time on tasks that don't warrant it. The advantages of spending many extra hours on particular jobs are often marginal, while the costs may be substantial. So wanting to do a brilliant job can lead to an impasse at either end—making it difficult to get started or to stop.

Perfectionism also causes us to become overly concerned with small flaws and mistakes, and to downgrade our achievements and successes. We fail to acknowledge the things we do well, but self-flagellate when our performance falls short of expectations. Frequent self-criticism leaves us feeling frustrated and dissatisfied. Perfectionist attitudes limit our ability to relax, enjoy healthy self-esteem and take pleasure in activities that are not focused on outcomes. Many people with perfectionist traits also set very high standards for other people—partners, friends, children or work colleagues—and are frequently critical as a result. This makes them hard to live with, and consequently their relationships suffer.

This is not to say that a perfectionist attitude is always inappropriate. Certain situations do require exacting standards. Surgeons, for instance, need to be perfectionists when conducting surgery because people's lives are at stake. Bomb-disposal experts and military personnel working in combat zones also need to be perfectionists, as small errors can have dire consequences. There are other critical or dangerous situations where it is absolutely necessary to be meticulous. However, for most people in most situations, perfectionist expectations are unnecessary and unhelpful.

> *Cassie works as a research assistant to a respected radio presenter who conducts regular interviews with high-profile guests. In addition to finding speakers for the program and researching their backgrounds, Cassie also does a pre-interview telephone chat with each guest in order to find out more about them. Being a perfectionist, Cassie believes that she has to read through all of her researched material before she calls each guest, and she becomes anxious if she hasn't done this first. While Cassie believes that the job itself is stressful, the truth is that Cassie's perfectionism is the main problem, as her belief that she has to have read all the material is unrealistic and impractical. Ironically, trying to do her job too well makes Cassie inefficient, as the additional gains of reading all the background notes are marginal at best. Interestingly, the quality of the final product—the interview—is always high, regardless of whether Cassie has spent hours reading her research notes or no time at all.*

Although perfectionism often manifests in attitudes towards our work and study, we can also have perfectionist attitudes in other areas, such as in the way we dress and groom ourselves, the things we buy, the expectations we have of our partners, friends and children, the way we play sport or partake in leisure activities, and even the way we maintain our house.

> *Raylene has a perfectionist attitude to housekeeping. While always having a clean and tidy house gives her a sense of pride, Raylene's perfectionist attitude has downsides. On the occasions when the house is not looking its best, Raylene feels stressed. When a friend drops by unexpectedly, Raylene worries that they might notice the mess and think badly of her. The problem is not the fact that Raylene likes to keep a beautiful house. Aiming for excellence in any area that interests us can be rewarding. The problem is her cognitive rigidity—the belief*

that her house must always look fantastic and her inability to say,
'That's OK' at times when it doesn't. Instead of adding to her pleasure,
Raylene's perfectionist attitude makes her anxious and lessens her
ability to enjoy her lovely house, as well as the company of her visitors.

BEHAVIOURAL DISPUTING

For those of us who, like Cassie, have perfectionist attitudes in relation to our work, behavioural disputing is the most effective strategy. Setting time limits on the tasks that we perform gives us the opportunity to observe the consequences.

Cassie decided to limit the time she spends reading her guest speakers' profiles to one hour. By discovering that this had no negative effect on her program preparation or the quality of the radio interview, Cassie's assumptions changed, and consequently allowed her to be more efficient in doing her job.

Raylene chose to leave the beds unmade for a week. While initially this made her more anxious, over time she discovered that lowering her standards did not result in negative consequences, and so her anxiety subsided. In addition, she resisted the urge to take three days off work to clean the house before her brother arrived from France, and once again discovered that this made no difference to the enjoyment of his stay.

Tarne's perfectionism creates problems in his work as a journalist, as
his need to do a perfect job causes him to procrastinate. He has learned
to overcome this problem by commencing with the aim of writing a
poorly worded draft. Once the draft has been written, his anxiety
drops, and he is then able to work on refining it.

*

Mario challenges perfectionist attitudes in relation to his writing by
checking his emails only once before sending them.

*

Todd chooses to deliberately make 'errors' in his weekly tennis game, to help him challenge perfectionist attitudes about the standard of his game.

*

Nicky commits to spending no more than ten minutes doing her make-up, and bans her usual habit of changing her clothes repeatedly before going out, in order to challenge perfectionist attitudes in relation to her appearance.

*

Adrian deliberately leaves his office in a slightly messy state each day, to challenge his obsessional attitudes about tidiness.

*

Freya starts cooking dinner at 5 pm when entertaining friends. Choosing to serve a simple pasta and salad instead of an elaborate gourmet meal, and allowing herself only a couple of hours to cook before her friends arrive, helps Freya to challenge perfectionist beliefs about the standard she needs to achieve when having friends for dinner.

EXERCISE 6.3

If you are a perfectionist, write down some examples of situations where your perfectionist attitudes manifest. Design some behavioural experiments that you can undertake to test the validity of your assumptions regarding the need for perfection, and put them to the test over the next few weeks. What are the consequences of modifying your perfectionist expectations?

EXCESSIVE NEED FOR CONTROL

Taking control over challenging situations (through things like problem solving or disputing negative thoughts) can help us to feel good. It enables us to reduce anxiety and feelings of helplessness, and creates a sense of mastery. However, an excessive need for control has the opposite effect—it maintains anxiety and gives rise to unhelpful behaviours.

People who are anxious by nature often have an excessive need for control. We try to make our world safe and predictable by minimising the chances that things will go wrong. Consequently we anticipate, search out, prepare, initiate, pre-empt, fix, warn, arrange, check, adjust, plan, explain and organise.

The problem is that there are many things that we cannot control, and trying to do so does not make us feel safe. Very often it has the opposite effect. It also wastes our energy, distracts our attention and prevents us from living a full and meaningful life. A more psychologically healthy attitude is to accept that many things are beyond our control, and not to try to control them.

> Do what you can but don't expect to be omnipotent.
> Many things are beyond your control.

Valerie's seventeen-year-old daughter, Cheryl, has recently announced that she is going to live with her boyfriend, Mark. Valerie is beside herself. Although Mark is always polite, Valerie finds him to be rather simple. He is not particularly well-educated or well-spoken and he lacks ambition. Valerie can't understand what Cheryl sees in him. She also thinks that Cheryl is too young to live with her boyfriend and that she will only end up getting hurt.

It is perfectly normal for Valerie to be concerned about Cheryl's welfare as, like any parent, Valerie wants to her daughter to be happy and safe. It is therefore important for her to talk to Cheryl, explain her concerns, point out some possible downsides of her plan, and perhaps suggest some alternatives (e.g. 'Why don't you just continue to go out for the next six months, and he can stay over on weekends? Then, if you still feel the same way at the end of the year, you can move in together.'). Depending on Cheryl's personality and her relationship with her mother, she may or may not take Valerie's advice. The point is that once she has talked to her daughter, there may be little else that Valerie can do. Like many parents of teenage children, Valerie may need to accept that she can no longer control her daughter's actions. Relinquishing control is painful but necessary. Our ability to let go of things we cannot change is a measure of good psychological health.

Valerie works on challenging her unhelpful thoughts and beliefs by disputing some of her cognitions.

SITUATION	Cheryl announced that she intends to leave home, to live with Mark.
FEELINGS	Anxious, angry, tense, physically aroused
THOUGHTS	Where does she get these ideas? She is much too young to live with Mark. She will end up getting hurt.
BELIEFS	Her decision is bad. I should be able to protect her from all future problems. If it doesn't work out, it will be terrible. She should do what I believe is right.
THINKING ERRORS	Shoulds, predicting catastrophe, black-and-white thinking
DISPUTE	She may end up hurt but, then again, she may end up very happy with Mark. If it doesn't work out she may learn from this experience. She can always come home. I wish she would do what I believe is right, but there is no law that says she must. She has the right to do what she thinks is best for her. If she is hurt through this experience, she will recover. Lots of things in life are painful, and I can't protect her from all possible pain.
POSITIVE ACTIONS	Talk to her. Explain the reasons for my concern. Suggest a compromise solution but accept that she is not obliged to agree to it.

BEHAVIOURAL DISPUTING

The excessive need to control things can be challenged using behavioural experiments—changing our behaviour and observing the consequences. For instance, if you normally feel the urge to 'fix things' for others, make a decision to not take responsibility for other people's problems. If you frequently try to control your partner or your children, consciously choose to let go, and observe the consequences. In the above example, Valerie initially disputed her unhelpful cognitions, and then chose to relinquish attempts to control her daughter's decision. When Cheryl moved in with Mark, Valerie discovered that the consequences were not so terrible after all.

Lucia is anxious by nature, and has an excessive need for control over her children. She frequently admonishes them for not studying enough, hanging out with the wrong friends, dressing badly and listening to the wrong type of music. When her teenage daughter came home with a tattoo Lucia was furious—she would never have allowed this! Lucia decides to challenge her need to control her children's lives by choosing to be less interfering. While she continues to provide normal parental guidance, Lucia gives her children greater freedom in the decisions they make, the way they spend their time and the things they like to do. By taking a more accepting stance Lucia discovers that there are no catastrophic consequences, that her children are happier and that they can make reasonable decisions for themselves.

*

Pip likes to have things his way. Whenever he goes out with his friends to see a movie or to have a meal, it must always be to a place that he chooses or approves of. If he does not get his way, Pip is in a bad mood for the entire evening, which makes things unpleasant for others. Pip can challenge his need for control by deliberately letting others make the decisions, and choosing to go along with them. In opting to 'go with the flow', Pip learns that things don't always have to be done his way. Letting others lead has no major adverse consequences and often has positive spin-offs, like not feeling responsible if the movie or the meal turns out to be a dud.

*

Glen insists that his colleagues should use a work system that he has devised, even though they prefer an alternative system. He is also reluctant to delegate jobs because he likes to have full control over every stage of projects. This causes Glen to be inefficient and creates tension with his staff. Glen decides to work on developing flexibility by adopting the system devised by his colleagues and objectively evaluating its pros and cons. In addition, choosing to delegate certain tasks enables Glen to learn that relinquishing some control has advantages, and ultimately makes his job easier.

*

Jana has a strong need for control over her weight and is totally inflexible with her eating habits. In order to challenge her obsession with weight, Jana commits to eating more spontaneously, having some non-diet snack food every day, and ordering dessert when eating out. Breaking her rigid food rules helps Jana to realise that no catastrophic consequences occur, and the massive weight gain that she had feared does not eventuate.

*

Peter gets anxious whenever his girlfriend, Claudia, talks to other guys. When they go out to social functions, he keeps a constant eye on her and if he sees Claudia speaking to a young man, he makes angry or sarcastic comments on the way home. He gives Claudia a hard time when she wants to go out with her friends because he is concerned that she might meet someone else in his absence. Peter's attempts to control Claudia's behaviour actually reinforce his insecurities and do not help him to overcome his fears. A good behavioural experiment for Peter is to relinquish his efforts to control Claudia's behaviour and to stop monitoring her activities. While initially this will increase his anxiety, with time Peter will discover that his relationship is safe, and that he does not need to control Claudia in order to keep her. In fact, Claudia may feel happier and more committed to the relationship when Peter's controlling behaviour ceases.

*

Felix feels a strong need for control over his life and seeks to have a regular, predictable routine each day. When unplanned events crop up, such as when friends drop in or call with suggestions for things to do, he naturally resists. Felix recognises that his lack of flexibility is unhelpful and decides to challenge his rigid behaviour. He makes it his policy to take up opportunities whenever they arise, even if this means deviating from his plans. For instance, Felix goes out for a coffee with an old acquaintance that he runs into on the way home from work, thereby allowing himself to change his plans when an alternative opportunity arises. Being less structured enables Felix to discover that he doesn't need to keep such a rigid routine, and that spontaneity adds some 'spice' to his life.

EXERCISE 6.4

Write down any areas where you have an excessive need for control. Design some behavioural experiments that can test the effects of relinquishing control and put them into practice over the next few weeks. What are the consequences of giving up control in these areas—does it result in the negative outcomes you feared? Are there any positive outcomes?

PROBLEM SOLVE

Whenever we find ourselves in a stressful situation, the most appropriate first step is to look for solutions. Problem solving increases our sense of control, and so the very decision to do something often makes us feel better. The amount of control we can exert in any situation varies. Sometimes, in spite of our best intentions, there is nothing we can do to change the situation. In these circumstances, our best option is cognitive flexibility—acceptance of situations that are beyond our control. In situations where possible solutions do exist, brainstorming some options is a good place to start.

Jeanette works as an editor in a large publishing company. The demands of the job have grown in the past twelve months, and over that time she has done her best to manage her workload. Recently Jeanette was given additional jobs with tight deadlines, and this sent her anxiety levels soaring. Being very conscientious, Jeanette felt obliged to deliver on time, but she couldn't see how this was possible. An unpleasant tightness in the chest started to trouble her, and sometimes she found it hard to breathe.

Jeanette recognised that she had to do something, as the stress of unrealistic deadlines was overwhelming, and impaired her ability to do her job. While she thought about resigning, this seemed like a drastic step, so she decided to explore other options. She wrote the following list of possible solutions:

➤ Prioritise my jobs and focus on the most urgent ones.
➤ Talk to Louise [work colleague] to see if she'd be willing to help out with some of my projects.
➤ Come in early and stay back late every night this week.
➤ Come in on the weekend and finish off the more urgent jobs.
➤ Talk to Beth [team manager], explain my situation to her and ask for help.

As Jeanette worked through these strategies, she found that prioritising her jobs and staying back until late each evening helped her to feel more in control. Her decision to come into work on the weekend, while not something she relished, gave her additional breathing space and lowered her anxiety. She also talked to her colleague, who was sympathetic but unable to take on any additional work. Her colleague strongly encouraged Jeanette to talk to Beth, as she is the person who could lighten her load.

ADDRESS OBSTACLES TO PROBLEM SOLVING

Although talking to her boss was an obvious and important step, Jeanette felt strong resistance to doing this. Upon reflection, she realised that this stemmed from her beliefs about asking for help: 'I should always do it all myself'; 'Asking for help means that I am incompetent'; 'Others will think less of me'. In order to flourish in her job Jeanette needs to develop cognitive flexibility. As she contemplates this issue, Jeanette writes the following disputing statements:

➤ I prefer to complete all of my assigned tasks, but that is not always possible.

➤ Asking for help when my workload is excessive is a sign of competence, not failure.

➤ Experience has taught me that people rarely judge me as harshly as I judge myself.

Once Jeanette acknowledged and challenged the psychological obstacles that were holding her back, she approached Beth and had a useful discussion. This resulted in the extension of some deadlines and a more realistic workload.

When we find ourselves feeling anxious about a particular issue, looking for solutions is often a good place to start. Partial or total solutions are often available when we think creatively and challenge the obstacles that get in the way of problem solving (see also Chapter 9).

EXERCISE 6.5

For each of the following situations suggest:
a   The thoughts and beliefs that contribute to anxiety;
b   Disputing statements that could be used to reduce anxiety; and
c   Possible problem solving that could help the situation. (Sample solutions are at the back of the book.)

1   Eve is anxious about going to a social function where she won't know anyone.
2   Barry feels anxious about running late for a doctor's appointment.
3   Kim is anxious about having to give a speech to a large audience of professional people.
4   Rick is anxious about having to confront a colleague about a potentially unpleasant situation.
5   Fay feels anxious about having to confront her neighbours about their dog, which is constantly barking.
6   Jeremy is anxious about an approaching job interview.
7   Clive feels anxious about having to return some goods to the shop.
8   Olivia feels anxious because her daughter has slept in and may miss her flight for the holiday that she has planned.

CHALLENGE CATASTROPHIC THINKING

The aim of CBT strategies is to develop healthy, balanced thinking. This means seeing situations in their proper perspective—recognising that most problems rate between 5 and 20 on the 'awfulness' scale, and not the 90 or 100 that we might perceive at times. In addition to acknowledging that most of our feared situations don't eventuate, it also means recognising that even if they do eventuate, we will cope. There are two important things to keep in mind:

1 OVER NINETY PER CENT OF THE THINGS WE FEAR DO NOT EVENTUATE

If you were to add up the number of times that you worried about some imminent disaster, and then compared this to the number of disasters that actually occurred, what do you think you would find? Invariably the vast majority of the things you worried about never eventuated. (If you are a frequent worrier, it is more likely that 99 per cent of the things you worried about never eventuated.) In spite of your worst fears, the speech was not the debacle that you feared; you survived the dreaded dinner party; and the company restructure did not affect you. Upon reflection, the sky rarely fell, and after each episode of angst, your life continued pretty well as before.

2 THE CONSEQUENCES ARE RARELY CATASTROPHIC

Even on those rare occasions when your feared situation did eventuate, the consequences were usually not that bad. In most cases, there is temporary inconvenience, discomfort or distress, but rarely the disaster that we anticipate. Of course, this is not to understate some of the serious situations that sometimes do occur. On rare occasions our worst fears are realised and have major negative consequences—the diagnosis of a life-threatening illness; abandonment by a partner; the loss of our home; the death of a loved one; or serious disability from an accident. These events have long-term consequences and it is normal to experience substantial distress when they occur. The point is, however, that the majority of times when we expect the worst, nothing terrible happens.

Marissa has been feeling particularly low in energy recently and has been drinking a lot of fluids. Her friend told her that she might have diabetes and that she should get herself checked out. The suggestion of a chronic health problem put Marissa into a state of panic. Thoughts of being ill, having to inject herself with insulin and not being in control over her life overwhelmed her, and anxiety soon turned to despair. Consultations with her GP subsequently confirmed Marissa's worst fears—she did indeed have diabetes. While initially this news appeared disastrous, with time Marissa adjusted to her situation. She learned how to manage the condition with diet, regular exercise and medication. Although she is not happy to have diabetes, Marissa discovered that what initially seemed like disaster is an inconvenience that she can manage.

Sometimes situations that appear to be disastrous can have some positive consequences.

Alan went through major anxiety as he tried to save his ailing business for two years. Throughout this period he was consumed with worries about his finances and had difficulty sleeping. Finally, after much soul-searching and angst, Alan decided to call it a day. Much to his own surprise, once the decision was made, he felt immediate relief. What's more, over time Alan found himself feeling happier and more relaxed. The closure of the business forced Alan to re-evaluate his priorities and make positive changes to his lifestyle. No longer having to work long hours enabled Alan to spend more time with his family, and to do things that he enjoyed. He developed some new leisure interests, including bushwalking, sailing and golf. The reduction in stress made him happier and easier to live with, and his relationship with his wife improved. So while the closure of the business seemed like a disaster at the time, in retrospect Alan realised that it was actually a good thing.

*

Barbara made a career move to a new company six months ago, and has been doing well. However, recently she made a mistake transferring money, which could have ended very badly. Although the error was found and corrected, Barbara feels anxious that people in management will find out. Barbara decides to dispute her cognitions using a thought-monitoring form.

SITUATION	Realised that I had transferred money into the wrong account. I fixed the error, but people in management are likely to find out.
FEELINGS	Anxious, tightness in the chest.
THOUGHTS	Everyone will know that I've made a mistake. They will think badly of me. This will undermine my credibility in the company.
BELIEFS	I should never make mistakes. If people find out, they will judge me harshly. Making this mistake means I'm incompetent.
THINKING ERRORS	Predicting catastrophe, jumping to negative conclusions, shoulds, labelling
DISPUTE	All people make mistakes—that is a normal part of being human. I do my job correctly 98 per cent of the time. People tend to judge others by how they perform most of the time, rather than by one-off events. People are rarely as judgemental of me as I am of myself. This is unlikely to have long-term effects on my career, but if it does, I will cope with it when it happens.
POSITIVE ACTIONS	Speak to my supervisor, explain how the mistake happened, and reassure her that it won't happen again.

SOCRATIC QUESTIONING TO ADDRESS WORRYING THOUGHTS

When we are in an anxious state, our mind is focused on threat. We pay attention to feared possibilities, overestimate the likelihood of worst-case scenarios and predict catastrophic consequences. As our perceptions are biased towards threat, our appraisals of danger are unreliable. (Just because you feel it doesn't mean it's true!) For this reason, it is helpful to use objective criteria to evaluate our situation.

The following Socratic questions can be helpful during times of high anxiety, when we are predicting catastrophe or worrying unnecessarily. Because these questions focus on evidence rather than gut feelings, they can help us to perceive our situation in a more realistic way.

SOCRATIC QUESTIONS TO ADDRESS WORRYING THOUGHTS:

1 Describe the situation you are worried about.
2 What specifically do you fear might happen?
3 Rate the likelihood that this will happen (from 0 to 100 per cent).
4 What evidence supports your worrying thoughts?
5 What evidence does not support your worrying thoughts?
6 If your feared situation did eventuate, what actions could you take?
7 Realistically, what is the worst thing that can happen?
8 What is the best thing that can happen?
9 What is most likely to happen?
10 Are there any useful actions that you can take now?
11 What would you tell a friend who was in your situation?
12 Realistically, re-rate the likelihood that your fears will be realised (from 0 to 100 per cent).

William has had a successful career as an artist; however, since the economic downturn, art sales have plummeted and William's income has been affected. He decided to take a stall at the coming Art Fair to try to get exposure for his work, make some new connections and, hopefully, sell some paintings. William paid $5,000 for the stall, and is now having second thoughts. Was this a really good idea? Could it end disastrously? He decides to use Socratic questioning to explore his worrying thoughts.

1 Describe the situation you are worried about.
I am worried about the coming Art Fair.

2 What specifically do you fear might happen?
I will not sell any paintings. I will be $5,000 out of pocket and will feel humiliated. It will be a waste of money and my reputation will suffer.

3 Rate the likelihood that this will happen (from 0 to 100 per cent).
50 per cent.

4 What evidence supports your worrying thoughts?

The market is quiet at the moment. My sales have dropped and other artists are also complaining about poor sales.

5 What evidence does not support your worrying thoughts?

I did sell three paintings in the last month. They fetched reasonable prices, although less than in previous years.

6 If your feared situation did eventuate, what actions could you take?

I could try to sell the paintings via my website and the South Australian gallery. I could also get in touch with some galleries in other states and send them images of my work.

7 Realistically, what is the worst thing that can happen?

I will not sell any paintings and will be $5,000 out of pocket. I will have given up time and energy preparing for the fair.

8 What is the best thing that can happen?

I will sell lots of paintings, and make new connections with art dealers and gallery owners that will have long-term benefits.

9 What is most likely to happen?

I might sell some paintings, but might not cover my costs.

10 Are there any useful actions that you can take now?

I can work on the remaining pieces to make them as saleable as possible. Make arrangements for setting up the display. Ask my partner to help me set up. Contact some of my previous customers and pass on my free tickets to the fair.

11 What would you tell a friend who was in your situation?

If you don't make any sales it will be disappointing, but it is not going to make the difference between success and poverty. Sometimes you have to try new things to find out what works and what doesn't—you won't know if you don't have a go. You can use these paintings for other exhibitions if they don't sell here. Other people are unlikely to notice or care, so any humiliation you might feel would be entirely in your own mind.

12 Realistically, re-rate the likelihood that your worst fears will be realised (from 0 to 100 per cent).

10 per cent.

Talia was very proud of her son's marks in his final year of high school,
and was happy to tell all her friends how well he did. However,
she subsequently realised that her friends' children did not have the
advantages of her son's excellent private school, and had not done as
well. Talia now feels very ashamed and anxious. She believes that
she has done a bad thing, and she assumes that her friends must feel
resentful towards her.

1 Describe the situation that you are worried about.
I am worried that I have offended my friends by boasting about Luke's marks.

2 What specifically do you fear might happen?
They feel hurt and resentful. They will dislike me and I will lose their
friendship.

3 Rate the likelihood that this will happen (from 0 to 100 per cent).
60 per cent.

4 What evidence supports your worrying thoughts?
I don't have any evidence but it feels true.

5 What evidence does not support your worrying thoughts?
I have spoken to three of the women since then, and their behaviour was the
same towards me as usual. There was no indication that they were feeling
hostile towards me.

6 If your feared situation did eventuate, what actions could you take?
I would apologise to those that I offended. I would still have other friends and
family members who would support me.

7 Realistically, what is the worst thing that can happen?
Some of my friends are annoyed by what I said and will feel wary of me.

8 What is the best thing that can happen?
None of my friends were offended or upset by my behaviour. Our friendships
continue the same as before.

9 What is most likely to happen?
Maybe some of my friends feel a bit annoyed, but it is unlikely to have any
effect on our friendships.

10 Are there any useful actions that you can take now?

I could speak to the women that I think I may have offended and apologise for being insensitive. Acknowledge that Luke went to an excellent school, and this provided him with a significant advantage.

11 What would you tell a friend who was in your situation?

You told them Luke's results because they asked. You didn't do anything terrible, and you didn't mean to hurt anyone. You tend to worry easily, so it is quite likely that you are catastrophising about this. You have no evidence that anyone is upset or thinks less of you. Your friends know that you are a kind person. Even in the unlikely event that someone did think you were boasting, it is still unlikely that they would 'write you off' for this (if they did, it would mean that it wasn't much of a friendship in the first place).

12 Realistically, re-rate the likelihood that your fears will be realised (from 0 to 100 per cent).

5 per cent.

EXERCISE 6.6

Think of an issue that you are currently worried about. Use the Socratic questions listed above to test the validity of your current perceptions.

IDENTIFYING ANXIOUS THOUGHTS

Although anxiety is a response to perceived threat, it is not uncommon for people to experience anxiety without knowing why. Some people say, 'I got anxious, but I wasn't thinking anything.' Others may wake up in the middle of the night with strong anxiety for no apparent reason. As we saw in Chapter 2, not all cognitions are immediately available to conscious awareness. Mindful observation of our inner state can help to bring them to awareness. Closing our eyes and observing what is happening on the inside helps us to connect with current thoughts, feelings and body sensations, and can bring cognitions to the surface.

Remy is often anxious when she gets home from work but she is not sure why. By bringing mindful attention to her thoughts and body sensations, Remy realises that her anxiety stems from being alone at home and not knowing how to use her time.

*

Charles was unable to identify the thoughts associated with his anxiety until he reflected mindfully on his current state. He subsequently realised that his anxiety was caused by procrastination over an unpleasant task.

FREE-FLOATING ANXIETY

Some people describe periods of ongoing anxiety that do not seem to be connected to any particular issue. 'Free-floating anxiety' is a response to perceived danger, where the source of threat is poorly defined. It is a common feature of anxiety disorders and situations where we have been on 'high alert' for long periods. Our world continues to feel unsafe, so we remain vigilant even when specific threats have receded or are not clear to us.

Sometimes free-floating anxiety is initiated by biological changes (e.g. premenstrual hormonal changes; high caffeine intake or withdrawal from medication) that produce physical arousal. However, in most cases, it reflects perceptions of threat that may not be immediately apparent. For individuals who have experienced episodes of anxiety in the past, any sign of arousal may trigger associations with anxiety. The perceived threat in this case is the anxiety itself, which gives rise to further anxiety.

SECONDARY ANXIETY

Anxiety about anxiety or '**secondary anxiety**' is a common feature of anxiety disorders. We may not be thinking about anything specific, but our brain perceives our anxiety and its associated physical sensations as a threat, and this maintains our anxiety in a self-perpetuating cycle.

Craig has been suffering from anxiety for the past two years, and is worried that it will never be resolved. Searching for signs of recovery,

Craig has become vigilant to any symptoms of anxiety. Consequently he becomes increasingly anxious whenever he notices tightness in the chest or butterflies in his stomach. Paradoxically, the very process of monitoring his anxiety keeps Craig vigilant and aroused, which in turn maintains his anxiety.

The fear that anxiety will last forever is a common concern for people who have suffered from anxiety in the past. Monitoring the body for anxiety maintains the problem because the more attention we give it, the more it remains a threat in our mind. For instance, the initial (primary) anxiety may be related to a stressful job, an interpersonal conflict or a financial problem, but subsequently the anxiety itself becomes the main source of threat. Checking our anxiety and wondering when it will end keeps us vigilant and aroused, and so perpetuates the anxiety.

Most individuals dealing with secondary anxiety are horrified at the idea of **accepting their anxiety** or 'giving up the fight'. 'I'll never give up!' is a common response. It seems counterintuitive to stop trying, as we know that many problems can be solved when we apply ourselves conscientiously. However, when we are caught up in the self-perpetuating cycle of anxiety about anxiety, giving up is the best thing we can do.

Releasing our attempts to control anxiety, and instead focusing on other aspects of our lives, provides space for anxiety to diminish, or at the very least to become easier to ignore. When we let go of self-monitoring, looking for signs of improvement or speculations about when it will pass, we release a central aspect of the self-perpetuating process.

BREAKING THE SELF-PERPETUATING CYCLE

- Try to notice each time your mind 'checks in' with your anxiety, looking for reassurance or hoping that it will go away.
- Label the process: 'self-monitoring again' and then return your focus to whatever you are doing at the time. Don't try to suppress the self-monitoring thoughts, but acknowledge their presence and label them each time you are aware of them. (Initially this may occur hundreds of times a day.)
- Accept that 'At this stage, anxiety is part of my life. It cannot be otherwise.'

- Let it be. Do not try to control your anxiety.
- Identify life goals that are important to you—relationships, family, work, learning, exercise, new interests, etc. Set specific goals and choose to pursue them, irrespective of the presence of anxiety in your life. Focus on your goals.
- Don't wait for your anxiety to pass before you can get on with your life. Get on with your goals now, irrespective of your anxiety. The anxiety will pass in its own time.

Paradoxically, when we give up our desperate attempts to eliminate anxiety we create the space that allows it to slowly drift away. If at times your anxiety feels overwhelming, mindfully focusing on neutral objects such as the breath, sounds or points of physical contact (such as our feet resting on the floor, or our buttocks on the seat of the chair) can help you to move through the discomfort. While not a permanent release from anxiety, this process can provide respite during uncomfortable periods (see also Chapter 12).

EXPOSURE

For situations that elicit strong fear reactions (such as public speaking, social anxiety, travelling on public transport while suffering from panic disorder or driving on a freeway after a car accident), exposure exercises are a particularly powerful method for reducing fear. This is because it allows us to **learn experientially** that our fears are unreasonable. Experiential learning enables us to go beyond rationally *knowing* that something is safe to *feeling* that it is safe. With repeated exposure our fears diminish.

CONFRONT YOUR FEARS

Avoiding situations that we perceive to be dangerous is a natural human response. However, when the danger is imagined rather than real, avoiding those situations reinforces our perception of danger because we have no opportunity to discover that our fears are misguided. If we do not confront our demons at some stage, we never learn to overcome them. Exposing ourselves to the things we fear enables us to discover that they are not harmful after all. The more often you stand up in front of that group of people, get on that dreaded plane, make that phone call or assertively say what you want, the easier it becomes to do it again next time.

The golden rule when it comes to anxiety—AVOID AVOIDANCE.

Ever since her husband died, Rene has felt anxious being alone at home at night. She has tried to manage this by staying at her daughter's house as often as possible, and sometimes arranging for her adult son to sleep over at her house. This provides temporary relief; however, it does not solve the problem—she cannot expect her children to be there all the time. By avoiding her most feared situation (being alone at night), Rene actually perpetuates her anxiety. Although she does not like the idea, Rene needs to repeatedly expose herself to the situation she fears. By choosing to sleep at home at night in spite of her fear, Rene gradually habituates to the new situation. She is no longer scared.

Sometimes, if the situation we fear seems too overwhelming, we may prefer to expose ourselves gradually, using whatever resources we can muster along the way. This is called **graded exposure** because we confront our fears one step at a time. For Rene, it might involve initially having one of her children spend some time with her each evening, but not stay the night. Then, after a week or two her children might speak with her on the phone each evening and, over time, reduce the length of their conversations to shorter periods. Graded exposure can be a useful option when full exposure feels too scary; however, the goal is always to move towards full exposure over time.

Frances worked as a senior administrator in a government department for five years. While she initially enjoyed her job, subsequent changes in staffing brought her into direct conflict with a new supervisor, and after a few months Frances resigned. As she felt emotionally bruised by the experience, Frances decided to give herself a few weeks to recover before applying for another job, but weeks

soon turned to months, and now Frances feels too anxious to apply
for another job. The problem with procrastinating is that the longer
she avoids looking for a job, the more threatening the idea of job-
seeking becomes. As difficult as it may seem, Frances needs to accept
her feelings of anxiety, and start taking some actions towards getting
back into the workforce.

As Frances lacks the confidence to apply for new jobs, she might start by easing herself in gradually. This may involve initially doing some voluntary work or helping out in her brother-in-law's business. Alternatively, she might start by taking some work in an area that she is overqualified for, and once her confidence returns she can apply for more challenging jobs. (See also Exposure Exercises, page 177.)

DEALING WITH PANIC ATTACKS

In situations where we are experiencing high levels of anxiety, the accompanying physical symptoms may become more intense. Heart palpitations, tightness in the chest, difficulty breathing, chest pain, tremors, sweating and dizziness frequently accompany high levels of anxiety. This can be experienced as a panic attack. Sometimes the perception of even mild physical symptoms can cause anxiety to increase and consequently trigger a panic attack. For instance, if you feel your heart pounding, your chest constricting or your breathing becoming difficult, you may find yourself having catastrophic thoughts like:

> ➤ I'm going to have a heart attack.
> ➤ I am going to collapse.
> ➤ I am going to run out of air.
> ➤ I am going to lose control and go berserk.
> ➤ I'm not going to be able to get out of here or get home.
> ➤ I'm going to die.

Thoughts like these cause the anxiety to escalate, which in turn increases physical arousal. Rapid breathing often results in **hyperventilation**, resulting in too much oxygen in the blood. This increase in oxygen levels relative to carbon dioxide gives rise to further unpleasant symptoms such as light-headedness, confusion, jitters, dizziness, numbness or tingling in the extremities, chest pain and sweating.

Panic attacks are triggered by unpleasant physical symptoms and become more intense as we panic about the symptoms themselves. This is sometimes referred to as the panic cycle because the physical symptoms of anxiety become a source of threat, causing anxiety to escalate. This in turn causes us to panic even more, which causes the symptoms to escalate further.

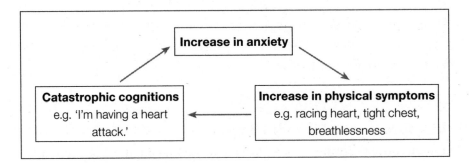

In order to short-circuit this process we need to correct the catastrophic cognitions that maintain it. Thoughts like 'I'm going to lose control' or 'I might run out of air' fuel the panic attack. It is important to realise that the physical symptoms that accompany anxiety and panic are **not harmful—they are just unpleasant**. Although you may feel unsafe, the reality is that the symptoms that accompany a panic attack are harmless. You will not have a heart attack; you will not be unable to breathe; you will not collapse or die; you will not run amok, go mad or damage your health. The worst thing that will happen is that you will feel unpleasant sensations.

SURF THE SYMPTOMS

Arguably the most powerful technique for defusing a panic attack is to let the symptoms be, without trying to stop them. The term 'panic surfing' was coined by Australian psychologists Ron Rapee and Andrew Baillie as a metaphor for a healthy response to panic. If you imagine that resisting panic is like swimming against the waves, panic surfing involves turning around and letting the waves carry you. You ride with the wave of anxiety in an accepting manner, rather than trying to stop or control it. Labelling the symptoms for what they are ('fight-or-flight response') and letting your body do what it needs to do allows the adrenaline surge to pass. Most people are amazed to discover that the unpleasant sensations fizzle out when they stop resisting or trying to control them.

RESPONDING TO A PANIC ATTACK:
Label the sensations: 'Fight-or-flight response' (which is harmless)
Surf the symptoms: Ride out the wave of anxiety—it builds up, peaks and then washes away.
Don't try to stop it or control it. Let your body do what it needs to do. Give it space to complete its process.

INTEROCEPTIVE EXPOSURE

Interoceptive exposure involves deliberately producing the body sensations that are experienced during a panic attack. While most anxious individuals are horrified by this idea, it is actually a very powerful technique because deliberately choosing to recreate the feared sensations ultimately reduces our fear of them.

The physical sensations that we experience during a panic attack can be simulated through methods such as hyperventilation, spinning in a chair, shaking our head from side to side, running on the spot or up and down stairs, putting our head between our legs and then quickly lifting it up (repeatedly), breathing through a straw or sitting in an overheated room. (Choosing a method that produces sensations that most closely resemble the symptoms we fear produces the best results.)

Deliberately creating the sensations at a time when we are not acutely anxious provides an opportunity to practise panic surfing, and helps us to desensitise to the physical sensations we fear. By choosing to let them be we discover that they fizzle out by themselves. This provides experiential learning that the symptoms will settle and helps us to stop feeling afraid of them. Many people feel empowered through this process, as learning that we can induce and manage panic sensations enables us to be less fearful of the sensations when they arise spontaneously. However, if the idea of doing this is too confronting, you might prefer to practise interceptive exposure with the help of a therapist.

CONTROLLING HYPERVENTILATION THROUGH SLOW BREATHING

An alternative method for dealing with panic attacks involves deliberately slowing our breathing (see 'Slow Rhythmic Breathing' exercise on page 185). Slow breathing stops hyperventilation, and so reduces the excess oxygen in the blood, with all of its associated physical symptoms. This has the same effect as breathing into a paper bag (the traditional treatment for panic attacks), restoring the normal balance of oxygen to carbon dioxide in the blood. Reducing the unpleasant symptoms of hyperventilation reduces threat perceptions and increases our sense of control. This in turn reduces arousal and other associated symptoms.

Both panic surfing and slow breathing help to switch off the symptoms of a panic attack, so which one is best? The advantage of panic surfing is that it can help to overcome fear of the physical symptoms that we dread so much. By facing the feared sensations without trying to stop them we learn not to be so afraid of them, and this reduces fear of panic attacks in the longer term. However, some people respond well to slow breathing, and find this option less scary in the short term. So trying both methods and deciding which works best for you may be the way to go.

SITUATIONAL EXPOSURE FOR PANIC ATTACKS

While the strategies described above help to switch off a panic attack when it arises (or is about to arise), they might not fully eliminate our fear of panic attacks. To do this, we need to repeatedly confront the situations we associate with having a panic attack. Repeated exposure to those situations leads to **habituation**—causing our fears to subside. It is enhanced by the realisation that the catastrophic consequences we had presumed would occur, do not in fact eventuate. The discovery that we do not die, we do not run out of air, we do not go mad and we do not get trapped in unwanted situations forever produces experiential learning that our catastrophic thoughts are unfounded. We also learn that **letting go of resistance** and **releasing our attempts to gain control** paradoxically enables us to gain control.

> *Ben had a disturbing experience when he was shopping in a large department store two years ago. He was feeling unwell at the time, and as he made his way towards the exit he became dizzy and disorientated. Ben became aware of his heart pounding and he struggled to catch his breath. For a moment he thought he might collapse.*
>
> *Ever since then Ben has been checking himself, trying to make sure that the symptoms don't return. On occasions when he notices his heart beating faster or his dizziness returning—usually at shopping centres, on public transport or at the movies—Ben escapes as quickly as he can. Ben tries to avoid going out to public places because having a panic attack there could be embarrassing and hard to escape. What Ben doesn't realise is that avoiding those situations perpetuates the problem because he does not get the opportunity to discover that his fears are unfounded.*

A second problem is that Ben is paying excessive attention to his physical symptoms. Because he is terrified of the prospect of further panic attacks, Ben constantly monitors his body for signs of arousal. This is called 'hypervigilance', and is self-defeating because focusing on his body sensations makes Ben more anxious, which in turn increases his physical arousal and the likelihood of further panic attacks.

EXPOSURE EXERCISES

A basic principle in psychology is that repeated exposure to the things we fear leads to habituation, so the fear diminishes over time. Repeated exposure enables us to learn experientially that the situation is not dangerous, as nothing terrible happens when we face our fears.

SECRETS OF SUCCESSFUL EXPOSURE

➤ **Repetition:** Do exposure exercises repeatedly—the more often the better.

➤ **Duration:** Stay in the feared situation for long enough to allow some habituation to occur.

➤ **Challenge:** Exposure exercises should be at least a bit anxiety-provoking. If it's too easy, it's not 'therapy'.

➤ **Daily practice:** Do some exposure exercises every day.

➤ **Spontaneous:** Take advantage of opportunities to practise exposure whenever they present themselves, including in unplanned situations.

To plan exposure exercises, it is useful to create an exposure schedule. This involves writing down all the situations that are currently associated with increased anxiety. If the idea of confronting these situations is too overwhelming, they can be arranged in a hierarchy, from those that are least anxiety-provoking to those that are most feared. This is called graded exposure.

Once our plan is complete, we are ready to commence exposure. This will involve physically putting ourselves in the situations that are specified on our exposure schedule and remaining in those situations for long enough to experience some reduction in our fear. It is important to maintain exposure for long enough to allow some habituation to occur—try not to run away at the first sign of anxiety. If you feel panicky during this process, then surf the symptoms (see instructions on page 174), allowing your body to do whatever it needs to do. The anxiety will surge and fall in its own time. Repeat exposure exercises as frequently as necessary for habituation to occur. Many situations will require just a few exposures, while others will require more.

EXPOSURE SCHEDULE

EXERCISE	TRIAL 1	TRIAL 2	TRIAL 3	TRIAL 4	TRIAL 5	TRIAL 6	TRIAL 7

Record: Date, length of exposure, highest level of anxiety experienced (0 = no anxiety; 10 = unbearable anxiety).

To overcome his fear of public places Ben wrote himself a plan for graded exposure exercises. He listed all the situations that provoke his fears, and then put them in order, from the least to the most anxiety-provoking. He then started the process of repeatedly confronting each situation, beginning with those that were least anxiety-provoking. Here is Ben's exposure schedule:

EXERCISE	TRIAL 1	TRIAL 2	TRIAL 3	TRIAL 4	TRIAL 5	TRIAL 6	TRIAL 7
Go to supermarket with wife.	4 May 15 mins 7	7 May 20 mins 6	11 May 35 mins 4	16 May 45 mins 3	22 May 15 mins 1	24 May 10 mins 1	
Go to supermarket alone.	12 May 15 mins 5	14 May 25 mins 6	15 May 10 mins 5	17 May 25 mins 3	20 May 15 mins 2	23 May 25 mins 1	26 May 15 mins 0
Catch bus for three stops during quiet period.	20 May 5 mins 8	22 May 5 mins 8	23 May 5 mins 6	26 May 5 mins 2	29 May 5 mins 1		
Catch bus all the way to the city during quiet period.	26 May 25 mins 7	29 May 25 mins 5	31 May 25 mins 6	6 June 25 mins 3	9 June 25 mins 1	13 June 25 mins 0	17 June 25 mins 0
Catch bus to city during peak hour.	10 June 35 mins 9	12 June 30 mins 4	15 June 35 mins 8	16 June 30 mins 4	19 June 35 mins 3	22 June 35 mins 1	
Go to movies.	1 June 1.25 hrs 8	6 June 1.5 hrs 7	9 June 1.5 hrs 4	12 June 2 hrs 5	19 June 2 hrs 2	26 June 1.5 hrs 1	
Catch a ferry.	14 June 30 mins 9	19 June 30 mins 9	25 June 35 mins 6	30 June 30 mins 7	3 July 30 mins 6	5 July 30 mins 2	10 July 30 mins 1

Doing exposure exercises every day helped Ben's anxiety to resolve. Repeatedly returning to the situations he feared resulted in a reduction in anxiety. As the panic attacks diminished, his fears and the desire to avoid public places also disappeared.

Exposure exercises are useful for overcoming all types of fears and phobias, including social phobia, specific phobias (such as spiders, flying, elevators and snakes) and the ubiquitous fear of public speaking. In each case, creating a schedule of situations we fear, and then deliberately putting ourselves in those situations for a period of time enables habituation to take place.

Although real-life exposure usually produces the fastest recovery, sometimes this is not practical as the object of our fear is hard to access repeatedly in the real world (e.g. spiders, snakes, thunderstorms, flying, etc.). For these situations, the internet is a rich source of imagery that can be used for repeated exposure exercises. Alternatively, we can use our own imagination for creating exposure situations. This is similar to real-life exposure; however, instead of physically attending the situations, we construct the scenes in our mind. We can do this by recording the scenes in vivid detail on a recording device (dictaphone, mobile phone, etc.) and listening to them repeatedly until our fear starts to diminish. Alternatively, we can do imaginal exposure; exercises through writing. This involves describing our scenes in writing (handwriting works best) and then repeatedly reading over them for 20 minutes a day. Over the following days we can add a little more to our script or add new scenes, and continue to read over our stories. While initially this process evokes high levels of anxiety, most people experience habituation following repeated writing and reading. As habituation occurs, we can move our story into more feared territory with each subsequent writing session.

> *Ross has a fear of flying, which is a major problem as his job in the corporate sector requires him to take regular flights. Ross commences an imaginal exposure program by writing a list of feared scenarios that he associates with flying:*
> * *In taxi on the way to airport*
> * *Going through security check at airport*
> * *Sitting at departure terminal*
> * *Sitting on plane prior to takeoff*
> * *Flying through turbulence*
> * *Start of descent towards landing.*

Ross commences imaginal exposure with the first scene on his list, describing it in detail while recording it on his dictaphone. He then listens to the recording repeatedly, and finds that after five occasions, his fear in response to the thought of being in the taxi on the way to the airport drops from 8 to 3 on a 10-point scale. He then proceeds to the next step, describing in vivid detail the image of himself moving through the security checkpoint at the airport. He then listens to this description on six occasions, until his fear reduces from 9 to 2 on the same scale. By repeating this procedure for each of the scenes in his hierarchy, Ross notices that his fear continues to diminish. While he originally rated his fear of flying as 9 out of 10, his fear has reduced to a 3 out of 10 after two weeks of intensive imaginal exposure.

RELAXATION TECHNIQUES

As we have already seen, anxiety is associated with strong physiological arousal and muscle tension. As long as we continue to perceive threat (real or imagined), we remain tense and physically aroused. The fear centre of our brain messages our body to remain vigilant and prepared for action, and we therefore instinctively stay on high alert. For this reason, relaxing the body during an intensely anxious state is difficult—our brain resists relaxation when the perception of danger is high. However, deep relaxation can be achieved while in a moderately anxious state.

Practising deep relaxation on a regular basis—ideally twice a day— helps to lower physical arousal and provides feedback to our brain that it is safe to relax. Doing this frequently helps to switch off hypervigilance and arousal, and therefore reduces anxiety in the longer term. Regular relaxation also teaches us to recognise the tension that we normally carry, and so makes it easier for us to identify and consciously release tension before it escalates.

Deep relaxation is not the same thing as the normal relaxation we experience when we put our feet up at the end of the day, go for a walk or listen to our favourite music. It is a deeper, more profound state, which is accompanied by physical changes. These include:

- ➤ a slowdown in the rate of our heartbeat;
- ➤ a slowdown in our breathing rate;
- ➤ a drop in blood pressure;
- ➤ a relaxation of muscle tension; and
- ➤ a drop in oxygen consumption (metabolic rate).

These changes are the opposite of what occurs during the fight-or-flight response. When we create a state of deep relaxation, we reverse the physical changes produced by fight-or-flight, and consequently release the unpleasant physical symptoms that accompany this state. In fact, it is virtually impossible to be deeply relaxed and anxious at the same time.

Deep relaxation practice is a useful maintenance technique which, when performed frequently, helps to reduce hypervigilance and arousal. As regular practice improves our ability to manage anxiety, this has psychological benefits beyond the immediate reduction in anxiety.

There are various methods by which deep relaxation can be achieved. These include progressive muscle relaxation, cue-controlled relaxation and calming visual imagery. In addition, breathing exercises can be used to lower arousal during times of intense anxiety.

PROGRESSIVE MUSCLE RELAXATION

This is a physical process that involves relaxing the body by systematically working through the major muscle groups—the feet, lower legs, thighs, tummy, chest, shoulders, arms, hands, neck and face. It is normally performed by sequentially focusing on each muscle group and consciously relaxing the muscles. Briefly tensing each muscle group for a few seconds before relaxing it produces deeper and more immediate relaxation. After relaxing each muscle group, we spend a little time observing the sensations and allowing the muscles to relax a little more before moving on to the next area. This process normally takes about 20 minutes. Once we have learned how to do this exercise, we may be able to achieve deep relaxation within a shorter period of time; however, we still benefit from remaining in a relaxed state for 20 minutes or more.

CUE-CONTROLLED RELAXATION

When we are in a deeply relaxed state we can utilise 'cue words' to form a mental association with that state. For example, we may think to ourselves 'breathe in' with each in-breath and 'relax' with each out-breath. By repeating these words with each in- and out-breath while we are in a deeply relaxed state, we create a mental association between those words and our physiological state. This association enables us to subsequently use those cue words to evoke deep relaxation in a shorter period of time. This can have advantages when we have limited time available for achieving a deeply relaxed state.

MEDITATION

The techniques described above aim to achieve a state of deep relaxation by deliberately releasing tension from the muscles. In contrast, meditation is a mental process that does not involve deliberately trying to create relaxation (although relaxation frequently occurs). The most commonly used meditation techniques involve **concentration** on a particular object, while passively releasing thoughts that arise during this process. The object of focus may be a part of the body (such as our lungs, heart or the point between our eyes); the breath; a word or sound that is repeated mentally or out loud (mantra); an external sound such as music, waves or bird sounds; a physical object (such as a candle or picture) or a visualised image or symbol.

In recent years **mindfulness meditation** has become very widely used in Western practice. As described in Chapter 12, this approach includes concentration meditation (such as concentrating on the breath), as well as observing aspects of one's current sensory experience, including thoughts, emotions and body sensations. Mindful attention can be brought to any experience, including intense emotions as they arise (including anger, fear and frustration) or activities of daily life (eating, bathing, cleaning, walking or swimming, etc.). We do not set out to deliberately produce relaxation or any particular state, but rather to be fully aware and connected to current experiences.

Most people find meditation to be more challenging than relaxation exercises because the mind is naturally inclined to wander. Maintaining our focus for more than a few seconds at a time is not easy and, like most skills, improves with regular practice.

BREATHING EXERCISES

While the relaxation techniques described above are useful for managing moderate levels of anxiety, they are difficult to apply during periods of acute anxiety or a panic. When our brain perceives high levels of threat, the body is usually resistant to relaxation. This is where breathing exercises can be helpful.

The way we breathe reflects the way we feel. When we are calm and relaxed, our breathing is slow and rhythmic. When we are anxious or panicky, our breathing is fast and shallow. While our breathing reflects our level of physical arousal, we can also use the breath to regulate arousal. By consciously slowing our breathing, we can prevent or switch off hyperventilation, lower our level of physical arousal, and eliminate many of the unpleasant sensations caused by hyperventilation. In addition, focusing on the breath distracts from catastrophic cognitions, and so can prevent the anxiety from escalating. Below are two types of breathing exercises that can be used to reduce arousal.

DIAPHRAGMATIC BREATHING

This involves consciously directing breath down into the lower part of the lungs. To do this we use our diaphragm (the muscle separating our lung cavity from the abdominal cavity) to direct air downwards into the lower lungs. You can monitor the movement of your breath by placing your hands on your chest at the bottom of your rib cage, just above the navel, so that the tips of your middle fingers just touch. As you direct your breath slowly into your lower lungs, you will feel your fingertips being forced apart slightly by the expansion of your abdomen. As you breathe out, you will feel your fingertips touching again.

SLOW RHYTHMIC BREATHING

This exercise is particularly useful for switching off hyperventilation during a panic attack. Take in one diaphragmatic breath, and hold it to the count of ten. Breathe out slowly, mentally saying the word 'relax' as you do so. Then breathe in to the count of three and out to the count of three, mentally saying the word 'relax' at the end of each out-breath. This process will slow your breathing rate to ten breaths per minute. Do this for ten breaths, and then take another diaphragmatic breath and count to ten, and return to slow breathing again. Keep repeating this process for five to ten minutes, or until your anxiety drops.

CALMING VISUAL IMAGERY

Calming visual imagery can help to reduce physical arousal and deepen our level of relaxation. It can be an adjunct to progressive muscle relaxation, or a standalone technique. It involves immersing ourselves in an image that we associate with peace and tranquillity. The most widely used images are nature scenes (rainforest, beach, countryside, waterfall, beautiful garden), dream-like imagery (floating on a cloud or on a magic carpet) or a guardian angel or inner guide. Adding sensory information such as sounds, colours, shapes, textures, smells, temperature and physical sensations makes the experience more vivid. For instance: 'Hear the crackling of leaves under your feet and the sound of the birds as you make your way through the forest. Smell the damp sweet odour of the undergrowth, see the brightly coloured wild flowers that grow near the track, feel the rough textures of the ancient trees ...'

GUIDED EXERCISES

There are many albums and tracks available for download on websites that provide guided instructions for practising meditation, progressive muscle relaxation and calming imagery. External guidance can be very useful when learning to practise these techniques (see also the Recommended Reading list on page 409 for relaxation CDs by the author).

IN SUMMARY

➤ Anxiety is a response to perceived threat. It is accompanied by changes to our thoughts, physiology and behaviours.

➤ Some anxiety can be protective; however, frequent or intense anxiety has many disadvantages and impairs quality of life.

➤ When we feel anxious, our perceptions become more threat-focused, so things appear to be more catastrophic than they really are.

➤ Avoidance and safety behaviours are common ways by which we try to protect ourselves from perceived threats. These are usually self-defeating and ultimately serve to maintain anxiety in the longer term.

➤ Disproportionate worrying, perfectionism and excessive attempts at being in control and trying to get approval are cognitive safety behaviours that serve to maintain anxiety.

➤ Confronting the things we fear helps to reduce anxiety over time. Repeated exposure and behavioural experiments enable us to learn experientially that many of the things we fear are not dangerous, or are highly unlikely to occur.

➤ Deep relaxation practice and breathing techniques can help to reduce arousal and physical tension, which in turn can reduce anxiety. Meditation techniques may confer additional benefits.

SEVEN

Maintaining self-esteem

The greatest thing in the world is to know how to belong to oneself.
MICHEL DE MONTAIGNE, *THE COMPLETE ESSAYS*

Our self-esteem is a perception—it is the way that we perceive our own worth as human beings. It can influence the meanings that we give to various life events, the way we respond to particular situations and the way we feel much of the time. Poor self-esteem can make us vulnerable to feelings such as guilt, defectiveness, shame, anxiety and depression. It affects our ability to relax and feel comfortable with others, and determines who we feel worthy of to have as friends and partners. Our self-esteem may influence the type of work we do, the risks we take and our willingness to be assertive in our dealings with others. Poor self-esteem increases our likelihood of becoming depressed (and conversely, during a depressive episode our self-esteem plummets). Most importantly, our self-esteem affects our ability to feel happy and safe in our world—to know that we have a right to be here, and that we are as worthy and valid as every other person on this planet.

Self-esteem is not the same thing as self-efficacy. We may be confident about our ability to do certain things, but still have low self-esteem. For instance, we may feel confident in our ability to do our job, give a speech, repair a computer, run a marathon, host a successful dinner party or perform at a concert. Knowing that we can do some things well does not mean that we perceive ourselves in a positive way. Our self-esteem is the way we appraise our total worth—not just our abilities in certain areas.

Since childhood, Susan has strived hard to be valued and accepted by others. She is bright, competent and attractive. At the age of 34, she had built up her own successful public relations company, and by the age of 40, she could afford to retire. Colleagues respect her and friends admire her; yet, in spite of her apparent success, Susan harbours feelings of inadequacy and self-doubt. She is highly sensitive to feedback from other people—even minor criticisms can send her into episodes of self-doubt and rumination. When things go wrong, Susan immediately blames herself and assumes that others must also be judging her harshly. Like many people, Susan has poor self-esteem. In spite of her confident outward appearance, Susan can't help thinking that she's just not good enough.

FACTORS THAT INFLUENCE OUR SELF-ESTEEM

Like all perceptions, the way that we think about ourselves is shaped by both our temperament and our life experiences.

TEMPERAMENT

While self-esteem is not genetically determined, our personality and temperament can influence the way that we interpret events, which in turn may influence our self-esteem. For instance, a person who tends to be anxious by nature is more likely to notice potentially negative information (e.g. 'She tuned out while I was talking to her') and might be more inclined to interpret ambiguous cues in a negative way ('She obviously doesn't like me'). A person with a shy temperament might make less effort to connect with other people and may therefore receive less socially reinforcing messages compared to someone who is friendly and outgoing. A person who is highly emotional and sensitive by nature may be more affected by negative experiences compared to someone who is more resilient, and their resulting overreaction may alienate others.

EARLY EXPERIENCES

Events that occur during childhood play an important role in shaping perceptions about ourselves and our world. While our parents are normally the most important influence, others (our siblings, grandparents, cousins, teachers and even school friends) also play a role. These people provide seminal information regarding our lovability and worth. Early messages suggesting that we were unimportant, defective, worthless or unlovable can have negative long-term consequences on how we perceive ourselves. In addition, negative events that occurred during our teenage years (e.g. being bullied, ostracised, ridiculed or rejected) can have long-term consequences on our self-esteem.

How effectively we manage to shake off beliefs about inferiority or defectiveness depends on subsequent events in our lives, as well as inherent resilience factors. Loving, supportive relationships developed later in life can sometimes override early perceptions of worthlessness. Having a resilient nature—being able to bounce back after setbacks—can also protect from the potentially scarring effects of early experiences.

RELATIONSHIPS IN ADULTHOOD

Our relationships with other people—friends, colleagues, acquaintances, partners and children—can influence our self-concept. Interactions and feedback that suggests we are loved, accepted and valued by others helps us to feel good about ourselves. For instance, a partner, friends or family members who tell you that you are wonderful, lovable and important to them helps to reinforce perceptions of worth. On the other hand, a significant other who frequently carps, criticises and puts you down can have the opposite effect.

FRAGILE VERSUS PERMANENTLY IMPAIRED SELF-ESTEEM

Negative life experiences and/or a vulnerable temperament can contribute to self-esteem that is either **fragile** or **permanently impaired**. Those of us with fragile self-esteem may feel OK about ourselves much of the time, but become vulnerable when negative life events occur. For instance, the loss of job, health, role or social status; a personal failure (in work, education, business or a family role) or an experience of rejection, can trigger strong feelings of self-doubt and inadequacy that may last for months or more. As time passes or our circumstances improve, our self-esteem bounces back.

On the other hand, positive events contribute to feelings of self-worth. Success in achieving particular goals, feeling competent in particular areas, or receiving praise and recognition from others helps to maintain a positive self-concept.

Some of us have had very difficult lives, starting in early childhood and continuing into adolescence. Individuals in this category are at greater risk of permanently impaired self-esteem. This means we feel inadequate and defective all the time—regardless of our personal strengths, achievements or relationships. Our early life experiences, as well as our temperament, can give rise to long-standing difficulties across a range of life situations, with interpersonal relationships being a key problem area. While positive events may temporarily make us feel better, permanent improvements in self-esteem may be difficult to achieve with self-help alone. For people in this situation, psychological therapy may be helpful (see also Recommended Reading on self-esteem on page 408).

SOCIAL CONDITIONING

In our society, certain traits, qualities and achievements are highly valued, while others are ignored or discounted. As a result, we develop beliefs about what we need in order to succeed in life, maintain relationships and be happy. If these beliefs are held in a rigid, inflexible way they have the potential to create distress and impair self-esteem (see 'Tyranny of the Shoulds' on page 21). As long as the terms of our beliefs are met (that is, we are achieving the things that we believe are important), we feel reasonably good about ourselves. However, problems arise when we are unable to live up to our rigid expectations (or shoulds). Beliefs that play a role in relation to our self-esteem fall into four main categories:

APPEARANCE
➤ I should be slim and attractive.
➤ I should be youthful and sexy.
➤ I should be tall, muscular and have a full head of hair.

CHARACTER TRAITS

➤ I should always be positive and psychologically healthy.

➤ I should be witty and extroverted.

➤ I should always be relaxed and in control of my emotions.

PERFORMANCE/ACHIEVEMENTS

➤ I should have a high-status, well-paid job.

➤ I should have a university education.

➤ I should be making lots of money.

➤ I should have an attractive and tidy house.

➤ I should have a successful business.

➤ I should have high libido.

➤ I should be good at sport.

SOCIAL RELATIONSHIPS AND INTERACTIONS

➤ I should have lots of friends.

➤ I should be able to connect easily with everyone.

➤ I should be married or in a committed relationship.

➤ I should be going out with lots of people and having fun.

➤ People should like and approve of me.

PATTERNS OF THINKING THAT DIMINISH SELF-ESTEEM

Common habits that both reflect and perpetuate poor self-esteem include comparing ourselves with others, rating our worth through our achievements, trying too hard to get approval and labelling ourselves on the basis of our experiences. These habits, as well as strategies for challenging them are demonstrated in the following section.

COMPARING

Recently Kathy ran into Anthea, an old school friend whom she hadn't seen for 15 years. After some reminiscing, Anthea invited Kathy and her husband to come over for dinner on Saturday night. What a night it was! It turned out that Anthea lives in a beautiful house, in a salubrious suburb. Her husband, a partner in a well-known law firm, was charming and handsome. Their children go to a top private school and were clever and sociable. The dinner was a culinary delight, beautifully presented and served. The conversation was stimulating, and Anthea's children entertained the guests with some pre-dinner piano recitals. It had all the makings of a great night. So why did Kathy leave feeling so depressed?

Kathy fell for the oldest trick in the book—comparing herself to others. Most of us do it. Like Kathy, we are particularly prone to comparing ourselves to people we regard as peers—those from our own social circle, family members, neighbours, people our own age and people in the same occupation as ourselves. We compare ourselves on things like achievements, material wealth, appearance, friends, partners and even the successes of our children. Kathy could have left the dinner feeling excited, impressed, pleased for her friend, amazed, inspired or even indifferent. But she left feeling inadequate and depressed because she compared her own life circumstances to those of her friend, and found herself wanting.

Comparing ourselves with others invariably gets us into trouble. The problem is that there will always be people who are smarter than we are; who are thinner and more attractive; who have more friends; who go out more; who have a better sense of humour; who have more exciting sex; who make more money; who live in nicer houses and own better cars and who have more interesting things to say.

While all of this might sound depressing, keep in mind that the opposite is also true. There are also people who are far less attractive, less clever, less well-off, less sociable and less privileged than we are. If our self-esteem is fragile, we tend to disregard those in this second category, and limit our self-comparisons to those we consider to be better than us in some way.

Some people try to deal with this issue by insisting that the so-called successful people of this world are not really all that happy after all—'Her husband is probably a lousy lover ... They probably fight when no one is around ... Their children will probably grow up to be boring lawyers and finance brokers.' It is true that external appearances can be deceptive—success may be an illusion. But we do not need to convince ourselves that other people are doing badly in order to feel OK about ourselves. A more healthy way of thinking is to acknowledge that some people are especially lucky, gifted or privileged, without begrudging their good fortune or using their success as a yardstick for our own worth. Instead, we can set goals that are realistic and life-enhancing for us, and enjoy working towards them without making comparisons.

Immediately after their graduation, Troy and his friend Peter started working at a large insurance company. In the six years that they have worked there, Peter has had several promotions and was recently promoted to a very senior position. Troy has also had some promotions; however, his career has not progressed as quickly.

SITUATION	Peter told me that he has been promoted to Operations Manager.
FEELINGS	Despondent, inadequate, anxious, hopeless.
THOUGHTS	What about me? I've only had two promotions in the time that Peter has had four. Why wasn't I promoted too? I am not good enough.
BELIEFS	Our career paths should move at exactly the same pace. Peter's rapid promotion means that my progress is poor.
THINKING ERRORS	Comparing, personalising, labelling
DISPUTE	Peter is very talented and has a sociable manner that gives him an advantage in work situations. Most people like him and he is good at what he does. That is his good fortune. I am making good progress in my role. It is pointless comparing myself to Peter. His promotions do not mean that my progress is poor.
POSITIVE ACTIONS	Focus on my own work. Set work-related goals that are realistic for me.

RATING OUR WORTH THROUGH OUR ACHIEVEMENTS

Many people rate their worth according to their accomplishments or possessions. A highly paid job, successful business, high-status friends or expensive possessions are status symbols to which many aspire. Fame, beauty, popularity and academic achievements are also commonly sought-after objects for building a sense of self-worth.

While there is nothing wrong with aiming for excellence, problems arise when our achievements or possessions become the basis of our self-esteem. This is **conditional self-acceptance**—I am OK, as long as I make lots of money, have a high-powered job, get that degree, buy that car or lose that weight. In their book *Self-Esteem*, Matthew McKay and Patrick Fanning describe how some people see themselves as empty vessels: 'You might see yourself as essentially worthless, a body that moves and talks. You believe you have no intrinsic value—only the potential for doing something worthwhile and important.'

One of the problems with equating our worth with achievements is that it makes us vulnerable. We may feel worthwhile when we are doing well, but worthless when things go wrong.

> *Dan has built up a lucrative importing business with an annual turnover of over $30 million. While the business was growing, Dan felt good about himself. However, recently Dan made some risky investment decisions that resulted in a significant loss, and this, coupled with a changing economic climate, created major difficulties. In the last twelve months, Dan has struggled to meet his financial commitments and it is not clear whether he will be able to avoid bankruptcy. Now Dan feels worthless and hopeless. He blames himself for making bad decisions and thinks of himself as a failure.*

As Dan's self-esteem has always been fragile, he has tried to earn his worth through work-related achievements. While his business was doing well, Dan felt worthy, but when it faltered he immediately felt defective and worthless. As his self-esteem rests solely on one criterion, problems in that area are quickly perceived as failure as a person. The resulting depression further impairs his self-esteem, and affects his motivation, as well as his ability to see things in perspective.

While it is appropriate for Dan to go through a period of sadness and reflection, continuing to blame and label himself as a failure is unreasonable and self-defeating. It is unreasonable because Dan is rating his entire worth as a human being on the basis of just one criterion. It is self-defeating because perceiving himself as a failure causes him to feel inadequate and depressed, and makes it harder for him to recover.

When we make mistakes, it is helpful to acknowledge that, with the benefit of hindsight, some of our judgements proved to be incorrect. As we always operate with the limited knowledge and awareness available at the time, it is unavoidable that some of our decisions will lead to negative outcomes. Sometimes we make mistakes, and sometimes it is just unfortunate life circumstances that intervene. Usually there are many factors that contribute to particular outcomes, and simple labels like 'I am a failure' or 'It's all my fault' are rarely accurate.

As we saw in Chapter 1, emotions play an important role in influencing our behaviours. To motivate behavioural change, emotions sometimes need to be painful. For this reason, when we make a serious error it may be adaptive to feel upset for a period of time. Indeed, we are more likely to remember events that were associated with strong emotions, so this may help us to learn from our experience. However, beyond a few days (or perhaps a little more, depending on the consequences of our mistake) ongoing self-criticism and negative ruminations provide no advantage. They simply maintain emotional distress, stifle motivation and limit our ability to make good decisions.

For any person in Dan's position, it would be reasonable to go through a period of sadness and regret as they contemplate their losses. Reflecting on his actions and their consequences may help Dan to make sense of the factors that contributed to his loss, and learn from the experience. He might also acknowledge that there are inherent risks in his industry, and perhaps he made the best decisions he could given the awareness and information that was available to him at the time. Once Dan has been through this process, there is no advantage in further rumination and self-flagellation. It is time to think about goals for the future. (Dan may even use this experience as an opportunity to rethink the course of his life, and make decisions that lead to a more healthy and balanced lifestyle from now on.)

EFFECT ON LIFESTYLE

A further problem with equating our worth with our achievements is that it often leads to a lifestyle that is unbalanced and stressful. Many people we regard as 'workaholics' are in fact desperately trying to earn their worth through their achievements. The constant striving and sacrifice is often accompanied by thoughts that they should be doing more. Similarly, people we regard as perfectionists are often motivated by the belief that achievements equal self-worth. Unrealistically high expectations means that they rarely feel satisfied with themselves or their performance.

> *Roy works extremely long hours in his job as a corporate lawyer. At 33 he is a very high achiever and hopes to become a partner of the firm within the next few years. In spite of all of his achievements, Roy has a self-esteem problem—he only feels adequate when he is performing brilliantly. Consequently, he has little interest in spending time with his family, maintaining friendships, reading, participating in leisure activities or doing things that do not directly contribute to success in his work. Holidays in particular are a gruelling experience, and Roy always takes work with him to make sure that he uses his time productively.*

It's not that Roy doesn't love his family—in fact, he will tell you that they are the most precious things in his life. It's just that in order to feel valuable, Roy believes that he must earn his worth by 'being the best'. In his mind, that means becoming a partner in the firm and earning large sums of money. Interestingly, even when he does finally become a partner, Roy's attitude does not change. Like most people who rely on achievements for self-worth, the promotion provides temporary elevation in self-esteem, which soon evaporates. In addition, his stressful and unbalanced lifestyle creates other problems that Roy does not have time to address—his marriage is disintegrating, his children barely know him, he has few friends and he has developed high blood pressure and other health problems.

SEEKING LOVE AND RESPECT

Many of us want to be outstanding in some area in order to win love, respect and admiration from others. So we try to excel in our career, be brilliant at some sport, keep an immaculate house, maintain a perfect body, be a fabulous cook, own the most beautiful objects, be the perfect hostess or achieve excellence in some other area. However, most people who do this will attest that in spite of their best efforts to excel, this does not win them the love, admiration or friendships they are seeking. While others might admire their achievements, excelling at something rarely makes people like us. (In fact, high achievers are sometimes a turn-off because they can make others feel inadequate.) We are far more likely to win people's affection if we share common values and interests, and demonstrate traits like friendliness, honesty, loyalty and a genuine interest in others. Paradoxically, instead of spending our time trying to being brilliant, we are more likely to get what we want if we devote more time to nurturing relationships and taking a greater interest in other people.

While for some, self-esteem is contingent on financial success, for others it requires academic achievements or impressive work. Take Margaret for example:

> *Margaret has spent most of her married life raising a family. Now that her four children have left home, Margaret feels useless. She believes that she has never achieved very much in her life, and doesn't have any particular talents or abilities. Many of Margaret's friends are university-educated, and have high-status, well-paid jobs. Recently Margaret met up with her friend, Rebecca, for a coffee and was struck by her friend's energy and enthusiasm when talking about her job. Margaret immediately thought to herself, 'Rebecca must think that I'm boring. I have so little to offer.'*

Margaret decides to evaluate her assumptions by doing a Reality Testing exercise (see also page 57):

1 What are the facts?

I met up with Rebecca, and she talked enthusiastically about interesting things that she is doing at work.

2 What are my subjective perceptions?

I'm inadequate. I'm not as good as Rebecca. She must look down on me.

3 Evidence for my perceptions?

Rebecca was excited about her job, and she knows a lot of interesting people. I had little to contribute when she was talking about her work.

4 Evidence against my perceptions?

Rebecca frequently calls me and always appears to enjoy my company. I have other university-educated friends who also like spending time with me. I contribute to conversation as much as anyone else, and my friends don't appear to care whether or not I have a university education.

5 Have my perceptions been wrong before?

Yes, I often worry about things unnecessarily.

6 Am I making any reasoning errors?

Comparing, shoulds, mind reading.

7 How else can I perceive this situation? (Or think of a calm, rational friend. How would they perceive this situation?)

People choose different paths, depending on their life circumstances and what is relevant to them at the time. I chose to have a family and bring up my children—that's been important to me. Having a university degree or a high-powered job is right for some people but it's not the path that I could have managed, as I wanted to be there for my children. The choices I made were valid for me. While it sounds glamorous, having a university degree or a high-powered job would not make me a better person. I don't have to prove my worth with jobs or qualifications. I appreciate my own lifestyle and freedom. I'm very lucky.

EXCESSIVE NEED FOR APPROVAL

We are all approval-seekers—instinctively, we want to be liked. However, the degree of approval we need varies. For some, approval from just a few significant people is enough—for example, from family, bosses or a few close friends—so they may be reasonably unaffected by what most other people might think. Others need approval from almost everyone. Consequently, they may feel embarrassed when buying personal products in the chemist, when fellow diners don't leave the waiter a tip or when a stranger hears them thinking aloud. The stronger our need for approval, the more vulnerable we become to anxiety, depression and feelings of low self-worth. We are also more likely to behave in self-defeating ways—trying too hard to please others and always putting our own needs last. Paradoxically, this behaviour frequently has the opposite effect—people often sense our desperation to be liked and respond with limited respect.

Wanting to be liked by everyone is unrealistic—we all have admirers and detractors. The secret is to acknowledge that one size does not fit all. Individuals have different preferences and are attracted to different human qualities. Some people seek out those who are loud and gregarious; others prefer those who are contemplative and good listeners. Some people value honesty and genuineness beyond all other human traits, while others are attracted to people who have social status, wealth or a pretty face. Some people are attracted to intelligent conversation; others to a sense of humour; and others value loyalty and kindness above all else.

As we cannot be all things to all people, we need to accept that we will not 'connect with' or appeal to everyone. There may be some people who, for complex reasons, do like not us—this is true for all of us. A psychologically healthy attitude is to accept that some social disapproval is a normal part of human experience.

Some people worry that they are different to others and put a lot of effort into trying to 'fit in'. They may be conscious of looking different, behaving differently, thinking differently and having different values from the people around them. They may believe that in order to be accepted by others, they should avoid saying or doing anything that might draw attention to their differences.

People with healthy self-esteem are authentic, and are often willing to say or do things that might make them stand apart from others at times. For instance, they might take a stand against a prevailing view, choose not to go where everyone else is going, choose not to laugh when they don't think it's funny or choose not to care if they don't think it matters. It may be reflected in the way that they dress or the things they say. Of course, at times it is appropriate to compromise—it may be perfectly valid to do things we don't particularly want to do out of consideration for others.

However, it is also important to be able to express ourselves honestly, even if this means standing out from the crowd.

> ➤ *Sharon isn't interested in going out drinking with her friends on Saturday nights.*
> ➤ *Ian doesn't enjoy the jokes shared by the other apprentice mechanics that he works with.*
> ➤ *Rita is the only one in her circle of friends who votes for the Labor Party.*
> ➤ *Yasmin is a practising Muslim in a predominantly Christian culture.*

How these people deal with their differences will determine how they feel about themselves. If they are ashamed, embarrassed or worried about how others will judge them, they are likely to feel diminished by their differences. If, on the other hand, they accept that they have a right to be different and are willing to express themselves honestly, they are more likely to feel comfortable with themselves.

Whether our differences are major or subtle, there is no rule that says we should all be the same. Variety is the spice of life. A healthy attitude is to accept our differences and to be tolerant of differences in others. Although we may think that people will judge us harshly for not conforming, people often take their cues from us. If we feel comfortable with who we are, most of the time others do too. In fact, people frequently admire those who have the courage to be authentic, in spite of social pressure to conform.

BEHAVIOURAL DISPUTING

In Chapter 6 (page 148) we saw how behavioural disputing can be used to challenge one's excessive need for approval. Instead of trying too hard to please or impress other people, we do exactly the opposite—use shame-attacking exercises and look for spontaneous opportunities to do things that might risk the possibility of disapproval. When we relinquish behaviours based on an excessive desire to please, we learn through experience that our assumptions are incorrect—that we do not need to try so hard to win people's approval. We cannot know that we are inherently likeable and OK until we abandon attempts to be someone we are not. In fact, the paradox of trying too hard is that the harder we try, the less attractive we become (see also 'Be Honest' on page 218).

> When we stop trying so hard to be liked,
> we give ourselves the chance to discover
> that we are in fact already likeable.

Many of us also live with ongoing dread that at some stage, people will discover our perceived shortcomings, failures or flaws.

➤ *Sean is terrified that people will find out that he has made some mistakes at work.*

➤ *Irving is afraid that people will see how nervous he is when he gives his public presentation.*

➤ *Claude is terrified that people will discover that he is gay.*

➤ *Shirene is afraid that people will notice her blushing when she feels socially anxious.*

➤ *Joe was charged for driving while under the influence of alcohol four years ago and is anxious that people will find out.*

➤ *Nathan suffers from depression and is anxious that his new girlfriend will reject him if she discovers it.*

➤ *Helena has carried huge shame for years—that she was not sufficiently attentive to her father when he was dying of cancer.*

For each of these people, keeping secrets reinforces the perception that their shame is justified, and that catastrophic consequences would follow if others should find out. This maintains their anxiety and feelings of defectiveness. One of the best ways to evaluate whether our beliefs are correct is to conduct a behavioural experiment—self-disclose to the relevant people and observe their responses. Once we 'come out', our anxiety drops because we no longer need to worry that people will find out. Most people's experience in these situations is that others are nowhere nearly as judgemental as they had predicted. This helps them to recognise that their perceived shortcomings are not so bad after all.

But what if others *are* judgemental? Behavioural experiments always involve some risk—sometimes our fears are realised. For instance, when Claude finally disclosed that he was gay, most people were very supportive; however, two of his friends were judgemental. Taking risks involves the possibility of disapproval, failure or rejection—that is what makes them a risk. However, we do not overcome our fears and self-doubts by staying in our comfort zone. If we only self-disclose when we have an iron-clad guarantee that people will respond favourably, we gain nothing. The most powerful learning occurs when we risk the possibility of disapproval and discover that in most cases it does not happen, and that even if it should happen, we can cope.

There may of course be some situations where it is better not to self-disclose, particularly if the stakes are high. Nonetheless, most of us are too quick to hide because we assume that if people really knew us they would not like what they saw. Keeping secrets prevents **disconfirmation**—we never learn that our negative beliefs are incorrect. It is also harder to accept ourselves while we believe that we are unacceptable to others.

LABELLING

At times we do things that have negative consequences. For instance, we might mishandle social situations or make comments we later regret. Sometimes our actions have negative consequences for our work, relationships, health, finances or career, and on occasions we fail to achieve some of our most cherished goals. Sometimes we are just not good at things that we would very much like to be able to do. This is the nature of things— human beings are intrinsically fallible and we all have our strengths and weaknesses.

In addition, many people perceive themselves to have character flaws that limit their potential. For instance, some perceive themselves as too shy, too old, too fat, too awkward, too weak or too lazy. Others believe they are not clever enough, not successful enough, not capable enough or simply not as good as other people. Many people habitually label themselves as bad or defective on the basis of perceived shortcomings. The labels we use may be verbal and conscious—'stupid', 'weak', 'failure' or 'hopeless', or they may be just a felt sense of inferiority or defectiveness. The problem with labelling is that we make gross generalisations about ourselves on the basis of limited events or characteristics.

> *Vicki unthinkingly passed on some information that was told to her in confidence, which unfortunately got back to her original source. Her friend is furious with her for 'shooting her mouth off', and Vicki is full of shame and remorse. She tells herself that she is a traitor and a heel and should never be trusted again.*

Clearly Vicki has some fence-mending to do—it may take some time before she regains her friend's trust. It is important to acknowledge our mistakes so that we don't repeat them. It is reasonable for Vicki to regret her actions and to acknowledge that she made a serious error: 'I did a very silly thing!'. Judging some of our behaviours as silly or wrong does not diminish our self-esteem because behaviours are specific and can be changed—we can do it differently next time. However, labelling ourselves as bad or defective impairs our self-esteem because we make a global judgement about who we are.

> *Kim feels like the odd one out at the advertising agency where she works. Although she has been there for almost a year, Kim doesn't feel particularly close to the other members of her team. Their values and interests are different to hers, and Kim regards much of their conversation to be pretty superficial and banal. Most of the staff seem to get on well, and at times Kim wonders if there's something wrong with her. She labels herself as an outsider. She writes the following on her thought-monitoring form:*

SITUATION	Sat through a staff meeting—there was lots of joking and carrying on, but I didn't find it funny—couldn't even manage a smile.
FEELINGS	Sad, lonely, tense, uncomfortable, inadequate.
THOUGHTS	I don't belong—I'm an outsider. There is something wrong with me. They noticed that I wasn't joining in—they must think I'm boring or strange.
BELIEFS	I should be like them. I should connect well in all social groups. If I don't connect in some situations, it means that I am defective. Others are judging me harshly.
THINKING ERRORS	Shoulds, labelling, mind reading
DISPUTE	I connect well with some people and not with others. People are all different—I got on well with the staff at my last job. Most people feel comfortable in some social situations and not in others. There is no reason why I should connect well in every situation. It would be nice to feel closer to the people here but, sadly, we have little in common. It's OK to be different. Our differences do not mean that I am inferior or defective.
POSITIVE ACTIONS	Be friendly and cooperative. Respect their right to be different from me. Focus on having good professional relationships.

BE SPECIFIC

Rather than labelling ourselves, it is more helpful to think of our behaviour or situation in specific terms.

> *Claire recently went to a party where she didn't know any of the other guests. As she was too shy to approach anyone to start a conversation, Claire spent much of the evening sitting on the couch, feeling awkward and self-conscious. When she left the party, Claire felt troubled. 'I'm socially incompetent,' she thought to herself.*

Many of us have been in Claire's situation at some time. Do we really need to feel bad about ourselves when we don't connect? Labels such as 'loser', 'inferior' or 'socially incompetent' make us feel defective. If Claire had been able to think in specific rather than global terms, she could have told herself, 'I'm shy in some social situations, especially when I don't know people' or 'I'm not very good at starting up conversations in a room full of strangers'. Acknowledging that we have limited skills in some situations does not diminish our self-esteem because we make no global assessment of our overall worth. Being specific protects our self-esteem.

LABELS (UNHELPFUL)	SPECIFIC STATEMENTS (HELPFUL)
I'm socially incompetent.	I'm shy with people I don't know well.
I'm an idiot.	I did a silly thing.
I'm a traitor.	I let her down—I made a mistake.
I'm a failure.	I didn't achieve some of my career goals.
I'm lazy.	I find it difficult to get motivated on some tasks.
I'm dumb.	I don't have very good general knowledge.
I'm damaged.	I suffer from depression at times.
I'm incompetent.	I'm not very good at using modern technology.
I'm pathetic.	I get upset easily.
I'm unlovable.	My ex was not interested in me.

OVERGENERALISATION

How do you respond when you make a mistake or fail to achieve a goal? Do you tell yourself that you never get things done? That you always mess things up? That everything is going wrong? The tendency to make overgeneralisations about personal failures or perceived shortcomings is a common reinforcer of poor self-esteem.

Jillian is in her mid–40s and decided to do an Arts degree as a mature-aged student. Although she believed that she would have no difficulty in coping with the course work, the reality proved to be quite different. Jillian found it hard to concentrate during lectures or to do the prescribed reading, and worrying about the possibility of failure made studying more difficult. Finally she decided to defer for a year; however, when she recommenced the course the following year, the same problem arose. Finally, after much anguish and self-flagellation, Jillian dropped out of the course. Since that time, her self-esteem has plummeted and she has become depressed.

Overgeneralising about her inadequacies diminishes Jillian's self-esteem. Instead of acknowledging that there are some things that she does well and others that she has difficulty with, Jillian tells herself that she cannot achieve anything worthwhile, and that she is unlikely to do anything useful in the future. This makes her feel inadequate as a person. To assess her situation more rationally, Jillian needs to think about her perceived failure as specific to one area of her life. That is, that she has difficulty studying at this stage.

SITUATION	Dropped out of course that I really wanted to do.
FEELINGS	Worthless; depressed.
THOUGHTS	This means I'm dumb; I'm a failure; I'm hopeless. I can't seem to achieve things any more.
BELIEFS	My achievements define my worth. I should be able to succeed in everything I set out to do. If I don't, it means I am worthless. I am not capable of achieving things now.
THINKING ERRORS	Labelling, overgeneralising, jumping to negative conclusions, shoulds
DISPUTE	Studying is difficult for me at this stage of my life. I find it hard to focus because I am anxious about the possibility of failure. That doesn't make me incompetent or defective as a person. I succeed at some things and not others. There is no reason why I must succeed in everything I set out to do. This course does not define my worth as a person.
POSITIVE ACTIONS	Focus on other areas of my life—friendships, interests, health. Set myself new, life-enhancing goals.

BE SPECIFIC

Sticking to the facts enables us to remain objective, and limits our tendency to distort information with overgeneralisations.

OVERGENERALISATIONS (UNHELPFUL)	SPECIFIC STATEMENTS (HELPFUL)
I'm not achieving anything.	I haven't achieved a goal that was important to me.
Everyone thinks I'm an idiot.	Phil's parents and my mother disapprove of my decision.
People reject me once they get to know me.	I have been rejected in three of my relationships.
The harder I try, the worse things get.	In spite of trying hard, I couldn't resolve this particular problem.
Women don't like me.	I don't connect well with some of my wife's friends.
I've been a hopeless mother.	I have made some mistakes in the way I brought up my children.
I'm not making any progress.	I have not made as much progress as I would have liked.
I have wasted a whole day.	I have achieved substantially less than I had planned.
I'm hopeless at job interviews.	I didn't perform very well at my last two job interviews.

UNCONDITIONAL SELF-ACCEPTANCE

> The value of human life is that it exists. You are a complex miracle of creation. You are a person who is trying to live, and that makes you as worthwhile as every other person … And in spite of all that is hard in life, you are still trying. This is your worth, your humanness.
>
> **MATTHEW MCKAY AND PATRICK FANNING, *SELF-ESTEEM***

The above quote from McKay and Fanning's book *Self-Esteem* describes the essence of unconditional self-acceptance. It means accepting ourselves for our very humanness; recognising that we do not 'earn' our worth through things like our job, qualifications, achievements, appearance or possessions. In spite of all our perceived flaws and shortcomings, our worth lies in the fact that we are human.

Learning to accept ourselves does not mean that we should stop trying to improve aspects of our life. Learning new skills, embarking on a healthier lifestyle, developing friendships or taking on new challenges can greatly enhance the quality of our lives. However, we don't need to achieve these things before we become worthwhile human beings. Self-acceptance means knowing that we are OK regardless of our successes or achievements. It also means accepting parts of ourselves that we don't like but are unable to change. This might include aspects of our history, personality, competence or physical appearance.

Howard went through a very troubling time when he was diagnosed with schizophrenia ten years ago. While he has managed to get the illness under control with medication, Howard perceived himself as 'damaged' and inferior to others, and this created shame and self-downing. As a result, Howard ended up with two problems—the first was his mental illness (which was largely under control); the second was his poor self-esteem, which interfered with other areas of his life. It was only when Howard finally learned to accept his illness as a part of him (not liking it, but accepting it) that he stopped feeling defective and was able to feel comfortable with himself.

*

Emma has been overweight for most of her life and has hated her body for as long as she can remember. She has spent much of her life desperately fighting fat, trying one weight-loss regimen after another, to no avail. Finally, at the age of 35, after attending a support group, Emma has learned to accept the body that she has. While she tries to eat a healthy diet and do some exercise every day, she has learned to accept that she will probably never be slim. Releasing her belief that she must lose weight before she can like herself has been liberating, and has freed Emma to focus on other areas of her life.

*

*Sandra sometimes feels inadequate when she goes out to social
functions with her friend, Anne. Anne has a natural warmth and
sparkle that draws people to her and attracts admirers wherever she
goes. Although Sandra makes an effort to be friendly and to initiate
conversations, she does not have Anne's easy, warm social manner.
Sandra perceives herself as rather boring when she is in Anne's
company, and this makes her feel self-conscious. In order to maintain
healthy self-esteem, Sandra needs to stop comparing herself with
Anne or insisting that she should be like her. She needs to accept that
it takes longer for people to get to know her, and remind herself that
when she is comfortable with people, she can also relate well and
have good friendships.*

WHATEVER YOU FOCUS ON BECOMES MAGNIFIED

We all have things that we don't like about ourselves. Perhaps you are
too short or too heavy or have bad skin. Or maybe you are ashamed
of some aspect of your past that you cannot put behind you. Or maybe
you believe that you are not interesting enough, or outgoing enough, or
clever enough.

Whatever we focus on becomes magnified. Have you ever noticed, for
instance, that when you go to a social function and worry about what you
are wearing, this concern dominates much of the evening? Other people
don't notice or care, but focusing on your appearance stops you from
having a good time. The more we focus on our perceived defects, the more
problematic they become. Paradoxically, it is not the perceived defect, but
the attention we give it that robs our confidence, inhibits our behaviour
and diminishes our self-esteem.

The assumption that others judge us as harshly is often incorrect—most
of us are our own harshest critics! When we can truly accept the things that
we don't like about ourselves, their importance diminishes. Our sense of
worth grows accordingly.

EXERCISE 7.1

1 Think of something you don't like about yourself but cannot change. Have you ever noticed that focusing on this contributes to feelings of inadequacy?
2 Are there any benefits in focusing on this feature?
3 What are the downsides?
4 What would be the effect of accepting this feature and no longer giving it any attention?

COGNITIVE FLEXIBILITY

Healthy, adaptive thinking means accepting those aspects of ourselves that we cannot change, and not expecting that things should be otherwise. While we may prefer to be different in some respects, and we might strive to change some aspects of ourselves that we can control, we nevertheless remain flexible in the way we think about ourselves.

It may be useful to identify the beliefs that affect your self-esteem, and then think about ways in which you could be more flexible in relation to these beliefs. The following table contains examples of observations that have the potential to impair self-esteem, and ways in which they can be modified. Notice that none of the observations are a problem unless they are accompanied by a 'should'.

OBSERVATIONS	SHOULDS	FLEXIBLE BELIEFS
I'm not as witty as some people I know.	And I should be as witty as they are.	I don't have to be. Some people have the gift of being very funny. That's their good fortune. There is no reason why I must be as witty as they are.
I am not very good at keeping a clean and tidy house.	And I should keep a clean and tidy house.	I don't have to. I wish I was tidier, but there is no reason why I must be. Keeping my house clean and tidy isn't something that I am interested in or particularly good at.
I have a low libido.	And I should have a high libido and I should be having lots of sex.	I don't have to have a high libido. There is no 'correct' amount of libido. Many people don't have a high libido—that doesn't make them defective or inferior. People are all different, and libido varies from person to person.

OBSERVATIONS	SHOULDS	FLEXIBLE BELIEFS
I don't work.	And I should be working.	There is no rule saying that I must work. I'm fortunate that I don't need to work at this stage of my life, so I can enjoy my freedom and spend time on the things I like to do.
I'm not a perfect parent.	And I should be a perfect parent.	I don't have to be. I do my best and usually I do a pretty good job. At times I make mistakes, but then so does everyone else. Perfect parents are hard to find.
I take myself too seriously.	And I shouldn't take myself too seriously.	I have the right to take myself seriously. It would be good for me to lighten up and enjoy myself more but I tend to be a fairly intense person by nature. That doesn't make me bad or defective.
I am not achieving as much as I used to.	And I should be achieving as much as before.	I don't have to achieve as much as I used to. At this stage of my life, I can't do all the things that I used to. I'm achieving enough.
I don't have a university education.	And I should have a university education.	I don't have to have a university education. I can be a totally worthwhile and interesting person even if I didn't go to university.
I'm not very good at sport.	And I should be good at sport.	I don't have to be good at sport. Some people are good at sport—that is their good fortune, but it isn't one of my strengths.

EXERCISE 7.2

Now it is your turn. Make up your own table with columns for 'Observations', 'Shoulds' and 'Flexible Beliefs'. Write down some observations about yourself that have caused you to feel inadequate—now or in the past. In the 'Shoulds' column, write some of the rigid beliefs that have made you feel that way. Then think about a healthier, more balanced way of perceiving your situation. In the 'Flexible Beliefs' column, write some more realistic ways of thinking about your situation that would help you to maintain healthy self-esteem.

ACKNOWLEDGE YOUR STRENGTHS AND QUALITIES

If our self-esteem is fragile, we are more likely to focus on our perceived flaws and weaknesses (as any event that seems to confirm them receives our immediate attention), while ignoring our strengths and achievements. An interesting exercise is to write two lists—one comprising all our perceived strengths and the other comprising our perceived weaknesses. Many people struggle to think of anything good to say about themselves, not because they have few strengths, but because they habitually focus on their weaknesses. Choosing to focus more on our qualities and to accept the things we don't like but can't change, can help us to maintain a more healthy self-image.

EXERCISE 7.3

Create a Strengths Inventory. Write a list of as many strengths, positive attributes and achievements as you can think of. Ask people who know you well to contribute their suggestions. Keep updating your Strengths Inventory as additional information becomes available to you.

BEHAVIOURAL STRATEGIES THAT ENHANCE SELF-ESTEEM

We saw earlier that behavioural disputing is a powerful strategy for changing the way we think and feel about ourselves. In addition, strategies such as setting goals and using honest and assertive communication can help us to maintain healthy self-esteem.

SET LIFE-ENHANCING GOALS

While self-acceptance is essential for healthy self-esteem, this does not mean that we should avoid striving to improve ourselves in areas where we can make a difference. Whenever we are dealing with a self-esteem issue, it is worth considering whether there are any practical things we can do to improve our situation. For instance, we might consider increasing our general knowledge, extending our social circle, improving our fitness, developing a new interest, learning some new skills, taking on a new challenge or updating our wardrobe.

While pursuing meaningful goals can be very satisfying, doggedly chasing unrealistic goals can be self-defeating. It is therefore important to set goals that are realistic, and to remain flexible in pursuing them. Many people underestimate what they are capable of; however, the opposite is also sometimes true—setting unrealistic goals can make us feel inadequate when we fail to achieve them.

James is seeking Ms Perfect, with whom he can share his life. She has to be slim, beautiful, clever, gregarious, financially independent and mad about him. While James has occasionally pursued women who looked like Ms Perfect, none of them has been interested in him. The problem is not that James is unlovable but that his expectations are unrealistic. Modifying his expectations would help James to find a suitable partner and enable him to avoid feelings of failure and inadequacy.

*

Candice is a stocky size 16 build but she desperately wants to get down to a size 10. She has tried various diets, exercise and alternative therapies, but time and again she has temporarily lost weight, only to put it on again. Given her build, it is unrealistic for Candice to expect a major drop in weight. However, it may be more realistic to aim for a healthy lifestyle, and to build up the fitness rather than focusing on weight loss.

*

Roberto is determined to earn his worth by making lots of money, and his goal is to own a $5 million house on the harbour by the time he turns 50. Given the nature of his business, this goal is unrealistic. Roberto is setting himself up for failure and disappointment.

When setting goals, it is sensible to consider our resources—what we have to work with, what we are capable of and what sacrifices we are prepared to make along the way. Taking those factors into account helps us to set realistic goals, which in turn increases our chances of success.

It is also important to remain flexible when pursuing our goals. This means doing our best, while accepting that we may not always succeed.

It also means not waiting until we have achieved the things we want before we can accept ourselves. We can practise self-acceptance from the outset, regardless of what happening in our lives. Healthy self-esteem can be nurtured by changing our thinking, as well as working towards life-enhancing goals.

> *Wendy is shy by nature. Over the past ten years that she has lived in Sydney, Wendy has made some new friends, but not as many as she would like. One of the women she works with has been in Sydney for only two years and seems to have made lots of friends in that time. Wendy feels inadequate for having limited success in making new friends. To improve her self-esteem, Wendy needs to accept shyness as part of her personality, without labelling herself as defective. It may therefore take her longer than others to develop new friendships, but she nevertheless is capable of making new friends. Wendy can also be more proactive in developing new friendship—this is where goal-setting is important. For instance, she may choose to become more involved in social activities and initiate more contact with people she knows. The following is Wendy's thought-monitoring exercise:*

SITUATION	It's the weekend, and I've got very few activities planned.
FEELINGS	Sad, hopeless, heavy sinking feeling.
THOUGHTS	How am I going to spend my time? I don't have any friends. Nadia has been here for two years and she knows lots of people. What's wrong with me? I'm not attractive to people.
BELIEFS	People don't like me. I should have lots of friends by now.
THINKING ERRORS	Comparing, labelling, jumping to negative conclusions, shoulds
DISPUTE	I'm shy with people I don't know—it takes me a while to get close to others. When people get to know me they often like me. I am capable of making close friends. The friends that I have made over the years like and value me—Jeanette, Sue and Judy really like me. Being shy doesn't make me inferior, but it means I need to work harder than some people to make new friends.

POSITIVE ACTIONS	Make more effort to take social risks. Join Toastmasters and go to fortnightly meetings. Join the bushwalking club. Sign up for lessons in ballroom dancing. Join the local tennis club and take lessons. Invite Cynthia (woman I get on with at work) to see a movie on the weekend and make more effort to self-disclose when appropriate.

Joanne has become self-conscious about her appearance. She has put on weight since menopause and is now avoiding social situations because she hates the way she looks. Unfortunately avoiding people keeps Joanne feeling low and maintains her poor self-esteem. Joanne would feel better about herself if she could accept the physical changes that have come with age, and return to her previous lifestyle, including going out with friends. She might also consider setting herself some goals in relation to her weight; however, she would need to maintain realistic expectations as to how much she can change (as significant weight loss is notoriously difficult to achieve and maintain, beyond the short-term). The following is her thought-monitoring form:

SITUATION	Ran into old friend that I haven't seen for years. She didn't recognise me.
FEELINGS	Embarrassed, devastated.
THOUGHTS	She was probably shocked at how bad I look.
BELIEFS	I look terrible. I should be able to maintain my previous appearance. People are judging me. They look down on me.
THINKING ERRORS	Labelling, shoulds, mind reading, awfulising
DISPUTE	I would like to look youthful and slim, but physical change is a part of ageing. Most people don't care much how others look—they mainly worry about themselves. If I don't focus on my appearance, others are also unlikely to care. Even if some people do judge my appearance, it's unlikely to have any practical effect on my life. If I can accept myself, others will too.
POSITIVE ACTIONS	Join the gym—start a regular exercise program. See a dietician for guidance on a more healthy diet. Initiate social contact with friends—start going out more.

Be who you are and say what you feel
Because those who mind don't matter
And those who matter don't mind.

DR SEUSS, *HORTON HATCHES AN EGG*

BE HONEST

Feeling connected to others via friendships and intimate relationships can protect our self-esteem because it provides direct evidence that we are likeable or lovable. To connect with others in a meaningful way, we need to be authentic. Poor self-esteem may cause us to try to be someone we are not. In an effort to be liked, we may say or do things to try to impress. We might also avoid honest communication for fear of making a bad impression. Some people hide behind a happy facade that they believe will make them likeable.

For most of her life, Helen strove to be the person she believed others would like. She attempted to win goodwill from her work colleagues by bringing them presents and baking them treats. Even when she felt down, Helen put on a cheerful facade because she believed that people would find this endearing. On the rare occasions when she disclosed a personal problem, Helen always followed up by saying, 'But that's OK,' in order to reassure others that she is a positive person. Helen tried to present herself as dynamic, knowledgeable and well-connected, so she told exaggerated stories about the people she knows and the things that she has been doing. She feigned expertise on subjects she knew little about and used jargon and long words in an effort to impress people.

Some people regard Helen as a phoney, some like her, and some think she tries too hard. The problem for Helen is that, as long as she pretends to be someone she is not, she will always find it difficult to accept herself. Even when some people like her, Helen is never sure whether they like the 'real' her or the mask she hides behind. Most of us appreciate genuineness in others, and we are often turned off by someone who tries too hard to impress us.

Always be a first-rate version of yourself instead of a second-rate version of somebody else.

JUDY GARLAND

An essential ingredient for healthy relationships is honesty—a willingness to take off our mask. It means being willing to reveal our thoughts, feelings and experiences without extensive censorship or trying to impress. It means not putting on airs or false cheerfulness, not exaggerating our achievements and not trying to be all things to all people.

Being honest can be scary because we are putting ourselves on the line, but it can also be rewarding. When we discover that people like us without our disguise, we realise that we are valued for who we are—not for who we pretend to be.

USE ASSERTIVE COMMUNICATION

The way we communicate—verbally and via body language—sends a message to others about how much we value ourselves. Choosing to communicate assertively is a form of behavioural disputing because changing our behaviour changes the way we think about ourselves. When we communicate assertively, we express our opinions, feelings or needs in a way that says 'I am as worthwhile as every other person.' We can say what we think and what we want. We are able to look people in the eye and speak in an appropriate tone and volume. Unassertive communication reflects low self-esteem—the belief that we are not as valid or significant as other people. It also helps to maintain low self-esteem.

THE SELF-FULFILLING PROPHECY

Ian believes he is inferior to others. As a result, he finds it difficult to look people in the eye, say what he thinks or ask for what he wants. When he talks to people, he usually looks down and speaks in a soft voice, as though he really doesn't want them to hear. Ian never expresses his thoughts or feelings—he presumes that people wouldn't be interested. He never asks for what he wants because he doesn't believe that he has the right to expect anything from others. Ian's behaviour and body language communicate his belief that he is inferior. Sadly, people often treat him accordingly.

Ian's behaviour is a good example of the self-fulfilling prophecy. That is, our beliefs influence our behaviours, which in turn influence our experiences, which in turn reinforces our beliefs. So when we believe that we are inadequate or inferior to others, we behave in a way that conveys this message via our body language and verbal communication. As a result, people start to perceive us as inadequate and behave towards us in a way that reinforces our sense of inferiority.

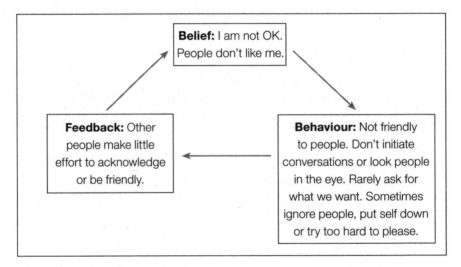

When we communicate assertively, we give out the opposite message: 'I am a person of equal worth to everyone else. I feel comfortable with other people because I know that I am OK. My thoughts, feelings and needs matter as much as anyone else's.' Not only does this reinforce the belief that we are as significant as every other person, but it also encourages others to treat us as equals. Assertive communication is one of the most valuable tools for maintaining healthy self-esteem and relationships. It also helps us to get our needs met more of the time. Chapter 10 provides further information on assertive communication (see also the Recommended Reading list on page 406).

IN SUMMARY

➤ Self-esteem is the perception of one's own worth. It has a major impact on many areas of our lives, including our relationships, mood and happiness.

➤ Our self-esteem is influenced by many factors, including our temperament, childhood and subsequent experiences, past and present relationships and messages from popular culture.

➤ Common faulty-thinking styles that diminish self-esteem include comparing ourselves with others, rating our worth on the basis of our achievements, trying too hard to get approval, overgeneralising and labelling ourselves.

➤ Self-acceptance is important for healthy self-esteem. This means accepting our perceived flaws without judging ourselves as defective. Being flexible, accepting that not everyone is going to like us and perceiving our flaws as specific rather than global helps us to maintain healthy self-esteem.

➤ Common symptoms of poor self-esteem include the need to please or impress others and to avoid self-disclosure and honest communication. These can be most effectively challenged via behavioural disputing.

➤ Setting and working towards realistic goals can also help to boost self-esteem.

EIGHT

Recovery from depression

Life is difficult.
This is a great truth, one of the greatest truths.
M. SCOTT PECK, *THE ROAD LESS TRAVELED*

Everyone feels sad or blue from time to time. Experiences of sadness are usually triggered by loss or disappointment—things go wrong, people let us down, we fail to get something we wanted, we lose something we valued. Sadness is a normal reaction to life's setbacks, and usually passes after a few hours or days, or perhaps after a good night's sleep. While we might be able to make ourselves feel better by talking to someone or distracting ourselves with a pleasant activity, sometimes we may simply allow ourselves to experience our sadness, knowing that it is a normal response and that with time it will pass. Occasional episodes of sadness are not usually a problem; however, if it lasts for more than a few days or occurs frequently, it is a good idea to learn some self-help strategies that can help us keep it in check.

At the other end of the misery spectrum is depression—a debilitating condition that interferes with our ability to experience pleasure, interact with people or participate in our regular roles at work or at home. Depression can have negative effects on our health and can even influence our perception of pain and physical symptoms. Unlike sadness, it can last for months or sometimes years.

Depression has been called the common cold of psychological disorders because it is one of the most common problems encountered by mental-health professionals. Approximately six per cent of Australians suffer a depressive episode each year, and 15 to 20 per cent will experience at least one episode of depression at some stage of their lives. While both men and women experience depression, women are affected twice as often as men. Episodes of depression are very often accompanied by anxiety, and about one third of depressed individuals also have an anxiety disorder at the same time.

The majority of people who become depressed do not seek help. This is a pity, as depression usually responds to treatment. While most people eventually recover even without therapy, receiving treatment from a qualified mental-health professional can speed up recovery by months or years, and may help to prevent future relapse. In addition to strategies described in this book, there are also self-help resources available on the internet (see Recommended Reading on page 409).

The cognitive behavioural techniques described in this chapter are useful for managing both sadness and mild to moderate depression. However, if you are experiencing more severe depression, these self-help strategies are extremely difficult to implement on your own because depression reduces motivation and physical energy, and impairs the ability to think rationally. If this is your situation, it is best to see a qualified mental-health professional, such as a psychologist or psychiatrist. It is particularly important to see someone if your depression interferes with your ability to function, if you are having thoughts about suicide or if you have already tried self-help strategies without success. While the information in this chapter will be a useful resource to complement your therapy, it is no substitute for treatment. If you would like to read more about how to manage depression, see the books in the Recommended Reading section on page 406.

DIFFERENT TYPES OF DEPRESSION

Although we tend to think of depression as one thing, there are in fact several types of depression.

DEPRESSED MOOD

This is a normal state of sadness that we all experience at times, usually in response to a disappointment. In this state we feel sad and low, and our perceptions take on a negative bias. For instance, we may perceive our friends, work situations or key relationships in a more negative light, and our own self-esteem may also diminish. In this state we might describe ourselves as feeling 'depressed'; however, we are actually experiencing a temporary depressed mood, which is likely to resolve within hours, days or weeks.

CHRONIC DEPRESSIVE DISORDER (DYSTHYMIA)

About six per cent of the population suffer from ongoing depressed mood at some point in their lives. This condition, which is experienced as a chronic mild depression, has sometimes been referred to as 'depressive personality', as the symptoms continue for years (at least two years to qualify for the diagnosis). In addition, the person might experience other symptoms, such as disturbed appetite and sleep patterns, low energy, poor self-esteem, poor concentration, difficulty in making decisions and feelings of hopelessness. People with this condition are at increased risk of experiencing episodes of major depression. They may see themselves as uninteresting and may therefore avoid social situations, which in turn increases their risk of depression.

MAJOR DEPRESSION

Different disorders relating to mood are described in the Diagnostic and Statistical Manual of the American Psychiatric Association (DSM-5). This guide to diagnosis is widely used by psychologists and psychiatrists in many Western countries, including Australia. According to DSM-5, a person can be said to be suffering **major depression** if they have at least five of the following symptoms over a minimum of two weeks, including at least one of the first two symptoms listed:

1   Depressed mood for much of the day.
2   Reduced interest in usually pleasurable activities.
3   Changes in appetite or weight.
4   Changes in sleep patterns.
5   Lack of energy.
6   Feelings of guilt or worthlessness.
7   Agitation or slowing down of physical movements.

8   Inability to concentrate or make decisions.

9   Recurrent thoughts of death or suicide.

The severity of depression can be classified as mild, moderate or severe. People with mild depression feel bad, but are still able to function. For instance, they may be able to go to work, do house chores and spend time with people, even though they experience little joy in doing so. Because their depression is not as crippling as the more severe forms, it is less likely to be noticed by others or to be treated.

People experiencing moderate depression have a greater degree of social and occupational impairment. For instance, they may go to work but achieve very little because of poor concentration and low levels of motivation. In their social relationships, they may be awkward and withdrawn.

People suffering from severe depression experience nearly all of the nine symptoms listed above, and their ability to do things is very limited. Even minor tasks like getting out of bed or getting dressed can be extremely challenging.

COMMON SYMPTOMS OF DEPRESSION

➤ **Emotions:** feel sad, despondent, hopeless, guilty, anxious, irritable, worthless, teary, numb.

➤ **Cognitive function:** poor concentration and memory; inability to make decisions or solve problems.

➤ **Thoughts:** negative bias (negative view of self, the world, the future); loss of interest in most things; narrow focus on perceived problems; negative ruminations; self-criticism; thoughts of suicide.

➤ **Behaviours:** inactivity; social withdrawal; avoidance; self-defeating behaviours such as abuse of drugs, alcohol or food; reduced productivity and effectiveness at work

➤ **Motivation:** lack of interest in most things, including work, social activities or hobbies; everything is an effort; difficulty in setting and pursuing goals

> **Physical functioning:** fatigue and low energy; disturbed sleep; disturbed appetite; feeling physically ill; loss of libido; slowness of movements; agitation.

DEPRESSION VERSUS GRIEF

Grief is a common human reaction to situations that involve major loss, such as the death of a loved one, diagnosis of a serious illness, loss of a job or break-up of a marriage. The symptoms of grief are often very similar to depression (including depressed mood; insomnia; loss of energy and interest in normally pleasurable activities; lack of motivation; loss of appetite and poor concentration); however, grief is not considered a disorder, but rather a normal response to major loss.

In recent years there has been a vigorous debate about whether the diagnosis of depression can be made when someone is facing bereavement. As this is probably the greatest emotional burden one is ever likely to bear, many experts argue that depressive symptoms are a normal response to this situation and should not be seen as a disorder. Others argue that if an individual experiences particular symptoms, such as feelings of worthlessness, suicidal ideas, physical agitation or slowing down, or very severe impairment of their overall functioning, this is beyond the normal symptoms that are likely to accompany bereavement, and suggests the presence of depression in addition to grief. This is the view that has been adopted in the most recent version of the diagnostic manual (DSM-5, released in 2013), which states that a diagnosis of depression can be made, even in the context of bereavement.

CAUSES OF DEPRESSION

Although thinking in a negative, self-defeating way increases the risk of depression, negative thinking alone is rarely the sole cause. Depression is the result of a combination of factors that may include:

> Biological (e.g. disturbances in neurotransmitter functioning);
> Historical (e.g. family history of conflict; alcohol use; early parental loss or neglect);

➤ Psychological: personality and cognitive style (e.g. habitual negative thinking);

➤ Environmental (e.g. stressful life events such as loss of job, illness, divorce); and

➤ Psychosocial (e.g. lack of close confiding relationships, social isolation).

Mental-health practitioners distinguish between depression that is primarily related to stressful life events, versus that which is largely attributable to biological factors, as this has implications for treatment. Depressions that are more biological in origin usually require biological treatments in the first instance, while those that arise largely in response to stressful situations are more likely to respond to self-help and talking therapies like CBT (although sometimes medication may still be required for a full recovery).

DEPRESSION TRIGGERED BY STRESSFUL LIFE EVENTS

The majority of depressions are triggered by a stressful event or long-term stressful circumstances. Events like the break-up of a relationship, loss of a job, onset of a serious illness or disability, bereavement, divorce, loss of reputation or business failure are common triggers for depression. So too are chronic stressors like poverty, a hostile or unpredictable domestic situation, a stressful work environment, social isolation, chronic physical or mental illness or being a caregiver to a family member with serious illness.

The likelihood of becoming depressed is greater when several negative events occur simultaneously or within a short period of each other. For instance, the loss of a job followed by the break-up of a relationship or the onset of an illness substantially increases the risk of becoming depressed. However, some people are able to get through several major hardships without becoming depressed. This reflects the role of personality and resilience, which influence how we respond to life's challenges. Resilience factors include things like one's style of thinking, biological disposition and the availability of resources such as friends, communication skills and interests.

People who have experienced previous episodes of depression are at increased risk of further episodes, particularly if they have had several prior episodes. As the number of episodes increases, the significance of the stressful events needed to trigger depression diminishes. So, while initial episodes may be triggered by a major event or loss, later episodes may be triggered by relatively minor issues. For people with recurrent depression, building resilience (e.g. through cognitive flexibility, a balanced lifestyle, regular exercise, social support, etc.) and utilising relapse prevention strategies (see page 260) can reduce the likelihood of further episodes.

DEPRESSION WITH STRONG BIOLOGICAL UNDERPINNINGS

MELANCHOLIC DEPRESSION

Depression often runs in families. Studies that compared the rates of depression among identical and non-identical twins have found that genes sometimes play a role in this disorder. Depression that is largely underpinned by biological factors is referred to as 'melancholic' depression, and accounts for up to ten per cent of all depressions. It is believed that people who are prone to melancholic depression have abnormalities in the delivery of neurotransmitters—the chemical messengers in the brain. The neurotransmitters most directly involved in the regulation of mood include serotonin, norepinephrine and dopamine. Antidepressant medications used for treating depression work by increasing their availability in the synapses between neurons (brain cells).

People with melancholic depression experience severe and debilitating symptoms that make it very difficult to function. These include a loss of pleasure in all things, and mood that rarely changes in response to positive events. Melancholic depression is associated with biological changes, which may be observed in **psychomotor retardation**—a slowing down in physical movements and thinking processes—or **psychomotor agitation**—feeling restless, irritable and unable to settle. It is also quite common for depressed mood to be more severe in the mornings, although this is not necessarily unique to melancholic depression.

Because of the strong biological underpinning, melancholic depression requires biological treatments (such as antidepressant medication) in the first instance. While psychological therapy is also beneficial, it is rarely effective as a stand-alone treatment for melancholic depression. Once mood starts to improve, good psychological therapy can promote further improvement. Although biological factors play an important role, stressful life events are frequently triggers for melancholic depression. For this reason, developing healthy psychological thinking and building resilience is beneficial for people who are prone to melancholic depression.

PSYCHOTIC DEPRESSION

About one per cent of people who suffer from depression experience a psychotic episode during their depression. This means that, in addition to severe depression symptoms, the person becomes delusional, and may believe all sorts of strange things. For instance, they may think that they have done something terrible and are going to be punished, or that others are out to 'get' them. Some may believe that their insides are rotting or that their thoughts are being controlled by aliens. Depression with psychotic features requires treatment with medication, and usually responds to a combination of anti-psychotic and antidepressant medication. Once it has been successfully treated, the psychotic features disappear, and the person will acknowledge that their thinking was abnormal at the time. (It is not the same as schizophrenia, where psychotic symptoms should be present for at least six months in order to qualify for diagnosis.)

PREMENSTRUAL DYSPHORIC DISORDER

About three per cent of menstruating women suffer a monthly depression in response to hormonal changes associated with their menstrual cycle. While up to 50 per cent of women experience some emotional, physical or behavioural changes prior to their monthly period, those who suffer from this disorder experience more severe symptoms within the week prior to menstruation. Symptoms include severely depressed mood, marked anxiety, irritability or anger, decreased interest in activities, social withdrawal and impaired ability to function.

POSTNATAL DEPRESSION

This condition is much more severe than the more common 'baby blues' that affect most mothers for a few hours or days shortly after childbirth. Postnatal depression affects about ten per cent of mothers and arises within three months of childbirth. It can last for a few weeks to years. In addition to the common symptoms of depression, mothers suffering from postnatal depression may also experience fluctuations in mood; anxiety or panic attacks; sleep and appetite disturbance; feelings of guilt, shame, anger, incompetence and hopelessness; suicidal thoughts and unrealistic fears regarding themselves, their baby or their partner.

BIPOLAR DISORDER

Around two per cent of the population experience depression that is part of an underlying mood disorder called bipolar disorder (previously known as 'manic depression'). People with this disorder experience episodes of severe depression, and have had at least one episode of feeling 'up' or 'manic' (being too happy, hyperactive, talkative or fast; having unreasonable thoughts and inability to sleep). People with bipolar disorder also often suffer from frequent or chronic anxiety or irritability and are at increased risk of alcohol and substance abuse (often used as 'self-medication' to manage distressing symptoms). People with a more severe bipolar disorder may find it difficult to function at work or to maintain healthy long-term relationships.

Bipolar disorder has been categorised into two types: bipolar I and II. While both types are associated with episodes of severe melancholic depression, people with bipolar I have episodes of full **mania** and may become delusional (out of touch with reality) in this state. People with bipolar II experience **hypomania**, which is a milder form of mania. They may for instance have episodes of high energy, feeling 'wired' and having little need for sleep, and they may be incredibly productive during this time. While some also have elevated mood, and see new and exciting possibilities, others are more prone to irritability during this time.

Because the symptoms of hypomania are more subtle than the mania that accompanies bipolar I, people with bipolar II are frequently misdiagnosed as having the more common 'unipolar' depression. This is a problem because it may prevent them from receiving appropriate treatment. As bipolar II is associated with an increased risk of suicide, as well as very severe depressions, early diagnosis and appropriate treatment is important.

During a manic or depressive episode, medication is normally a key part of treatment. Mood-stabilising medication is frequently prescribed, and other types of medication may also be prescribed, depending on severity. Psychological therapy such as CBT is often a good adjunct to medication during bipolar depression, but without accompanying medication it has limited benefits due to the strongly biological underpinnings of the disorder. Treatment with adjunctive CBT can help to speed up recovery, as well as help the individual manage mood swings, anxiety and self-esteem in the longer term. Reducing predictable stressors and learning to regulate emotions when stressful events arise can also decrease the risk of future episodes.

OTHER BIOLOGICAL CAUSES OF DEPRESSION

Sometimes depression is caused by physical illness or drugs. Certain endocrine disorders (e.g. lupus, Cushing's disease, diabetes), neurological disorders (e.g. Parkinson's disease, epilepsy, multiple sclerosis) and allergies may for some sensitive individuals cause depression. The use of certain prescribed medications (e.g. anti-hypertensive drugs, analgesics, migraine medication), and withdrawal from legal and illicit drugs (e.g. alcohol, nicotine, cocaine, cannabis, amphetamines) can also trigger episodes of depression.

In some situations, changes in hormone levels can also cause depression. For instance, depression sometimes occurs when an underactive thyroid gland produces too little thyroxin, a condition known as hypothyroidism. Fluctuations in sex hormones (oestrogen and progesterone) can trigger depressive symptoms in women who are premenstrual, pregnant, premenopausal or who have recently given birth.

Even seasonal reductions in daylight during the winter months can cause depression among some sensitive individuals—a condition known as Seasonal Affective Disorder, or SAD. This condition is rare in Australia but affects people who live in countries that have little sunlight during the winter months. Treatment involves exposure to artificial lighting.

Different types of depression benefit from different types of treatment, including various psychological approaches, biological treatments or a combination of both. For this reason, identifying the underlying causes, and maintaining factors is important. Seeing an experienced mental-health practitioner who has a tailored approach to treatment (as opposed to 'one size fits all') increases the likelihood of good outcomes.

THE EFFECTS OF DEPRESSION

People 'wear' their depression in different ways. Some look unhappy; talk in a flat, emotionless voice; become irritable or withdrawn and cry easily. Others are able to conceal their pain and manage to put on a brave face to the outside world. The downside of this approach is missing out on the support that friends and family members could otherwise provide. Disclosing the fact that we feel depressed may also help others to understand why we are (for instance) more irritable, withdrawn or distant than usual, and they are therefore less likely to take it personally. Educating family members about the effects of depression, and the specific things they can do to help, increases the resources available to assist with recovery. If the depressed individual is not receiving professional treatment, family members may encourage them to do this, as depression is treatable.

THE EFFECTS OF DEPRESSION ON COGNITION

Once depression has been triggered, something strange happens to our thinking: we develop a sense of **global pessimism**. Our mind becomes preoccupied with negative thoughts and everything feels bad and pointless. We cannot remember or relate to positive events from our past, and we cannot imagine that we will ever feel good again. Our problems seem overwhelming and insurmountable, and we feel helpless to resolve them. Minor mishaps such as misplacing our keys or missing an appointment may be perceived as evidence that we are losing our mind, and that our lives are out of control. We ruminate (see following) and find it hard to detach from our internal world. Yet our thoughts occur so automatically and without awareness that we don't even notice what we are thinking—we just accept them as truth.

EFFECTS OF RUMINATION

Depression gives rise to rumination—repetitive thoughts that focus on our problems; futile attempts to analyse past mistakes; speculation on the possible reasons and cogitation about the past and future consequences:

> *'Why did this happen? ... If only I had done 'this' instead of 'that' ... It's my fault ... Why do these things happen to me? ... Other people have good lives ... I am missing out ... It's too late to change things now ... It's never going to get better ... I used to be happy, but I've lost that now and I'll never get it back ... When did I lose my ability to be happy? ... I wish things were different ...'*

The **rumination** and **worry** that accompany depression have much in common. Both are pointless repetitive cognitive processes that maintain depression and anxiety. While worry focuses on bad things that could happen in the future, rumination focuses on past and present events. These processes have been likened to a caged rat running on a wheel—our mind goes around and around in circles, but gets nowhere.

So why engage in a process that is pointless and self-defeating? The answer is, because it *feels* like we are doing something useful. At an unconscious level, rumination is an attempt to escape our misery by trying to find solutions. By moving from one thought to another, considering every aspect of our problem, over-thinking and over-analysing, we assume that the answer will come. The ruminative thoughts feel important and necessary, and many people describe feeling 'compelled' to keep engaging with them—it is as though letting go of these thoughts might mean that we miss something vital.

Unfortunately it doesn't work. Research has shown that rumination is associated with *less* proactive behaviour and *reduced* attempts to find solutions (perhaps because it makes us feel more depressed). Rumination keeps us stuck in self-defeating thoughts and behaviours, and contributes to the downward spiral of depression.

Although rumination usually happens inside our minds, sometimes we do it aloud with friends or family members. Wanting to be supportive, our friends may listen and encourage us to talk. While communicating with a person who cares is often therapeutic, getting stuck in rehashing the same theme over and over again usually is not. We may be simply 'co-ruminating'— ruminating aloud in the presence of another person. If you find yourself doing this, consider initiating some activity such as playing cards, going for a walk, looking at photos, playing computer games or cooking a meal together. Activity helps to break the ruminative cycle, as it switches our attention to the external world.

THE DEPRESSION SPIRAL

Once we start to feel depressed, the negative cognitions and loss of motivation that accompany low mood often cause a downward spiral into deeper depression. Inactivity makes us feel bad. Spending too much time alone gives our ruminations room to roam, and these thoughts only make us more despondent. The more we withdraw, the more we ruminate, and the more we ruminate, the more miserable and sedentary we become. We then become self-critical for doing so little, which only serves to reinforce or exacerbate our low mood. In this way depressive episodes are perpetuated, and what may begin as low mood may spiral into a more severe depression.

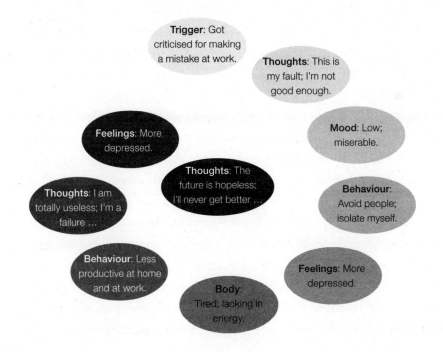

THE COGNITIVE TRIAD

Psychiatrist and early pioneer of CBT Aaron Beck, observed that depression causes people to take a negative view of themselves, the world and the future. These three areas of negative perception have been referred to as the **cognitive triad**:

➤ **The Self** e.g. I am no good; useless; worthless; defective.
➤ **The World** e.g. people are harsh; uncaring; critical; indifferent.
➤ **The Future** e.g. things will never get better; it will be this way forever.

These distorted cognitions are typically accompanied by feelings of hopelessness, helplessness and worthlessness.

HOPELESSNESS

One of the most debilitating aspects of depression is the sense of hopelessness that accompanies it—the perception that one's problems are insurmountable and permanent. In this state, many people believe they would be better off dead as it is hard to imagine that things will ever improve.

HELPLESSNESS

Low energy, lack of motivation and diminished ability to solve problems brings feelings of helplessness—the perception that we have no control over our lives. We feel overwhelmed by problems that we are unable to solve, and our helplessness contributes to feelings of hopelessness.

WORTHLESSNESS

Depression affects our self-esteem. In a depressed state we see ourselves as defective and worthless, and we are sure this is fact. We may blame ourselves for not being in control over our lives, and attribute negative events to our perceived deficiencies, such as laziness, incompetence or lack of effort.

Typical thoughts and themes that arise during depressive episodes include:

➤ Everything is hopeless. It will never get better.

➤ Life is meaningless. There is nothing to look forward to.

➤ My problems are too great. It's impossible to solve my problems.

➤ Given the magnitude of my problems, it's impossible not to feel depressed.

➤ I am defective. I am a failure. I have nothing.

➤ Everything is my fault. I don't deserve to be happy.

➤ I'm inferior to others. People look down on me.

➤ Nobody cares. I'm a burden to everyone.

➤ Everyone else has a good life, and I am missing out.

➤ I have ruined my life and now it's too late to change.

COGNITIVE STRATEGIES FOR DEPRESSION

As negative thoughts and ruminations are important factors in the maintenance of depression, strategies that enable us to recognise the negative bias in our thinking, correct faulty perceptions and disconnect negative ruminations enable healing to commence.

LABEL THE FAULTY THINKING

Once we are aware of the negative thoughts that pop into our mind, it is helpful to label the thinking errors associated with them (see 'Discovering Faulty Thinking' on page 27). Labelling helps to create some 'distance' from our thoughts, and reinforces the idea that thoughts are not 'truth'. The following questions can help to identify faulty thinking styles:

AM I ...	LABEL
Assuming that the very worst thing will happen?	Predicting catastrophe
Condemning myself as a person, on the basis of one or two events?	Labelling

AM I ...	LABEL
Assuming that I know what other people are thinking?	Mind reading
Focusing on the negative aspects of my situation, but ignoring the positive?	Filtering
Seeing things in absolutist, black and white, inflexible terms?	Black-and-white thinking
Blaming myself for things that aren't my fault?	Personalising
Making gross generalisations on the basis of just a few experiences?	Overgeneralising
Overreacting about things that are really not catastrophic?	Awfulising
Telling myself that I should have known something that I couldn't have known at the time?	Hindsight vision
Ignoring my strengths and focusing on my weaknesses?	Filtering
Comparing myself to others?	Comparing
Blaming myself or others?	Blaming
Assuming that things should always be fair?	Just world fallacy
Making assumptions on the basis of limited information?	Jumping to negative conclusions

SELF-CRITICAL THOUGHTS

Once we become depressed, our thoughts become self-critical, and we often blame ourselves for the very things that depression inflicts on us. For instance, we might perceive ourselves as bad or weak for becoming depressed or for not recovering more quickly. If we fail to achieve our own expectations (perhaps we may not manage to get out of bed, do our daily walk or abstain from drinking) we ruminate about our failure. We convince ourselves that the future is hopeless and things will never change. Although these thoughts are unreasonable and incorrect, they feel true. For this reason, it is helpful to notice their presence in our mind. The following table lists some of the common critical thoughts that accompany depression, as well as a more reasonable perspective.

SELF-CRITICAL THOUGHTS	REASONABLE PERSPECTIVE
This is my own fault—I'm a weak person for becoming depressed.	Depression affects one in six people at some stage in their lives. It is not a measure of character or personal worth. It affects people from all walks of life.
I'm totally egotistical—I am totally obsessed about my own problems.	Focusing on my problems is a symptom of the depression. It doesn't mean that I am egotistical or conceited. I don't focus on myself when I am not depressed.
I'm so lazy. I should be doing more. It's wrong to be so inactive.	Lack of motivation and lethargy are part of depression. They are not signs of laziness or weak character. I am trying to be active, but I can't always achieve this.
I'm causing family members to suffer. People are worried about me. It's my fault—I'm a bad person.	Depression is not something that I choose to have—it is not my fault. The people I love worry about me, and if our situations were reversed I would worry about them. That's the price we pay for caring relationships.
I should have recovered by now. When will it ever end?	There is no set time period for depression. Recovery can be a slow process, with two steps forwards and one step backwards. Rather than ruminate about how long it will last, I can choose to focus on my goals and try to do some things that are important to me.
I'll never get over this. I'll be depressed forever.	It feels like this will never end, but this perception is caused by the depression itself. Feeling hopeless about the future is part of depression—not an accurate view of reality.
My brain is deteriorating—I'll never be able to think normally again.	Depression affects people's ability to think and make decisions. These are not permanent changes, and they do not cause brain damage or deterioration.

EXERCISE 8.1

Make up your own form with columns titled 'Self-critical Thoughts' and 'Reasonable Perspective'. In the left-hand column, write your own negative or self-critical thoughts, and write some more reasonable ways of thinking in the column on the right.

DISPUTING NEGATIVE THOUGHTS: THE TWO-COLUMN TECHNIQUE

While depression generates lots of negative thoughts, certain themes tend to dominate. These focus on topics such as personal failure and past errors, negative appraisal by others and the hopelessness of our current circumstances.

Given the frequency of negative thoughts, a useful alternative to the standard thought-monitoring form is the two column technique. In the left-hand column, we record the 'automatic' negative thoughts that pop into our mind and label the faulty-thinking style that underlies them. In the right-hand column, we describe a more reasonable, balanced way to perceive our situation.

NEGATIVE AUTOMATIC THOUGHTS	REASONABLE, BALANCED PERSPECTIVE
Faulty thinking? ❏ Shoulds ❏ Awfulising ❏ Black-and-white thinking ❏ Blaming ❏ Personalising ❏ Overgeneralising ❏ Mind reading ❏ Labelling ❏ Filtering ❏ Jumping to conclusions ❏ Predicting catastrophe ❏ Just world fallacy ❏ Comparing ❏ Hindsight vision	

At the age of 44, Victor has developed depression. As he looks back on his life, Victor perceives a string of failures. In the search for his ideal vocation, Victor worked in several areas, none of which ultimately led to the career success he had hoped for. Working long hours has put Victor's marriage under strain, and he has spent little time with his wife and children. Years of neglecting his health have also taken their toll, and he is overweight and suffers from high blood pressure and headaches. When Victor thinks about his life, he can see so many mistakes. It seems as though he has failed at everything that matters—

his career, his family and his health. Victor's mind is full of negative
thoughts including 'Nothing has worked out for me ... I have wasted
my life ... I have achieved nothing ... I am a failure ... I should have
done things differently ... Now it's too late ...'

Victor's ruminations perpetuate feelings of hopelessness. It would therefore be helpful for him to challenge the unreasonable aspects of his thinking. When Victor writes his negative thoughts on the left side of the form, he is able to label the faulty aspects of his thinking. He then talks to his therapist, who helps him to come up with a more reasonable perspective, which he records in the right column. (Depression makes it hard to come up with rational thoughts, so getting some help from a friend, family member or therapist can be useful.) Once he gets the hang of this, he continues to challenge his negative thoughts without assistance.

NEGATIVE AUTOMATIC THOUGHTS	REASONABLE, BALANCED PERSPECTIVE
Nothing has worked out for me. *Black-and-white thinking* *Overgeneralisation*	I have achieved some of my goals but not others. I have done quite well in some vocations and provided a comfortable living for my family. Some things did not work out the way that I had hoped.
I have wasted my life; I have achieved nothing and now it's too late. *Black-and-white thinking* *Overgeneralisation*	My life has been full of experiences and I achieved many things, although I didn't achieve everything I would have liked. While I can't change the past I can choose how I live my life from now on.
I am a failure. *Labelling*	It is irrational to label myself as a failure on the basis of particular events. I have succeeded in some areas and not in others, at various times. 'Success' and 'failure' are unrealistic descriptors of a whole person.
I should have done things differently. *Hindsight vision*	The decisions I made were based on the knowledge and awareness that were available to me at the time. They were reasonable decisions, given the circumstances at the time. I don't know if things would have been better if I had done things differently. They could have worked out worse.
What's the point of trying? I can never make it work. *Jumping to negative conclusions*	I can't change the past but I can work on making the second half of my life more meaningful and satisfying. It is not too late to make positive changes to my life.

LIFESTYLE CHANGES

In addition to changing his thinking, Victor is re-evaluating his lifestyle and planning actions to improve his quality of life. He sets new goals which include improving his diet, exercising daily, learning to meditate, communicating more with his wife and children and learning to play golf. These lifestyle changes will help Victor develop greater resilience by improving his health, increasing his energy and building coping resources.

MINDFULNESS

Victor starts to practise mindfulness meditation twice a day, initially for 10 minutes at a time, and then gradually building up to 30 minutes twice a day. At the start this is very difficult, as his mind constantly wanders. With practice, Victor finds that he is able to focus on his breath for a minute or so before being distracted by thoughts. These periods of mental stillness give him a sense of clarity and calm. During meditation, Victor allows himself to sit with and observe feelings of hopelessness and 'heaviness' in his body without judging or resisting them. Over time, this helps Victor to release the 'despair about his despair' that normally makes him feel worse. It feels strangely peaceful to just let things be.

In addition, Victor starts to pay more attention to his thoughts and feelings during daily-life situations. He notices that his mind returns to common themes such as past mistakes, personal failures and the view that he has let down his family. Whenever he catches himself immersed in rumination, Victor acknowledges this ('I notice that I am ruminating again') and then switches his attention to whatever he is doing at the time. While his mind frequently returns to rumination, Victor is now more aware of times when it is happening, and he simply reminds himself that it is just rumination.

Through the practice of mindfulness, Victor starts to recognise that his thoughts are objects produced by his mind (strongly influenced by his depressed mood) rather than reflections of reality. This helps to create some distance from his thoughts.

DEALING WITH SETBACKS

As people start to recover from a depressive episode, they often begin to notice 'good days', where they might feel close to 'normal' again. It is therefore very disheartening when setbacks arise. The sense of hope that comes with perceiving that we are on the path to recovery may be dashed as our mood plummets again.

Setbacks are typically triggered by events—an error at work; an upsetting comment from a friend or family member; a return to self-destructive habits (drinking, taking drugs, bingeing, smoking); not coping effectively in a social situation or having a panic attack. The event itself is not the problem, even though it may feel hugely important at the time. The real problem is the negative thinking that arises in response to the event, as it has the capacity to derail our progress: 'I thought I was getting better, but now I can see that I was wrong ... Will I ever recover? ... I don't think so ... What will my life be like when I am permanently depressed?' This type of thinking creates feelings of hopelessness, and so impedes recovery.

During the recovery period the frequency of 'bad days' starts to diminish, however **setbacks invariably arise**. A healthy response is to accept setbacks when they occur—they are a normal part of the process. Interestingly, some people actually choose to be pessimistic when they start to feel better, for fear of subsequent disappointment. While this might seem protective, it is actually counterproductive. It is far more helpful to enjoy and appreciate the good days, accept the bad days and to allow time and space for our mood to gradually improve.

THE ROLE OF METACOGNITIVE BELIEFS

When we are depressed, our negative thoughts feel true, and in a strange way we feel drawn to them. Many of the self-critical and pessimistic thoughts that accompany depression are driven by metacognitive beliefs. These are the beliefs that we hold about our own cognitive processes. At some level, it feels like self-criticism is necessary and appropriate—as though it will motivate us to try harder.

In fact, the opposite is true. Self-critical thoughts make us feel worse, and perpetuate depressed mood. We would be far better off accepting that we feel depressed right now, without judging or blaming. It may be helpful to remind ourselves that we are doing our best, particularly given the challenges that depression metes out to us.

> *Amanda has been depressed for the past two months and worries that she will never recover. She has started applying some self-help strategies, including increasing her activity levels, for example, with morning walks; challenging her negative thoughts using the two-column technique and practising mindfulness meditation. Since commencing these strategies, Amanda's mood has improved and she has started to feel better. However, on Friday night, when Amanda was at a low ebb, she ended up drinking half a bottle of gin. When she awoke the following morning, hungover and miserable, negative ruminations flooded her mind: 'I am such a weak person. ... What have I done? ... Drinking alone is so desperate ... Why don't I have any willpower? .. I am just hurting myself. ... When am I ever going to learn? ... I am wasting my life ... Will anyone be able to help me? ... What will I do if I never recover? ... Is this how I am going to live the rest of my life? ... What am I to do?' These ruminations caused her mood to plummet further, and for the next few days Amanda stayed in her pyjamas and comforted herself with chocolate and crisps.*

While Amanda perceives her problem to be the lack of willpower that led to her binge, this is not actually the case. Amanda's main problem is the thinking that followed this event. A stream of negative, self-critical ruminations perpetuates her depressed mood, sapping her energy and further diminishing her motivation. Paradoxically, Amanda's ruminations are moving her further away from where she wants to be.

As Amanda observes her thoughts, she notices that her mind keeps going back to the same themes. As is typical of individuals with depression, Amanda feels drawn to her ruminations. At an unconscious level those pessimistic thoughts feel 'productive'—as though continuing to ruminate will help her to find solutions to her problems. Amanda also believes that being self-critical is the only way to motivate herself to change her behaviour: 'If I feel really terrible about it, maybe I won't do it again?' Unfortunately it doesn't work. The relentless stream of self-critical thoughts is demoralising and demotivating. It makes Amanda feel worse, and so increases the likelihood of further binge drinking in the not-too-distant future.

POSITIVE BELIEFS ABOUT RUMINATION

Positive beliefs about the value of worry and rumination are common obstacles to recovery, as they motivate us to engage in futile thought processes. Recognising and challenging these beliefs can help us to disconnect from rumination, and therefore hasten our recovery. The following table provides examples of beliefs that promote rumination during depression, and ways in which those beliefs can be challenged.

POSITIVE BELIEFS ABOUT RUMINATION	CONSEQUENCES	ALTERNATIVE, REALISTIC VIEW
If I keep criticising myself, this will motivate me to 'lift my game'. I should feel guilty or I won't learn.	Ongoing negative ruminations and self-blame. Guilt, hopelessness, despair.	I'm doing my best, and self-criticism does not motivate me to do better. It just makes me feel hopeless. I can motivate myself by acknowledging my achievements, however small, and focusing on small daily goals. I don't need to judge myself when I don't achieve them.
If I keep asking these 'why' questions I will find answers, and that will help me recover.	Ongoing rumination and preoccupation with pointless thoughts. Hopelessness. Poor concentration.	There are no answers to these questions. They are pointless ruminations that lead nowhere, and there is no benefit in pursuing them. They do not help me in any way.
Expecting and thinking about not recovering, and other worst-case scenarios, prepares me for the worst. At least I won't be disappointed if they should happen.	Feelings of hopelessness. Loss of motivation.	Focusing on worst-case scenarios is unrealistic and unhelpful. I can choose to focus on small achievements instead of pointless speculations about worst-case scenarios.

POSITIVE BELIEFS ABOUT RUMINATION	CONSEQUENCES	ALTERNATIVE, REALISTIC VIEW
If I start to feel hopeful on days when I'm feeling better I may jinx myself and therefore not recover. It's best to remain pessimistic, even when I have good days.	Remain depressed, even when I see signs of improvement.	There are no downsides to feeling encouraged on days when I'm feeling better. I can value and enjoy my improvements, whether they are temporary or ongoing. Ups and downs are a normal part of the process. There are no benefits in remaining pessimistic.
I should feel guilty that my family members are worried about me. If I don't feel guilty, it means I am a bad person.	Guilt. Anxiety over feeling pressure to recover.	I wish my family members did not worry about me, but my guilt does not help them or me. Feeling guilty does not make me a better person or speed up my recovery. My depression is not a lifestyle choice—I am doing the best that I can.
If I keep worrying about whether I will ever get better, this helps me to stay in control, and increases my likelihood of recovery.	Worry, anxiety. Physical arousal and tension.	Worrying about the future is my way of trying to stay in control, but it doesn't work. It wastes my energy and makes me anxious. I can focus on goals one day at a time, and leave the future alone. Worrying provides no advantages.

Now that Amanda is aware of her metacognitive beliefs (beliefs about her own thought processes), she makes a commitment to try to notice whenever she engages in self-chastising thoughts. Her opportunity came very soon, as on the following day Amanda missed her regular morning walk, and before long she was chastising herself for being lazy and undisciplined. As Amanda realised that she was back in self-critical thinking, she promptly reminded herself that she can choose not to continue. She reminds herself that she is doing the best that she can, and accepts that she will not always be able to meet her own expectations. Being aware that self-criticism will not motivate her to improve her performance (in fact, it will have the opposite effect), and nor will it help her to recover from depression, Amanda is now more willing to give it up. While she continues to have the occasional 'hiccup', Amanda no longer engages in self-punishing thoughts. Consequently, her mood bounces back more quickly, which in turn gives her the energy to do more. As a result, her mood improves further.

EXERCISE 8.2

Reading through the table on the previous pages, can you identify any positive beliefs about rumination that are relevant to you? (Remember, these beliefs are held on an emotional or 'gut' level. You may logically know they are irrational, but still feel them.) Read through the alternative, realistic view that can be taken in response to each of these beliefs.

1   If you were able to take these on board, what difference would this make to the way you think and feel?
2   Write down your own positive beliefs about rumination, and then write an alternative, more realistic view in response to each of these beliefs.

BEHAVIOURAL STRATEGIES FOR MANAGING DEPRESSION

Behavioural strategies are particularly powerful in the management of depression because they have both direct and indirect effects on mood. Certain behaviours, such as physical exercise, listening to music or spending time with friends have a direct mood-enhancing effect—doing them can lift our mood. In addition, some behaviours have an indirect effect on our mood by influencing our cognitions. For instance, communicating honestly with a friend can help us to challenge the belief that no one likes or cares about us, which in turn gives us a psychological boost. Fixing something, cleaning out a cupboard, cooking a meal or completing an outstanding task can challenge perceptions of helplessness, and this can also make us feel better. In fact, any behaviour that gives us a feeling of achievement can lift our spirits. Most importantly, engaging in activity disrupts the negative ruminations that perpetuate depressed mood. In the section below, we will look at the specific activities that are often helpful.

Action is the antidote to despair.

JOAN BAEZ

ACTIVITY

Depression drains our energy and depletes our motivation, so that even minor tasks like getting dressed or making breakfast can feel difficult. Our struggle to get things done adds to our sense of helplessness, which in turn makes us more depressed. As our mood plummets, so too does our motivation, and the less we do, the more depressed we become.

One way to break out of this spiral is to engage in activity, despite our overwhelming desire to lay low. By shifting our focus to the external environment, activity distracts us from rumination, and so provides a space for our mood to lift. Activity scheduling is also a form of behavioural disputing because when we take control over parts of our lives, we realise that we are not completely helpless after all. Although our motivation is low, once we get started we nearly always feel better, so it's important to push ourselves, even when we can't be bothered.

> Do the opposite to what your depression tells you to do. If you are inclined to stay in bed, then get out. If you don't want to go to the concert, then go. It's important not to let your down moods take control and guide the way you act.
>
> **SUE TANNER AND JILLIAN BALL,** *BEATING THE BLUES*

SCHEDULE POSITIVE EVENTS

Two types of activity are particularly helpful for overcoming depression— activities that give us a sense of **pleasure** and **achievement**.

PLEASURE

Activities that are intrinsically pleasurable improve our mood and lift our spirits. It is helpful to incorporate pleasurable activities into our lives regardless of our mood, but it is particularly important during periods of depression. Here are some examples:

- talk on the telephone
- have a bath
- look through some old photos
- watch a funny video
- go for a walk
- listen to music
- have a massage
- write in a diary
- do some stretching
- play with your pet
- work on a hobby
- sing

- write poetry
- go for a swim
- play computer games
- play a musical instrument
- work on a puzzle
- cook a nice meal
- listen to a relaxation CD

- dance
- sit in the sun
- go shopping
- say a prayer
- play golf
- read
- play cards

- visit a neighbour
- do some art work
- sexual activity
- see a play
- go on a chat site or Facebook
- have a meal with a friend
- watch a movie

ACHIEVEMENT

Getting things done is intrinsically satisfying whether or not we feel depressed, and it reduces the feeling of helplessness that so often accompanies depression. Activities that give us a sense of achievement are also good spirit-lifters. Here are some examples:

- get out of bed before 9 am
- repair something
- work in the garden
- finish an incomplete job
- make an appointment
- drive someone somewhere
- do the ironing
- work on some special project
- make a phone call
- mow the lawn
- initiate some social contact
- do some knitting

- do a routine chore
- do some sewing
- write a letter
- clean up the bedroom
- do some exercise
- pay a bill
- clean out a cupboard or spare room
- cook a meal
- initiate some activity with your children
- wash the dishes
- go to work
- help someone else

When we feel depressed we may be reluctant to engage in normally pleasurable activities because depression robs us of the capacity for enjoyment. It is true that most activities are less fun during depression; however, we will usually feel better doing something, as opposed to doing nothing.

> Carol used to enjoy singing in the community choir, but since the onset of her depression she gets little pleasure from her singing. It is tempting for Carol to think, 'What's the point? I'm not enjoying it anyway.' However, when she compares the way she feels when she goes to choir practice with the way she feels when she stays at home, Carol can see the value of making the effort.

GOAL SETTING

Setting goals is the means by which we move towards the things that we want. Goals give us a sense of direction and purpose, and provide a focus that helps us to achieve things. Goals can provide:

A SAFEGUARD AGAINST DEPRESSION

Working towards goals keeps us focused and motivated. The sense of purpose gives our lives meaning and reduces our risk of becoming depressed.

A TOOL FOR OVERCOMING DEPRESSION

When we feel depressed, setting goals gives us direction and reduces feelings of helplessness. Achieving goals produces a sense of achievement, which lifts our mood.

While goals should always be realistic and attainable, this is particularly the case when we feel depressed. Setting unrealistic goals can lead to failure, and so reinforce feelings of helplessness.

When we feel depressed (or even if we are not), a **weekly goals list** can help us to focus on the things we want to achieve, and boost our motivation to stay active. In addition, a **daily 'To Do' list** provides a useful guide for things to do each day. The following is an example of a weekly goals list:

WEEKLY GOALS LIST:

This week I plan to:

- ❏ Get out of bed and shower by 8 am each day.
- ❏ Walk around the park at least four times.
- ❏ Eat dinner with my family each day, even if I'm not hungry.
- ❏ Answer my phone when someone calls.
- ❏ Do at least one sketching session this week.
- ❏ Listen to music for half an hour before going to bed.
- ❏ Go to bed by 10 pm each evening.
- ❏ Re-read Chapter 7 of Change Your Thinking.
- ❏ Do some gardening.
- ❏ Make an appointment to see a psychologist.
- ❏ Enrol in an adult-education class.
- ❏ Practise daily meditation.

When setting goals, it is important to express them in a way that is objective and measurable. This means defining specific behaviours rather than vague concepts. Setting goals such as 'I'm going to be more positive,' or 'I'm going to be calm' can be problematic because they are vague and difficult to measure. On the other hand, defining specific behaviours gives us concrete steps that are more easily implemented and achieved. Below are some examples of vague versus objective goals:

VAGUE GOALS	OBJECTIVE GOALS
Be more positive.	Do thought-monitoring exercises every day.
Improve my eating habits.	Eat three meals every day.
Try to get out more.	Go for a walk each morning, go to classes on two evenings a week, baby-sit my niece once a week and go out for lunch with a friend at least once a week.
Stay calm.	Practise meditation at least four times per week.
Take more social risks.	Make telephone calls to at least three people each week. Initiate two social outings each week.
Increase my leisure activities.	Go to the movies once a week, go sailing each weekend and do my sketching for at least two hours per week.

SCHEDULING AND MONITORING ACTIVITY

In addition to setting daily and weekly goals, it is often helpful to keep a record of the things that we actually did. This is called an Activities Log, and can be recorded daily or weekly.

A **Daily Activities Log** (see next page) is a record of the things we do each day. Keeping a record can in itself motivate us to do more, as well as provide feedback on how we are spending our time. It can also highlight activities that are particularly mood-enhancing. By scoring each activity on 'P' for pleasure and 'A' for sense of achievement, we have useful information on activities that are worth scheduling in the future. (When rating yourself on achievement, make sure your score reflects your sense of achievement given how depressed you felt at the time, rather than an objective measure of how much you accomplished. For instance, getting out of bed or having a shower may be a major achievement on days when you feel very low.)

DAILY ACTIVITIES LOG

Time	Activity	P-score /10	A-score /10
7.00–8.00 am			
8.00–9.00 am			
9.00–10.00 am			
10.00–11.00 am			
11.00 am–noon			
12.00–1.00 pm			
1.00–2.00 pm			
2.00–3.00 pm			
3.00–4.00 pm			
4.00–5.00 pm			
5.00–6.00 pm			
6.00–7.00 pm			
7.00–8.00 pm			
8.00–9.00 pm			
9.00–10.00 pm			
10.00–11.00 pm			

P: Sense of **pleasure** experienced while doing this activity
A: Sense of **achievement** experienced after doing this activity

Leonie has been struggling with depression ever since the last of her children left home. As part of her treatment, she is setting daily and weekly goals to motivate herself to stay active. Each evening she plans her activities for the following day, and at the end of each day she completes an Activities Log, recording what she did that day, and scoring each activity on pleasure and achievement out of 10. The following is a page from her log:

LEONIE'S DAILY ACTIVITIES LOG
DAY/DATE: Tuesday 17 August

Time	Activity	P-score /10	A-score /10
7.00–8.00 am			
8.00–9.00 am			
9.00–10.00 am	Got up and went for a walk.	4	6
10.00–11.00 am	Shower, breakfast.	3	4
11.00 am–noon	Did the laundry.	3	6
12.00–1.00 pm	Made lunch.	2	3
1.00–2.00 pm	Picked up Emma [granddaughter] from kindergarten and dropped her off at Katy's.	6	4
2.00–3.00 pm	Stayed and talked to Katy. Played with Emma.	6	3
3.00–4.00 pm	Came home. Didn't do much.	2	0
4.00–5.00 pm	Watched TV.	1	0
5.00–6.00 pm	Watched TV.	1	0
6.00–7.00 pm	Had take-away dinner with Sam.	4	0
7.00–8.00 pm	Phone calls—talked to Marilyn, Kim.	4	5
8.00–9.00 pm	Worked on computer.	3	4
9.00–10.00 pm	Watched TV in bed .	2	0
10.00–11.00 pm	Watched TV in bed.	2	0

Knowing that she will be recording and reviewing her activities at the end of the day motivates Leonie to do a little more than she otherwise would. In addition, when Leonie reflects on the activities in her log, she notices that she experienced more pleasure when she was spending time with people—for example, talking to her friend, Marilyn and her husband, Sam; or being with her granddaughter, Emma and daughter Katy. Leonie also noticed that activities like going for a walk, doing the laundry and working on her computer also made her feel better. On the other hand, she felt at her worst when she watched TV or just sat around. Leonie keeps this information in mind when setting goals over the next few weeks.

WEEKLY ACTIVITIES LOG

Some people prefer to log their activities on a weekly rather than daily basis. The Weekly Activities Log opposite provides a template for weekly monitoring.

GENERALLY UNHELPFUL BEHAVIOURS

Although individuals find different activities to be helpful, there are some behaviours that are generally unhelpful when we feel depressed. These include:

➤ staying in bed for hours during the day;

➤ inactivity—watching TV for hours or sitting around unoccupied;

➤ avoiding people and isolating yourself;

➤ avoiding any situation that reminds you of your problem;

➤ short-term comfort activities, such as eating snack foods, drinking alcohol or taking drugs; and

➤ discouraging people who care about you from giving you their support.

PROBLEM SOLVING

Although the factors that contribute to depression vary, it is common for its onset to be triggered by stressful life events (such as a relationship breakdown, difficulties at work or onset of a health problem) or ongoing

WEEKLY ACTIVITIES LOG

TIME	MONDAY		TUESDAY		WEDNESDAY		THURSDAY		FRIDAY		SATURDAY		SUNDAY	
	A	P	A	P	A	P	A	P	A	P	A	P	A	P
7.00–8.00 am														
8.00–9.00 am														
9.00–10.00 am														
10.00–11.00 am														
11.00 am–noon														
12.00–1.00 pm														
1.00–2.00 pm														
2.00–3.00 pm														
3.00–4.00 pm														
4.00–5.00 pm														
5.00–6.00 pm														
6.00–7.00 pm														
7.00–8.00 pm														
8.00–9.00 pm														
9.00–10.00 pm														
10.00–11.00 pm														

chronic stressors (such as loneliness, poor self-esteem or ongoing family conflict). These situations often present problems that need to be solved. In addition, depression itself creates problems, such as diminished productivity at work, difficulty sleeping, neglect of important tasks and breakdown of social connections.

Responding effectively to depression involves not only changing our thinking but also addressing the problems we are facing. A good way to begin is to make a list of the specific problems that we need to address. This imposes order on the chaos—a mass of overwhelming difficulties can be reduced to specific items that can then be worked through. Try to avoid writing vague statements such as, 'My life is a mess' or 'Everything is terrible'. Using precise descriptions helps to make the situation more manageable. For example:

> *Since I have separated from Tim:*
>> *I'm afraid that I won't be able to find somewhere to live.*
>> *I am avoiding people.*
>> *I am unable to sleep.*
>> *I feel financially insecure.*
>> *I have poor self-esteem.*
>> *I'm afraid of being alone for the rest of my life.*

Once we have defined our specific problems the next step is to look for solutions. This will involve examining each individual problem and working out how to address it. Sometimes it is useful to brainstorm various possible solutions and then identify those that are most viable (see page 273). It is often a good idea to get other people's input during this process, as depression impairs our ability to think creatively. It also causes us to see obstacles in response to every possible solution, so be aware of this as you encounter resistance to problem solving. By focusing on aspects of our situation that we can control, deciding what needs to be done and following through with specific actions, we can often improve our circumstances and feel better as a result.

Tina has been an active and energetic woman for most of her life. In her earlier days, Tina did lots of ballroom dancing and by the age of 30 she was a proficient dancer. She also enjoyed writing, reading and entertaining. Early in her marriage, the family home was always full of interesting people wining, dining and exchanging ideas. After her three children left home, Tina started to focus on her own career and eventually set up a successful public relations consultancy. When her marriage broke up eight years later, Tina sold her business and her house, and went travelling overseas for three years. After she returned, Tina rented a flat by the beach and set herself a new goal—to write a book about her travels.

At age 52, Tina was totally unprepared for the depression that descended on her shortly after she moved into her flat. For weeks she had difficulty sleeping and found it hard to get out of bed. She lacked the motivation to do even basic things and found it impossible to work on her book. Tina soon realised that writing is a solitary business and, without an outside job or reason to leave the house, she had few opportunities to meet with other people. In addition, being away for so long had caused her to lose contact with many old friends and now that she was depressed she felt incapable of reconnecting with them. Tina was also reluctant to call on her children because she did not want to burden them with her own problems.

Tina defined her problems as:

➤ I have lost my motivation to do things, including my writing.
➤ I feel lonely and disconnected from people—I'm spending too much time alone.
➤ My days have very little structure—I have too much time on my hands.
➤ Other than writing, I have no interests.
➤ I have difficulty sleeping.

Her next step was to explore possible solutions for each of the problems that she identified. After doing some brainstorming and generating additional ideas from talking to a friend, Tina resolved to take the following steps:

1 Get a part-time secretarial job for two to three days per week.
2 On the days when I'm not at my job, work on my book each day until 1 pm.
3 Ring up some of my old friends. Re-establish contact. Invite them around for dinner and make more effort to see them.
4 Talk to my children. Tell them how I'm feeling at the moment and ask for their support.
5 Arrange to baby-sit my granddaughter two afternoons a week.
6 On the days when I work on my book, go to the gym at 3 pm every afternoon. On the days I work in my secretarial job, go to the gym in the evenings.
7 Take up dancing again—go along to the dance club on weekends and one evening per week.
8 Get back into reading—join a book club.
9 If I still have too much time on my hands, consider doing some courses through the local adult education centre.
10 Practise deep relaxation exercises before going to bed.

As Tina involved herself in more activities and re-established contact with old friends, her mood started to improve. Now, two years later, Tina has developed a more balanced lifestyle that gives her personal satisfaction and protects her from falling back into depression.

SOCIAL SUPPORT

> And in the sweetness of friendship
> Let there be laughter and sharing of pleasures
> For in the dew of little things
> The heart finds its morning and is refreshed.
> **KAHLIL GIBRAN, *THE PROPHET***

Strong, supportive relationships are one of the best safeguards against depression. Studies have found that good social support helps to protect both psychological and physical health. Connecting with others is inherently pleasurable and lifts our mood at times when we feel low.

People can provide us with many important things:

➤ emotional support;
➤ practical assistance and information;
➤ a different perspective on our problems;
➤ a sense of personal worth and belonging; and
➤ ideas for problem solving.

Depression makes us feel alone. We may feel friendless or unable to connect. Normal social interaction may become difficult, and there is a heaviness in our heart that can make even basic conversation feel like hard work. As we assume that we have nothing to offer, it is easy to withdraw—physically and emotionally. While our instinct is to disappear into our shell, doing so gives us space to dwell on our problems. The more we ruminate, the worse we feel.

Friends might suspect that something is wrong, while some may misinterpret our withdrawal as rudeness, indifference or rejection. For this reason, it is helpful to talk to the people in our lives and explain our struggle. Doing so will relieve the pressure to pretend, and may lead to a more empathic response. It is particularly important to communicate with the people we are closest to—our family members and close friends.

GETTING SUPPORT FROM OTHERS

While sharing our concerns can build bonds and make us feel better, sometimes this leads to an unintended effect—people try to help us by telling us what to do. 'Why don't you leave that bastard? I would!' or 'You've got to be more assertive' or 'Lose some weight, buy yourself some new clothes and start flirting!' The problem with getting advice is that other people's solutions may not be right for us—we are all different. Also, it is easy to give advice when you don't have to take it yourself. This is not to say that suggesting possible solutions is always unhelpful. Receiving suggestions and brainstorming strategies can be useful, as long as we don't feel pressured or told what to do.

The best way to avoid unwanted advice is to tell people how they can help. Let them know that you appreciate their support and their willingness to listen, and that this in itself is helpful. Also let them know that they cannot solve your problems (although you might value some suggestions) as only you can work out what is right for you. This may actually come as a relief—once people realise that they don't have to fix your depression, they can relax and just be there for you.

A second thing to be aware of is other people's limits. Talking too much and for too long about our problems can sometimes drive people away. While some friends are happy to listen indefinitely, others may find this wearing. Try to be sensitive to people's needs and to know when to stop. (If you feel a strong need to talk about your issues try writing in a diary, talking into a recorder or seeing a therapist.)

One of the best ways to use our available social support is to share activities with others. Accompany your friend to a movie, go out for lunch or a coffee, go for a walk or do dinner and a show. If you feel up to it, challenge yourself with something more energetic, such as a game of tennis, a jog in the park, a swim or a game of golf. Activities like these provide the opportunity to enjoy the company of others and disconnect from thinking about our problems. If you are able to focus on the activity itself and take an interest in the people around you, this will also make you feel better.

> The depressed person is constantly chewing on himself. He needs to find something else to chew on. The form of diversion is not important, but the act of diversion is.
>
> **PENELOPE RUSSIANOFF,** *WHEN AM I GOING TO BE HAPPY?*

RELAPSE PREVENTION STRATEGIES

People who have had previous episodes of depression are at increased risk of further episodes. Creating a lifestyle that is meaningful and satisfying not only contributes to personal wellbeing, but may also protect against future episodes of depression. The following section describes some strategies that can reduce the risk of relapse.

DEVELOP MEANINGFUL INTERESTS—FIND YOUR PASSION!

*Develop interest in life as you see it—in people, things, literature, music.
The world is so rich, simply throbbing with rich treasures, beautiful souls
and interesting people. Forget yourself.*

HENRY MILLER

We all know someone who has a passion for something they love doing. We
know that it is a passion because they talk about it with great excitement
and they want to do it as often as they can. The object of their passion
may be totally remote from anything we can relate to—steam trains, base
jumping, seventeenth-century baroque music, model aeroplanes, scuba
diving, motorcycles, poetry, football, playing the guitar or bird watching.
It is not the activity that defines a passion, but the enthusiasm with which
it is pursued.

In his book *Flow*, Hungarian-born psychology professor Mihaly
Csikszentmihalyi describes a state of total involvement and immersion in
an activity that is satisfying and meaningful. In this state of 'flow' we are so
absorbed in what we are doing that we are barely conscious of other things
around us. For instance, we might not notice noises, other people's presence
or the passing of time. We feel in harmony with the object of our attention.
Any activity we love doing or that absorbs us in this way may also provide
protection from depression. Activities that involve active participation
(rather than mere observation) and some interaction with other people are
usually the most protective.

Ask yourself, 'What do I love doing? What is my passion?' If at this
stage your answer is 'Nothing', it is a good time to consider your options.
Think about some activities that you might enjoy. Keep in mind that a
passion is very often acquired over time. It starts as an interest and gradually
develops into something more as we keep doing it. It may take months or
even years to find something that we truly love doing. That's OK. In the
meantime enjoy exploring!

A good place to start is with courses offered through adult education
centres, or by joining activities that your friends enjoy. Another great

source is the internet. Websites like Meetup.com provide opportunities to get involved in a range of interest groups and to connect with people with similar interests who are also seeking to make friends. Choose one or two activities that sound interesting and commit yourself to giving it a go for at least six months. (Don't give up too quickly as it sometimes takes months before we come to appreciate new interests.)

To start you thinking, here are some activities that some people get passionate about:

- tennis
- sailing
- weightlifting
- going to the gym
- cricket
- fishing
- pottery
- print making
- patchwork quilting
- amateur theatre
- writing short stories
- card games
- computer games
- internet chat sites
- watching movies
- playing a musical instrument

- golf
- roller-blading
- scuba diving
- soccer
- rowing
- bird watching
- leadlighting
- sculpturing
- computer graphics
- singing in a choir
- writing poetry or plays
- collecting stamps
- playing chess
- joining a singles club
- going to the theatre
- joining a foreign language club

- bushwalking
- dancing
- skiing
- softball
- touch football
- sketching
- woodwork
- embroidery
- reading books
- cooking
- visiting art galleries
- public speaking
- painting
- joining a bridge club
- yoga
- joining a political movement or group

... when we commit ourselves, particularly together with other people, we become part of something larger than ourselves. And we are distracted from the despair of a life lived in solitary, obsessive fixation on ourselves. Our headlights again are turned outwards, illuminating the wonder of the world around us, instead of inward, blinding us to everything but our own unhappiness.

PENELOPE RUSSIANOFF, *WHEN AM I GOING TO BE HAPPY?*

EXERCISE

Doing regular physical exercise, such as brisk walking, jogging, swimming, cycling, rowing or working out in a gym, enhances our mood and provides protection from depression. Studies have found that regular exercise can be as effective as antidepressant medication among people with mild to moderate depression. There are different theories on how it works, from boosting the production of endorphins (the body's natural opiates) to increasing mood-elevating neurotransmitters such as norepinephrine and dopamine. Regular exercise also increases our energy levels in the longer term, which gives us greater reserves with which to manage stress. By turning attention to our bodies, exercise also provides a distraction from negative thoughts. It also enhances our self-efficacy, as the commitment to participate in something challenging, yet important helps us to feel good and increases our perception of control. The commitment to regular exercise can be a symbol of our active participation in life—the willingness to work on something that is challenging, but makes us feel physically and psychologically well.

DEVELOP YOUR RESOURCES

Everyone experiences negative events at times, but not everyone gets depressed. How we respond largely depends on the resources available to us. These are the things that help us to cope during difficult times, including:

➤ **cognitive flexibility:** the ability to adapt to stressful or challenging situations, and to be able to perceive things in a balanced, reasonable way;

➤ **healthy self-esteem:** the belief that we are as important and worthwhile as everyone else;

➤ **self-efficacy:** the belief that we are able to solve our problems and achieve the things that we want;

➤ **effective communication skills:** the ability to express our thoughts, feelings and wants in a clear and reasonable manner;

➤ **social support:** having friends, family and social networks that we connect with;

➤ **interests:** the things that we engage in beyond our regular commitments, for pleasure and stimulation; and

➤ **a sense of purpose:** having things in our life (e.g. work or an involvement in a cause) that give us meaning and purpose; believing that what we do matters.

Our resources are not fixed at birth—they are accrued over the course of our lives. We can make a deliberate decision to develop or enhance some of our resources. For instance, we can develop cognitive flexibility by reading books, using online CBT programs, noticing and challenging biased and unreasonable thoughts, and practising mindfulness techniques. We can work to improve our self-esteem by consciously relinquishing self-diminishing habits (see Chapter 7) and we can improve the quality of our relationships by using effective communication strategies (see Chapter 10). We can develop a more extensive and supportive network of friends by joining interest groups, taking social risks, improving our communication skills and initiating social contacts. We can develop new interests by searching for activities that appeal to us, enrolling in courses and joining clubs. Much of the information presented in this and other self-help books provide strategies for increasing our resources and motivating ourselves to access and utilise them in a way that enriches our lives. It is useful to think about the resources that we already have, and to identify any areas that we would like to improve.

EXERCISE 8.3

1 Describe the resources that are available to you, which help you to feel good and protect you from becoming depressed.
2 Describe any additional resources that you would like to acquire. What would you need to do in order to develop these resources?

MAKE A RELAPSE-PREVENTION PLAN

The onset of a depressive episode usually begins with signs, such as depressed mood, social withdrawal, loss of motivation and rumination. A relapse-prevention plan can prevent the escalation of symptoms and may avert a relapse to a major depressive episode. If you have experienced depression in the past, it is a good idea to make a plan of how you will respond if depressive symptoms start to re-emerge. Prevention is always better than cure, and taking pre-emptive steps is preferable to seeking treatment after depression has spiralled.

Because Anna has suffered previous episodes of depression, she is familiar with the symptoms that signal the potential onset of a new episode. Anna has written the following relapse-prevention plan, which she starts to implement as soon as signs of depression start to emerge.

➤ Get out of bed by 7 am, no matter how I feel. This is not negotiable.
➤ Go for a brisk walk every day—at least 45 minutes. Listen to my favourite music while walking.
➤ Call my supportive friends, Susie, Bronny or Jill, and tell them how I feel. Don't isolate myself.
➤ Practise mindfulness meditation—at least 30 minutes per day.
➤ Monitor my thoughts in daily life, label 'ruminating again' when I notice ruminations, and remind myself that these are 'just thoughts' when I am caught up in negative thinking.
➤ Stay active—keep going to work, write in my journal, talk on the phone, play computer games, cook dinner and clean up my room.
➤ Read *Change Your Thinking*. Fill out thought-monitoring forms every day.
➤ Work through the Moodgym online self-help program.
➤ Talk to my partner about how I am feeling.
➤ If I'm not feeling better in three days, see my psychologist.

MEDICATION

People's ability to respond to 'talking therapies' like CBT depends on the type of depression they are experiencing, as well as their coping resources and self-awareness. While CBT is normally very useful, not everyone recovers with psychological therapy or self-help strategies alone. For those who experience little improvement, the option of medication is normally considered. Mental-health practitioners often recommend medication for people who have biologically based depression or severe depression that is not responding to treatment, for those who are suicidal and those whose depression seriously impacts on their ability to function. Antidepressant medications frequently reduce anxiety as well as depression, and so provide benefits for individuals who are experiencing mixed depression and anxiety. (They are also frequently helpful in the management of anxiety disorders.)

Doctors and psychiatrists can prescribe antidepressant medications. They are most commonly prescribed by general practitioners (GPs)—usually the first port of call for people who are depressed. Sometimes depressed people are referred to psychiatrists because they have expertise in the pharmacological therapies, and can therefore prescribe suitable medications. Clinical or counselling psychologists have expertise in the use of talking therapies for treating psychological problems and disorders, but they cannot prescribe medication. Thus psychologists who believe that antidepressant medication is appropriate will normally refer clients to their GPs for medication. Antidepressants are usually given as a temporary measure, with the length of treatment depending on the nature of the depression (frequently six to twelve months). For people who have suffered previous episodes of depression, longer treatment is often recommended—sometimes two years or more.

Many people benefit from a combination of antidepressant medication and CBT. Adding CBT to medication has been found to reduce the risk of future relapse when compared to treatment with medication alone.

Antidepressant medication sometimes produces side-effects. Common side effects include dry mouth, agitation, insomnia, nausea, headache, tiredness, mild tremor and diminished libido. While many side effects decrease or disappear after a few weeks, some people are unable to tolerate them. It is not uncommon for people to try different medications before they find one that suits them.

There are dozens of medications on the market and research continues into the development of new and better varieties. Although chemically different, most work through increasing the availability of neurotransmitters (such as serotonin, norepinephrine and dopamine) within the brain. The decision as to which particular antidepressant medication should be prescribed is usually based on the individual's specific symptoms and what has worked in the past. For instance, some antidepressant medications also have a sedating effect and are therefore useful for people who have trouble sleeping. Some appear to have less adverse effects on libido, which makes them suitable for people who are particularly concerned about impaired sexual function. Certain antidepressants have also been shown to be effective in the treatment of particular disorders, such as bulimia or obsessive compulsive disorder, and are therefore prescribed for people with those disorders. Some medications are not suitable for people who have cardiac disease, and a few have negative interactions with other drugs and are therefore not prescribed for those individuals. Certain types of depression do not respond well to treatment with one category of medication, but respond better to other categories. The person prescribing medication normally takes these issues into account.

Studies have found that about two thirds of people respond to treatment with antidepressant medication. Some feel dramatically better, some only a little better and others experience no change at all. From the time of commencing medication, it often takes two to four weeks before a substantial improvement is felt, although most people who are going to respond start to feel some improvement in the first ten days. Sometimes the dose needs to be increased before the full benefits can be felt. Any change in the recommended dose should be done with the supervision of a doctor or psychiatrist.

When an antidepressant medication starts working people often feel significantly better. If you have been taking antidepressant medication for three to six weeks but have not experienced any improvement, you should see the prescribing clinician to have the dose adjusted or change to another medication. It is not uncommon for people to try two or three different types of medication before they find one that suits them.

OTHER BIOLOGICAL TREATMENTS

ELECTROCONVULSIVE SHOCK TREATMENT (ECT)

For many people ECT brings to mind images from *One Flew Over the Cuckoo's Nest*, where Jack Nicholson's character was 'zapped' in order to make him compliant. In spite of the bad 'look', ECT is often highly effective, and is particularly useful for melancholic and psychotic depression. Its use is limited to severe depression that does not respond to other treatments.

Modern procedures have eliminated most of the unpleasant effects that used to be associated with ECT. The patient is given a short-acting general anaesthetic and a muscle relaxant before an electric current is applied to a carefully selected site on one side of the brain. The convulsive spasms caused by the current are barely perceptible to onlookers, and the patient awakens a few minutes later, remembering nothing about the treatment. To reduce the risk of relapse, ECT is given in a series of treatments (usually between four and fifteen) about two or three times per week. The most common side effects are loss of short-term memory and confusion. ECT works more rapidly than antidepressant drugs and is generally regarded as safe and effective; however, it does not prevent the recurrence of future depressive episodes.

BIOLOGICAL TREATMENTS CURRENTLY UNDER INVESTIGATION

Research is currently being conducted on other treatments that involve directly stimulating the brain. These include **direct current stimulation** (which involves passing a weak current through the scalp to the front part of the brain), **transcranial magnetic stimulation** (which involves applying an electric coil that uses rapidly changing magnetic fields to induce small electrical currents in the brain) and **magnetic seizure therapy** (which involves the induction of a brief seizure through magnetic stimulation rather than electrical current). As these treatments are less invasive than ECT and side effects are minor or rare, there is a great deal of interest in their possible benefits and applications for people with depression. It is hoped that the current research will lead to new effective treatments for people who do not respond to, or cannot tolerate existing treatments for depression.

IN SUMMARY

➤ Depression is often triggered by stressful life events; however, biological factors, personality, cognitive style and coping resources also play a role in its onset and features.

➤ During a depressive episode, cognitions become negative and self-defeating. This in turn perpetuates depressed mood and decreases energy and motivation. The resulting inactivity gives rise to further negative thoughts, which maintain or increase depressive symptoms via a self-perpetuating spiral.

➤ The ruminations that accompany a depressive episode contribute to its maintenance.

➤ Positive beliefs about the value of self-criticism, rumination, and negative thinking encourage maintenance of these habits. Challenging these beliefs can motivate us to release unhelpful thinking habits that perpetuate depression.

➤ Activities that provide a sense of achievement or pleasure tend to elevate mood and distract from negative ruminations. Social activities and physical exercise are particularly helpful.

➤ If depression does not respond to self-help strategies, it is advisable to see a mental-health practitioner. In some cases, antidepressant medication may be recommended.

NINE

Taking charge

It is in the process of meeting and solving problems that life has its
meaning.

M. SCOTT PECK, *THE ROAD LESS TRAVELED*

Life is full of problems. Some are minor irritations, while others are major
hardships that can trouble us for years. Problems arise in our relationships,
finances, health, work and home. On top of that, there are the normal
demands and frustrations of everyday life: deadlines, traffic, teenage kids
and mounting bills. As some problems get resolved, new ones appear. That
is the nature of things.

➤ *Henry has high blood pressure. Following his recent medical
assessment, he has been told by his doctor that he is at serious risk
of having a heart attack.*

➤ *Lee is struggling with his repayments on his mortgage, due to
rising interest rates.*

➤ *Simon has made some incorrect statements on his tax return and
has been summoned by the tax office for an audit.*

➤ *Helen's daughter has dropped out of school and spends her time
watching TV.*

➤ *Ross has been caught driving under the influence of alcohol and is
likely to lose his driver's licence.*

➤ *Mary has discovered that she is pregnant following a casual
Saturday night liaison.*

➤ *Lucy has lost her job.*

➤ *Eleni will have to sell her lovely house in order to finance her divorce settlement.*

➤ *Nancy has had a fiery argument with her boyfriend, and now it seems that the relationship is over.*

One of the challenges of being human is to confront and solve problems. Our ability to solve problems affects our sense of control and quality of life. When we see our problems as a challenge, we feel motivated to look for solutions. The very act of contemplating, planning and implementing a strategy makes us feel good and increases our perception of control. This is important, as it is the feeling of not being in control that frequently creates stress. Feeling helpless drains our energy and makes us miserable.

Approaching life's challenges with the spirit of problem solving benefits us in two ways:

1   It increases the likelihood of finding solutions and, therefore, getting our needs met more often.

2   It gives us a psychological boost. We feel empowered when we take control.

Do the thing, and you will have the power.

EMERSON

But sometimes we find ourselves in situations where there is nothing we can do to fix or modify a problem. In those circumstances, our challenge is to **practise acceptance**—to acknowledge that the situation is beyond our control and to accept that this is how it is. (In fact, the ability to accept situations that are beyond our control is actually a way of exercising some control—we *choose* to let it go.)

In many situations, however, there are things we can do to either resolve the problem or reduce its impact. Sometimes the solutions are obvious; at other times, we need to explore the options to discover what might work. While the answers are not always clear-cut, the secret is to see problems as a challenge—a puzzle to be solved. When you start with the presumption that solutions exist, you are more likely to find them.

If it's going to be, it's up to me!

SOLVING PROBLEMS

Our ability to overcome our difficulties depends on both the situation itself and the available personal resources we have to respond to it. These include our attitudes, beliefs, knowledge, strategies and problem-solving skills.

PRESUME THAT SOLUTIONS EXIST

An exercise that I occasionally do in workshops is to ask participants to come up with 50 possible uses for a paper clip. Sounds impossible at first, but when I reassure people that our record is 102, the creative juices start to flow. After some time, I ask participants to join up with four other people and continue brainstorming in groups. At this stage, the ideas come flooding in. Not only can we get more ideas from other people, but there is a synergy that happens when we bounce ideas off others. The list of ideas grows and grows.

There are two main lessons that we can learn from this exercise. Firstly, when we believe that solutions exist, we are more willing to look for them, and therefore are more likely to find them. Secondly, when we recruit the support of other people, we can usually come up with more, and often better, ideas. People are great resources.

FINDING SOLUTIONS

Some situations lend themselves to problem solving more easily than others. Sometimes the solutions are obvious and, while we may not always be keen to make the effort, we know what we need to do. Henry, for instance, who has recently discovered that he is at risk of a heart attack, knows exactly what he needs to do—stop smoking, improve his diet, embark on a regular exercise regime and make some lifestyle changes to reduce his stress levels. Lee, who is struggling to keep up with his mortgage repayments, also has some options—re-negotiate the terms of his bank loan, borrow some money from his father or sell some of his shares to give himself breathing space.

But what about the tough ones—those difficult situations for which no obvious solutions exist? Just like the exercise with the paper clip, these situations challenge us to think creatively. Brainstorming possible options and then narrowing them down to a short list is the best way to work out what needs to be done.

> The will to succeed is important, but what's more important is
> the will to prepare.
>
> **BOBBY KNIGHT**

STRUCTURED PROBLEM SOLVING

To solve a problem, we need to decide what we want to achieve and how to go about it. Setting clear goals is an important part of the process. Sometimes the steps may be as simple as 'call and explain'; more often, working towards goals requires thought and planning. The following steps can be useful when we are dealing with more complex problems:

1 DEFINE THE PROBLEM CLEARLY.

When we feel overwhelmed by life's circumstances, the problem may appear large and insurmountable. Clearly defining the problem makes the situation feel more manageable and draws attention to the things we need to work on.

2 BRAINSTORM POSSIBLE SOLUTIONS.

When solutions are not obvious, we need to think creatively. Brainstorming helps us to explore a wider range of options and can lead to better solutions. Because this is a creative process, it is important to think laterally and to write down all ideas, even those that initially seem silly or impractical (silly ideas can sometimes lead to clever ideas). It may also be helpful to ask other people for their suggestions and to add their strategies to your list.

3 IDENTIFY THE BEST SOLUTIONS.

The next step is to think about the ideas you have generated and eliminate those that are not feasible or realistic. Identify the most potentially workable solutions—the ones that feel worthy of consideration. Once again, it may be helpful to talk to other people during this process.

4 SET CLEAR GOALS.

From your list of potentially workable solutions, write down specific goals. These will become the focus of your future actions.

5 BREAK DOWN YOUR LARGER GOALS INTO SUBGOALS.

For more complex goals or those that require some planning, it is often helpful to break them down into small chunks or 'subgoals'. These are the stepping stones to your main goals. Setting a deadline for each step can provide an additional psychological boost.

> *Chris has been running a busy real-estate agency for the past ten years. For most of that time the business has been successful; however, in the past two years sales have plummeted. While part of the problem has been a downturn in the economy, the biggest contributor has been low morale and lack of motivation among the sales staff. Chris knows that unless things improve, he will be facing bankruptcy in the next twelve months.*

Chris decides to do some problem solving to come up with strategies that will help him turn things around. He invites a colleague who also works in real estate to discuss options. Chris writes the following notes:

1 DEFINE THE PROBLEM.
- Large drop in sales over the last two years.
- Currently operating at a loss.
- Poor performance and low morale among the sales team.
- High staff turnover.

2 BRAINSTORM POSSIBLE SOLUTIONS.
- Sack the entire sales team and employ a new team.
- Sack three employees who are performing particularly badly.

- Implement more financial incentives for staff to work harder.
- Do a major restructure of staff positions, responsibilities and salaries.
- Offer a voluntary redundancy package to low-performing staff.
- Run motivational sessions to build up enthusiasm and team spirit.
- Team building weekends—invite sales team and their partners to come sailing on the weekend.
- Organise motivational workshops.
- Schedule weekly staff meetings to discuss performance and productivity issues.
- Send some of the sales team off to do training programs.
- Revise their pay structure to create greater incentive to sell.
- Close the business and invest the money in managed funds.
- Lay down the rule, 'If your sales fall below our minimum level three months in a row, you're out.'
- Initiate regular training exercises with the sales team.
- Talk to each employee individually and get their perspective on the problem.
- Invite a management consultant to come in, assess the problem and give advice.
- Talk to other real-estate proprietors for further ideas.

3 IDENTIFY THE BEST SOLUTIONS.

After exploring each idea generated in the brainstorming session, Chris identified the following as the most viable solutions:

- Call a staff meeting and talk to them as a group—ask them for their suggestions.
- Talk to each employee individually and get their perspective on the problem.
- Schedule weekly staff meetings to encourage more open communication.
- Revise pay structure to create greater incentives to sell.
- Run motivational sessions to build up enthusiasm and team spirit.
- Provide funds for training in sales and marketing.
- Be open to making other changes, based on feedback from staff.

4 SET GOALS.

Once he had compiled his list of possible solutions, Chris noticed that they fell into three main areas. From these, Chris identified three goals:

- Goal no. 1: Improve communication with the sales team.

- Goal no. 2: Create greater financial incentives for the sales team to boost their sales.

- Goal no. 3: Provide additional training programs.

5 BREAK DOWN YOUR LARGER GOALS INTO SUBGOALS.

Chris then proceeded to write subgoals for each of his three main goals:

- Goal no. 1: *Improve communication with the sales team*.
  Monday to Thursday: Talk to each member of sales team individually
  and get their perspective on our current problems.
  Friday: Call a staff meeting for the sales team and get their joint
  feedback and suggestions. Schedule weekly staff meetings to
  encourage more feedback and open discussion.
  From now on: Try to communicate more openly with staff. Be friendly
  and remind them that my door is always open. Be responsive to their
  ideas—don't dismiss anything out of hand.

- Goal no. 2: *Create greater financial incentives to boost sales*.
  Wednesday: Talk to finance about revising salary structure. Work out
  structure that provides greater rewards for higher sales. Announce
  additional bonus to employees who achieve quarterly sales above our
  target figure.
  Next week: Consult individually with each employee regarding revised
  packages.

- Goal no. 3: *Provide additional training programs.*
  Monday: Get Rosemary to call 'Training Solutions' to find out about
  training programs in sales and marketing. Bring up training at next staff
  meeting.
  Tuesday: Arrange motivational program for next month for entire staff.
  1 July: Review staff training needs. Arrange further training if
  necessary.

Now that Chris has worked out his goals and subgoals, he faces the greatest challenge of all—the follow-through. To achieve his goals, Chris will need to act on each subgoal that he has set. This means that he will communicate more openly with his staff from now on, arrange regular meetings, talk to his accountant, change the salary packages, arrange training programs and be more open to receiving feedback from his employees.

Following through with action does not mean that we must never deviate from our plan. At times when obstacles arise or new ideas emerge, it may be appropriate to revise our plans, and possibly set new goals. However, if we do choose to deviate from our original goals, this should be based on a considered decision rather than low frustration tolerance or a lack of commitment.

IDENTIFYING THE OBSTACLES

If it is simply a matter of exploring solutions, planning appropriate actions and then taking the necessary steps, why don't we just do it? Why do we find ourselves stuck in unhappy, frustrating situations when we could be making life easier for ourselves? For a variety of reasons we procrastinate, make excuses and rationalise: 'What's the use? It won't work anyway … I'll do it later when I am ready.' The desire for change may be there, but not the drive to follow through. Obstacles get in our way.

> … the elusive goal is translating intentions into action and resolutions into results. The gap between *knowing* and *doing* remains a weak link in most of our lives.
>
> **DAN MILLMAN, *NO ORDINARY MOMENTS***

When we look at the obstacles that prevent us from getting what we want, they fall into two main categories—**psychological** and **logistical**. Psychological obstacles, such as a lack of confidence, fear of failure or criticism, inertia and low frustration tolerance, are often the most challenging of all. In addition, we need to confront logistical obstacles, such as other people's needs, and lack of time, money, energy or skills. Although different, the two types of obstacles are interrelated. Confronting our psychological obstacles can clear the way for solving logistical problems. For instance, it is a lot easier to address other people's needs or find the time to work on our goals when we have overcome our own fears and doubts about our ability to achieve them.

LOGISTICAL OBSTACLES

Psychological obstacles are largely determined by our cognitive style—they may not be a problem for others if they are in our shoes. Logistical obstacles stem from the realities of our situation—others who were in our situation would also need to deal with them. Logistical obstacles challenge us to take some sort of action to address them, so that we are able to make progress towards our goals (e.g. communicate with someone; reorganise the way we spend our time; give up other competing responsibilities or change aspects of our lifestyle). Common logistical obstacles include:

TIME CONSTRAINTS

Having limited time in which to do all the things required to get what we want.

FINANCIAL CONSTRAINTS

Having insufficient funds to be able to afford working towards particular goals.

LOW ENERGY

Lacking the stamina needed to work towards our goals. This may be the result of things like stress, fatigue, age, illness, a demanding lifestyle or mental-health issues.

NEEDS OF OTHER PEOPLE

The time and commitment involved in pursuing particular goals may affect our partners, family members, work colleagues or friends. The needs or desires of other people can make it difficult to work towards our goal, especially if they do not support the things we want to achieve.

CONFLICTING GOALS

Pursuing some goals makes it more difficult to pursue others. For example, you may want to develop a business (which requires working long hours) and at the same time maintain a healthy lifestyle (which requires making time for regular exercise and not pushing yourself too hard). Or you may want to spend more time with your children but also want to get a university degree. In situations like these, we need to prioritise—work out which goals are most important at this time, and which other goals need to go on hold for the time being.

LACK OF SKILLS

Sometimes we do not have the skills to enable us to get what we want. This might be overcome by working to develop new skills (such as effective communication, time management, budgeting, cooking or internet technology). Sometimes, however, we may need to recognise that a particular goal is incompatible with our inherent aptitude and abilities, and may therefore be unrealistic, or achievable only at enormous personal cost. In these circumstances, it may be wise to reassess our goals, and perhaps come up with alternative, more realistic objectives.

PSYCHOLOGICAL OBSTACLES

These are the thoughts, feelings and attitudes that stop us from making progress on our goals. They include:

POORLY DEFINED GOALS

Vague or poorly defined goals are a common obstacle to success. Wanting things to change is not enough. To achieve specific goals we need to clearly define what we want, make a decision to actively pursue it and create a plan of action.

FEAR

Fear can stifle our motivation and keep us stuck in unhappy situations for years. Common fears include fear of failure, fear of disapproval, fear of discomfort, fear of change, fear of making the wrong decision and fear of future difficulties.

INERTIA

Humans are creatures of habit. We have a tendency to continue doing things that we have always done. Creating change requires us to confront our natural tendency to maintain established routines.

LOW FRUSTRATION TOLERANCE

Working towards goals requires self-discipline—we need to be able to tolerate the frustration and discomfort that arises along the way. We may need to give up things we enjoy, sacrifice our short-term desires for longer-term rewards, consciously move away from distractions, tolerate and deal with other people's doubts or disapproval and do things that are difficult and unpleasant. In the process we are likely to experience anxiety, frustration, boredom and guilt, with their accompanying physiological and psychological discomfort. The ability to tolerate unpleasant experiences is a strong predictor of one's ability to persevere and succeed in the longer term. (See 'The Marshmallow Test' on page 282.)

LOSING SIGHT OF OUR GOALS

Most people have busy lives, and are responding to demands from various quarters—family, work, financial obligations, health issues etc. It is not uncommon for people to commit to goals with the best of intentions, only to get sidetracked by other demands. Recognising distractions when they arise and having strategies in place to address them and then return to our goals is an important ingredient for success.

LOW SELF-EFFICACY

Self-efficacy is the belief in one's ability to get things done. When self-efficacy is low, we lack confidence in our ability to achieve our goals. Therefore we are not motivated to invest much energy in working towards them. Sometimes we need to work on building self-efficacy at the outset. In order to make progress, we need to recognise our own skills and resources, and believe that success is possible.

POOR TASK APPROACH

Many people fail to achieve particular goals because they go about it the wrong way. Whether our goal is losing weight, strengthening family relationships, starting a new business, renovating the house, motivating a child to study or improving our health, the way we approach the task is crucial to success. Poor planning and defective strategies often lead to failure. Accessing good information (which may include paying for professional help or talking to others who have had personal experience in the area) can vastly improve our chances of success.

ANXIETY

While low to moderate levels of anxiety can motivate goal-focused behaviour, high levels of anxiety often have the opposite effect. Because working towards particular goals is often anxiety provoking, many people procrastinate. This is an avoidance strategy—we keep putting it off. In addition, anxiety increases threat perceptions and so reduces confidence in our likelihood of success. This diminishes our motivation and keeps us stuck. Anxiety also contributes to sleep disturbances, poor concentration and physical exhaustion, all of which discourage goal-focused behaviour.

DEPRESSION

Like anxiety, depression impairs one's ability to concentrate, think clearly and make rational decisions. It also causes disturbed sleep, apathy and depleted energy levels. Because depression has a strong impact on physical energy and cognitive function, it is usually unrealistic to expect to be able to achieve significant goals in the presence of depression. While working towards small, short-term goals is helpful, large goals are often best set aside until the depression has resolved.

THE MARSHMALLOW TEST

In the late 1960s, psychologist Walter Mischel at Stanford University launched a now famous experiment. A succession of 4-year-olds were left in a room with a bell and a marshmallow. If they rang the bell, the researcher would return and they could eat the marshmallow. But if they were able to wait 15 minutes, they would get two marshmallows. The children's performance varied widely. Some ate the marshmallow almost immediately, while others managed to hold out for the full 15 minutes.

A follow-up study conducted many years later found that the children who waited 15 minutes on the marshmallow test subsequently achieved much higher scores on their Scholastic Aptitude Test at the end of high school. They were also rated as more dependable in surveys completed by their teachers and parents, and had less behavioural problems than those who could not wait 15 minutes. By age 32, they had lower body mass indexes, more successful careers and were less likely to have drug-related problems. These findings suggest that the ability to exercise self-control can be seen at an early age, and the trait strongly influences achievements and wellbeing further down the track.

Subsequently, researchers have found that teaching the children mental strategies to help them delay gratification enabled them to exercise much better self-control on the marshmallow test. Whether this translates into other areas of life remains to be seen. However, there is no doubt that learning to delay gratification and tolerate frustration can increase our likelihood of achieving our goals. Sometimes we need to tell ourselves: 'Don't eat that marshmallow!'

CONFRONTING OUR OBSTACLES

Once we have defined our obstacles, our next step is to plan strategies to overcome them.

> ➤ *Leonard has tried to give up smoking on a few occasions but has not succeeded.*
> ➤ *Steve would like to ask his friend to repay the $1,000 which he lent him more than two years ago.*
> ➤ *Ruth needs to do an evening course at university to upgrade her qualifications but she keeps putting it off.*
> ➤ *Helen would like to initiate a friendship with a woman at work.*

These people want particular outcomes in order to improve their lives in some way, yet all are procrastinating. Some know why they are stalling; others have a sense of wishing things to be different but have not made a commitment to taking action. Their first step is to set clear goals—define what they want to achieve and plan how they will go about it. The second step is to identify the obstacles that are likely to get in their way and plan strategies to overcome them.

DEALING WITH LOGISTICAL OBSTACLES

Logistical obstacles test our resolve. Something is in our way and we need to work out strategies that enable us to move forward. Sometimes we may need to forgo a comfortable lifestyle for a period of time, take out a loan, get into the habit of rising early in the morning or do a stress-management program. Sometimes we may need to get advice from other people, do some research or just try doing things differently for a while. Sometimes we may need to communicate with the people who will be affected by our actions to try to win their support. Sometimes we need to re-prioritise—put some of our goals on hold while we work towards our highest-priority goals. Most problems have potential solutions and the most appropriate strategies will depend on our specific circumstances and the resources available to us.

For instance, Leonard may need to change the way he spends his leisure time for the next six months so that he can avoid the people and situations that trigger his desire to smoke. In addition, he could use nicotine patches to reduce physical cravings and exercise daily to remind his lungs how good it feels to breathe. Leonard might also reward himself with a treat every fortnight, using the money he has saved through not buying cigarettes.

Steve would find it easier to ask his friend to repay his debt if he had better communication skills. It may therefore be helpful for him to read about assertive communication and to carefully plan what he is going to say. He might also consider doing an assertiveness training course so that he can get a better sense of his rights, and learn how to ask for what he wants without feeling guilty.

Ruth will need to cut down on some of her commitments so that she can concentrate on her university course over the next two years. She will also need to talk to her family to help them understand why her studies are important, and discuss with them how they can best support her.

Identifying possible solutions is usually not the hard part. Far more challenging is the follow-through—taking the necessary actions and persevering when the going gets tough. This involves moving outside of our comfort zone, and acting in spite of inertia, fear, frustration, low self-efficacy and other contributors to internal resistance. When we sort out our psychological obstacles, the logistical obstacles often become less daunting. When self-doubt and fear dissipate, problem solving usually becomes easier.

ADDRESSING PSYCHOLOGICAL OBSTACLES

Sometimes we know exactly why we are procrastinating. At other times we have no idea—we simply know that we find it hard to proceed. Our first task is to identify the source of the problem—the cognitions that underlie our resistance. The following exercise may be useful at times when we are procrastinating but don't know why.

Mindfully observing our inner state can provide useful information, including cognitions that underpin our resistance. These can subsequently be targeted using cognitive and behavioural strategies.

The following table displays cognitions that underlie procrastination among the people described in our earlier examples:

AREA OF PROCRASTINATION	UNDERLYING COGNITIONS
Leonard—giving up smoking	It's too hard. I've tried and failed before, so I am unlikely to succeed now.
Steve—asking for a debt to be repaid	He will be annoyed with me if I ask for my money back. I will feel terrible if he has negative feelings towards me. Everyone should like me.
Ruth—updating qualifications	Studying is very difficult—I may not succeed. If I fail, it will mean I'm not a very competent person. Others may think less of me. The risk is too great.
Helen—initiating a social connection with a woman at work	She will think I am desperate. If she says 'no' I will be humiliated. It's better to avoid the possibility of rejection.

Our greatest weakness lies in giving up. The most certain way to succeed is always to try just one more time.

THOMAS EDISON

CHALLENGING LIMITING THOUGHTS AND BELIEFS

Identifying the limiting thoughts and beliefs that keep us stuck can be motivating in itself. When we look at our negative cognitions, we can often see the lack of logic in our thinking, and the beliefs that can be challenged.

Our next step is to write statements that directly challenge our limiting beliefs. These statements are not magical thinking but realistic perceptions regarding what we can achieve. The process of writing and reading over these statements helps to increase motivation by challenging the cognitions that keep us stuck (see table below).

LIMITING THOUGHTS AND BELIEFS	MORE REASONABLE PERSPECTIVE
Leonard It's too hard. I've tried and failed before, so I am unlikely to succeed now.	Many ex-smokers have made repeated attempts to quit before they succeeded. Previous failures have taught me the traps. I better understand what to look out for and avoid. I now have additional strategies to help me get through the most difficult period.
Steve He will be annoyed with me if I ask for my money back. I will feel terrible if he has negative feelings towards me. Everyone should like me.	He is the one who has acted badly—I don't need to feel guilty in this situation. He may or may not be annoyed. If he is annoyed, it will be unpleasant but I will cope. This is an opportunity to develop assertiveness skills. I prefer people to like me, but I can cope if some individuals don't.
Ruth Studying is very difficult—I may not succeed. If I fail, it will mean I'm not a very competent person. Others may think less of me. The risk is too great.	I have no guarantee of success, but nothing will change if I don't give it a go. I prefer to succeed but even if I don't, it is not going to have terrible consequences. It is unlikely to affect my reputation—most people don't care either way. The only thing I am risking is my time and effort—it's not such a huge investment.
Helen She will think I am desperate. If she says 'no' I will be humiliated. It's better to avoid the possibility of rejection.	It is normal and reasonable to initiate social events, particularly as we seem to get on well. She may or may not be available. Initiating social activity does not indicate desperation—people do it all the time. There is nothing inherently shameful about initiating a social event. It is better to risk the possibility of rejection and learn to cope with it if it should happen than to always avoid risks.

The following table provides further examples of limiting thoughts and beliefs, and ways in which they may be challenged:

LIMITING THOUGHTS AND BELIEFS	MORE REASONABLE PERSPECTIVE
It may be hard or unpleasant. I should always avoid things which might be hard or unpleasant.	It may be hard or unpleasant, and that's OK. There is no reason why I must always avoid things that are hard or unpleasant. Confronting things that are difficult makes it easier to deal with difficult things in the future and makes me stronger.
It might involve lots of stress or hassles. I should avoid situations that may involve hassles.	It might involve stress or hassles, but hassles are a normal part of life. It's OK to experience hassles in the process of working towards the things I want. Confronting hassles is a good learning experience. If I can achieve my goal, it's worth the hassles.
It's too much work.	It's a lot of work, but it's not too much work. If I take one step at a time, and have reasonable expectations of how much I can achieve each day, it's manageable.
I might not succeed. It would be awful to try and fail. I should never attempt things unless I'm guaranteed success.	I have no guarantee of success but I'm guaranteed that nothing will change if I don't give it a go. I prefer to succeed but I can cope even if I don't succeed.
I can't do it. I don't have the ability to succeed.	I can achieve many things when I put my mind to it. I have achieved lots of things already. If I do my research, get good advice, and apply myself, I can optimise my chances of success.
I've already tried and failed in the past. Past failure means that it's impossible to succeed in the future.	Some things require several attempts before we finally succeed. Thomas Edison failed hundreds of times before he finally succeeded in inventing the light bulb.
The problem is too complex. Complex problems can't be resolved.	Complex problems can be tackled by breaking them down into small, manageable chunks. If I do this, and then take one step at a time, it will be less complex. It's OK to tackle complex problems.
If I fail, I'll feel awful. Failure would be a terrible thing.	Better to have tried and failed than to never have tried. There is no shame in failure—only in not giving things a go. If I try, at least I'll know that I've given it my best shot.

LIMITING THOUGHTS AND BELIEFS	MORE REASONABLE PERSPECTIVE
Other people might not like it. I should never do anything that others may disapprove of.	I need to explain to them why this goal is important, and try to recruit their support. They may not like it but they may still be willing to support me. I prefer people to approve of everything I do, but I can choose to do some things, even when certain people don't approve.

THE PLAN OF ACTION

After defining the problem, brainstorming solutions, setting goals and identifying obstacles that might get in the way, we come to the final stage—our **plan of action**. This is a blueprint for what we want to achieve and the steps we need to take to get there. In addition to our plan, we should also consider obstacles that are likely to arise, and the strategies we will use to address them.

PLAN OF ACTION

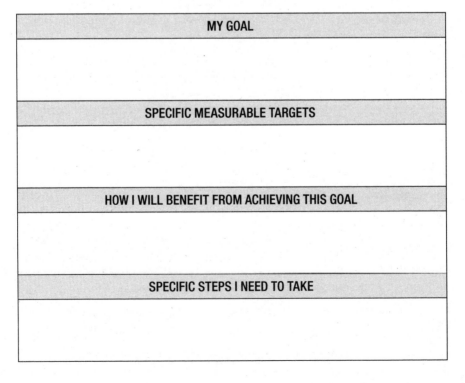

MY GOAL
SPECIFIC MEASURABLE TARGETS
HOW I WILL BENEFIT FROM ACHIEVING THIS GOAL
SPECIFIC STEPS I NEED TO TAKE

OVERCOMING THE OBSTACLES

LOGISTICAL OBSTACLES	STRATEGIES TO OVERCOME THEM

PSYCHOLOGICAL OBSTACLES	STRATEGIES TO OVERCOME THEM

Janice is in a rut. Until her mid-30s, Janice used to be a picture of health and fitness. However, since commencing a new job and working long hours, she has stopped paying attention to her health. Janice has developed the habit of eating lots of fast food, and drinking wine in the evenings to relax. Drinking at night makes it difficult for Janice to get out of bed the following morning, and consequently she has given up her regular morning jogs. Janice feels unfit and overweight. She feels particularly frustrated at not being able to get into some of her favourite clothes.

After months of concern about the direction her life is taking, Janice decides do something about it. She writes the following plan of action:

MY GOAL
I want to have a healthy lifestyle—lose weight, improve my fitness, and eat healthy food.
SPECIFIC MEASURABLE TARGETS
Lose three kilos in the next two months *by 1 November.* Jog or walk around the park (4 kilometres) on five mornings per week—*from next Monday.* Eat healthy, home-cooked meals on at least five evenings per week—*from today.*
HOW I WILL BENEFIT FROM ACHIEVING THIS GOAL
I will be healthier. I will have more energy and feel better physically and mentally. My mood will improve. I will be able to sleep better. I will feel more in control over my life. I will be able to fit into my favourite clothes.
SPECIFIC STEPS I NEED TO TAKE
• Get up at 6 am each morning on Monday to Friday and go for a jog around the park. • Buy some healthy lifestyle cookbooks to give me ideas for making healthy meals. • Go to the market every Saturday morning; buy lots of fruit and vegetables. • Choose healthy snacks, like nuts, fruit or yoghurt. Don't buy unhealthy snack foods. • Cook and freeze healthy meals to eat during the week. • Eat out on weekends only. Be selective with the meals I order—choose healthier dishes. • No alcohol during the week. Have alcohol only on weekends or special occasions. • Relax in the evenings by doing mindfulness exercises, listening to my favourite music, talking to friends or playing with my dog.

Janice now proceeds with the second part of her action plan, which involves identifying possible obstacles and planning strategies to overcome them.

LOGISTICAL OBSTACLES	STRATEGIES TO OVERCOME THEM
I find it hard to get up early in the morning to exercise. I am usually too tired.	Will go to bed at 9.30 pm from now on and read until I'm sleepy. If I stop drinking at night, I will feel less tired the next day.
My husband Jason enjoys eating out and he may not like my home-cooked meals as much.	Talk to Jason—tell him how I feel. Explain why I need to make these changes and ask for his support. Encourage Jason to take an interest in healthy food and lifestyle. Agree to eat out on weekends.
Working long hours, I don't have much time to shop and cook during the week.	Buy fruit and vegetables for the week on Saturday mornings. Cook large quantities on the weekend and freeze meals for use later in the week. Cook simple meals mid-week.
PSYCHOLOGICAL OBSTACLES	**STRATEGIES TO OVERCOME THEM**
I enjoy drinking wine at night—it helps me to relax. It will be hard to stop that now.	I am learning strategies to relax from the 'inside' without alcohol: weekly yoga classes, 20 minutes of mindfulness meditation each evening, relaxing music while cooking, playing with Rover and listening to my audio books.
I don't believe I can really change much. This could be beyond my control.	I gave up smoking four years ago, which was very difficult, so I know I can change my habits. Once I get used to feeling well and have more energy, it will be easier to stick to my new plan. I will need to remain vigilant and frequently review my goals.
I feel impatient to lose weight—like I need to get instant results.	Losing weight slowly and having realistic goals is the best way to succeed. If I focus on changing my lifestyle rather than monitoring my weight, I can get a sense of achievement straight away.
If I have a setback, it proves I can't succeed.	Setbacks and 'hiccups' will invariably occur. My job is to not to let them derail me when they occur. When I have setbacks I will not criticise myself, but I will focus on ways to get back on track, and my plans for tomorrow.

BEHAVIOURAL DISPUTING

We have already seen that behavioural disputing—changing behaviours in order to challenge cognitions—is a powerful method for altering perceptions. For instance, we might challenge the belief that certain people deserve our contempt by deliberately being pleasant towards them; we can challenge the belief that we must always be in control by deliberately choosing to relinquish control in some situations; or we might challenge the belief that rejection would be unbearable by taking social risks and experiencing the possibility of rejection.

Behavioural disputing is particularly useful when we are dealing with cognitions that dampen our motivation, such as 'It's too hard', 'I can't do it' and 'I'll probably fail'. A good way to dispute these cognitions is to make a start, in spite of the desire to put it off. Once we make progress on things we thought we couldn't do, our cognitions adjust accordingly. Experiencing even a small degree of success challenges the 'I can't do it' belief, and increases our motivation. We develop confidence in our ability to succeed as we realise that it is not so hard after all.

> Courage is not the absence of fear. It is the willingness to act,
> in spite of the fear.
>
> **M. SCOTT PECK, *THE ROAD LESS TRAVELED***

INGREDIENTS FOR SUCCESS

➤ a belief that change is possible;
➤ self-efficacy—the belief in our ability to succeed;
➤ clearly defined goals;
➤ a plan of action; and
➤ a willingness to confront the obstacles that will arise.

EXERCISE 9.2

Describe a goal that you would like to achieve or an issue that you want to resolve.

1 Are there any logistical obstacles that you need to overcome? If so, write them down.

2 Suggest some actions that could help you to overcome these obstacles.
3 Are there any psychological obstacles that might impede your ability to succeed? If so, write them down.
4 Suggest some strategies that may help you address these obstacles.
5 Can you do any behavioural disputing to challenge the obstacles that have held you back so far?

SELF-EFFICACY

Self-efficacy is the belief in our ability to achieve the things we want. Our self-efficacy varies from one task to another. For instance, you might feel confident when it comes to using a computer, fixing an electrical appliance or building a boat but not when it comes to making friends, cooking or selling yourself at a job interview.

Our self-efficacy plays an important role in the things we are willing to attempt and our motivation to persevere. It determines how hard we try and how long we are willing to persist. For example, if you have little confidence in your ability to stop smoking, improve your diet, make new friends, get a university degree or set up your own business, low self-efficacy will be a major obstacle to success.

Our self-efficacy is largely influenced by our experiences—the things that we have been able to achieve in the past. Whenever you experience success in a particular area, your self-efficacy grows for this type of task. It may even encourage you to extend yourself to more challenging tasks. Experiences of failure often have the opposite effect. To try and fail can reduce our self-efficacy, and so diminish our willingness to try again. This is particularly the case if we have experienced repeated episodes of failure.

> Whether you think you can or you think you can't, you are right.
>
> **HENRY FORD**

BUILDING SELF-EFFICACY

Self-efficacy is a perception. Like many of our perceptions, it can be modified and sometimes radically overhauled. Acknowledging our skills and abilities, as well as our past achievements can help to build self-efficacy.

ACKNOWLEDGE YOUR SKILLS AND PAST ACHIEVEMENTS

Some people who are keen to succeed set themselves unrealistic expectations, and then become self-critical when they fail to meet them. Perfectionist thinking can cause us to focus on our failures and faults, while ignoring our strengths, abilities and past successes. Self-criticism may be our way of trying to motivate ourselves to try harder. While this might seem like a good idea, it doesn't work.

A basic rule of human motivation—we are far more likely to achieve our goals when we believe that we can succeed. For this reason, it is much better to focus on our successes, strengths and achievements than to think about our shortcomings and failures. Acknowledging our skills, abilities and past successes reinforces the perception that we can succeed. Visualising some of our past successes and achievements can strengthen that belief, because we take in that information through a more emotional channel.

> No matter how well you do, it only becomes an accomplishment when you tell yourself that you did well.
>
> **BOB MONTGOMERY, *THE TRUTH ABOUT SUCCESS AND MOTIVATION***

EXERCISE 9.3
Do the self-efficacy booster exercise below and notice how your perceptions change when you recognise your existing strengths and abilities.

SELF-EFFICACY BOOSTER
1 Write down a goal—something that you would like to achieve.
2 List all the skills, abilities and strengths that you already have that will help you to achieve this goal.
3 Write down any past achievements or successes that suggest that you are capable of achieving this goal.
4 Close your eyes and visualise those past successes, as well as the things you did in order to achieve them.
5 Now visualise your new goal. Picture yourself doing things that you need to do in order to achieve the goal, as well as the final outcome. Make the imagery as vivid as possible and bring it to mind several times a day.
6 Describe any limiting thoughts or beliefs that cause you to doubt your ability to succeed and, next to each of these, write some statements that directly challenge those cognitions.

Bob has worked as an architect at a large firm for the past 15 years. While he doesn't mind the work, Bob believes that he is poorly paid and not appreciated. For this reason, a recent job advertisement for a senior position at another company caught his eye. Bob would dearly love to apply, but he is not sure that he has what it takes. It has been a long time since Bob attended a job interview, and he is not sure he can perform well under pressure. In addition, he is not sure he is good enough to do the job. Perhaps they want someone younger, with more management experience?

As long as Bob's self-efficacy is low, he is not likely to get very far. Even if Bob does manage to get to the interview, his lack of confidence will be visible in his manner, body language and the things that he says. His performance at the interview is likely to suggest that he is not up to the job. It would therefore be useful for Bob to consider his skills and realistically reflect on his strengths and abilities. To help him do this Bob completes a self-efficacy booster:

1 Write down a goal—something that you would like to achieve.
I would like to get the advertised position at Design Solutions.

2 List all the skills, abilities and strengths you already have that will help you to achieve this goal.
- I have lots of experience—I have done this type of work for the past 15 years.
- I am self-disciplined and hard-working and I enjoy doing this type of work.
- I pick up new information and concepts quickly.
- My designs have led to many new contracts at my current workplace.
- My performance appraisals have always been positive.
- I get on well with the people I work with.
- I am highly regarded by the people in management.

3 Write down any of your past achievements that provide evidence that you are capable of achieving this type of goal.
- I secured that large government contract, when most people thought it was impossible.
- I have maintained a good relationship with clients—we have had lots of repeat business and recommendations.

- I made some useful connections at the trade fair last year, which led to new projects.
- I learned to use some of our new technically complex computer software.
- In the days when I used to apply for jobs, I was successful on most occasions.

4 Close your eyes and visualise those past successes, as well as the things you did in order to achieve them.

Bob started to visualise his earlier experiences of success, as well as the preparations he made along the way that contributed to those successes.

5 Now visualise your new goal. Picture yourself doing things that you need to do in order to achieve the goal, as well as the final outcome. Make the imagery as vivid as possible and bring it to mind several times a day.

Bob started visualising himself preparing for the interview at Design Solutions, as well as seeing himself at the actual interview. Initially this generated a lot of anxiety, but after repeating the exercise several times his confidence grew. He subsequently saw himself employed at the company, sitting at his desk, and working on an exciting new project. Bob brought the imagery to mind several times a day, most often when lying in bed in the morning, when on the train to and from work, and while resting in his armchair in the evenings. It felt feasible and Bob started feeling excited.

6 Describe the limiting thoughts or beliefs that cause you to doubt your ability to succeed and, next to each of these, write some disputing statements that directly challenge them.

LIMITING THOUGHTS AND BELIEFS	DISPUTE
This position must require someone with a lot more ability than I have.	I already have lots of skills and abilities—I am highly qualified. I'll be honest with them at the interview, and if I'm not what they're looking for, that's OK.
To earn so much money, I would have to be a super-performer.	I am used to getting paid less, but that doesn't mean that I am not worth more. Many people who are paid more than me are not particularly outstanding workers.

LIMITING THOUGHTS AND BELIEFS	DISPUTE
I am 45 years old—perhaps that's too old to take on a new, high-powered position? Am I still smart enough to learn all the new things that I'll have to learn?	Being 45 gives me the advantages of experience, maturity and accrued skills. I know that I can learn new concepts, ideas and systems without difficulty.
I haven't applied for a job in a long time—I'm not sure I'll be able to sell myself.	I can sell myself effectively when I recognise my strengths and achievements. I also need to put together a good resumé and prepare myself for the interview.

You might be saying to yourself, 'That's all very well for Bob, he's performed well throughout his career. Now all he needs to do is realise it. But what about those of us who have made major mistakes, or failed at some of the things we dearly wanted to achieve?' It all comes down to how we think about 'mistakes' or 'failures'.

SEE MISTAKES AND FAILURES AS A LEARNING EXPERIENCE

The trouble with mistakes or failures is not the event itself but the negative beliefs that they may generate—'I've failed in the past, so I'll fail again.' Repeated failures are discouraging because they reduce our expectations of future success.

Developing self-efficacy involves more than recognising our strengths and achievements. It also involves acknowledging past mistakes without exaggerating or distorting their importance. The challenge is to learn from our mistakes and to use those lessons in our new endeavours, so that we increase our chances of future success.

> Let's expect to make some errors in judgement and welcome them as part of the learning process. Also, if we don't take ourselves too seriously, it is a whole lot easier to live with a few mistakes.
>
> **ANDREW MATTHEWS, *BEING HAPPY***

AVOID PERFECTIONISM

Although perfectionism is a common trait of many ambitious people, those who excel are rarely perfectionists. More often they are people who set themselves goals, aim for excellence but remain flexible enough to accept mistakes and setbacks as part of the process. In fact, perfectionism has the potential to crush motivation because we feel dissatisfied with our achievements much of the time. Unrealistic expectations can leave us feeling frustrated, discouraged, anxious or even paralysed. On the other hand, realistic expectations allow us to move forward, because it doesn't feel like there is quite so much at stake.

> Anyone who has never made a mistake has never tried anything new.
> **ALBERT EINSTEIN**

USE A REALISTIC DEFINITION OF SUCCESS

Several writers have provided definitions of the word 'success', but probably the best one I have seen is that of Dr Bob Montgomery, in his book *The Truth about Success and Motivation*. He defines success as having 'done your personal best at this stage, given your genes, past experiences and present situation'. Note that this does not mean that you always get things right or achieve what you want. It means that you do your best, given the information, abilities, energy, skills and current life circumstances that are available to you at the time. When we are able to accept that we can only do our best, given our available resources, we can be kinder to ourselves and feel successful more often.

USE SUBGOALS

Facing the challenge of an important new goal can be daunting. It is easy to feel overwhelmed and discouraged by the sheer size of the task, especially when completion is a long way off. Working towards a goal that takes months or years to achieve, such as getting a university degree, building a successful business, changing careers or writing a book, can be hard work if there is little to keep us going along the way.

This is why setting subgoals is so important. Breaking down our main goal into small chunks makes the task more manageable and adds a sense of achievement along the way. While our final target may be a long way off, our subgoals are within reach. Subgoals keep us motivated as we work our way towards the bigger target, and as we attain each subgoal our self-efficacy grows. Achieving subgoals gives us a sense of making progress, even if it happens at a slower pace than we would ideally like.

> Perseverance is not a long race; it is many short races one after the other.
>
> **WALTER ELLIOT**

SET REALISTIC SUBGOALS

As with our main goals, it is also important to be realistic with the subgoals we set for ourselves.

> *Mary is hoping to write her history essay over the next week. She has planned to do the background research on Monday, develop a rough draft on Tuesday, write the main section on Wednesday and finish off the remainder on Thursday. Like many students, Mary is finding that her essay is taking much longer to write than she had planned, and consequently she feels frustrated and discouraged. Today Mary spent the entire afternoon working on the discussion section of her essay but she has completed only half of what she had planned. Mary thinks to herself, 'Today was a total waste of time—I barely achieved anything.'*

Setting overly ambitious subgoals can leave us feeling discouraged. Mary could have saved herself a lot of frustration by setting more realistic subgoals. In addition, telling herself that she had 'wasted the entire day' is unrealistic and unhelpful. Mary would have felt better if she had acknowledged that she has made some progress, despite the fact that she did not achieve as much as she would have liked.

Telling ourselves 'I didn't do as much as I had planned but I did make some progress' helps to reinforce the idea of success and keeps us feeling optimistic. Remember, the time we spend working towards a goal is never a complete waste, even if we achieve no more than discovering what doesn't work.

WRITE A DAILY 'TO DO' LIST

A very simple yet amazingly effective tool for motivation and achievement is to write a daily 'To Do' list. This is a list of the tasks that we plan to do each day. Crossing off the items on our list as they are accomplished boosts our sense of achievement as we acknowledge our progress.

If we are not achieving many of the tasks that we had planned, it may be worth examining the reasons why. Just as it is useful to identify the obstacles to achieving our greater goals, it is also useful to reflect on the obstacles that stop us from achieving our daily goals.

COMMON OBSTACLES TO ACHIEVING DAILY GOALS

Unrealistic expectations: We were overly ambitious in what we had planned for one day.

Lack of focus: We lose sight of our goals because we don't refer to our 'To Do' list.

Low frustration tolerance: We lack the self-discipline to confront the tasks because we find them challenging or boring.

Giving way to distractions: We allow ourselves to get distracted by emails, phone calls, TV, conversations and social media.

Lower priority tasks: We engage in other, lower-priority activities because we can mentally justify them to ourselves—after all, they need to be done. However, they are not the things that we need to be working on right now.

Low energy: We find it hard to work on our tasks because our energy is low.

Anxiety: We know what we need to be doing, however, the thought of doing it makes us anxious, so we procrastinate.

Depressed mood: We feel too low to motivate ourselves to work on our goals.

Other people: Others make demands on our time, and we respond to them.

EXERCISE 9.4

Write a daily 'To Do' list for the next two weeks. At the end of each day, cross off the tasks that you have achieved. For every task you did not achieve, fill in the following form:

TASKS THAT WERE NOT ACHIEVED TODAY:

_____

_____

_____

_____

WHAT WERE THE OBSTACLES?	LESSONS LEARNED? STRATEGIES TO OVERCOME THESE OBSTACLES?
❏ Unrealistic expectations	
❏ Lack of focus	
❏ Low frustration tolerance	
❏ Giving way to distractions	
❏ Lower priority tasks	
❏ Low energy	
❏ Anxiety	
❏ Depressed mood	
❏ Other people	
❏ Other:	

KEEP IT GOING—REINFORCEMENT

Once we start to make progress, we feel good—we are on the way! It is easy to feel inspired in those initial days or weeks, but what about later? One of the biggest obstacles to getting what we want is losing sight of our goals over time. We get distracted. We forget. We stop trying. We give up.

> Persistence is a secret.
> Successful people know the secret—
> they realise that it is the main ingredient in winning at anything.
> **ANDREW MATTHEWS,** *BEING HAPPY*

Whether or not we succeed depends largely on our willingness to persist—to continue working towards our goals for as long as it takes to get there. To remain motivated over time, it is important not to lose sight of our goals. Just as certain strategies can inspire us to get started, others can help us keep up the momentum.

DISPLAY GOAL PROMPTS

The very act of defining our goal and writing a step-by-step plan for its achievement boosts our motivation—that is why preparing a plan of action is so important.

In addition, writing and displaying goal prompts helps us to stay on track. A goal prompt is a word or short phrase that represents our goal and serves as a reminder of the things we want to achieve. For instance, the word 'vitality' may remind us of our decision to build up our fitness; 'lighten up!' may remind us of our plan to take things a little less seriously; and 'communicate' may remind us of our decision to remain open and available whenever our partner brings up an issue that needs to be resolved. Display your goal prompts in prominent places to remind you of your commitment. Consider setting the goal prompt reminders on your phone or computer, or stick reminders on the fridge, the inside of your wardrobe door, the bathroom, or on a business card in the clear section of your wallet.

Every time you see your prompt, stop and ask yourself: 'Have I done anything today in relation to that goal? What can I do today or tomorrow that will bring me closer to achieving it?'

DISPLAY PHOTOS AND PICTURES THAT REMIND YOU OF YOUR GOAL

Visual images can evoke powerful emotional responses that inspire us on a deeper level. A photo or drawing that captures the spirit of what you want to achieve can serve as a compelling impetus to persist. A picture of the divan you would like to buy can remind you of the need to keep saving. A photo of you and your partner during happier times can serve as a motivator to keep working on that relationship. A picture of a dream holiday from a brochure or website can remind you of the reward that you will give yourself after you finish that important project.

VISUALISE

Research suggests that we are more likely to perform a new behaviour if we have visualised it first. As imagery has stronger links to our emotions than words, visualising can make us feel excited about our goal, and helps to keep it at the front of our mind. After you have defined your goal and made a plan of action, visualise yourself working towards it, going through each of the steps that you will need to take along the way. The more senses you employ within your imagination—sounds, textures, images, colours and smells—the more vivid the experience and the more powerful the effect.

It is also helpful to visualise the final outcome as well as the process of working towards it. After visualising yourself working towards your goal, see yourself having achieved it, enjoying the fruits of your success. For example, you might see yourself studying at home, swotting in the library, doing your exams and checking the noticeboard for your grades. Then see yourself on graduation day, stepping up to the podium as you are about to receive your diploma. Finally, see yourself working in a rewarding new job—the product of persevering with your studies.

TALK ABOUT IT

Talking about our goals reinforces our commitment and helps to keep us focused. Talking with people who share similar goals, or to those who strongly support our desire to succeed, is particularly motivating. It is also important to talk to the people who will be affected by our efforts—those whose goodwill we need to nurture along the way. When people understand what we want to achieve and why our goal is important, they are more likely to come on board, particularly if they have our best interests at heart.

Accordingly, recruiting support from your partner, children, friends, boss or work colleagues can help to smooth the path ahead.

FOCUS ON THE REWARDS THAT YOU STAND TO GAIN

The desire to receive rewards and avoid punishment is a key motivator for most animals, including humans. When we perceive the punishment associated with a course of action to be greater than the rewards, we are not motivated to act. So focusing on the possible problems, difficulties, frustrations and hassles that we might encounter as we work towards our goal is a major turn-off. On the other hand, acknowledging the challenges that are likely to arise along the way, planning strategies to address them and focusing on the rewards will have the opposite effect.

Stay mindful of all the benefits that you stand to gain—write about the rewards and visualise them on a regular basis. Be sure to include all the incidental rewards that come with success, such as improved self-efficacy and self-esteem, benefits to others and a sense of personal satisfaction.

REWARD YOURSELF

Although the joy of achieving a goal is usually its own biggest reward, sometimes setting an additional prize that is conditional upon completion can provide extra motivation. Make the size of your reward proportional to the amount of effort you will need to put in. Rewards such as a massage, a new outfit, a night out at a special restaurant, a weekend away, an overseas holiday or a new car may be appropriate, depending on the effort involved. Be sure to make your reward conditional on achieving your goal—if you plan to reward yourself regardless of your achievement, it will not be an effective motivator.

USE QUOTES THAT INSPIRE YOU

Just as certain pictures can arouse emotional responses that intensify our desire to succeed, so too can words. A poem, a quote or a short piece of prose that is meaningful to you can provide additional inspiration to strengthen your desire to persist. Here are examples of quotes that some people find inspiring. If any of these move you, use them for your own spark of inspiration. Alternatively, you might prefer to look at other sources for quotes that are meaningful to you.

'Do the thing, and you will have the power.' RALPH WALDO EMERSON

'Just do it!'

'Action is the antidote to despair.' JOAN BAEZ

'If it's going to be, it's up to me.'

'Don't wait for a light to appear at the end of the tunnel.
Stride down there, and light the bloody thing yourself.'
SARA HENDERSON

'The secret to getting ahead is getting started.' AGATHA CHRISTIE

'The way we live is determined
Not by what we read or hear or think
But by the things that we do.'

'Victims spend their time pointing to the problems.
Winners spend their time looking for solutions.'

'Sucess is stumbling from failure to failure with no loss of enthusiasm.'
WINSTON CHURCHILL

IN SUMMARY

➤ Problems are an unavoidable part of life. Taking responsibility for solving problems increases our perception of control and enables us to get our needs met more often.

➤ Accepting situations that are beyond our control and focusing our efforts on situations that are changeable is both practical and psychologically healthy.

➤ For more complex problems, a systematic process of problem solving can help us find solutions. Once we have identified useful goals, it is helpful to break them down into small steps and work through them, one step at a time.

➤ When people fail to achieve their goals, it is because certain obstacles get in their way. Obstacles can be psychological (such as low self-efficacy, fear of failure, inertia and low frustration tolerance) or logistical (such as other people's needs, lack of time, money or skills). We can increase our likelihood of success by recognising obstacles that are likely to get in our way, and planning strategies to overcome them.

➤ A plan of action can keep us focused and motivated while working towards our goals. Other motivational strategies include goal prompts, visualisation, focusing on the rewards, and inspiring quotes.

TEN

Effective communication

A sweet life is a shared experience. Our greatest joys, our most precious moments, our toughest challenges and our most loving times are mostly shared with people … To have a memorable stay on this planet we must be prepared to knock down some barriers—make a special effort to meet, be with, get close to people.

ANDREW MATTHEWS, *MAKING FRIENDS*

Communication is the process through which we connect with people, share information, disclose our concerns and negotiate solutions to our problems. Good communication is essential for successful relationships. It enables us to make friends and develop bonds. Without communication, we would be isolated in our own solitary world. We would also be unable to solve many of our problems or get our needs met most of the time.

Dennis is constantly getting into trouble in his personal relationships. Whenever he needs to resolve a problem, his attempts at communication invariably end in unpleasant confrontations that upset both himself and the other person. Over time, Dennis has managed to alienate many of the people that he deals with, both at work and in his private life. Finally, he concludes that trying to resolve issues by communicating only makes things worse and he decides on a new strategy—say nothing. Although this enables Dennis to avoid unpleasant confrontations, it also prevents him from getting his needs met and causes him to feel frustrated and resentful much of the time.

'No matter what I do, I just can't win,' he thinks to himself. Like many people, Dennis doesn't realise that it is not communication in itself, but the way that he communicates that gets him into trouble.

Many people have poor communication habits and so, like Dennis, they frequently find themselves alienating people and experiencing tension within their relationships. Others communicate pretty well most of the time but get into difficulties when they need to confront someone or ask for what they want. Being an effective communicator is much more than having a good command over the English language—in fact, many people have a great vocabulary but do not communicate well. Effective communication means expressing ourselves in a way that increases mutual understanding and promotes goodwill. When we communicate effectively, people understand what we think and how we feel, and do not feel threatened or under attack. Although other people will not always agree to do what we want, effective communication also increases our likelihood of getting our needs met.

Throughout our lives, we experience hundreds of thousands of situations in which we need to negotiate or resolve a problem by communicating with someone—a partner, family member, friend, work colleague, supervisor, neighbour, tradesman, shop assistant or stranger. The issue may be as minor as having to ask someone to move their car or as significant as informing a partner that the relationship is over. Regardless of the circumstances, the way in which we communicate will determine the tone of our discussion, how effectively we resolve the problem, how we feel afterwards and how amicable our relationships remain in the longer term. Applying the techniques that are described in this chapter can make a big difference to the way we interact with people and can determine whether our relationships are based on mutual understanding or distrust.

POOR COMMUNICATION HABITS

When we look at the reasons why people experience problems in their relationships, we invariably find poor communication habits. The most common of these are avoidance and alienating messages.

AVOIDANCE

Good communication involves saying what we think, feel or want in a way that increases mutual understanding and reduces the perception of threat and the likelihood of conflict. When we are dealing with an issue that we believe other people will not approve of, the idea of communication often makes us feel anxious or uncomfortable. Low frustration tolerance and fear of conflict or disapproval may cause us to withdraw, procrastinate and avoid the issue. We put off saying what we need to say to avoid the discomfort that comes with tackling potentially unpleasant situations. The trouble with avoidance is that it prevents problems from being discussed and resolved, and consequently it leads to tension and resentment. So while we evade the short-term pain of raising issues that make us uncomfortable, we sabotage our greater goals—to solve problems and have healthy relationships.

Some people habitually avoid any possibility of confrontation. They are loath to initiate discussions about issues that they are concerned about and refuse to engage in conversations that make them feel uncomfortable—they may literally walk out of the room when someone brings up issues that are potentially distressing. While it is reasonable to occasionally postpone discussion when we feel very angry or upset, sooner or later issues need to be dealt with—even those that make us feel uncomfortable. The trouble with refusing to discuss important issues is that they do not get resolved, and consequently resentment grows, tension increases and relationships deteriorate.

Some of us choose to avoid the possibility of conflict by giving incomplete messages—conveying only part of the story. Instead of clearly saying what we think, feel or want, we drop hints, mutter under our breath or make vague comments alluding to the issue and hope that the other person will work it out. For instance, we might bring up an issue but avoid saying how we feel about it, or we might agree to do something that we don't want to do and then express our objection through brooding, withdrawal or unfriendly body language. Incomplete communication is another form of avoidance because we steer away from saying what we need to say.

COMMON BELIEFS THAT CAUSE AVOIDANCE

➤ Raising the issue will result in conflict and disapproval.

➤ I must avoid conflict or disapproval at all costs.

➤ Everyone should like and approve of me.

➤ If someone is hostile towards me, it's awful and I can't stand it.

CHALLENGING BELIEFS THAT CAUSE AVOIDANCE

➤ Raising the issue does not necessarily result in conflict. Good communication skills can actually help to minimise the likelihood of conflict.

➤ It is important to discuss certain issues, even if there's a chance that doing so may generate some conflict or disapproval.

➤ I prefer to be liked but I can cope even if some people don't like or approve of me.

➤ I prefer to avoid conflict but I can cope with conflict if it should arise. If someone is hostile towards me, it's unpleasant, but I can stand it.

ALIENATING MESSAGES

While avoidance stems from fear of conflict or disapproval, alienating messages stem from anger, defensiveness or a lack of skills. Alienating messages are expressed in a hostile, uncompromising or threatening way and therefore put others on the defensive. When others feel threatened, they stop listening to what is being said because they start planning their counterattack. As a result, it is not possible to achieve mutual understanding and goodwill.

Typical alienating messages are designed so we get our way or win an argument. It is not only the things we say but the way we say them that can alienate other people. Our facial expressions, body language and tone of voice play a huge role in the way our messages are perceived. Speaking in a belligerent tone or using hostile gestures makes people feel threatened, which in turn causes them to respond defensively or aggressively. In this atmosphere, tension escalates, and ultimately no one wins. Although we may sometimes believe that we have won the argument, it is a hollow victory if we are unable to solve problems or have good relationships.

In some situations alienating messages can intimidate others into submission or cause them to withdraw from communicating altogether. In families and workplaces, we occasionally see individuals who rule the roost through threat and intimidation. While the frequent use of alienating messages gives those people power over others, the resentment and bitterness that it generates makes for an unhappy environment and unhealthy relationships.

Alienating messages are usually expressed as 'you-statements'. Metaphorically speaking, we point our finger at the other person and suggest that they are wrong or bad. This tends to put them on the defensive and frequently triggers a hostile response. Typical alienating messages include:

LABELS

- ➤ You only think of yourself.
- ➤ You're a hopeless communicator.
- ➤ You're stingy.
- ➤ You're so neurotic!
- ➤ You're manipulative and deceitful.
- ➤ You need professional help!

OVERGENERALISATIONS

- ➤ You're never happy until you get things your own way.
- ➤ Every time you say you'll do something, you never do it.
- ➤ You always take, but you never give.
- ➤ Whenever I suggest anything, you're always negative and critical.
- ➤ You're always telling me what to do.

INFERRED MOTIVES (MIND READING)

- ➤ You conned me into doing all that extra work because you knew you could get away with it.
- ➤ You're just jealous because I've met someone and you're still single.

➤ You feel threatened when you see me with other people because you're insecure; you'd prefer it if I had no friends.

➤ You tried to make a fool of me in front of all those people.

SARCASM

➤ You're just so clever—you know everything.

➤ When was the last time you had your hearing tested? You obviously have a hearing problem.

➤ That's great! I really like the way you take my needs into account!

THREATS

➤ If you don't change your attitude, I'm going to leave you.

➤ If you ever treat me that way again, I'll tell everyone about your big secret.

➤ You do that again and you can get out of the car and walk!

Threats are not conducive to good relationships because they are based on power and intimidation rather than negotiation. One person tries to make another do what they want by threatening to hurt them in some way if they do not comply. This is the opposite of good communication, which involves respect for the other person's rights.

There are, however, some occasions where it may be appropriate to point out the consequences of another person's actions. When all reasonable communication has failed and we believe that our current message is not being heard, it is appropriate to describe the consequences if things do not change—e.g. 'If you continue to lie to me, I'm not willing to stay in this relationship'; 'If you're not prepared to complete the job satisfactorily, I'm going to lodge a claim with the Fair Claims Tribunal' and 'If you don't clean up your room, I'm not going to give you any pocket money this week'. Pointing out the negative consequences can be a useful strategy after more conciliatory negotiation has failed. However, it is effective only if it is used sparingly and if we are fully prepared to act on the consequences that we describe.

EFFECTIVE COMMUNICATION HABITS

Steering away from poor habits such as avoidance and alienating messages is an important aspect of good communication. In addition, using the following principles and communication strategies can make a substantial difference to the quality of our communication.

BE CONCILIATORY

Good communication enables us to maintain goodwill in our relationships with other people. This means that we avoid messages that are alienating. We look for win-win solutions in our negotiation with others, so that both parties feel good and no one feels disadvantaged. The secret is to always be reasonable, even when it seems that the other person is not. We do not make demands or idle threats, we do not blame or finger-point and we accept that we may not necessarily get what we want. However, we are willing to communicate how things are from our point of view.

Conciliatory = I want what's fair for all of us.

'But why should I be conciliatory, when they're not the slightest bit concerned about my feelings?' asks Dennis. The answer is that being conciliatory increases your chances of getting what you want. It gives you power. It also lets you avoid the stress and agitation that come with a bad-tempered exchange or an escalation of conflict. It is in your interests to be conciliatory, Dennis! While sometimes it may seem easier to lash out and say what's on your mind, ultimately this doesn't help you to get what you want.

BE ASSERTIVE

Many people think that being assertive simply means standing up for your rights. While this is one aspect of assertive communication, it is not the whole story. Being assertive means that we are willing to honestly express our thoughts, feelings and needs in a way that also takes into account the rights of other people. The spirit of our communication is: 'We both matter—let's try to understand each other.' Assertive communication enables people to have healthy relationships based on mutual respect.

The willingness to communicate assertively comes from recognition of our own self-worth. We do not see ourselves as superior to others but we recognise that our needs are just as valid as anyone else's. This does not mean that we are inflexible and insist that we must always get our own way—good relationships involve negotiation and compromise. However, we are willing to express ourselves honestly and clearly and we are prepared to ask for what we want.

MAKING REQUESTS

An important aspect of assertive communication is the ability to make requests or express our needs to others. Often all that is required is a brief statement describing what we want:

> ➤ Marcella, I'm taking the train into work today, so would you be able you pick me up from the station this afternoon?
> ➤ I'd like to spend the weekend with my daughter. Is that OK with you?
> ➤ Lorraine, I need to talk to you about the project. Will you be available at 10 this morning?
> ➤ I have to work back until late this evening. Can you cook the dinner tonight?
> ➤ Luc, I'm finding it difficult to concentrate with all the noise—could you please turn the TV down?
> ➤ Tony, I need those accounts by this afternoon. Will you be able to have them ready by then?
> ➤ Ricki, it worries me that you spend so much time on the internet. Could you finish your homework first, before you do that?

In the majority of situations, asking for what we want is reasonably straightforward. However, sometimes we may expect that others will feel threatened, annoyed or put out by our request. In these situations, the way we communicate can make the difference between a happy resolution or a major brawl. The following techniques are particularly useful when more skilful negotiation is called for.

CREATING CONCILIATORY MESSAGES

I-STATEMENTS

I-statements are a simple and effective technique for communicating messages in a conciliatory way. When we use I-statements, we describe our own feelings and preferences without blaming or criticising the other person. By pointing the finger at ourselves, we reduce the likelihood that others will feel threatened, which then opens the door for conciliatory negotiation.

When someone has said or done something that we are unhappy about, making an I-statement can help to communicate our concerns in a non-threatening way. Typical I-statements describe the person's behaviour that is problematic to us, the way we feel about it and the alternative behaviour that we would prefer:

When you … I feel … I'd like (or prefer) …

➤ Bill, when you criticise me in front of other people, I feel embarrassed and upset. I'd like you to treat me with respect, whether we're with other people or on our own.

➤ Sally, when you keep giving me extra jobs while I'm still working on earlier projects, I feel overwhelmed. I'd prefer it if some of those new projects were distributed among our support staff.

➤ Dad, when you tell me that I'm neglecting my children, I feel angry and hurt. I'd like you to have faith in my ability to look after my kids.

➤ Jimmy, when you stay out late without letting me know where you are, I feel very worried. I'd like you to call me if you are going to come home after midnight.

➤ Sarah, when you interrupt me when I'm telling a story, I feel frustrated and annoyed. I'd like to you allow me to finish what I am saying, without trying to edit it.

A major advantage of using I-statements is that they focus on behaviours rather than the person. This is an important distinction because behaviours are something that people can change. When we focus on behaviours, we are not attacking the person but describing the way their actions affect us and the changes we would like.

As a general rule, when people know how we feel and what we want and they do not feel under attack, they are more likely to respond in a conciliatory way. Although there are no guarantees, in most situations clear, non-threatening statements increase the likelihood of getting our needs met.

WHOLE MESSAGES

I-statements are useful for conveying our feelings and preferences in situations that are reasonably straightforward. However, some situations are more complex, and using an I-statement may not adequately convey why we think and feel the way we do. In these situations it is often useful to provide a more complete picture of how things look from our point of view. This is particularly the case in potentially threatening situations, where we want to minimise the likelihood of conflict.

In the book *Messages*, Matthew McKay, Martha Davis and Patrick Fanning describe the use of whole messages for communicating in a clear and conciliatory manner.

Whole messages describe:
- ➤ observations,
- ➤ thoughts,
- ➤ feelings and
- ➤ needs.

Whole messages are a form of I-statements, in that they describe the problematic behaviour, how we feel about it and what we want. However, they also provide a description of our own observations and thoughts, and therefore convey a more complete picture of how things are from our point of view.

Communication using whole messages is particularly useful at times when we need to discuss issues that we believe might generate disagreement, disapproval or conflict. A whole message clearly communicates what we need to say in a reasonable and non-threatening way. This increases the likelihood of constructive engagement with the other person. As we develop confidence in our ability to use whole messages, we discover that discussing contentious issues does not necessarily result in conflict. In fact, it very often helps to clear the air and enables potential conflicts to be resolved. Consequently, the idea of raising a difficult issue or responding to one that has been raised by someone else becomes less daunting. While communication using whole messages does not always resolve the issue, it opens the door for non-threatening engagement and therefore increases the chances of reaching a mutually acceptable solution.

OBSERVATIONS

These are statements of fact—things that we have experienced, seen or heard. For example:

➤ I arrived half an hour late for my appointment.
➤ Katy asked me why Daddy doesn't come home any more.
➤ I haven't had a holiday for two years.
➤ I heard that you told them that I was leaving the company.
➤ Tom is starting a new job next week.

A central feature of whole messages is that our observations are **objective** and unbiased. We avoid making emotive statements, jumping to conclusions or trying to interpret the other person's motives.

EMOTIVE STATEMENTS	OBJECTIVE STATEMENTS
When you made a fool of me in front of all those people …	When you said that I'm 'not very bright' in front of all those people …
You're just playing power games with me.	You've become very quiet and uncommunicative lately.
You're blaming me because you don't see your son, Adam, very often.	Whenever we talk about Adam, you become quiet and you look upset.

THOUGHTS

These are our perceptions and opinions. When we describe our thoughts, we reveal subjective information about how things are from our point of view. For example:

➤ I think you're being very hard on yourself—you're doing your best.

➤ I sometimes wonder if your heart is in the job.

➤ It seems unfair that I work full-time and do most of the housework as well.

➤ I'm not sure if I'm going to be able to cope with all that extra pressure.

➤ I think it would be good if you saw the children more frequently.

FEELINGS

Feelings are statements that describe our emotional response. For example:

➤ I feel upset that you made that decision without consulting me first.

➤ I'm so grateful that you've been here for me during this difficult time.

➤ You say your friendship with Marieta is platonic, but I can't help feeling threatened.

➤ I feel relieved that we're finally making progress.

➤ I feel anxious that I won't be able to do a good job.

NEEDS

These are statements describing what we need or want. It's important that our needs are not expressed as demands, but as requests or preferences.

➤ I need some help with this project—do you think you can spare some time for me?

➤ I'd like you to take some more responsibility with doing the housework.

➤ I want you to tell me if you're unhappy with something I have done, rather than withdrawing or brooding.

➤ I'd like you to be more affectionate towards me, and show me that you care.

➤ Could you give me a hand with bathing the kids and putting them to bed?

When we use whole messages, we make a statement describing our observations, thoughts, feelings and needs (not necessarily in that order). In some situations, we may not need to describe either our thoughts or our feelings because they are implied by the rest of our statement. For this reason, in the examples below we see Thoughts/Feelings displayed as one item. The heading actually implies Thoughts and/or Feelings.

Sandra is angry that her husband, Matt, rarely makes an effort to talk to her girlfriend, Dianne, when she comes to their home. Sandra had said nothing for weeks (avoidance), until one day she exploded, 'You're such a pig! Would it kill you to talk to her?' (alienating message). Not surprisingly, this generated a defensive response from Matt, and a major row ensued.

Let's take a look at how she might have communicated using a whole message.

Observations: Whenever Dianne comes over, you seem to ignore her. Usually you avoid coming into the room and, on the rare occasions that you do, you don't say 'hello' or chat to her.

Thoughts/Feelings: I think she feels uncomfortable when you act like that and I suspect she thinks you're rude. I feel embarrassed and awkward when you behave that way. It upsets me that you can't be more friendly towards her.

Needs: I would like you to make an effort—to say 'hello' and to chat for just a couple of minutes—so that she feels welcome when she comes here.

Last night Tom and his girlfriend, Sheila, were with a group of friends. Tom's friend, Ralph, had recently lost his job and was describing how difficult it has been to get up in the morning with no plans and no idea of how he's going to spend the day. Much to Tom's irritation, Sheila made light of parts of Ralph's story and kept relating it to her own experiences.

Alienating message: In the car on the way home, Tom exploded, 'Can't you just listen to what someone else has to say? Why do you have to bring everything back to yourself?' Not surprisingly, Sheila became defensive, and the atmosphere became very icy between them.

Let's take a look at how Tom could have communicated using a whole message.

Observations: Sheila, I don't know if you were aware of this, but when Ralph was describing how difficult it's been for him since he lost his job, you interrupted him several times and you kept bringing up your own experiences. In the end, Ralph didn't get a chance to finish his story and he stopped talking.

Thoughts/Feelings: I felt uncomfortable. It seemed to me that Ralph was trying to talk about something very personal, and that you were making light of his story and not giving him a chance to finish.

Needs: I'd like you to be a bit more sensitive to people's feelings. If someone is telling their story, just let them finish, instead of interrupting them and talking about your own experiences.

Ian's sister, Paula, tends to become forceful, almost aggressive, whenever she expresses her opinion, especially if someone says something she disagrees with. Ian would like to be close to her but he often avoids bringing up issues because she is likely to respond badly and he doesn't want the 'aggro'. As family relationships are important to Ian, he decides to talk to her about this.

Alienating message: Why do you have to jump down my throat every time I disagree with you? Why can't you accept that people don't have to always see things your way?

Let's take a look at how Ian might have communicated using a whole message.

Observations: I don't know if you're aware of this, but often when I say things that you don't like or that you disagree with, you get very intense and a bit aggressive in your response. For instance, when I mentioned that Mum and Dad seemed lonely, you became irate and accused me of saying that you don't do enough for them. And last week, when I mentioned that Kath [Ian's daughter] was doing really well at school, you seemed annoyed and said that she's at a private school so why wouldn't she do well … You seem to get upset easily, and I find myself avoiding many issues because I don't want to end up in an argument.
Thoughts/Feelings: I feel frustrated and disappointed at the way we are communicating, as there are often things that I would like to talk to you about, but I hold back. I think that, in the end, censoring what we talk about creates distance between us.
Needs: I'd like us to be close and to be able to talk to you honestly without feeling that you're going to get angry if I say something you don't like.

PRELIMINARY STATEMENTS

Sometimes we feel anxious about raising an issue because we expect that the other person will respond aggressively to what we have to say. Making a preliminary statement acknowledging our discomfort reduces our anxiety and decreases the likelihood of a hostile or defensive response. When the other person understands that bringing up the issue is difficult for us, their perception of threat decreases, and they are therefore less likely to respond defensively. A typical preliminary statement may be:

> ➤ I want to discuss something with you, but I'm uncomfortable about bringing it up. I'm hoping that you are willing to listen with an open mind.

> ➤ I'd like to talk to you about something but I feel anxious that you're going to take it personally or get upset.

Let's take a look at how this can work in practice:

Whenever Lucy and her husband, Frank, go to dinner at Lucy's parents' place, Frank switches on the television immediately after dinner and watches TV for the rest of the night. Lucy feels upset about Frank's behaviour, but has been reluctant to bring it up with him because she doesn't want to have an argument. Finally, she has decided to talk to him about it.

Alienating message: You're so selfish—you do it every time! Is it so hard for you to just sit and talk to them?

Here is how Lucy could have communicated using a preliminary statement.

Preliminary statement: Frank, I want to bring up something that is bothering me but I don't want us to have a fight about this. I'd like you to listen with an open mind and not get annoyed.

Observations: Every Friday when we go to Mum and Dad's for dinner, immediately after the meal you sit on the couch and watch TV for the rest of the night.

Thoughts/feelings: It upsets me that you make so little effort to talk to them. I think Mum and Dad feel disappointed because it means a lot to them that we come over and they want you to be part of our discussion. When you put on the TV you withdraw from the rest of the family.

Needs: I know that you're not terribly interested in what they have to say, but could you make a bit more effort to talk to them?

Another type of preliminary statement that takes the heat out of a potentially confronting situation is a **positive acknowledgement**. This involves starting our communication by acknowledging something positive about the other person or their behaviour. For instance:

*'Frank, I really appreciate that you're making an effort with Dianne—
it's made the situation much more comfortable. But now I'd like to talk
to you about Mum and Dad.'*

*'Jolan, you've been so much more flexible since we had our talk, and I
think it's been great for both of us. But there are still times when you
overreact, such as when I told you that I had to work late on Monday.
Are you OK to talk about it?'*

*'Kim, you've been meticulous with your record-keeping since our last
review, which is a great improvement, but I still have some concerns
about your telephone manner.'*

Starting our communication with a positive statement 'lowers the
temperature' by reducing the other person's perception of threat. This
reduces the likelihood of a defensive response and consequently keeps open
the channels of communication. We are far more likely to have constructive
communication when people do not feel threatened.

REVISITING AN ISSUE

Most people are willing to bring up an issue once, but what happens if
we need to raise it again? Perhaps you have successfully negotiated an
agreement with someone, only to find that over time old habits re-emerge?
Teenage kids who agree to keep their room tidy sometimes renege after
only a few days; employees who agree to stop spending too much time on
personal phone calls may fall back into long-held habits; and a husband
who agrees to make more of an effort with the in-laws sometimes goes back
to watching TV. The re-emergence of previous behaviours usually reflects a
natural tendency to return to old patterns rather than a deliberate decision
to renege. Unless the commitment to change their behaviour is strong in
people's minds, they often lose sight of it over time.

In these circumstances, many of us make the big mistake of concluding
that communication does not work and we give up. For instance, Hugh has
already talked to his wife about her making social arrangements without

consulting him. 'She agreed to change her behaviour but now, after two weeks, she's doing it again.' Hugh thinks to himself, 'Communication gets you nowhere.' But Hugh is wrong. Good communication does work, but sometimes we need to restate our message—people need to be reminded.

'But I don't want to keep reminding her,' Hugh protests, 'it makes me feel bad to have to bring it up again.' It is true that many of us feel uncomfortable revisiting an issue that has already been dealt with, but if it remains unresolved, then that is what we need to do. The challenge is to communicate skilfully, so that our reasons for revisiting the issue are clear, and our discussion does not get bogged down in hostile accusations. In situations where people have failed to act on their promises, skilful communication can result in a stronger commitment to do the right thing the next time around.

When revisiting an issue that has already been discussed, it is a good idea to make reference to the earlier agreement, and to point out that the problem has re-emerged. If you feel uncomfortable about raising the issue for a second or third time, then acknowledge this in your message.

> *Although Ben agreed to put out the garbage when his mother asked him, an hour later he still hadn't done it. Finally she asked again, and this time he said, 'In a minute.' Half an hour later, the garbage has still not been taken out. Now his mother is tempted to do it herself; however, she decides that this would set a bad precedent—Ben would simply learn that if he procrastinates, Mum will do it for him.*

Alienating message: I can't rely on you for the smallest thing. You expect me to do things for you, but you're not willing to give an inch!

Ben's mum decides to use the situation as an opportunity to practise her communication skills. She makes the following whole message:

Observations: Ben, I asked you to put out the rubbish earlier this afternoon, and you said that you'd do it. I asked you again before, and you said that you'd do it in a minute. Now it's half an hour later and the garbage is still sitting there.

Thoughts/Feelings: I hate asking you again because it makes me feel like I'm nagging. It upsets me that I have to ask you so many times, but if I don't remind you, it seems that it doesn't get done.

Needs: I don't want to have to keep asking you to take out the garbage or keep reminding you of your commitments. I'd like to think that when you tell me that you're going to do something, I can count on you to do it.

> *Lorna has approached her landlord on two occasions regarding the broken hot water unit in her flat, and on each occasion he has told her that he will come over the next day to repair it. Now, five days later, he still hasn't come, and Lorna is still without hot water.*

Alienating message: This is your responsibility—how many times do I have to ask you? I'm going to get a tradesman to repair it and send you the bill!

Let's have a look at how Lorna could have communicated using a whole message.

Observations: I've already called you a couple of times about the hot water unit, and each time you said that you were going to come over the next day to repair it. But now five days have gone by, and you still haven't come. As you know I have no hot water at all, which means that I can't use the shower, and it's difficult for me to wash the dishes or do the laundry.

Thoughts/Feelings: I feel very frustrated because it's been almost a week, and I still don't have any hot water.

Needs: I appreciate that you're busy, but this matter needs your urgent attention. If you're not able to come immediately, then I'd like your agreement for me to call a tradesman, so that it can be repaired as soon as possible.

RESPONDING TO AN ALIENATING MESSAGE

Even though we may have good communication skills and understand the importance of making our messages reasonable and non-threatening, often other people do not. So how do you respond when someone talks to you in a threatening, hostile way? It is important to remember that, even if someone disagrees with you or is unhappy with something that you have said or done, you have the right to be treated with respect and you are not obliged to put up with abuse. So a good place to start is with an I-statement describing how you feel and what you want. For example, 'Bill, when you speak to me in that angry tone, I feel intimidated and uncomfortable. I'd like to discuss this with you, but I don't want to have an argument or get into personal abuse. Now, we can either talk about it reasonably or else we can put it off until later, after you've cooled down.'

EXERCISE 10.1

For each of the following examples, write down whole messages that convey your observations, thoughts and/or feelings and needs in the following situations. (Sample solutions are at the end of the book.)

1   Someone has borrowed a book from you and has not returned it. They have had it for a long time, and when you finally asked them to give it back, they said, 'If I can find it.' They have never mentioned it again. It's quite precious to you, and you would like it back.

Observations:

Thoughts/Feelings:

Needs:

2 When a friend asked you to come to a trivia evening at their child's primary school, you were caught off-guard and agreed to go. The more you think about it, the more you really don't want to go. You'd like to get out of it but you feel bad about letting them down.

Observations:

Thoughts/Feelings:

Needs:

3 Your partner has been extremely irritable lately, and you feel concerned and upset about it. You suspect that s/he might be under a lot of stress, and you would like to talk about it.

Observations:

Thoughts/Feelings:

Needs:

COMMUNICATION DOS AND DON'TS

In addition to using whole messages, there are a number of general rules that can help to make our communication more effective. The following DOs and DON'Ts provide some useful guidelines.

DO—ASK FOR WHAT YOU WANT

When we do not express our needs clearly, we usually end up feeling angry and resentful. An important aspect of effective communication is to clearly express what we want. This means that we do not drop hints or make vague references and we do not give the other person the silent treatment until they work out that something is wrong. Of course, stating what we want does not mean that we demand that things must go our way—only that we are willing to honestly communicate how things are from our perspective.

Some people insist that others should know what they want—'He should know that I need help with preparing for Sunday's barbecue—why doesn't he offer?'; 'She should know that I need some peace and quiet while I'm studying—I shouldn't have to ask'; 'He should know that I need special attention when I'm sick—he should have offered to come to the doctor with me'. The problem is that other people often think differently to ourselves—they have different needs, different concerns, make different assumptions and focus on different issues. If we don't tell them what we want, very often they don't know.

> If you're not happy about something that someone is doing
> and you want things to change, tell them.

Rick was feeling frustrated because it was Sunday morning, and Julie was at her computer, working away on the business accounts. Finally Rick asked her, 'How long are you going to work on those accounts?' Julie replied, 'Oh, I suppose until about 2 o'clock.' Rick walked away feeling angry and dejected because it was Sunday, and he wanted to go out with Julie and do something leisurely. Meanwhile Julie was totally engrossed in her work and oblivious to Rick's frustration. Rick stewed all afternoon, until a major argument blew up between them later that evening.

While Rick blamed Julie for being inflexible and tied to her work, the truth is that much of the problem stemmed from Rick's poor communication. By asking a question ('How long are you going to work on those accounts?') instead of making a statement ('I feel disappointed that you want to stay at home and work—I'd like to go out for brunch'), Rick failed to clearly communicate what he wanted. As a result, Julie did not notice his frustration and disappointment. Where there is goodwill in relationships, solutions can often be negotiated, but we need to clearly express what we want.

Harold is cross with the young people who live next door because they often play their music loudly late into the night. He is annoyed at their lack of consideration and has decided to teach them a lesson. One night Harold put an amplifier against the adjoining wall, and at 2 o'clock in the morning he blasted them with some old-time classics at full volume. 'That will teach them,' he thinks to himself. Ask Harold whether he'd actually talked to the neighbours and told them that their music was a problem, and he'll tell you, 'Well, they sure know now!'

They may have got the message, Harold, but then again, they may not have—some people aren't aware of their own noise and may not even make the connection. And even if they did get the message, why bring out the big guns and create bad feelings when a reasonable request might have done the same job?

As so often happens in our dealings with other people, when we avoid saying what we want, our resentment grows, and we often end up behaving with unnecessary antagonism. Harold is quick to point out that being assertive doesn't always solve the problem. That's true, but it increases our likelihood of getting our needs met and is a good place to start. It is never too late to take firmer action, such as calling the police, ringing the real estate agent or complaining to the local council, but starting with conciliatory communication often saves us the need to do this. It also enables us to avoid the stress and bad will that comes with hostile actions.

DO—BE WILLING TO SAY 'NO' AT TIMES

Just as people have the right to say 'no' to our requests, we also have the right to say 'no' to requests for things that we do not want to do. Being assertive does not mean that we always put our own needs first. Sometimes we may choose to go out of our way for other people because they are in need and we are happy to help out—good relationships involve making sacrifices and doing things for others at times. However, sometimes it is perfectly appropriate to say 'no' to requests for things that we do not want to do. Learning to say 'no' is particularly important for people who are habitually unassertive.

> *Tony has a broad taste in music and has over a thousand CDs in his collection. He was somewhat taken aback when his friend Sean looked through his collection and pulled out some CDs. Sean had brought CDs from his own collection and wanted to swap them with those that he had removed from Tony's shelf. Although Tony doesn't like to trade his CDs, he likes Sean, and he didn't want to disappoint him. So Tony agreed to the swap and then felt annoyed about it for weeks—'That mongrel! Why can't he buy his own CDs?'*

When we agree to do things that we really don't want to do or when we say 'OK' when it's really not OK, we feel angry and resentful. That's the price that we pay for not being assertive.

BELIEFS THAT INHIBIT ASSERTIVE COMMUNICATION	RATIONAL BELIEFS
If someone asks me to do something, I should always do it.	If someone asks me to do something, I'm not obliged to do it. It's OK to say 'no'.
I should never put my own needs before the needs of others.	It's OK to put my own needs first at times.
I should never say or do things that some people may disapprove of.	I have the right to say or do things, even if others disapprove. It's OK to behave in accordance with my own values and beliefs.

BELIEFS THAT INHIBIT ASSERTIVE COMMUNICATION	RATIONAL BELIEFS
I shouldn't ask for what I want or people won't like me.	It's OK to ask for what I want. People have the right to say 'no', but I have the right to ask.
I should be like other people—I should try to 'fit in'.	It's OK to be different. There's no reason why I have to think, feel or behave the same way as other people.
If someone gives me advice, I should always take it.	It's OK to ignore other people's advice.
I am not important—other people matter more than I do.	I am no less important than anyone else. I have the right to say what I think and to ask for what I want.
If someone is in trouble, I should always help them out.	It's OK for me to not take responsibility for other people's problems.

DON'T—DELAY YOUR COMMUNICATION: DO IT NOW

What do you do when you need to resolve an issue but the idea of communication makes you feel uncomfortable? Procrastinate? Drop hints? Put it in the too-hard basket and hope that you might have the courage to deal with it some time in the future? The desire to avoid potentially unpleasant situations can undermine our ability to have healthy relationships with our partners, family members, friends and work colleagues.

Confronting difficult issues now rather than later prevents escalation and reduces stress. Once our issues are out in the open, they can be dealt with, and if our communication is reasonable, very often they can be resolved. While there is no guarantee that communication always gets us what we want, we can be pretty sure that things will stay the same if we do not say anything.

Nothing changes unless something changes.

When we delay or avoid communication, issues that need to be dealt with remain unresolved and tensions escalate. When we do finally address these issues, accrued resentment has often distorted their magnitude, leading to angry outbursts.

Val became upset when she discovered that Sharon, one of her work colleagues, had lent their heater to someone in a neighbouring office. As Val uses the heater a lot, she was particularly annoyed that Sharon had not consulted her first. Instead of politely telling Sharon that she would like it to be returned, Val sulked. She said almost nothing the whole day, except for occasional mutterings under her breath. Finally Sharon asked her whether something was wrong, to which Val angrily exploded, 'Why do you just give our things away? Don't I have any rights? Why couldn't you have asked me first?' Although it may have been reasonable for Val to feel annoyed, her alienating statements created unnecessary hostility and resulted in icy relations between the two women for the next two weeks. As is often the case, delaying our communication causes tension to escalate and creates unnecessary bad feelings between people.

If there is an issue that needs dealing with, do it now. The only exception to this rule is in situations where we feel very angry, in which case a cooling-off period may be a good idea. Delaying the discussion for a few hours or a few days gives us time to calm down and helps us to see things in a more rational perspective.

DO—BE HONEST

> When you are honest with people—
> - they admire and appreciate you
> - they trust you
> - they know where you stand
> - you can get more of what you want.
>
> Don't you appreciate people giving it to you straight?
>
> **ANDREW MATTHEWS, *MAKING FRIENDS***

Most of us are a little dishonest at times. When we tell lies, it is usually because we want to be nice or we want to protect someone's feelings. Sometimes we lie to protect ourselves or to avoid conflict or disapproval; e.g.

'If I'm honest, she'll get offended' or 'If I tell him the truth, he'll get angry'. Some people lie in order to try to impress others or to manipulate others into doing what they want.

It might be argued that on rare occasions a 'white lie' or omission can save someone unnecessary hurt or offence. Telling someone that you have a prior engagement when the truth is you just do not want to come to their party, or telling a distressed friend that their new unflattering haircut 'looks fine' may occasionally be justifiable. However, in most cases lies create barriers between people; they prevent us from dealing with the real issues and impede others from knowing what we really think and want. Lies break down trust—an essential ingredient for healthy relationships. Once we know that we have been lied to, it is hard to trust that person in the future. While it is important to be kind and tactful and to respect other people's feelings, healthy relationships are based on honest communication. This means that we express ourselves truthfully, without ulterior motives or hidden agendas.

> Being straight also means that you tell the truth. You state your real needs and feelings. You don't say you're tired and want to go home if you're really angry and want more attention. You don't angle for compliments or reassurance by putting yourself down. You don't say you're anxious about going to a couples therapist when actually you feel angry about being pushed to go. You don't describe your feelings as depression because your mate prefers that to irritation … Lies cut you off from others. Lies keep them from knowing what you need or feel.
>
> **MCKAY, DAVIS AND FANNING, *MESSAGES***

Mandy has just started dating a man whom her best friend, Rachael, detests (Rachael calls him a 'complete jerk'). Because Mandy wants to avoid Rachael's disapproval, she omitted telling her friend about her new boyfriend. At times she was evasive and occasionally she lied to Rachael about who she was going out with. When Rachael eventually discovered the truth, she was furious with Mandy, not because of who she was dating but because she had lied. Paradoxically, Mandy had not

been honest with Rachael because she wanted her approval but, in the
end, lying created distance and disapproval.

Dishonesty feels like betrayal—it destroys trust and can ruin a friendship. Being assertive means being prepared to tell the truth, even when we know that others won't necessarily approve.

> *Laura has poor self-esteem and consequently she tries to boost her*
> *image by exaggerating some of her achievements. Over the years Laura*
> *has made a number of exaggerated claims, including non-existent*
> *university degrees, famous people she's friends with, impressive jobs*
> *she's held and high incomes she's earned in the past.*

The problem with making false or exaggerated claims is that eventually we get found out, and we lose our credibility. Laura stretches the truth because she wants to impress people but the harder she tries, the less impressive she becomes. When we know that someone has been dishonest, they lose our respect—lies push people away.

DON'T—GET AUTOMATICALLY DEFENSIVE

Perhaps the greatest obstacle to effective communication and problem solving is the tendency to feel threatened and to become defensive when we receive criticism or negative feedback from others. Some people are particularly sensitive and perceive criticism even when none is intended. This tendency usually stems from low self-esteem—doubts about our own worth put us on the lookout for possible threats to our self-esteem. Core beliefs such as, 'If someone criticises me, then it means I'm not OK' and 'Criticism means rejection', make negative feedback from others feel like a life-or-death issue. Consequently, we get defensive or go on the attack. On the other hand, people with healthy self-esteem are much less concerned about criticism or negative feedback. An inherent belief that we are 'OK' enables us to accept negative feedback without feeling threatened.

Just as we appreciate it when other people take our comments on board without becoming defensive, so too do others appreciate it when we are willing to take their comments on board. The ability to listen and respond constructively to criticism is an invaluable quality that helps us to learn about ourselves. It enables us to reach an understanding with other people and to work cooperatively at finding solutions. Ultimately, it helps us to get along with others and to have good relationships.

DO—VALIDATE

While it may sometimes be appropriate to argue our case when someone is upset or angry about something that we have done, often this just inflames the situation. Trying to prove at all costs that we are right and they are wrong may miss the point—often all people want is to be heard. How would it be if instead of arguing or being defensive, you validated the other person's feelings and concerns? When we validate, we make a statement acknowledging that we can understand how it is from the other person's point of view. (Of course, if you really don't understand, you may need to ask them to explain it first.) If we feel responsible for the situation, we acknowledge our responsibility and if we are genuinely sorry, we apologise: 'I can see that it must be very upsetting for you. I'm really sorry.'

When we validate a person's concerns, it does not mean that we necessarily see things the same way or that we agree with what they have said. Thus, we do not take responsibility or apologise unless we genuinely believe that we are at fault. However, at a minimum level we state that we can understand how it is from the other person's point of view. For the person who is angry or upset, having one's feelings validated is one of the most satisfying experiences. It can resolve all hurt and resentment, and sometimes enables people to let go of issues that have troubled them for months or even years.

Since childhood, Sylvia has always believed that her parents loved her younger sister more than they loved her. For years this had been a great source of pain to her and finally, at the age of 38, she decided to talk about it with her mother. Without blaming or condemning her parents, Sylvia reflected on numerous childhood memories of situations where she believed she had received unfair treatment. She described how unloved or dejected she had felt at times.

While this type of message is likely to be confronting for any parent, Sylvia's mother could either add fuel to the fire by responding defensively or she could help her daughter to resolve the pain of the past by validating her experience. Compare the likely outcomes of the two types of responses below:

Defensive response: This is complete nonsense. We loved you both equally—this is all in your mind. You're always looking to blame us for all of your problems.

Validating response: Darling, I had no idea how difficult things must have been for you at the time. We were struggling with our own problems and we didn't know much about parenting, so I guess we made lots of mistakes. It must have been very painful for you to feel second-best so much of the time.

Validating can be used for issues (such as in the above example) that have been a sore point for years, as well as for more common issues that arise in our daily-life situations:

➤ I know it's frustrating to be kept waiting—I'm so sorry I'm late.

➤ I understand that it's hard for you to feed, bathe and put the kids down on your own, without my help. It must be absolutely exhausting. At the moment things are pretty chaotic at work so I can't leave any earlier, but I'll try to change things when this busy period has passed.

➤ It must have been very upsetting to have been spoken to like that—I'll follow it up with the manager.

DO—GIVE POSITIVE FEEDBACK

While it is important to communicate our concerns when someone does something that we are unhappy about, it is equally important to communicate our appreciation when they do things that make us feel good. Positive feedback helps to create bonds between people and reinforces behaviours we want to encourage. When people know that we appreciate certain things, they are more likely to continue doing them. Giving positive feedback may be as simple as saying:

> I really appreciate that you're making more of an effort to talk to my friends.
> I'm so glad that we're both being more open and honest with each other now.
> I can see that you're making an effort to help with the housework—I really appreciate it.
> Now that you're not angry all the time, I enjoy spending time with you—it's so much easier to talk to you these days.
> I know that you wanted to go to that match—I'm very grateful that you're here instead.
> I like the way that you've become more assertive—it means that I know what you want.
> You've been a great friend to me. I'm grateful for your support.

A crucial step in making your relationship rewarding is to share your good feelings. A basic law of human behaviour is that people are more likely to do things which make them feel good. If your partner does something that makes you feel good, and you would like him to do it more often, reward it! Tell your partner how she made you feel good.

BOB MONTGOMERY & LYNETTE EVANS, *LIVING AND LOVING TOGETHER*

DON'T—BRING UP RED HERRINGS

In the middle of an argument or an angry exchange we may sometimes find ourselves bringing up 'red herrings'—issues that are not really related to the subject under discussion. Usually these involve past hurts, injustices or disappointments—e.g. 'What about the time you let me down when I really needed your help?'; 'How come you've never acknowledged the things that I did well?' or 'You showed more loyalty to your mates than to me'. These past hurts are sometimes marginally related to the current issue and sometimes not at all, but we bring them up to bolster our defences, as if to say, 'You're bad, and here's the evidence.'

In their book *Really Relating*, David Jansen and Margaret Newman refer to the 'gunny sack' that we carry on our back. The gunny sack is a metaphor for the collection of past hurts and resentments that we carry around with us—'All the angers, resentments, hurts, grievances that we haven't talked about and resolved.' These issues may fester silently for years until they finally pour out during a fit of rage in an argument over some other matter.

The problem with bringing up past hurts is that they derail the communication process and impede problem solving. Suddenly we are arguing about peripheral issues and losing sight of the main game. The challenge during any discussion is to stay focused on the current issue. This is not to say that revisiting unresolved issues from the past is a pointless exercise. In some situations, talking about past hurts can be healing and worthwhile, but the question here is one of timing. It may be worth choosing some other time to talk about unresolved issues; however, it is rarely helpful to raise them in the context of an argument about other things.

DO—KEEP YOUR COOL

A major disadvantage of anger is that it limits the opportunities for constructive problem solving. Once we lose our cool, people feel threatened and tensions escalate. For this reason, it is important to be aware of our voice and body language, as well as the things we say. Try to set the tone by speaking calmly and reasonably, avoiding alienating messages and not being sidetracked by irrelevant issues. If the tone of the discussion becomes hostile, it is useful to point this out to the other person—'We seem to be getting angry again. Let's try to speak calmly and stay focused on the issue.' If the discussion remains heated, it may be best to suggest a cooling-off period, and to return to the issue when tempers have settled down.

DON'T—WALK AWAY FROM A DISCUSSION

Talking honestly about our thoughts and feelings can make us uncomfortable at times. Some people deal with their discomfort by literally walking away. While this may give them temporary relief, it does not solve the problem and usually creates new ones. With a few exceptions, walking away from a discussion is one of the most unhelpful ways of dealing with a problem in a relationship. Avoiding communication usually stems from beliefs such as, 'Talking about it will make me feel uncomfortable, and it's bad to feel uncomfortable' and 'If we don't talk about it, the problem will disappear'.

In some situations, people deliberately walk away from a discussion to punish the other person—usually a partner or family member. The knowledge that doing this causes frustration to others gives some people a sense of power—'I know that she wants to talk about it, so I'm not going to give her the opportunity!' Of course, walking away is totally self-defeating because if problems are not resolved, it is impossible to have satisfying relationships—in the end, no one benefits.

> *Over the ten years of their marriage, Justine had often tried to discuss some of her concerns with her husband, Noel. Every time she tried to talk, Noel became annoyed and literally walked out of the room. After years of frustration and unresolved issues, Justine had finally had enough. She packed her bags and moved out, leaving only a short note saying that she couldn't take any more. Noel was devastated. To him the break-up came totally out of the blue. 'Why didn't she tell me that she was so unhappy?' he asked himself. 'If I had known, I would have done things differently.' She tried to talk to you, Noel, but you kept walking away, remember?*

Although walking away from a discussion does not always result in the breakdown of a marriage, it does ensure that problems are unresolved and resentment grows. When issues cannot be discussed, relationships invariably suffer.

DO—ASK FOR CLARIFICATION

Sometimes we get messages that are ambiguous or unclear—someone seems cold and irritable; someone appears to ignore us for no reason;

someone hints at an issue; or someone hasn't called for ages and we assume that they are probably angry. Misread messages can result in unnecessary hurt, tensions and bad feelings. If you are unsure of the message you are receiving, ask for clarification.

➤ You seem very quiet lately. Have I done something to upset you?

➤ I haven't heard from you for a long time—is everything OK?

➤ When we first talked about the idea, you seemed excited about it, but now you sound less enthusiastic. I'm wondering if you have changed your mind.

➤ You seemed keen to see me when we spoke on the phone, but now that I am here, you appear put out. Is something the matter?

➤ You have talked about people in relationships needing to take breaks from each other. Are you saying that that is what you would like us to do?

EXERCISE 10.2

For each of the following situations:

a   Describe what you would probably do if you found yourself in this situation. (Be honest!)

b   For those situations in which you would *not* respond assertively, write down:

  i   the beliefs that might stop you from being assertive

  ii more reasonable perceptions that would help you to respond assertively.

c   Write down a brief assertive statement that would be appropriate for the situation. (Sample solutions are given at the back of this book.)

1   A friend asks you to tell a lie to someone on his behalf. You feel uncomfortable with this.

2   The salesman has been serving you for over 40 minutes and he has been extremely pleasant and helpful. You have found something that is OK, but you're not really sure. You are aware that you've taken up a lot of his time.

3 You get a call from someone you met while travelling overseas two years ago, and she wants to stay at your place for 'a while'. You're not too happy about the idea.

4 You have had dinner with friends at an expensive restaurant. You have not had any alcohol, while the others have drunk a lot. Although the alcohol alone comes to over $30 a head, when the bill is being worked out, no one suggests that you should pay less.

5 One of your colleagues at work has a habit of sitting down next to you and talking while you are trying to work.

6 You have already asked the two people sitting behind you in the cinema to stop talking. Now, ten minutes later, they have started talking again.

7 You are watering your front garden when a dog that is being walked by its owner poos on your nature strip. The owner does not pick it up.

8 A group of friends is at your house, and one of them lights up a cigarette. You have a no-smoking policy at your house.

9 The coffee you ordered at a restaurant arrives lukewarm.

10 A friend borrowed $200 from you four months ago and seems to have forgotten about it.

IN SUMMARY

➤ Effective communication skills enable us to get on with people, solve problems and get our needs met a lot of the time.

➤ Avoidance and alienating messages are the most common cause of poor communication within relationships.

➤ Alienating messages are perceived as hostile and therefore put the other person on the defensive. This reduces the likelihood of successful communication.

➤ We are far more likely to get our needs met and to maintain healthy relationships when our communication is conciliatory and respectful of the needs of others.

➤ Communication techniques that increase our chances of successful negotiation include assertive requests, I-statements and whole messages.

➤ Important ingredients for good communication include respect for the rights of others, clear and honest communication, validating the feelings of other people and positive feedback to others when appropriate.

➤ Poor communication habits include hostile manner or statements, defensiveness, walking away from a discussion, delaying communication and bringing up unrelated issues from the past.

ELEVEN

Being happy

Why search for personal happiness? Because you'd damned well better! If you don't achieve some measure of your desires, your goals, your values, who will get them for you?

ALBERT ELLIS

The desire for happiness motivates many of our decisions and actions. Whether we behave selfishly or altruistically; work until we are 65 or retire early; enrol in a university degree or drop out of a course; keep the house spotless or neglect the housework; take frequent holidays or stay at home; search for a new relationship or end an existing relationship; have children or choose not to have children; join a gym or join the couch potato club, it is the desire to feel good and to be happy, now or in the future, that underlies most of our behaviours.

Although we all want to be happy, few of us can clearly define what happiness is. Psychologists, like philosophers and sociologists, have struggled with the term. The most widely accepted, yet inadequate definition is: a state of subjective wellbeing. There is much disagreement about the characteristics of happiness. Some experts argue that happiness is an enduring human trait—an ongoing perception that life is good, meaningful and pleasurable. Others argue that it is a temporary state—that people have experiences of happiness rather than an ongoing sense of being happy. However we choose to define happiness, it does appear that some people are more predisposed towards feeling happy and satisfied with their lives than others.

Since the 1960s, studies examining the issue of happiness have been reported in the research literature. Many sought to measure people's level of happiness and to identify the factors that predict whether or not they feel happy. In the late 1980s, two American social psychologists, David Myers and Ed Diener, analysed the results of international studies across sixteen countries based on the responses of 170,000 people. They looked at people's ratings of happiness in countries all over the world, and what sort of factors predicted whether or not they were happy. One of their surprising discoveries was that the factors that predict happiness are very similar across different countries and cultures. Here is what they found.

FACTORS ASSOCIATED WITH BEING HAPPY

Wealth: There is good evidence for the old cliché, 'Money doesn't buy happiness.' People on high incomes tend not to be much happier than those on low incomes. The exception is for those who live in poverty, who tend to be much less happy than other people. For instance, in the poorest countries, such as India and Bangladesh, poor people are much less happy than those who are better off. It seems, however, that as long as people have enough to buy the necessities of life, they can be happy, and having much more does not make people much happier.

Age and gender: These are not related to people's level of happiness. There are equal numbers of happy and unhappy people at every age group and among both men and women. People's race and level of education are also not associated with their level of happiness.

Work: This can play an important role in people's level of happiness. Those whose work provides them with a sense of vocation, identity, purpose or connection with others are more likely to feel happy.

Consuming interests: These can also contribute to human happiness. Having a passion for something that we do (e.g. golf, gardening, music, writing, tennis, bridge, bowls or dancing) and indulging in it on a regular basis increases the likelihood of feeling happy.

Goals: These can also play a role in people's overall sense of happiness. Having a sense of mission, purpose or working towards something that we consider important helps us to feel happy.

Relationships: One of the strongest predictors of happiness is the quality of our relationships. Close, committed, enduring relationships are associated with higher levels of happiness. People who have intimate relationships are more likely to be very happy than those who have lots of superficial relationships but little intimacy. Being happily married is also a strong predictor of overall happiness, but people who are single tend to be happier than those who are unhappily married.

Religion: People who are highly spiritually committed are more likely to be happy than those who have no spiritual commitment. This may be because religious beliefs give people a sense of connection and purpose, which makes their lives meaningful. People with strong religious beliefs also frequently have good social support through 'communal fellowship', which may also explain why they are more likely to feel happy.

Active lifestyle: Happy people live active, robust lives, and are less focused on themselves than people who are unhappy.

PERSONAL ATTRIBUTES OF HAPPY PEOPLE

In addition to lifestyle factors, the researchers found that four key personal attributes were associated with higher levels of happiness.

Good self-esteem: People who feel good about themselves are more likely to feel happy than those who have poor self-esteem.

Sense of control: People who feel in control over the things that happen in their lives are more likely to be happy.

Optimism: People who feel optimistic about the future are also more likely to be happy.

Extroversion: People who are outgoing and who associate easily with others are more likely to report feeling happy.

The conclusions drawn from this and other research suggest that human happiness is partly determined by our personal characteristics (such as our level of self-esteem, sense of control, extroversion and optimism) and partly determined by the way we live our lives (our work, interests, goals and interpersonal relationships).

Much of the focus of this book has been on our thoughts—knowing ourselves better, identifying the cognitions that make us feel unhappy (i.e. angry, sad, anxious, depressed, frustrated or worthless) and consciously working towards changing those cognitions. Using the cognitive and behavioural techniques that we have looked at throughout the book can help us to feel better in situations where we might otherwise feel bad. It can also help us to develop more of the traits that are associated with human happiness—a sense of control over our experiences, good self-esteem, optimism and greater willingness to take social risks and connect with people.

> In the midst of winter I finally learned
> there was in me
> an invincible summer.
> **ALBERT CAMUS, 'RETURN TO TIPASA'**

LIFESTYLE

The way we spend our time from day to day, week to week and month to month can have a huge impact on the way we feel. Our lifestyle can influence whether we feel happy or sad, stressed or relaxed, lonely or connected, healthy or ill, bored or stimulated, contented or unfulfilled. The way we spend our time often reflects our beliefs about what we think is important. For instance, if you spend much of your time on work-related activities, it is probably because you believe that work and the things that it gives you are important. If you spend a lot of time on leisure activities, chances are you believe that having fun is important; and if you spend a lot of time studying, it is because you believe that education and the things that it will ultimately bring are worth the effort.

Sometimes, however, our beliefs fall out of step with the way we live our lives. For instance, you may believe that your health is important, but actually spend very little time on exercise or healthy lifestyle habits. Or you might believe that relationships are important but make little effort to maintain friendships or spend time with people you like. Or you might believe that leisure is important, but spend very little time doing things you enjoy.

While there is no correct way to spend our time, it can be useful to reflect on our current lifestyle and ask ourselves whether it is consistent with our values and goals. The lifestyle self-assessment questionnaire at the end of this section (page 353) can help us review different aspects of our lifestyle and identify areas that might be worth changing.

ASK YOURSELF:
➤ How satisfied are you with your current lifestyle?
➤ Does it reflect your beliefs about the things that are important?
➤ Is it conducive to happiness and good health?
➤ Will your current lifestyle bring you the things you want in the future?

For most people, having a balanced lifestyle increases the likelihood of feeling happy. This means spending time and energy on a range of activities and not putting all our eggs into one basket. As people who have relied too much on one area of their lives can testify, if we drop our basket (as a result of retrenchment, divorce, health problems or financial problems) we can get into all sorts of trouble. Spending energy on a range of activities is not only a safer bet for the future, but also makes our lives richer and more satisfying in the present.

While there are many different types of activity that people find rewarding, a good balance includes spending some time and energy on each of the following areas:

➤ work/regular commitments;
➤ interests/leisure activity;
➤ mental stimulation;
➤ health maintenance; and
➤ relationships.

WORK/REGULAR COMMITMENTS

Do you feel satisfied with the way you spend your time during the week, either at work or doing other things?

Most people feel good when they are involved in some sort of regular work or activity. Although there is no reason why it should consume five days of every week or fall within certain hours, a commitment to regular activity—be it paid work, voluntary work, education or an interest—can have many benefits. Regular commitments provide a structure to our week and give us a reason to get up in the morning. Even though we may instinctively prefer to sleep in, the discipline that comes with routine seems to make most of us feel and function better.

Work or some regular activity can also provide other benefits—mental stimulation, social contact, enjoyment, a sense of purpose, a sense of achievement, self-efficacy, personal satisfaction and high self-esteem. It also reduces our risk of becoming depressed. In fact, satisfying work is one of the key predictors of overall life satisfaction.

Of course, work can also be tedious, stressful and soul-destroying and, for some people, resigning or retiring is the most life-enhancing decision they can make. One of the ironies about work is that it can be our greatest source of happiness and satisfaction, or the greatest source of misery, stress, isolation and health problems.

Having too much time on our hands or too few interests puts us at risk of unhappiness and depression. People who are not in paid work can experience many of the benefits that come with satisfying work (such as routine, social contact, stimulation, sense of purpose and so on) through participating in activities such as voluntary work, education or regular hobbies.

INTERESTS/LEISURE ACTIVITIES

What sort of things do you do for leisure/recreation? Do you have enough fun in your life?

Leisure activities are anything we do for enjoyment and relaxation. Different people enjoy doing different things. Common leisure activities include sports, crafts, bushwalking, sailing, movies, eating out, social media, artwork, bridge, playing a musical instrument, computer games and dancing. Leisure activities are a source of pleasure and relaxation, and provide an escape from one's regular routine. They also provide a counterbalance to the demands and stresses that exist in other areas of our lives. One of the benefits of not being in a work situation is that it gives us more time to participate in leisure activities.

In modern Western countries like ours, watching TV is the most popular form of leisure activity. Some people are highly critical of TV because of the poor quality of many of the programs and the frequent advertisements on commercial TV stations. Watching TV is also a passive pastime—it draws our time from other activities and discourages social interaction or engagement in more creative or challenging activities. This can particularly be a problem for children, who often watch for several hours a day. While TV can be a great source of entertainment, information, relaxation and mental stimulation, when used excessively or unwisely, it can have a negative influence on our lives. Excessive TV watching robs us of other, more worthwhile pursuits—we could be reading, talking to people, solving a problem, walking, discussing, entertaining, playing sport or doing any one of myriad other activities. Watching indiscriminately also means exposing ourselves to mindless junk and inane commercials—why do that to ourselves when there are so many other, more beneficial things we could be doing?

> When people say to me, 'How do you do so many things?'
> I often answer them, without meaning to be cruel 'How do you do so little?' It
> seems to me that people have vast potential. Most people can do extraordinary
> things If they have the confidence or take the risks. Yet most people don't.
> They sit in front of the telly and treat life as if it goes on forever.
> **PHILLIP ADAMS**

Some people feel guilty when they engage in leisure activities because they believe that they should always be 'productive' in their use of time. This comes from rigid beliefs, often learned in childhood, that things that are pleasurable are somehow less valid than those that involve hard work and produce tangible outcomes. However, if we do not engage in leisure activities with a spirit of guilt-free pleasure, we deny ourselves the full enjoyment the experience has to offer. Is there any point in participating half-heartedly?

MENTAL STIMULATION

What sorts of things do you do for mental stimulation?

Our brain loves stimulation. For most people, acquiring new knowledge, thinking critically, challenging our own ideas and solving problems are among our most satisfying experiences because they exercise our minds. Many activities can give our minds a workout—reading, writing, studying, solving puzzles, working, watching good quality TV programs, listening to the radio, playing games, seeing films, going to the theatre and having discussions with other people. In fact, many of us like nothing more than engaging in a good debate with friends over a meal.

Mentally stimulating activities are enjoyable in themselves and add richness to our lives. Exercising the brain also helps us to retain good mental functioning into our old age. The old saying, 'Use it or lose it' applies to the brain, just as it does to other parts of the body. In addition, activities that affect the 'right side of the brain'—things that move us on a 'spiritual level', such as music, art, poetry, dance, theatre, meditation or any creative interest—also help us to maintain a healthy balance between intellectual and creative parts of our mind.

HEALTH MAINTENANCE

How much responsibility do you take for looking after your health?

Among earlier generations, physical health was often presumed to be a matter of luck—if you were fortunate, you had good health; if not, you became ill or died young. As medical research established the relationship between behaviours and health over time, we have come to realise the importance of healthy lifestyle choices, such as not smoking, regular exercise, a balanced diet, adequate sleep and avoiding excessive amounts of alcohol or drugs. More recently, stress management and supportive social relationships have been added to the mix of healthy lifestyle habits. Although there is still an element of luck in the 'genetic lottery' that determines one's predispositions, our lifestyle choices can make a huge difference to how well we feel and how long we live. Given that most of us already know what we need to do to maximise our chances of staying healthy, it is amazing that so many of us don't put these things into practice.

The ability to exercise self-discipline in relation to healthy lifestyle habits partly depends on one's capacity to tolerate frustration. Low frustration tolerance can sabotage the desire to achieve our goals because we give in to immediate gratification at the expense of our long-term interests (see Chapter 4). Motivating ourselves to give up self-defeating behaviours such as smoking, overeating, drinking too much, abusing drugs or not exercising, requires our health to be one of our top priorities. In addition, we need to set clear goals, make a plan of action and prepare to deal with the obstacles that inevitably arise along the way (see Chapter 9).

RELATIONSHIPS

How much time do you spend with people you like? Are relationships a priority for you?

Humans are social animals. We enjoy talking to and being with others because that is our nature—we are genetically programmed to affiliate. Although we can be perfectly happy spending time by ourselves, at an instinctive level we like to be with people.

The quality of our social relationships is a strong determinant of our overall happiness. Therefore, activities that improve our connections with others also tend to increase our level of happiness. Good relationships provide us with many benefits—both emotional and practical. They satisfy our need for social connection and belonging, help us to feel secure and contribute to feelings of self-worth. They also provide enjoyment, entertainment and mental stimulation. When we are trying to solve problems, other people can give us ideas, useful information, a fresh perspective and sometimes, practical assistance. Several studies have found that strong supportive relationships are beneficial not only for our psychological wellbeing but for our physical health as well.

There are some interesting differences in the social behaviour of men compared to women. In most families, men take little responsibility for maintaining social connections, other than with their partner and immediate family. Women are more frequently responsible for making social arrangements and are more likely to initiate contact with friends. They are also more likely than men to have close friendships with people outside their family unit—usually other women. Although good social support is just as important for men as it is for women, men are generally less inclined to initiate contact or maintain social relationships, and therefore tend to be more dependent on their partner for friendship, intimacy and social support. For this reason, men often have fewer resources to help them cope at times of marital breakdown or bereavement. In fact, losing one's spouse often has a more devastating impact on the health of men than of women, largely because of the more limited support that is available to men.

While a loving and supportive primary relationship is a wonderful thing to have, relying on one person to satisfy all of our emotional needs is risky—a bit like putting all of our eggs into one basket. A safer and psychologically healthier approach is to develop at least a few close friendships, instead of relying on one person to meet all our social and emotional needs.

There are two essential ingredients for maintaining satisfying relationships—time and communication. Maintaining supportive relationships involves making ourselves available—spending time with people and initiating contact at times. People who lead busy lives may find this difficult. The demands of a stressful job, family responsibilities or a new love interest can cause us to fall out of touch with friends. If we are lucky, we realise the error of our ways in time to do something about it; if not, loneliness, isolation or depression will eventually bring home the cost of neglecting our friendships. Sharing a regular activity, such as going to movies, concerts, dinners, sporting events, taking walks or playing a sport can provide a structure for ensuring that we stay in touch.

The second ingredient for good relationships is open communication. Self-disclosure—talking honestly about our experiences, thoughts and feelings—is the stuff that connects us to other people. Communication that is consistently polite, formal or 'edited' keeps a wall between people, no matter how much we want to connect. Good relationships involve self-disclosure and honest communication. Of course, this doesn't mean that every conversation should be filled with deep and meaningful descriptions of our innermost feelings. However, it does mean that we are willing to talk candidly, and to disclose our feelings at times. With communication as with everything else, balance is the key.

HOW BALANCED IS MY LIFESTYLE?

Now that we have looked at different components of a balanced lifestyle, it might be useful to check our own. The following exercise can serve as a guide for reflecting on the various aspects of our lives and may help to highlight areas that could do with some changes. There are five lifestyle categories, and under each of these are ten statements. Read each one and circle a number between one and five to indicate how true that statement is for you. When you have finished, add up the numbers you have circled and write down the total (out of 50) in the space at the bottom of each category.

SELF-ASSESSMENT EXERCISE—HOW BALANCED IS MY LIFESTYLE?

For each of the following statements, circle a number to indicate how true the statement is for you.

1 = not true at all; 3 = somewhat true; 5 = very true.

A WORK/DAILY ACTIVITIES

1 I feel productive/useful in the way I spend my time during the day.	1	2	3	4	5
2 The work/things that I do during the day are enjoyable.	1	2	3	4	5
3 My work/daily activities suit my personality, interests and temperament.	1	2	3	4	5
4 My work/daily routine is mentally stimulating.	1	2	3	4	5
5 My work/daily routine involves some enjoyable social interaction.	1	2	3	4	5
6 My physical environment during the day is pleasant.	1	2	3	4	5
7 I feel valued by the people around me.	1	2	3	4	5
8 I feel adequately rewarded for the things that I do.	1	2	3	4	5
9 The demands that are made of me are reasonable and manageable.	1	2	3	4	5
10 The time I spend at work/in my daily activities is balanced and leaves me enough time to do other things that I value.	1	2	3	4	5

TOTAL SCORE   /50

B HEALTH

1	I make a conscious effort to look after my health.	1	2	3	4	5
2	I do some form of exercise (walking, swimming, etc.) at least four times per week.	1	2	3	4	5
3	I don't smoke.	1	2	3	4	5
4	I drink no more than a moderate amount of alcohol, consistent with guidelines recommended by health authorities.	1	2	3	4	5
5	I eat a balanced and healthy diet.	1	2	3	4	5
6	I avoid eating junk foods.	1	2	3	4	5
7	I do not have a highly stressful lifestyle.	1	2	3	4	5
8	I don't push myself too hard—I make sure I get lots of rest.	1	2	3	4	5
9	Most nights I sleep well and get adequate sleep.	1	2	3	4	5
10	I rarely feel stressed to the point of experiencing physical symptoms.	1	2	3	4	5

TOTAL SCORE   /50

C MIND

1	I frequently read material that is thought-provoking.	1	2	3	4	5
2	I often have challenging discussions/debates with others.	1	2	3	4	5
3	I have interests that are mentally stimulating.	1	2	3	4	5
4	I am constantly developing my thoughts, ideas and knowledge.	1	2	3	4	5
5	I actively participate in activities, rather than just observe.	1	2	3	4	5
6	I like to ask questions and think critically about issues.	1	2	3	4	5
7	Much of my entertainment (e.g. TV, films, radio) is thought-provoking.	1	2	3	4	5
8	I frequently partake in activities that move me on a spiritual level (e.g. music, dance, art, meditation).	1	2	3	4	5
9	I am constantly seeking to learn new things.	1	2	3	4	5
10	Many of my daily activities are mentally stimulating.	1	2	3	4	5

TOTAL SCORE   /50

D LEISURE

1	I have some hobbies/interests that I enjoy.	1	2	3	4	5
2	I frequently indulge in pleasurable activities.	1	2	3	4	5
3	I have lots of fun.	1	2	3	4	5
4	Watching TV is not my main leisure activity.	1	2	3	4	5
5	Some of my leisure activities involve doing things with others.	1	2	3	4	5
6	I take regular holidays and breaks from my usual routine.	1	2	3	4	5
7	When I participate in leisure activities I can really let go and enjoy myself.	1	2	3	4	5
8	When I indulge myself, I never feel guilty.	1	2	3	4	5
9	I let go and relax on a regular basis.	1	2	3	4	5
10	I enjoy most of the things that I do.	1	2	3	4	5

TOTAL SCORE   /50

E SOCIAL SUPPORT

1	I find it easy to self-disclose about my experiences, thoughts and feelings.	1	2	3	4	5
2	I have enough people in my life, with whom I share a trusting and intimate relationship.	1	2	3	4	5
3	I socialise a lot.	1	2	3	4	5
4	I am generally friendly and supportive to others.	1	2	3	4	5
5	I have a good network of social support.	1	2	3	4	5
6	I feel relaxed and comfortable with most people.	1	2	3	4	5
7	I am willing to take risks in initiating friendships.	1	2	3	4	5
8	I spend sufficient time connecting with the significant people in my life.	1	2	3	4	5
9	When I need emotional or practical support, I always have people that I can turn to.	1	2	3	4	5
10	When I need emotional or practical support, I do not hesitate to ask for it.	1	2	3	4	5

TOTAL SCORE   /50

After completing this exercise, look at your scores for each of the five areas. As a general rule, those areas in which you scored above 40 appear to be working well for you—it is likely that they are contributing to a sense of wellbeing and personal satisfaction. Areas in which you scored between 30 and 40 may not be quite as satisfying, and making some changes within those areas could improve your quality of life. Lower scores tend to reflect lower levels of personal satisfaction or possible problems. Scores below 30 often point to areas that may be in need of attention. Making positive changes in these areas could help to improve your quality of life and, ultimately, enable you to feel happier.

The aim of this exercise is to help you reflect on your current lifestyle and identify areas that might be worthy of some attention. If you already feel perfectly satisfied with your current lifestyle, then that is more significant than your scores on this or any other questionnaire, and there is no need to consider making changes. If you would like to reflect on your current lifestyle, the questions in the following exercise are worth thinking about.

EXERCISE 11.1

1   How balanced is your current lifestyle? Are there some areas that are missing out?
2   What sort of changes could you make to enhance your lifestyle?
3   What obstacles will you need to overcome in order to make these changes?
4   Write a plan of action (see page 288) for the things that you need to do to make these positive lifestyle changes.

Whether or not you resolve to make any changes to your lifestyle, remember that the best decisions are those based on rational, considered judgements—as opposed to simply giving into inertia or low frustration tolerance.

LIVING PURPOSEFULLY—SET LIFE GOALS

We have already seen that setting and working on goals can help us to overcome depression and increase our resilience in the longer term (see

Chapter 8). Setting goals can also help us to solve problems and take control over some of life's challenges (see Chapter 9). Finally, setting goals can also motivate us to make meaningful changes to our lives.

Identifying what we want, making a plan of action and working through it is the means by which we can accomplish many of the things that are important to us. Defining life goals helps us to focus on the things we want, and motivates us to mobilise our resources to work towards them.

> I went to the woods
> because I wished to live deliberately ...
> and not, when I came to die
> discover that I had not lived ...
> I wanted to live deep
> and suck the marrow out of life ...
>
> **HENRY THOREAU, *WALDEN***

Most of us live our lives from day to day. While we sometimes plan for future events—home renovations, next year's holiday, dinners, dentist appointments, job interviews, retirement—most of the time we respond to the pressures and demands of our daily-life situations as they arise. There is, of course, nothing wrong with this, if the things we do contribute to life satisfaction. However, sometimes it may be worth reflecting whether the current direction of our lives is where we want to go. Have you ever asked yourself, 'What is it that I want? What things are important to me? Where do I want to be in five years' time?'

VISUALISATION

A good way to clarify the things that are important to us is to visualise our lives at some time in the future—perhaps three to five years from now. The best way to do this is to get someone else to read you this prepared script very slowly, while you sit with your eyes closed and visualise what is being said. Alternatively, you can record the script and play it back to yourself while sitting in a comfortable chair with your eyes closed. With all visualisation and relaxation exercises, the secret is to pace yourself. Speak very slowly, and pause for about 15 seconds between each sentence to give yourself time to create and experience the images. The following is a text that I recommend. You can use it or modify it to make it more personally meaningful to you:

> *Within your mind's eye, see yourself moving forward through time. Perhaps you can see spirals and psychedelic colours and patterns as time flies before your eyes. And now, you find yourself at another point in time, [five] years into the future. Think of what year it is. How old are you now? You are walking towards the place where you live—see it from the outside—and now you walk in the front door, and step inside. How does it feel to be at home? Watch yourself, doing some things around the house. What sort of things are you doing? How do you look? Do you look healthy and well? How do you feel? Is there a bounce in your step? Are you happy with your life? Are you a happier person than you were [five] years ago? What has changed? What are the good things in your life? Now you can see the people who are important to you at this stage of your life sitting in the lounge room with you, talking and laughing. Who is there? What are they talking about? How do you feel about the people who are there with you? Who are your closest friends? Now let your visitors fade away, and see yourself at your place of work or the place where you spend much of your time during the week. Where are you? What are you doing? Is there anyone there with you? Are you enjoying the things that you do? Now let that scene fade away and see yourself engaging in some leisure activity that you frequently enjoy. What sort of things do you do for fun or relaxation? What are your interests? Look back over your life so far. What do you feel proud of? What are you especially glad to have done? What sort of things give you personal satisfaction? Just allow yourself a little time to enjoy your fantasy. And now, see the passage of time moving backwards, once again in spirals and psychedelic patterns, taking you back to the present time. Feel yourself gently returning to the*

here and now, back to the room that you're in at this point in time,
back to the present moment. And when you feel ready, you can open
your eyes.

After you have taken a little time to think about the images that came to you during this exercise, it is a good idea to write them down. In particular, focus on areas that you would like to work towards.

The following are some of the broad areas in which people often choose to set some of their life goals. You might like to select one or more of these and write down specific changes that you want to make within that area.

When writing down your goals, try to be specific. Avoid vague statements. For instance, not 'Have good relationships', but 'Have a close, open and honest relationship with my daughter'; not 'Improve my health', but 'Stop smoking, get my blood pressure down to 140/70'; not 'Improve my attitudes' but 'Write down an alternative perspective whenever I catch myself having self-critical thoughts'.

AREAS FOR SETTING LIFE GOALS
➤ health
➤ relationships
➤ attitudes
➤ leisure
➤ knowledge
➤ interests
➤ work
➤ material
➤ spiritual
➤ self-development
➤ other.

Once you have identified your life goals, it may be worth re-reading Chapter 9 on formulating an action plan in order to guide you through the process of converting intentions into action.

EXPECTATIONS

Whether we are happy or miserable depends on our expectations.
It depends not on the things that we have, but on what we expect to have.

In nearly every way, our lives are easier and more comfortable than they were for people of previous generations. Technological advances and economic growth in the past few decades have given us access to material goods our grandparents would not have dreamed of. We own houses, cars, TVs, mobile phones, MP3 players, computers and fancy equipment for home entertainment. We take more holidays than previous generations and we go overseas more often. We own devices that save us time and energy—washing machines, dishwashers, refrigerators, vacuum cleaners and microwave ovens. Most of these things have made our lives easier and freed us from the tedious aspects of domestic life. In addition, we have more opportunities than our predecessors—to study, travel, change careers, move house, develop our talents, indulge our passions and leave an unhappy marriage. With all of these new-found freedoms and creature comforts, one would think that life in the new millennium would be much happier than in any previous period in history.

Yet there is little evidence of increased happiness—in fact, some sections of the community are less happy now than in the past. This is the paradox of the 21st century. According to a World Health Organization report, depression is currently the third leading cause of disease and disability in the world, and is predicted to rise to first place by the year 2030. Drug abuse, loneliness, youth suicide and divorce are increasingly common symptoms of personal unhappiness and social alienation. While many factors, including urbanisation, unemployment and changing social habits and values have contributed to these problems, an important but often unacknowledged factor is our changing expectations.

It was the ancient stoic philosopher Seneca who first pointed out the role that our expectations play in determining our level of happiness. In AD 50, Seneca observed that people who are dissatisfied with their lives often have unrealistic expectations about how things should be. Today, with the mass media promoting tantalising images of success, beauty, romance, popularity and wealth, the perceived gap between our own lives and those of the people we compare ourselves with has never been greater. Consequently we are more likely to feel dissatisfied with our lot than ever before. We have so much, yet we expect so much more. Because we tend to compare our lives with those of other people, we are left with the impression that we are somehow missing out—that our lives are not good enough the way they are.

> Comparing yourself with idealised images of others
> is guaranteed to make you miserable.

People living in modern Western countries often have unrealistic expectations about how things should be. We want to retain our youthful looks for ever, and we become despondent as we discover that we have little control over the ageing process. We expect to have perfect friendships, and so we become easily disillusioned when friends and family members fail to live up to our expectations. We expect to have well-paid, stimulating and satisfying work and so we feel frustrated and dissatisfied because we have not found the perfect job. We expect to be married or in a committed relationship and so we despair because we have not found our ideal mate. We want to have perfect children and happy harmonious families and we feel disappointed when ours do not live up to expectations. We want to own an attractive home with lots of material comforts and we want to accomplish lots of important things. In short, many of our expectations leave us feeling unsatisfied with what we have.

CHANGING OUR EXPECTATIONS OVER TIME

As we move through the various stages of our lives, new circumstances constantly challenge us to modify our expectations. One of the greatest challenges is in relation to ageing. Over the course of our lives, we will need to change our expectations in relation to our appearance, and our physical and mental abilities. Age brings with it a series of physical changes—our skin starts to sag, and wrinkles appear; our hair thins and goes grey; our thighs and tummy get bigger, and a lot of flabby bits appear where they never used to be; our eyesight, hearing and memory deteriorate; and even our sense of smell and taste decline. None of this is in itself a problem, as long as we modify our expectations along the way.

With the passage of time, we also need to adjust to the changing stages of life—from childhood to adolescence, adulthood, parenthood, working life, retirement and old age. With each new stage come new challenges, responsibilities and rewards. Recognising that life is composed of a series of stages, and adjusting our expectations as each new stage unfolds helps us to make smooth transitions over the course of our lives. Unrealistic expectations or failing to modify our expectations over time can leave us feeling frightened, angry or depressed.

> *When petrol first went up to $1 a litre in 2001, Australians were horrified—we had been used to paying 80 cents, so the new price felt exorbitant. But when the price subsequently climbed to $1.40, $1 a litre suddenly sounded incredibly cheap. What previously seemed outrageous now seemed like a steal. Although $1 a litre was still $1 a litre, it felt very different. It is not the price we pay, but our expectation of what the price should be that determines whether we believe we are being fleeced or getting a bargain.*

A Chinese peasant celebrates because the abundant rice crop harvested this year will be sufficient to feed his family over the coming winter. In another part of the world, a businessman contemplates suicide after the net worth of his assets has fallen from $27 million to just $7 million. He will be depressed for years. It is all about expectations.

CONDITIONAL HAPPINESS—WAITING FOR THE RIGHT CIRCUMSTANCES

Many people believe that they could be happy, if only they were able to overcome a particular obstacle to their happiness—a rotten job, a difficult child, an unpaid mortgage or an unhappy marriage. As a result, we focus on our difficulties and postpone our happiness, assuming that one day, when all of our problems have been resolved or we have achieved some important goal, then we will be able to sit back and feel happy.

➤ When I finish my studies, then life will be so much easier.
➤ When I find the right job—something that makes me feel fulfilled—I will be content.
➤ When I move out of home, then I'll feel much happier.
➤ When I'm earning enough to feel financially secure, I'll be able to relax.
➤ When I meet the right man, then I'll be happy.
➤ When I have children, I will feel fulfilled.
➤ When the children finally leave home, then I'll be able to relax at last.
➤ When I finish writing this book, then maybe I'll get a life.

Happiness is not a place to arrive at—it is a manner of travelling.
MARGARET RUNBECK

Waiting for things to fall into place before we can feel happy is a precarious strategy for two reasons. Firstly, we miss the opportunity to fully experience and enjoy the present moment—to feel good now. And that is a waste because today is the only chance we will ever get to experience today. Remember the saying, 'This is not a dress rehearsal—it's the real thing'? Postponing our happiness to some future time means that we miss out on today. And once today has passed, it's gone and we don't get another chance to live it again.

Secondly, when we make our happiness conditional on solving our problems, we may never be happy, as problems will always be with us. As some are resolved, new ones emerge—that is the nature of things. The challenge is not to expect that all of our problems should disappear, but to fix what is fixable, accept what we cannot change and focus on all the many good things that we already have.

IT'S WHAT WE FOCUS ON

I cried because I had no shoes
Until I met a man who had no feet.
AUTHOR UNKNOWN

Making a conscious effort to redirect our focus from themes that make us miserable to those that make us feel good can make a big difference to the way we feel.

THEMES THAT MAKE US FEEL MISERABLE	THEMES THAT MAKE US FEEL HAPPY
All the things that have gone wrong	All the things that have gone right
Injustices	Our good fortune
Rejections	People who care about us
Our failures	Our achievements
Our shortcomings	Our strengths and qualities
Things we've missed out on	Things that we've been lucky enough to have or experience
What we've lost	What we've gained
Other people's faults	Other people's qualities

We have already seen that unrealistic expectations and focusing on the things that we believe are missing from our lives contributes to unhappiness. The reverse is also true—having reasonable expectations and being in the habit of acknowledging all the good things we have helps to make us feel fortunate and satisfied. Everyone has both positive and negative aspects in their lives—achievements and failures, pleasures and disappointments, losses and gains, illnesses and recoveries. The secret is to focus on all the good things that we already have. We take so much for granted! There is much to celebrate, if only we open our eyes.

DAILY GRATITUDE LIST

One way to stay mindful of all the good things we have is to write a daily gratitude list. This involves taking five minutes each morning or evening to think of all the things we have that we can feel grateful for. Gratitude has long been the domain of prayer—most religions urge followers to express gratitude for various blessings, including food on the table, a roof over one's head and the good health of loved ones. Gratitudes do not need to exclusively focus on big-ticket items. We can learn to appreciate every positive aspect of our lives, no matter how small—an outstanding task finally accomplished; an invitation to dinner; a fascinating program on TV; the affections of our pet; the sunshine beaming through our window; or the sweet, curious questions of a child. Keeping a daily gratitude list need only take up a few minutes a day, and can make a significant difference to the way we feel. For example, these are the gratitudes that I wrote down yesterday:

I feel grateful for:
1 *The laughter that I shared with Sue on the phone this evening.*
2 *The pleasure of reading today's newspaper.*
3 *The revived energy and sense of wellbeing that I felt after my morning walk.*
4 *The gradual healing of a wound—a problem that has troubled me is fading.*
5 *My back is feeling better.*
6 *That phone call that I had been putting off has now been made.*
7 *The peace of mind that I am experiencing right now.*
8 *My ability to think and write today.*
9 *The progress that I've made on my book.*
10 *Living in a t-shirt—Sydney's great weather.*

Don't ignore the small pleasures.
They are the things that make life delightful!

EXERCISE 11.2

Write down a gratitude list for today. Record the things that are going well in your life, the things that you enjoy or appreciate, and the things you are lucky enough to have. Repeat this exercise every day for a week, and see how you feel. Consider making this a lifelong habit.

IN SUMMARY

➤ Research from studies around the world suggests that people who have satisfying work, absorbing interests, close supportive relationships or religious affiliation are more likely to be happy than those who don't. Personal attributes of people who describe themselves as happy include good self-esteem, optimism, extroversion and a sense of being in control.

➤ A lifestyle that balances regular commitments with leisure activity, mental stimulation, social interaction and health maintenance is also conducive to psychological wellbeing.

➤ Setting and working towards goals can help us to achieve life-enhancing changes, and is a satisfying process in itself.

➤ Unrealistic expectations are a common cause of unhappiness. It is often useful to identify and challenge some of the expectations that limit our ability to be happy. It is also important to modify some of our expectations as we get older, and as our life circumstances change.

➤ Focusing on the good things that we already have, rather than the things we are missing, can help us to feel happy. A daily gratitude list is a useful way of maintaining this focus.

TWELVE

Mindfulness

The automaticity of being lost in thought without knowing that we're thinking is really the string upon which all of our suffering is strung.

**SAM HARRIS,
'INSIGHT INTO PRACTISING MEDITATION WITH SAM HARRIS', YOUTUBE VIDEO**

ABOUT THIS CHAPTER

This chapter has been added to the third edition of *Change Your Thinking* because of growing evidence that mindfulness techniques confer psychological benefits, and because they are now frequently integrated with CBT techniques by mental-health practitioners. The aim here is to outline basic components of mindfulness practice, describe the mechanisms that might underlie possible benefits and explain how they may be added to the CBT strategies described in this book. This chapter is not intended as a complete guide to mindfulness practice. There are many excellent books that describe the practice comprehensively (see Recommended Reading on page 407). Readers might also consider attending a course in mindfulness meditation, downloading guided meditation from the internet or using a guided meditation CD.

THE EMERGENCE OF MINDFULNESS IN WESTERN PSYCHOLOGY

The principles of mindfulness practice stem from Buddhist traditions that developed over 2,000 years ago as a path leading to the cessation of suffering. In the past two decades, mindfulness has been transformed from a largely Buddhist concept into a mainstream psychological approach used by Western mental-health practitioners. Stripped of its religious and cultural traditions, the practice has been described in therapist manuals and consumer self-help books. Studies conducted around the world have evaluated the effects of mindfulness techniques for managing various psychological conditions (including anxiety disorders, depression, relationship problems, pain and substance abuse), many with promising results.

Various claims have been made about the benefits of mindfulness practice, some well ahead of rigorous scientific research to support it. The potential uses and benefits of the practice are yet to be fully understood, and its capacity to resolve particular mental-health problems is yet to be established. Nevertheless, there is growing evidence that mindfulness practice, when undertaken frequently and consistently, does confer benefits. The most frequently reported benefits include:

➤ **Increased metacognitive awareness**—greater awareness of the cognitive processes occurring in one's mind, and increased ability to recognise that one's thoughts are just thoughts, rather than reality or truth.

➤ **Reduction in 'elaborative' thought processes** such as rumination and worrying. Individuals who practise mindfulness appear to be able to recognise unhelpful repetitive thought streams more readily, and experience a reduction in these processes over time.

➤ **Enhanced emotion regulation**—improved ability to remain mindfully aware as unpleasant emotions arise, and to avoid their escalation. Regular practitioners of mindfulness appear to have less emotional reactivity and therefore a greater ability to remain calm in response to stressful events.

➤ **Improved attentional capacities**—regular practice of mindfulness meditation appears to improve one's ability to concentrate and to ignore potentially distracting thoughts and information.

➤ **Reduced risk of mental-health problems**—when incorporated into a treatment 'package' called 'Mindfulness-based Cognitive Therapy', the practice has been found to halve the risk of recurrence for people with a history of depression. There is also some evidence that mindfulness practice can improve outcomes for people who are currently depressed, and assist in the management of anxiety disorders.

➤ **Pain management**—when delivered as part of a pain-management program, mindfulness practice improves one's ability to manage pain and other unpleasant physical symptoms.

➤ **Other benefits**—there is some evidence that regular practice produces long-term changes in mood and levels of wellbeing, which may be life enhancing and protective in the longer term. Studies currently being undertaken at research centres around the world are investigating other possible benefits, and these are likely to be reported over the next few years.

Western interest in mindfulness was initially sparked in the late 1970s, with the introduction of mindfulness training for patients with chronic pain at the University of Massachusetts Medical School. The 'Mindfulness-based Stress Reduction' (MBSR) program was the brainchild of Jon Kabat-Zinn, Professor of Medicine Emeritus at the Medical School. The program attracted referrals of patients with serious illness and chronic pain, frequently from doctors who could offer them nothing more. While not claiming to cure disease, the aim of the program was to equip patients with a way of responding to their illness that freed them from the anxiety, depression and distress that compounded their suffering.

In the past 20 years, psychologists have started incorporating mindfulness techniques as an adjunct to their therapies, and new treatment approaches that utilise mindfulness began to spring up. These included Mindfulness-based Cognitive Therapy (MBCT), which was developed by a group of psychological researchers (Zindel Segal, Mark Williams and John Teasdale) in collaboration with Jon Kabat-Zinn. The program combined many elements of Kabat-Zinn's original MBSR program with components of CBT for the prevention of recurrence of depression. Interest in mindfulness grew after two high-quality studies found that individuals who had experienced three or more prior episodes of depression halved their risk of a recurrence following participation in the MBCT program.

Other therapies that have adopted mindfulness practice as part of a combined treatment package include Acceptance and Commitment Therapy (ACT), which encourages individuals to mindfully accept painful experiences, clarify personal values and set goals that contribute to a more vital and meaningful life; and Dialectical Behaviour Therapy (DBT) which aims to reduce self-harm and suicidal behaviour in individuals with borderline personality disorder.

WHAT IS MINDFULNESS?

Mindfulness is not an emotional state, such as being happy or free of anxiety. It is a state of awareness where one is fully present with whatever is happening in this moment, without judging any aspect of the experience. In *Full Catastrophe Living*, his seminal book on the subject, Kabat-Zinn described the essence of mindfulness as 'a way of bringing conscious awareness and attention to the present moment, with an attitude of openness and curiosity'. In this state, sensory information (including sounds, smells, tastes, body sensations, thoughts, feelings and things we see) may be observed with curiosity. Thoughts and emotions are watched dispassionately, as objects of the mind rather than reflections of truth or reality. They are noted without over-identifying with them, judging or trying to change them.

Mindfulness practice is not directed at avoiding painful experiences, but at developing tolerance for them. It is held that the struggle against unwanted thoughts, feelings and bodily sensations creates inner turmoil. Responding with aversion to one's current experience exacerbates negative feelings and increases distress. For this reason, the attitude that accompanies mindfulness is central to the practice. Present-moment experience is observed with an attitude of **non-judgement, non-striving** and **non-attachment**. All aspects of current experience are approached with curiosity and openness. We take in whatever is there exactly as it is, without seeking or longing for something else. Instead of resisting emotional or physical pain, we turn towards it and observe its qualities with a curious and open mind.

> If you are tense, then just pay attention to the tension. If you are in pain, then be with the pain as best you can. If you are criticising yourself then observe the activity of the judging mind. Just watch. Remember, we are simply allowing anything and everything that we experience from moment to moment to be here, because it already is.
>
> **JON KABAT-ZINN,** *FULL CATASTROPHE LIVING*

Mindfulness can be practised as **meditation** (usually in a seated position, but may be while standing or walking) or as an **enhanced state of awareness** during daily-life situations. Although mindfulness does not necessarily involve meditation, the ability to experience mindful awareness is developed through regular meditation. The practice typically involves concentration meditation (usually focusing on the breath) as well as observing current sensory, mental and emotional experience (e.g. thoughts, emotions, body sensations, sounds and movement).

Mindfulness meditation provides the mental training that develops understanding of our own mind, and enhances our ability to practise mindfulness in daily-life situations. During the practice we pay attention to the objective reality of the present moment. Thoughts and feelings that arise are observed and accepted. We do not try to change or escape from them, but simply note their presence. Importantly, we do not respond to thoughts or emotions by judging them, resisting them, elaborating on them or thinking about how to stop them.

WHY PRACTISE MINDFULNESS?

Humans are thinking creatures—our mind is engaged in mental 'chatter' almost every moment of the day. Our thoughts arise constantly and automatically, usually without our awareness, yet their nature determines how we feel most of the time. Whether the majority of our experiences are characterised by feelings of contentment or dissatisfaction, and whether we are fully engaged with life or disconnected from it, is determined by the nature of our thoughts. This includes the 'background chatter' that occupies our minds much of the time, as well as the more prominent conscious thoughts in the 'front' of our minds when we contemplate specific issues. Given their very significant impact on our lives, it is perhaps surprising that we pay so little attention to our thoughts most of the time.

> The character of the conversations we have with ourselves engineers our suffering and the mediocrity of our lives in every present moment.
>
> **SAM HARRIS,**
> **'INSIGHT INTO PRACTISING MEDITATION WITH SAM HARRIS', YOUTUBE VIDEO**

Most of us tend to assume that our ability to feel happy is driven by the events in our lives—such as the people we deal with, the work we do, the state of our health and the objects we own. But is that true? There is no doubt that having good things, such as close relationships, a sense of purpose, enjoyable interests, mental challenges, a nice place to live and robust health contributes to wellbeing and life satisfaction. But they don't make us happy. Even when our life circumstances are excellent, many of us don't feel happy. We can sit under a tree and watch a beautiful sunset or take ourselves off to a favourite holiday destination, and still not feel happy. Our thoughts can make us miserable even in the best of places. Life events, no matter how good, do not protect us from our thoughts. When we are not connected to the present moment, we leave ourselves open to the vagaries and vicissitudes of our own mind.

This is ironic, because the present moment is not a bad place to be most of the time. If we were to stop and reflect on the present moment at random times during our week, we would probably discover that most of the events happening during those times are not too bad. But this may not be reflected in the way we feel. Our thought processes disconnect us from 'the now' and take us to all sorts of unhappy places. As our mind turns to problems, threats, criticisms, resentments, frustrations, shoulds, regrets, fears, injustices and other unhelpful notions, we disconnect from the present and create our own unhappiness.

A common feature of our everyday experience is how little choice we seem to have over where we place our attention. Unconscious mental processes shaped by our history and temperament direct our attention to thoughts that create suffering. For instance, you might find yourself paying attention to an event that made you angry; creating an imaginary conversation that you wish you had had; focusing on some perceived personal flaw you can't seem to overcome or thinking about some object that is missing from your life. Your thoughts may keep returning to a particular theme, such as missing out, failure, being judged or uncertainties of the future. You may think about these issues consciously, or keep them stored in the 'back' of your mind, where they continue to sit and prevent you from engaging fully with things happening now. Paying attention to problems (real or imagined) when we are not problem solving, or focusing on things that we can't control keeps us stuck in an unhappy place, even when the events occurring in our present moment are positive.

Of course, this doesn't mean that we can live in the present every moment of our lives. There are good reasons why our brains have developed the capacity to remember the past and plan for the future. Reflecting on past events—both happy and unhappy—enables us to learn and improve aspects of our lives, and provides context for our current experiences. Past events also shape our values and clarify what is important. This helps us in making decisions and planning for the future.

Similarly, contemplating the future is healthy and beneficial at times. Thinking about what we want in life, setting realistic goals, making plans and working towards them can help us create a rich and meaningful life, and may increase our wellbeing in the longer term.

However, there is a world of difference between, on the one hand, constructively thinking about the past and contemplating the future and, on the other hand, ruminating, worrying, fretting and engaging in pointless speculations about past injustices or possible future threats. These disconnect us from the present moment, and take us on futile journeys to nowhere. Unwittingly we confuse worrying and rumination with problem solving and planning.

Tuning our attention to the present moment helps us to become aware of these pointless meanderings. By acknowledging their presence, observing them with curiosity and labelling them for what they are ('mental chatter', 'rumination', 'worry thoughts'), it becomes easier to detach from the process. Or, at the very least, we are able to see how we create our own suffering.

MINDFULNESS IN DAILY LIFE

Although mindfulness is often practised as a sitting meditation, mindful attention to the present moment can be practised in any daily-life situation. Regular activities such as walking, eating, washing, waiting or putting out the garbage present opportunities for developing mindfulness skills. When we give our full attention to aspects of our current experience such as thoughts, feelings, sounds, smells, tastes or physical sensations, we are in a mindful state.

In addition, the onset of unpleasant emotions, such as anxiety, anger, guilt or frustration, provide an ideal opportunity to engage in mindful awareness. The observation 'I notice that I am having these thoughts' or 'I notice that I am experiencing these feelings' helps to reduce emotional reactivity by inserting a space between the event and our response to it. Stepping back and observing the process can help to defuse the automatic emotional response. However, even if this does not occur, the ability to observe our mind, body and emotions at work increases our awareness of the complex relationship between life events and the way we react to them. This is a useful step in learning to better manage our emotional responses.

PRACTISING MINDFULNESS MEDITATION

This practice involves two basic components:

Concentration meditation—focusing on specific objects or sensations, and

Insight meditation—understanding one's own mental processes that lead to suffering.

CONCENTRATION

Concentration meditation is a key foundation skill of mindfulness practice. It involves maintaining our attention on a single object while disengaging from thoughts, feelings or other distractions that arise. Since ancient times, the breath has been used for concentration meditation, and it is still the most commonly used point of focus today. However, other objects such as sounds and body sensations, when still or during movement (such as walking, yoga movements or stretches, or swimming) can also be used.

Concentration meditation keeps our attention anchored in current experience, so that thoughts, feelings and sensations can be detected as they arise in our stream of consciousness. It trains the mind to attend, enhancing our ability to focus on the task at hand in other areas of our daily life. It helps to stabilise the mind, reducing mental chatter and improving our ability to detect and disconnect from it during daily-life situations. The process has been likened to the concept of a glass of muddy water. Our thoughts keep stirring the water, keeping it cloudy, but if we choose to sit quietly, the mud will eventually settle. Concentrating on a single object while releasing the urge to engage with thoughts allows 'the mud to settle', and connects us to the stillness or 'clear water' that remains.

INSIGHT

Concentration is not the end goal of mindfulness meditation, but a skill that opens the door to insight and self-knowledge. When the mind is still, we are better able to connect with other aspects of our current experience. During mindfulness practice, we step back and observe the flow of consciousness within our own mind. We notice each object within that stream of consciousness—thoughts, emotions, states of vigilance, body tension, 'background chatter' and urges. We learn to discriminate between the different types of experience, and observe how they interact with each other. The process of observing creates a deeper understanding of how our mind works, beneath its usual perceptions and biases. We learn experientially that our thoughts and emotions are not reflections of reality or a permanent part of ourselves, but simply transitory occurrences.

Mindfulness has been described as a way of tuning in to ourselves, because we become acutely aware of our present-moment experience, based on information coming to us from our senses. The term 'the observing self' has been used to describe that part of our mind that is able to step back and watch our own cognitive processes, emotions and body sensations in action. It enables us to notice when we get caught up in thought streams, and how they affect us emotionally and physically. This ability to view our inner world as it reacts to various stimuli (e.g. our own thoughts or body sensations, other people's behaviours, life events) enhances our ability to understand the healthy and unhealthy habits of our own mind. By labelling our thoughts, feelings, urges and body sensations as they arise, we are better able to experience them objectively. We create a 'space' between our thoughts and the way we react to them, making it easier to detach from their messages.

> By observing your thoughts and emotions as if you had taken a step back from them, you can see much more clearly what is actually going on in your mind. You can see your thoughts arise and recede one after another. You can note the content of your thoughts, the feelings associated with them, and your reactions to them. You might become aware of agendas, attachments, likes and dislikes, and inaccuracies in your ideas. You can gain insight into what drives you, how you see the world, who you think you are—insight into your fears and aspirations.
>
> **JON KABAT-ZINN, A DESCRIPTION OF MINDFULNESS MEDITATION IN *MIND/BODY MEDICINE*, 1993**

FOCUSING ON THE BREATH

The most basic form of mindfulness meditation is focusing attention on the breath. It sounds simple—just sit quietly, breathe naturally and concentrate on the process of breathing. However, anyone who has tried this knows how incredibly difficult it is. Our mind is naturally inclined to wander, and staying focused on one particular object is extremely challenging. The ever-present stream of mental 'chatter' inevitably leaks into our consciousness as we try to meditate.

When we discover that our mind has wandered, our task is to simply acknowledge the experience and then return our attention to the breath. Rather than engaging with thoughts, emotions and sensations, we simply notice them when they arise and let them pass without being drawn into them. The process of switching attention back to the breath may occur dozens of times during a meditation session. Our mind repeatedly drifts to thoughts—e.g. things we need to do, reflections on past events or things that may happen in the future. We may also get caught up in thoughts about the process of meditation itself—that we are not making progress, that we are wasting time or that we have more important things to do. We might notice feelings such as impatience, boredom or frustration, or unpleasant physical sensations such as muscle tension or back pain. When this occurs, our task is not to judge any aspect of the experience, but to simply acknowledge what is occurring and return our attention to the breath.

By recognising and labelling thoughts when they arise and then returning our attention to the breath, we change our relationship with our thoughts. We switch from being 'inside' the thoughts to watching them 'from the outside'. In Buddhist writings, the idea of observing but not holding on to thoughts is described in metaphors such as thoughts being leaves that float along a stream, or clouds floating across the open sky. We experience our thoughts as temporary objects that pass through the landscape of the mind, and do not require any special attention. When we notice that we are engaged in a thought, we can let it move on—floating along the stream or as a cloud across the sky, without processing it further.

SIMPLE MINDFULNESS EXERCISE:

Sit upright in a chair. Close your eyes and let your attention focus on the physical sensations of your breath moving in and out of your nose. Notice that when air enters your nose it is slightly cool, and when it leaves your nose it is slightly warm. Keep breathing naturally, focusing on cool air entering and warm air leaving through your nose (for 2 minutes). Now, turn your attention to the sensations of your chest, expanding and contracting with each breath. Remain focused on the movement of your chest (for 2 minutes). Now continue to breathe naturally, focusing your attention on both sensations

> at once—air moving in and out of your nose, together with the movement
> of your chest as it expands and contracts with each breath (for 2 minutes).
> Whenever a thought pops into your mind, acknowledge its presence and
> return your attention to your breath.

As may be become apparent when you start to practise, mindfulness meditation is a dynamic process that involves controlling where we place our attention. We regulate our thought processes through:

➤ **sustained attention**—focusing on the breath or a fixed object;

➤ repeatedly **switching attention**—returning to our point of focus when the mind has wandered; and

➤ **inhibiting elaborative thinking**—choosing not to get caught up with the content of random thoughts.

MINDFULNESS AND RELAXATION

Unlike deep relaxation exercises that we use to release physical tension and arousal, mindfulness is not a relaxation technique. We can practise mindful awareness while experiencing intense emotions, including anger, fear, frustration, guilt and resentment, or while participating in physical activities such as eating, walking, bathing, cleaning or swimming. (It is usually very difficult to practise deep relaxation during periods of intense emotion as our body becomes tense and aroused when emotions are 'hot'.)

Although we do not deliberately set out to produce a particular physical state when practising mindfulness, relaxation is frequently an unintended consequence. One reason for this may be that, by being fully engaged with the present moment, we disconnect from other stresses or threat-focused cognitions. This includes conscious thoughts at the 'front' of our mind, and less conscious cognitions at the 'back' of our mind. These perceptions may keep us tense and vigilant, even when we are not consciously thinking about them. Focusing on present-moment experience can disconnect us from both conscious and unconscious perceptions, and therefore allows the body to relax.

MINDFULNESS OF THOUGHTS

As we develop mindfulness skills, our thoughts are increasingly used as objects for observation—both during meditation and in our daily lives. Instead of getting caught up in their content, we step back and observe the process. For instance, we might notice thought streams—how one thought leads to another, the way particular thoughts come and go and how the mind keeps returning to certain themes. Some thoughts feel trivial while others feel weighty and elicit strong emotion. We may notice how some thoughts are very prominent for a period of time and then disappear, while others seem to be sitting in the 'back' of our minds nearly all the time.

One of the most valuable insights to be gained from observing our thoughts in action is the realisation that they are just mental events, rather than 'truth', 'reality' or 'me'. Observing the flow of consciousness enables us to recognise that each thought and feeling is produced by our mind, and has no more inherent value than what we attribute to it. (This awareness reinforces a basic tenet of CBT, as understanding that our thoughts are just mental events helps us to downgrade the importance of their messages.)

The awareness that 'This thought is just a thought' has been referred to as **decentring** or **defusing**—a process that can change the meaning we give to our experiences. Instead of automatically accepting the validity of our thoughts, we come to see them as products of our mind. For example, perceptions such as 'I am a failure ... People think badly of me ... I am unsafe ... Things will never change' are recognised as 'just thoughts'. Since they are not reality, we do not need to take them too seriously, and we do not need to ruminate to find a solution. We can treat them like clouds floating by in the landscape of our mind without engaging with them further.

Observing thoughts as they arise also enables us to notice **elaborative thought processes** such as worry and rumination. When we discover that we are caught up in these processes, we can label the experience. For instance, 'That's worrying'; 'I notice that I am ruminating again' or 'There's my mental chatter'. Providing labels creates some distance from our thoughts, and enhances our ability to disengage from them. Although it does not necessarily switch off repetitive thought streams, bringing conscious awareness to the thought processes changes the way we relate to them. We understand that they will run their course, and if we choose not to engage with them each time they surface, they will fade over time.

> *During the course of an evening with friends, Noreen made some comments which she now believes put her in a negative light. The next day Noreen ruminates about what she said, what she should have said and what her friends must be thinking. Noreen's thoughts feel like 'truth', and she is very immersed in them.*
>
> *Although she is not aware that she is thinking, Noreen is aware that she feels upset. This prompts her to sit down and spend some time paying mindful attention to her inner state. Noreen notices thoughts about perceived failure—both recent and from the distant past. She notices feelings of anxiety and despair, as well as tension in her tummy and chest. Noreen observes these with curiosity, and notices the urge to keep re-engaging with her thoughts. She labels her thoughts 'ruminations', and each time she becomes aware of their presence, Noreen reflects, 'I notice that I am ruminating again.' Noreen imagines her ruminations as leaves floating along a stream—whenever she detects their presence, she imagines the words written on a leaf and sends it floating down the stream. Noreen is neither suppressing nor actively engaging with her thoughts, but just acknowledging them and letting them pass. This provides space for the thoughts to decay, and prevents her distress from escalating.*

MINDFULNESS OF EMOTIONS

During mindfulness practice, emotions—both pleasant and unpleasant— are observed without judgement or resistance. It is held that while trying to eliminate or suppress unpleasant emotions turns them into 'the enemy', observing and accepting them has the opposite effect. Paradoxically, turning towards unpleasant emotions and observing their qualities with curiosity and openness reduces the perception of threat that normally accompanies them. It also increases our ability to tolerate unpleasant emotions, and so prevents us from becoming excessively distressed by them.

When we stop trying to force pleasant feelings, they are freer to emerge on their own. When we stop trying to resist unpleasant feelings, we may find that they drift away by themselves.

WILLIAMS, TEASDALE, SEGAL AND KABAT-ZINN,
THE MINDFUL WAY THROUGH DEPRESSION

MINDFUL AWARENESS EXERCISE:
Sit upright in a chair. Close your eyes, take a few moments, and then ask yourself 'What's going on for me right now?' Notice whatever is present in your field of awareness. This may include:

Body sensations (such as points of contact with the chair, clothing touching your skin, internal tension, arousal, discomfort, etc.);
Mood (general background feeling—is it positive, negative or neutral?);
Emotions (for example, are you excited, sad, angry, frustrated, anxious, guilty, resentful, insecure?);
Issues at the 'back of the mind' (concerns that sit in the 'background', often without conscious awareness, creating feelings of unease and tension); and
Transient thoughts (these pop into your mind, and disappear—usually replaced by other thoughts).

Observe whatever is present with curiosity. Do not try to change anything— just be aware of what is happening in this moment (for 5 to 10 minutes).

SECONDARY EMOTIONS

A common difficulty for people who experience psychological problems is the emotional distress that arises in response to them. Thoughts like 'This depression is awful ... I just want it to go ... What if it never goes away?' produces a secondary problem. Despair about feeling depressed increases depressive symptoms and perpetuates or exacerbates the depression. Similarly, feeling anxious about one's anxiety or in anticipation of future anxiety, despondent at one's unhappiness or frustrated at one's stress levels creates secondary emotions that invariably make things worse. The emotions themselves become a source of further distress.

Mindfulness invites us to abandon the struggle with unpleasant feelings. By opening up to uncomfortable experiences, we release resistance. This increases our capacity to tolerate unpleasant feelings, and paradoxically reduces their intensity. While not a traditional CBT strategy, observing unpleasant emotions without judging or resisting them makes a lot of sense in situations where the emotions themselves have become a source of threat. Learning not to judge prevents the escalation of unpleasant emotions and mental-health problems because we avoid 'distress about distress'.

> *During a stressful period last year Sean experienced sleep difficulties that lasted for several weeks. Subsequently he started worrying about the possibility of not being able to sleep. The resulting anxiety produced further insomnia. While the original stress had passed, Sean developed a secondary problem—anxiety about the possibility of not sleeping. Sean's reaction to his insomnia and his unhelpful attempts to prevent it keep him hypervigilant and anxious, which in turn maintains the problem.*

To break the cycle, Sean would benefit from releasing his efforts to eliminate insomnia, and remaining open to whatever experience presents itself. Even if he is unable to sleep, this is far less of a problem than the anxiety produced by his desperate attempts to control it. By accepting insomnia if it should happen without catastrophising about it, Sean actually reduces his anxiety, and therefore creates space for the problem to disappear on its own.

> *Five years ago, Paddy went through a period of depression and anxiety following the break-up of a relationship. It was an extremely difficult time, and Paddy thinks back to that period as the low point of his life. In the past few weeks, Paddy has been dealing with a stressful work situation that has caused his mood to plummet. As his thoughts return to the earlier depression, Paddy starts thinking about the possibility that it could recur. Paddy desperately wants to avoid another depressive episode, and noticing his growing anxiety and plummeting mood makes him feel increasingly distressed. Paddy's reaction to his own internal*

state produces more anxiety and despair. This secondary effect—distress about his distress—exacerbates the original problem and prevents him from getting over it.

Paddy benefits from mindfully sitting with and observing the thoughts, feelings and body sensations that are part of his current experience, without trying to stop them. Observing the feelings with a curious and open mind, just letting them be without fighting against them eliminates the secondary distress that was created by feelings of aversion and resistance. This creates a space that allows the feelings to pass.

> Rather than seeing them as 'bad and threatening things', a view that triggers avoidance and gets us stuck in suffering, we begin to see unpleasant experiences for what they are: passing mental events—bundles of bodily sensations, feelings and thoughts. As best we can, we greet them with a sense of interest and curiosity, rather than with a sense of unease, hatred, and dread. We welcome them in, as they are already here anyway.
>
> **WILLIAMS, TEASDALE, SEGAL AND KABAT-ZINN,**
> *THE MINDFUL WAY THROUGH DEPRESSION*

MINDFULNESS OF BODY SENSATIONS

The body is a finely tuned messenger of our current emotional state. All emotions, including those that are pleasant (such as joy, surprise and excitement) and unpleasant (such as anger, anxiety, frustration, guilt, resentment, disgust or shame) are felt directly through the body. Interestingly, most of us are largely unaware of the continuous messages that our body transmits. When we are not in tune with our internal state, we miss important information, including feedback from our body. For this reason, it is not uncommon for people to experience high levels of tension and arousal, rapid breathing and knots in the tummy without even being aware that they are anxious.

Mindful attention to body sensations alerts us to what is happening within us, and so enables us to take remedial action. For instance, we may notice our chest becoming tight as we contemplate an unpleasant task, a knot in our stomach as we worry about some future threat, or our neck and shoulders tensing up during the course of the stressful day. As we become aware of these sensations we may also notice thoughts (e.g. 'So much work to do and so little time …'), emotions (e.g. anxiety, frustration, resentment) and behaviours (e.g. angry comments, eating, fretting). This increased level of awareness may motivate us to take remedial action. For instance, we might spend some time mindfully focusing on our breath, doing some progressive muscle relaxation, going for a walk or taking some practical steps to address the stressors we are facing.

Mindfulness of body sensations can also be useful in the management of pain and other unpleasant physical sensations and, in some cases, may help to resolve them. As anxiety produces a range of physiological responses, it is not uncommon for symptoms like headaches, neck pain, tightness in the chest, back pain, difficulty swallowing, diarrhoea, dizziness, fatigue, nausea, tremors, twitches, tingling, numbness, jaw pain and heat surges to be directly attributable to anxiety. Once these unpleasant physical symptoms arise, focused attention to these sensations (called 'hypervigilance') maintains anxiety and therefore arousal, which maintains the physical symptoms in a self-perpetuating cycle. The more we fear and resist them, the more they persevere. Adopting a mindful attitude to the presence of unpleasant body sensations and learning not to resist or struggle against them can result in a significant decrease or resolution of symptoms.

Even when unwanted symptoms are clearly physical in origin, our psychological response to them affects the degree of distress they produce. For example, physical pain that is accompanied by frustration, despondency, resistance or despair creates additional suffering, beyond the pure sensation of pain. Changing our response to pain changes the experience. Tinnitus (ringing in the ears) that is accompanied by frustration, anxiety and constant monitoring creates more suffering than tinnitus that is fully accepted and, therefore, largely ignored. (Failure to accept means that we end up with two problems—the sound in our ears plus ongoing psychological distress.) From the common cold to cancer, the experience of any physical malady is strongly influenced by the psychological response that accompanies it.

Accepting unwanted body sensations reduces suffering because it eliminates the emotional distress that accompanies the sensations—a key principle used in pain management programs. Increasing our tolerance of unpleasant sensations allows suffering to diminish and enhances our ability to get on with other aspects of our lives.

> We cultivate acceptance by taking each moment as it comes and being with it fully, as it is. We try not to impose our ideas about what we should be feeling or thinking or seeing on our experience, but just remind ourselves to ... accept it because it is here right now.
>
> **JON KABAT-ZINN, *FULL CATASTROPHE LIVING***

Yael started to experience frequent dizziness following a period of intense anxiety two years ago. She is now hypervigilant to her physical sensations, constantly watching her body for signs of dizziness, desperately hoping that it will not return. Although she is unaware of her self-monitoring, this process is Yael's unconscious way of trying to exercise control. Unfortunately it has the opposite effect. It is only when Yael learns to develop a mindful attitude towards the sensations (not judging, not resisting, not trying to control, but being open and accepting to whatever arises) that she starts to experience relief. As she gives up futile attempts to prevent or control her symptoms, Yael's hypervigilance diminishes and, paradoxically, her anxiety and related dizziness also recede.

Mindfulness strategies focus on **accepting** rather than **trying to get rid of** unpleasant experience. Paradoxically however, adopting a truly mindful attitude towards pain or other unpleasant sensations often results in the sensations diminishing, or becoming less significant in our lives.

EXPOSURE

Although the approaches may seem quite different, being mindfully present with distressing thoughts and feelings has much in common with exposure exercises that are used in CBT to manage anxiety. As we saw in Chapter 6, repeated exposure to situations we fear (such as lifts, tunnels, public speaking, flying, needles, spiders, driving etc.) leads to habituation. Exposure produces experiential learning—we discover that those things are not so bad after all, and we are able to tolerate them. As we repeatedly face our fears, they stop being a source of threat.

The process of sitting mindfully with distressing thoughts, emotions and body sensations is similar to the exposure exercises used in CBT. Being fully present with aspects of experience that are unpleasant or painful diminishes fear of them over time. Being open and receptive increases our ability to tolerate unpleasant experiences, including physical and emotional pain. As we sit with aversive sensations, fully accepting whatever is present, we learn to endure them. Things we don't resist become less prominent in our awareness. With time they matter less and may eventually disappear from consciousness. At the very least, when we learn to accept unwanted experiences, they become less significant in our mind. Not fighting or resisting things that we can't control allows us to get on with other aspects of our lives, even when our situations are less than ideal.

Malcolm has been feeling sad and anxious since he was diagnosed with prostate cancer three months ago. His prognosis is uncertain, and it feels like a 'black cloud' is hovering above him, preventing him from thinking about other things or getting on with life. When he tries to push negative thoughts away and tells himself not to worry, the thoughts keep returning.

With the guidance of a therapist, Malcolm starts to practise mindfulness meditation for 25 minutes, twice a day. Sometimes he simply observes his breath, while other times he observes his emotions, thoughts and body sensations. Malcolm notices feelings of fear, sadness and guilt, as well as thoughts and images related to dying. He also notices tension in his chest, stomach and shoulders. He sits with and observes the thoughts, images, emotions and sensations with an open and accepting mind. He labels the emotions that he notices: 'scared', 'guilty', 'sad', and observes them more closely. Choosing to be fully present with these experiences feels strangely liberating. By releasing resistance and futile attempts to block distressing emotions, Malcolm frees himself of fear and his preoccupation with his illness. With time Malcolm comes to accept his situation, with its uncertainty about the future, and starts to re-engage with other, more meaningful areas of his life that he has been neglecting until now.

MINDFULNESS VERSUS CBT

The philosophy underlying mindfulness practice is that **suffering arises from our reactions to our experiences** rather than the experiences themselves. While this is consistent with the philosophy of CBT, the strategies that form the two approaches are clearly different. CBT strategies frequently involve identifying cognitions that contribute to distress, labelling the faulty thinking and challenging or reframing the unreasonable aspects of our thinking (using behavioural as well as cognitive strategies). We may also use behavioural experiments to discover the effects of changing our behaviours, or deliberately expose ourselves to unpleasant or feared situations in order to habituate to those fears. In other situations, we work to problem-solve issues that produce distress.

On the other hand, mindfulness practice invites us **not to judge or resist** current experience, including painful emotions, body sensations and unwanted behaviours. Instead of trying to change things, we maintain a curious, nonjudgemental stance with all experience, including physical or emotional pain. As these two approaches appear to be quite different, you may ask yourself, 'Which is correct?'

The answer is that there is value in both approaches, and often the two can be integrated. Indeed, studies that have evaluated MBCT suggest that combining mindfulness practice with components of CBT can produce substantial benefits. Learning to practise mindfulness does not require the abandonment of CBT strategies that have proven highly effective for many psychological conditions. However, adding mindfulness-based techniques or undertaking a complete program of mindfulness training can provide further resources, which may confer additional benefits.

The attitudes that accompany mindfulness practice have the potential to increase **cognitive flexibility,** as we learn new ways of using the mind and responding to challenging experiences. Learning not to be afraid of unpleasant emotions and discovering that they usually pass when we accept them provides valuable insight, and may increase tolerance for emotional distress. This is a particularly useful for individuals who have a strong fear of negative emotions such as anxiety or depression, or who have an excessive need for control.

Although the philosophy of mindfulness does not involve challenging the content of our thoughts, mindfully observing the processes of our inner world increases awareness of our current thoughts, as well as the cognitive processes that underpin them. The ability to identify thoughts that are normally difficult to access may be helpful when using CBT strategies. This is particularly the case in situations where our emotional reactions are difficult to make sense of. For instance, it is not uncommon for people to notice feelings of anxiety, dread or sadness, but not know why they feel that way.

For her 30th birthday, Tegan's boyfriend organised a weekend away at a chalet in the mountains. From the moment she arrived, Tegan's anxiety grew. 'Why am I feeling so anxious?' she wondered. 'Everything is perfect—I have no reason to feel this way!' Later that day as Tegan sat mindfully observing her internal state, the cognitions came to awareness: 'This place is so beautiful and cost so much, if I remain anxious I'll ruin it!'

Once Tegan recognised the cognitions: 'I must not be anxious ... If I'm anxious I'll ruin it,' it became easier for her to address them, using both cognitive and mindfulness strategies. 'That's just my perfectionist, black-and-white thinking,' she reminded herself. 'I don't need to control every aspect of my experience. It's okay to allow myself to experience whatever arises. This is a good opportunity for me to practise mindful acceptance. I can go with whatever unfolds.'

In addition to challenging the belief that she must not be anxious (a cognitive strategy), Tegan chose to observe her responses with an open and accepting mind, and to relinquish her attempts to stop the anxiety. This was difficult, as her instinct was to resist the unpleasant sensations, but there were times when she was able to forget her anxiety. At other times, when her anxiety felt overwhelming, Tegan focused her attention on her breath or on aspects of her current environment. Tegan noticed that her anxiety was not constant, but came and went, and there were times when she was not aware of it at all (such as when they went for walks in the bush). Whenever she noticed her anxiety rising, Tegan reminded herself to 'just let it be' and then returned her attention to whatever she was doing at the time.

The combination of cognitive and mindfulness strategies enabled Tegan to manage her anxiety. Although it did not disappear, Tegan's attitude of acceptance allowed it to come and go without escalating. Releasing the urge to monitor and control her anxiety paradoxically reduced its impact, and freed Tegan to be more present with the experiences of that weekend.

PROBLEM SOLVING STILL MATTERS

Whether we use mindfulness to occasionally supplement cognitive and behavioural strategies, or embrace it as a central practice in our lives, there will always be a need to solve problems. Practising mindfulness does not mean going through life simply observing upsetting thoughts and feelings while not responding to their messages. After all, emotions play an important role—they alert us to potential problems and motivate us to seek solutions. To dismiss all emotions as simply objects of the mind could result in missed opportunities to improve aspects of our lives. For instance, emotions related to financial problems, relationship difficulties, problems at work, physical or mental-health problems or other difficulties alert us to issues that may require both attention and action. Identifying solutions, setting goals, planning strategies and working through them can help to resolve existing or potential problems, and make our lives easier. Indeed, the decision to practise daily mindfulness may itself be a goal that stems from the desire to manage stress and improve the quality of our lives.

On the other hand, when we are immersed in unhelpful thought processes such as persistent worry, rumination, over-analysing and over-thinking, we may unconsciously confuse this for problem solving. It is not the same thing. Indeed, the emotional states that accompany these thought processes (such as anxiety, guilt, resentment and depressed mood) impede our ability to think clearly and to find solutions. Effective problem solving is best done in a deliberate and conscious way (see 'Structured Problem Solving' on page 274). It involves defining the problem, brainstorming possible solutions, identifying various options and choosing specific strategies. This is quite different to the futile 'chewing over' of problems—real or imagined.

Corey suffers from social phobia—a problem that prevents him from making friends, getting promoted at work and enjoying a normal social life. He has participated in a mindfulness meditation program and is now practising daily. While the practice gives him greater insight and self-awareness, it does not cure his social phobia.

Corey embarks on a process of problem solving. He writes a plan of action, which includes getting more information about his condition, seeing a psychologist and talking to his family about the problem. In his search for solutions, he discovers an online chat site for people with social phobia, which directs him to various resources for managing the condition. He also starts seeing a psychologist. Part of his treatment involves undertaking exposure exercises to various social situations that he fears. He starts with less threatening exercises such as joining a bush-walking club and enrolling in a cooking class. Gradually he works through more challenging tasks, such as speaking up at staff meetings and initiating a social event with a colleague.

Mindful attention to his thoughts makes Corey aware that he is constantly self-monitoring in social situations. He discovers that this safety behaviour is self-defeating because it disconnects him from others. Corey learns to switch his attention back to the conversation, and this enables him to remain more engaged with others. Corey also stops planning and rehearsing conversations beforehand, and bans post-

*event analysis (e.g. 'Did I sound like an idiot?'). The combination of
exposure to feared social situations, challenging his catastrophic beliefs,
labelling 'mind reading' and 'jumping to negative conclusions' when
it occurs, mindful awareness of self-focused attention and consciously
switching his attention back to the conversation enable Corey to break
the bad habits that have maintained his social anxiety. This helps him
to develop healthy relationships over time.*

Recognising that he had a problem, planning solutions and actively working towards them enabled Corey to make significant progress in developing his social confidence. Mindfulness practice in isolation did not cure Corey's social phobia. However, mindful awareness of his thoughts (before, during and after social situations), and learning to switch his attention back to the conversation contributed to Corey's improvements.

As far as is known to date, mindfulness practice is rarely a complete solution or cure for specific psychological disorders; however, when combined with other effective treatment strategies, it provides a valuable resource. Mindfulness-based practice also appears to be an effective tool for managing stress and upsetting emotions in daily-life situations. Given the large amount of research that is currently investigating its effects, we can expect to know more about the benefits of mindfulness practice within the next few years.

IN SUMMARY

➤ Mindfulness has been a central component of Buddhist practice for over 2,000 years. In the past two decades it has been popularised in the West as a method of managing stress and approaching psychological problems.

➤ Studies around the world are evaluating the effects of mindfulness practice for various psychological conditions. There is good evidence that MBCT can reduce relapse among sufferers of repeated depressive episodes, and a growing evidence base for other benefits.

➤ Mindfulness has been defined as a way of bringing conscious awareness and attention to the present moment, with an attitude of non-judging openness and curiosity.

➤ Mindfulness can be practised as a meditation or by bringing mindful attention to daily-life experiences.

➤ Both mindfulness and CBT are based on the tenet that cognitions are products of the mind rather than truths or reality. Although the philosophy of mindfulness does not involve challenging the content of one's thoughts, mindfulness techniques can be integrated with CBT strategies.

Solutions to exercises

These are sample solutions to the exercises. There are no definitive answers.

EXERCISE 2.1

1 Personalising: I am totally responsible for my children's decisions and lives.
2 Filtering, shoulds: I should always sound intelligent. I should never say anything silly. People should think highly of me.
3 Comparing: I am not as good as my friends.
4 Predicting catastrophe: A restructure means that I will lose my job. If I lose my job, the consequences will be disastrous, and I will never find another one.
5 Filtering: Everything that I have done is useless, and all of my life experiences have been bad.
6 Black-and-white thinking: My performance must be perfect—otherwise it's a complete disaster.
7 Predicting catastrophe: The worst possible outcome is likely to occur.
8 Hindsight vision: I should have known then what I know now.
9 Mind reading: People must be looking at me and thinking there is something wrong with me.
10 Labelling: Not establishing a business means that I am a failure.
   Overgeneralising: I have never achieved anything worthwhile.
11 Comparing: I should achieve the same level of wealth as my friends.
12 Labelling: He is 100 per cent bad. He has no merit as a person.
13 Personalising: If they are unable to come, it means they don't like me.
14 Black-and-white thinking: Unless our marriage is perfect, it's no good and it won't work.
15 Labelling: If I had problems in my previous job, it means I am no good and will continue to have problems in other jobs.
16 Predicting catastrophe: If I have unpleasant physical symptoms, it must be life-threatening.
17 Personalising; mind-reading: He is doing the housework because he wants to punish me.
18 Just world fallacy: People should not be able to get away with doing things that are unfair.
19 Hindsight vision: I should have known in the past what I would be thinking now.

20 Overgeneralising: If I forget things occasionally, it means I am forgetting everything.

21 Filtering: She is focusing on information that supports her beliefs, while ignoring information that does not support it.

22 Jumping to negative conclusions: If he is not contributing to the conversation, it must be because he doesn't like the company.

23 Just world fallacy: It should be 100 per cent fair.

24 Jumping to negative conclusions: It might work for other people, but not for me.

EXERCISE 3.1: PRACTISE LOGICAL DISPUTING

The neglected birthday

DISPUTE: Not making a fuss about my birthday doesn't mean that he doesn't care about me. Birthdays are important to me but not to him—he has different priorities and values to me. He shows me he loves me in other ways.

POSITIVE ACTIONS: Talk to him. Tell him that birthdays are important to me, and I'd like to feel special on this one day of the year. Tell him what I would like for my next birthday.

The frustrated public servant

DISPUTE: It's disappointing that I didn't achieve very much today, but I did achieve some things. I can't change what has been, but I can organise myself better so that I'm more productive tomorrow. Although I prefer to be productive, this is unlikely to result in catastrophic consequences.

POSITIVE ACTIONS: Set clear goals for tomorrow. Prepare what I am going to work on, so that I can get straight into it first thing in the morning. Learn from the experience and avoid falling into the same traps in the future.

The forgotten breakfast arrangement

DISPUTE: I prefer to be reliable and I nearly always am, but it's human to occasionally make mistakes. I don't know why I forgot on this occasion but I didn't do it on purpose—she knows that. As long as I explain how sorry I am, chances are she'll understand. I have been a good and loyal friend over the years, and it's unlikely that she'll write me off for this.

POSITIVE ACTIONS: Apologise profusely. Perhaps send her a bunch of flowers with a note reiterating how sorry I am.

EXERCISE 3.2: PRACTISE BEHAVIOURAL DISPUTING

1 Speak up in class as often as possible. Observe whether there is any evidence that people think badly of you for speaking up.

2 Take as many flights as possible. Even though you might initially feel anxious, observe that you don't collapse or go mad, and nothing terrible happens.

3 Speak your own mind as often as possible. Observe whether there is any evidence that people like you less if you don't always agree with them.

4   Stop procrastinating—make decisions. Observe whether there was a right or wrong decision. Notice that even when you don't make the best decision, the consequences rarely lead to disaster.

5   Take social risks—approach people at conferences. Notice that people usually respond if you take the first step and that even if they don't, no disastrous consequences follow.

6   Once you have done a reasonable job on your essay, stop and hand it in. Set yourself a time limit. Observe that not being a perfectionist does not make a huge difference to the end result, and frees you to be productive on other things.

7   Make yourself get up in the mornings and exercise. Observe that there is no evidence that getting up early to exercise is too difficult.

8   Challenge yourself to be alone at times. Do things by yourself—go for walks, to the movies, to a coffee shop. Take a holiday at a health resort on your own. Observe that it's not awful to be alone at times.

EXERCISE 3.3: PRACTISE GOAL-FOCUSED THINKING

1   Does demanding that my mother shouldn't be there help me to enjoy my party? Getting upset about my mother's presence won't change the fact that she's there, but will spoil the evening for me. I want to have a good time at my party. I don't need to worry about the fact that she's there. It doesn't need to be my problem and it's not worth getting upset about.

2   Does 'giving him the cold shoulder' help us to have a good relationship? Not speaking might punish him but it also creates tension in our relationship and makes us both feel bad. I want us to be happy together. Not communicating whenever I feel upset does not help us to have a good relationship. It's better to talk about it so that he understands how I feel.

3   Does telling myself that I shouldn't have come help me to feel good or do well in my exam? I'm here now—I may as well try to relax and enjoy the movie. In retrospect I can see that it wasn't a great idea to come, but telling myself that I shouldn't be here doesn't help with my exam preparation and only makes me feel bad. It's not worth worrying about it now—just relax and enjoy the movie.

4   Does focusing on her behaviour help me to enjoy my work? Focusing on her unethical behaviour doesn't change the situation. It stops me from enjoying my job and distracts me from what I'm meant to be doing. I've chosen not to say anything to her or my boss, so the best thing for me to do is not worry about it. She's not my problem.

EXERCISE 5.4

1 Someone you considered to be a friend was not available to help you when you needed them.

ACTIONS: Communicate—tell your friend how you feel (see Chapter 10).

BELIEFS: My friends should always be available when I need them. They should behave towards me as I would towards them. If they don't, they are horrible and deserve my utmost condemnation.

DISPUTE: It's disappointing that she was not there for me when I needed her, but I accept that this is one of her limitations. She has enough likeable qualities for me to want to keep our friendship, even though I have learned that I can't always count on her support.

2 Your partner has behaved very rudely in a social situation.

ACTIONS: Communicate. Explain how you feel, and why the behaviour upset you (see Chapter 10). Perhaps negotiate that the next time you socialise with people he doesn't like, he need not come along.

BELIEFS: He should always behave appropriately in social situations. It's awful when he doesn't. I am responsible for the way that he behaves. People will think badly of me.

DISPUTE: I need to talk to him about his behaviour and negotiate a solution but ultimately I am not responsible for him. It is unlikely that people will dislike me because of his behaviour.

3 A friend is constantly late. You have made a lunch arrangement with her and have been kept waiting for over an hour.

ACTIONS: Communicate. Tell her how you feel and what you would like (see Chapter 10). Perhaps in future, bring a book with you; arrive late yourself or don't make further social arrangements with her unless others are also going to be present.

BELIEFS: Everyone should have the same values as I do. It's very bad to be kept waiting.

DISPUTE: This is who she is. If the friendship is worth keeping, I may need to accept this aspect of her behaviour and find ways to avoid getting bored or angry.

4 Someone keeps putting their garbage in your paper recycling bin when you leave it out for collection.

ACTIONS: Talk to the neighbours. Try to identify who is doing it, and then speak to them directly. Put a sign on your recycling bin.

BELIEFS: People should always do the right thing. It's awful when things like this happen.

DISPUTE: Although most people do the right thing, some people don't. I don't like it, but I can accept it. I am doing what I can to resolve the problem.

5 You told someone something in confidence and now you have discovered that they have told others about it.

ACTIONS: Communicate (see Chapter 10).

BELIEFS: People should always do the right thing. Anyone who betrays my confidence is a terrible person and deserves my contempt.

DISPUTE: It's disappointing but I've learned a lesson. Although I can trust some people, I can't trust everyone. This person has some nice qualities but on this occasion she has let me down. I don't have to hate her for this.

6 You are extremely inconvenienced by some ridiculous bureaucratic procedure imposed by a particular government organisation.

ACTIONS: Communicate (see Chapter 10).

BELIEFS: Things should proceed easily and smoothly. Bureaucratic rules and procedures should benefit members of the public. They should be simple and efficient, and it's awful that they're not.

DISPUTE: I have tried to negotiate a simpler solution but I have not been successful. Bureaucratic organisations often have cumbersome, silly rules. I don't like it, but I can accept it. It is a pain in the neck but it's not a disaster.

7 You are kept waiting in a telephone queue for half an hour each time you try to call a particular telecommunications company.

ACTIONS: Try to call at less busy times. Keep yourself occupied with other tasks while waiting for a response. Use email or written correspondence whenever possible. Check out the competitors and consider changing to another company, if practical.

BELIEFS: The service should be prompt and efficient. It's awful to be kept waiting. They should put customers before profits.

DISPUTE: Telephone queues are a pain in the neck but they're part of the modern world we live in. I don't like it but I can stand it. Getting upset over something I cannot control only makes me feel bad and doesn't solve the problem.

8 You have been substantially overcharged by a tradesman.

ACTIONS: Communicate (see Chapter 10). Explain why you believe the bill to be excessive and suggest a compromise fee. Contact the Department of Fair Trading for advice. Consider sending what you regard to be reasonable payment.

BELIEFS: I am being ripped off. My perspective is the correct one. It's terrible to be overcharged.

DISPUTE: I've learned a lesson—in future I need to clearly negotiate the fee before I start. I have done what I can. Are my expectations reasonable? Perhaps it's not as outrageous as it sounds. For my own peace of mind, it may be better to just pay the bill and let it go this time.

9 The company you work for has a ruthlessly exploitative policy towards its employees.

ACTIONS: Communicate specific grievances to the relevant people (e.g. HR manager, management). Look for another job.

BELIEFS: It's a terrible situation, and I don't have a choice—I have to put up with this.

DISPUTE: My health—both psychological and physical—is 'number one'. No job, no matter how high-status and well-paid, is worth jeopardising my health. I have choices—I don't have to put up with this.

10 Someone is rude to you for no reason.

ACTIONS: Communicate or ignore them, as appropriate.

BELIEFS: If I am nice to other people, they should always be nice to me. It's awful if they're not. Rude behaviour is personal.

DISPUTE: I prefer people to treat me courteously, and most of the time they do, but I can stand it if on occasions some people do not. People behave badly for all sorts of reasons, and often it's more about them than me. I don't have to take this personally.

EXERCISE 6.5

1 Eve is anxious about going to a social function where she won't know anyone.

THOUGHTS/BELIEFS: I may end up standing by myself all night. People might look at me and feel sorry for me. They might think I have no friends or that I am a loser. If I am at a social function, I must be seen to be talking to people and having a good time. It's bad to be seen alone.

DISPUTE: Chances are I'll end up talking to people for at least part of the night—that has been my experience to date. Even if I am on my own for some or all of the night, it's unlikely that people will think badly of me for that. Most people can relate to not knowing anyone at a social function. Even if I stood on my own, and some people thought I had no friends, that's too bad. It's not my problem. At worst it may be a boring night, but it's unlikely to be a disastrous night.

POSITIVE ACTIONS: Tell the hostess that I don't know anyone—ask her to introduce me around. Offer to take plates of savouries around to the guests. Move out of my comfort zone—make an effort to go up and talk to people. Perhaps take a friend with me. If I'm totally bored, I can go home after a couple of hours.

2 Barry feels anxious about running late for a doctor's appointment.

THOUGHTS/BELIEFS: This is bad. I may miss my appointment. They will be cross with me. I should always be punctual. It's bad to be late. The consequences of arriving late are likely to be disastrous.

DISPUTE: I know from past experience that even when I am running late, I am never excessively late, and it's never a disaster. The worst possible thing that might happen is that I may miss my appointment, and I will have to pay for this one and make another appointment. That would be inconvenient but it would not be the end of the world. I could cope with it, if it should happen.

POSITIVE ACTIONS: Pull up for a moment, call the surgery on my mobile and let them know that I'm running a bit late. Relax.

3 Kim is anxious about having to give a speech to a large audience of professional people.

THOUGHTS/BELIEFS: They are professional people—they might know more than I do. They will see how nervous I am. They will think I'm incompetent. I might do a bad job or I might even fall apart. I must do a brilliant job. It would be awful if they could see that I was nervous or if they didn't think I was any good.

DISPUTE: Just because they are professional people, doesn't mean they are knowledgeable in my area. I have enough expertise on the subject to do a good presentation. I prefer to do a great speech and I'll do my best, but even if it's not brilliant, the consequences are unlikely to be disastrous. Even if I look nervous, that's OK. Many people get nervous when they're giving a speech. It's highly unlikely that I'll fall apart or that the audience will think that I'm incompetent. I have never fallen apart or done a terrible speech in the past. At worst, it may not be a great presentation but it won't be a disaster.

POSITIVE ACTIONS: Prepare thoroughly. Practise the speech in front of my friends. Record it onto a tape recorder and listen to it a few times.

4 Rick is anxious about having to make a potentially unpleasant phone call.

THOUGHTS/BELIEFS: He'll probably hate me. He might get aggressive. This might be very unpleasant. Everyone must like and approve of me. I should avoid conflict/disapproval at all costs. If he became aggressive, it would be awful, and I couldn't stand it.

DISPUTE: I don't know how he will react—he may or may not react badly towards me. I prefer to be liked (and many people do like me), but I accept that not everyone has to like me. It's OK if some people don't like me. I prefer to avoid conflict, but I am willing to risk conflict and I can cope with it if it should arise.

POSITIVE ACTIONS: Plan what I'm going to say—make some brief notes to jog my memory. Do it now—don't procrastinate.

5 Fay feels anxious about having to confront her neighbours about their dog, which is constantly barking.

THOUGHTS/BELIEFS: They will not like me if I complain. They might be hostile towards me. I should avoid the possibility of conflict with my neighbours. If they became aggressive, it would be awful, and I couldn't stand it.

DISPUTE: They have been friendly towards me in the past. I have no evidence that they will respond badly to me. If I communicate in a conciliatory way, chances are they will be reasonable. Even if they are not reasonable, I won't like it but I will stand it. It's important that I say something. If I don't communicate, they won't know that I have a problem.

POSITIVE ACTIONS: Plan what I'm going to say. Do it now.

6 Jeremy is anxious about an approaching job interview.

THOUGHTS/BELIEFS: They may ask me questions that I won't be able to answer. I may come across poorly or make a total fool of myself. I may not get the job. I should perform really well. I should be able to impress them. I should get the job. It would be awful if I performed poorly or didn't get the job.

DISPUTE: I'd like to do well, and I'll do my best, but if I don't do a fantastic interview, it will be a learning experience and not a disaster. It would be great to get the job, but if I don't, I can accept that. This is not a do-or-die situation. I may need to go to several job interviews before I am successful. That's part of the process for most people.

POSITIVE ACTIONS: Prepare thoroughly. Read up about the company. Prepare answers to some of the possible questions that they might ask.

7 Clive feels anxious about having to return some goods to the shop.

THOUGHTS/BELIEFS: They may feel put out by my request for a refund. They may not like me. They may end up being very unpleasant. People should always be nice to me. It's awful when people are rude or unpleasant. It's wrong for me to return goods to the shop.

DISPUTE: I have the right to return goods to the shop. They have the right to say 'no', but I have the right to ask. They may be perfectly reasonable. I know from past experience that when I expect the worst I am often pleasantly surprised. Even if they refuse to give me a refund, I will lose nothing by trying. I prefer people to be nice to me but I can cope even if they are not.

POSITIVE ACTIONS: Do it now. Don't procrastinate.

8 Olivia feels anxious because her daughter has slept in and may miss her flight for the holiday that she had planned.

THOUGHTS/BELIEFS: Jenny might miss her flight. It will be an absolute disaster if she does. This is my responsibility.

DISPUTE: It will be unfortunate if Jenny misses the flight, but if she does, chances are she will be able to get on another one. Other people also sometimes miss flights and, as far as I know, they always end up getting other flights. At worst, she may need to wait around for hours for the next available flight. It will be a hassle, but she will manage. Jenny is 22 years old—it is her responsibility to get up in time to catch her flight. I can do what I can to support her but I am not responsible for her in this situation.

POSITIVE ACTIONS: Help her get ready. Drive her to the airport.

EXERCISE 10.1

1 Someone has borrowed a book and has not returned it.

OBSERVATIONS: Pam, I lent you my copy of *The Road Less Traveled* in September last year, and when I asked you about it a few weeks ago, you said that you don't recall whether you still have it.

THOUGHTS/FEELINGS: The book is very precious to me, and I'm feeling rather upset at the possibility of not getting it back.

NEEDS: I'd really appreciate it if you had another look and made a special effort to find it.

2 You agreed to go to the trivia evening, but now you don't want to.

OBSERVATIONS: Jo, you remember I agreed to go to the 'Trivial Pursuits' night at St Joseph's on Saturday week?

THOUGHTS/FEELINGS: I feel bad about saying this, but I really don't want to go. At the time, I thought it was really nice of you to invite me, so I didn't want to be a bad sport. In retrospect, I wish I had been more honest with you.

NEEDS: I'm really sorry about backing out of it at this stage but I hope that you'll understand.

3 Your partner has been extremely irritable lately.

OBSERVATIONS: Ken, you seem to be very irritable lately. You have been getting upset about fairly minor issues, like when the paper didn't arrive on Thursday, and when Johnny didn't wash his hands before dinner. You've also been pretty uncommunicative with me in the past few weeks.

THOUGHTS/FEELINGS: I'm wondering if there's something wrong? Perhaps you're under a lot of stress at the moment? It really worries me when you're like this.

NEEDS: I'd like us to be able to talk about things and support each other if there's a problem—would you like to talk about it?

EXERCISE 10.2

1 A friend asks you to tell a lie to someone on his behalf. You feel uncomfortable with this.

BELIEFS: If someone asks me to do something I should always do it. She will disapprove of me if I say 'no'. I should never do things that might disappoint my friends.

DISPUTE: It's OK to say 'no' to requests for things that I don't want to do, even when the request comes from a friend. It's not really fair for her to put me in this position. If she is a good friend, she will respect my right to say 'no'.

ASSERTIVE STATEMENT: Jane, I really don't feel comfortable lying to Toby. I feel bad about saying 'no' because you're a close friend and I care about you. I hope you'll understand why I'm not able to help you with this.

2 The salesman has been serving you for over 40 minutes and he has been extremely pleasant and helpful. You have found something that is OK, but you're not really sure. You are aware that you've taken up a lot of his time.

BELIEFS: If a salesperson gives me good service I am obliged to buy something. He will be annoyed if I don't buy anything. It's important for him to like me.

DISPUTE: He gave me very good service, but he was doing his job. People who work in sales frequently have customers who spend a lot of time but don't buy anything. That is a normal part of their experience. I am not obliged to buy something if I haven't found what I want. Chances are he won't be annoyed but if he is, that's not my problem. I can acknowledge the good service without having to buy anything.

ASSERTIVE STATEMENT: You've been very attentive and helpful and I really appreciate it. Unfortunately, I still haven't found anything I really want. Thank you for all your help.

3 You get a call from someone you met while travelling overseas two years ago, and she wants to stay at your place for 'a while'. You're not too happy about the idea.

BELIEFS: If someone asks me to do something, I should always say 'yes'. She won't like me if I say 'no'. Everyone must like me.

DISPUTE: I have the right to put my own needs first. I am not under any obligation to put her up. It's OK to say 'no' if it doesn't suit me. If she doesn't like me, that's too bad. I can cope with that.

ASSERTIVE STATEMENT: I'd be happy for you to stay for a day or two while you are looking for accommodation, but it really doesn't suit me for you to stay here for more than a couple of days.

4 You have had dinner with friends at an expensive restaurant. You have not had any alcohol, while the others have drunk a lot. Although the alcohol alone comes to over $30 a head, when the bill is being worked out, no one suggests that you should pay less.

BELIEFS: I shouldn't speak up or they'll think that I'm tight. I should just go along with what other people expect. It's tacky to stand up for your rights when you're dealing with money.

DISPUTE: As the alcohol contributed to a major part of the bill, it is reasonable for me to not pay as much as everyone else. Speaking up is unlikely to cause people to disapprove of me, but if someone does, I can live with it. It's not going to make any difference to my life. It's OK for me to stand up for my rights, whether I am dealing with money or any other issue.

ASSERTIVE STATEMENT: As I've had no alcohol tonight, I'm going to put in my share, minus the drinks. I hope that's OK with everyone.

5 One of your colleagues at work has a habit of sitting down next to you and talking while you are trying to work.

BELIEFS: Asking him to leave is likely to offend him. I should never say anything that might offend people. I should never put my own needs before the needs of others. It's better to put up with it than to risk the possibility of his disapproval.

DISPUTE: It's OK to put my own needs first in this situation. It is appropriate for me to tell him that I'm busy—it's better to be honest than to feel resentful.

ASSERTIVE STATEMENT: Bill, I hope you'll excuse me. I really have a lot of work that I need to get on with.

6 You have already asked the two people sitting behind you in the cinema to stop talking. Now, ten minutes later, they have started talking again.

BELIEFS: Asking once is OK, but asking a second time might make them mad. It's not OK to make the same request a second time. They will think I am a pest if I ask again—they might be rude or abusive to me.

DISPUTE: It's OK for me to ask again. Some people need to be reminded about their noise because they are oblivious to the people around them. If I ask politely, I'm unlikely to get a hostile response, but if it happens, I'll deal with it.

ASSERTIVE STATEMENT: I'm sorry to ask you again, but it's still a problem. Would you mind not talking during the film?

7 You are watering your front garden when a dog that is being walked by its owner poos on your nature strip. The owner does not pick it up.

BELIEFS: If I say something, he'll get aggressive. People don't like being told what to do. It's better to say nothing.

DISPUTE: Dog owners have a responsibility to clean up after their dogs. It's reasonable for me to ask him to clean up the mess, as it affects me. He knows that it's his responsibility. If I ask him nicely, he is unlikely to be rude or aggressive; however, even if he is, I can handle it.

ASSERTIVE STATEMENT: Excuse me, your dog just did a poo on my nature strip. Would you mind cleaning up the mess?

8 A group of friends are at your house, and one of them lights up a cigarette. You have a no-smoking policy at your house.

BELIEFS: I shouldn't say anything because these are my friends. She won't like me if I ask her to smoke outside. When it comes to friends, I should put my own needs last.

DISPUTE: It's perfectly valid for me to ask her not to smoke in my house. These days, smokers are aware of other people's rights and are used to being asked not to smoke. It's highly unlikely that asking her not to smoke in the house will cause any bad feelings.

ASSERTIVE STATEMENT: Karen, would you mind going out on the balcony while you're smoking?

9 The coffee you ordered at a restaurant arrives lukewarm.

BELIEFS: Asking them to replace it with a hot cup of coffee will cause an inconvenience to the staff. I should never say anything that might inconvenience the staff, especially if they are busy. My needs are not that important.

DISPUTE: I am paying for the coffee—it's reasonable to expect to get what I paid for. It may be a slight inconvenience to them, but it's inconvenient to me to get lukewarm coffee. My needs matter, and it's OK for me to ask for what I want.

ASSERTIVE STATEMENT: Excuse me. This coffee is lukewarm. Would you mind getting me a hot cup of coffee?

10 A friend borrowed $200 four months ago and seems to have forgotten about it.

BELIEFS: Asking people to repay their debt is tacky. She might think that I am tight. She won't like it and she may not like me as a result.

DISPUTE: It's OK to ask her to repay the money that she borrowed from me. The money was lent on the understanding that it would be repaid, so it is not unreasonable to expect this. It is unlikely that she will dislike me for bringing it up, but if she does, that reflects poorly on her. If our friendship relies on me bailing her out and being totally submissive, it is not a very healthy friendship.

ASSERTIVE STATEMENT: Ruth, remember you still owe me $200 from when we went to the club? It's been four months now since I lent it to you, so could you arrange to pay it back?

Recommended reading

ANGER

Carter, L. & Minirth, F. (2012). *The Anger Workbook: An interactive guide to anger management*. Tennessee: Nelson.

Schiraldi, G. R. & Hallmark-Kerr, M. (2002). *Anger Management Source Book*. Chicago: Contemporary Books, Inc.

ANXIETY

Antony, M. & Norton, P. (2009). *The Anti-Anxiety Workbook: Proven strategies to overcome worry, phobias, panic and obsessions*. New York: Guilford Press.

Antony, R. & McCabe, R. (2004). *10 Simple Solutions to Panic: How to overcome panic attacks, calm physical symptoms and reclaim your life*. Oakland, CA: New Harbinger Publications.

Brantley, J. (2007). *Calming Your Anxious Mind: How mindfulness and compassion can free you from anxiety, fear and panic*. Oakland, CA: New Harbinger Publications.

Bourne, E. (2005). *The Anxiety and Phobia Workbook*. Oakland, CA: New Harbinger Publications.

Knaus, W. J. & Carlson, J. (2008). *The Cognitive Behavioral Workbook for Anxiety: A step-by-step program*. Oakland, CA: New Harbinger Publications.

Leahy, R. L. (2010). *Anxiety Free: Unravel your fears before they unravel you*. Carlsbad, CA: Hay House Inc.

DEPRESSION

Aisbett, B. (2000). *Taming the Black Dog: A guide to overcoming depression*. Sydney: HarperCollins Publishers.

Gilbert, P. (2009). *Overcoming Depression: A self-help guide using cognitive behavioral techniques*. London: Robinson Publishing.

Greenberger, D. & Padesky, C. A. (1995). *Mind Over Mood: Change how you feel by changing the way you think*. New York: Guilford Press.

Parker, G. (2004). *Dealing with Depression: A commonsense guide to mood disorders*. Sydney: Allen & Unwin.

Tanner, S. & Ball, J. (2012). *Beating the Blues*. Sydney: NewSouth Books.

Williams, M., Teasdale, J., Segal, Z. & Kabat-Zinn, J. (2007). *The Mindful Way through Depression*. New York: Guilford Press.

EFFECTIVE COMMUNICATION

Alberti, R. E. & Emmons, M. L. (2008). *Your Perfect Right* (9th ed.). San Luis Obispo, CA: Impact Publishers.

McKay, M., Fanning, P. & Paleg, K. (2006). *Couple Skills*. Oakland, CA: New Harbinger Publications.

McKay, M., Davis, M. & Fanning, P. (2009). *Messages*. Oakland, CA: New Harbinger Publications.

Paterson, R. J. (2000). *The Assertiveness Workbook*. Oakland, CA: New Harbinger Publications.

GENERALISED ANXIETY DISORDER; WORRY

Forsyth, J. P. & Eifert, G. H. (2007). *The Mindfulness and Acceptance Workbook for Anxiety: A guide to breaking free from anxiety, phobias, and worry using acceptance and commitment therapy*. Oakland, CA: New Harbinger Publications.

Gyoerkoe, K. L., Wiegartz, P. S. (2006). *10 Simple Solutions to Worry: How to calm your mind, relax your body, and reclaim your life*. Oakland, CA: New Harbinger Publications.

Leahy, R. L. (2005). *The Worry Cure: Seven steps to stop worry from stopping you*. New York: Harmony.

MINDFULNESS MEDITATION

Brantley, J. (2007). *Calming Your Anxious Mind: How mindfulness and compassion can free you from anxiety, fear and panic.* Oakland, CA: New Harbinger Publications.

Kabat-Zinn, J. (2012). *Mindfulness for Beginners.* Boudler, CO: Sounds True.

Williams, M. & Penman, D. (2011). *Mindfulness: Finding peace in a frantic world.* London: Piatkus.

Williams, M., Teasdale, J., Segal, Z. & Kabat-Zinn, J. (2007). *The Mindful Way through Depression.* New York: Guilford Press.

MOTIVATION

Burka, J. B. & Yuen, L. M. (2008). *Procrastination: why you do it, what to do about it now.* Cambridge, MA: De Capo Press.

Emmett, R. (2000). *The Procrastinator's Handbook: Mastering the art of doing it now.* Toronto: Doubleday Canada.

Pink, D. H. (2011). *Drive: The surprising truth about what motivates us.* New York: Riverhead Books.

OBSESSIVE COMPULSIVE DISORDER

De Silva, P. & Rachman, S. (2009). *Obsessive-Compulsive Disorder: The facts* (4th ed.). New York: Oxford University Press.

Foa, E. B. & Wilson, R. (2001). *Stop Obsessing: How to overcome your obsessions and compulsions.* London: Bantam Books.

Hyman, B. & Pedrick, C. (2010). *The OCD Workbook: Your guide to breaking free from obsessive compulsive disorder.* Oakland, CA: New Harbinger Publications.

St Clare, T., Menzies, R. & Jones, M. K. (2008). *DIRT [Danger Ideation Reduction Therapy] for Obsessive Compulsive Washers: A comprehensive guide to treatment.* Bowen Hills, QLD: Australian Academic Press.

Vaccaro, L. D., Jones, M. K., Menzies, R. G. & St Clare, T. (2010). *DIRT [Danger Ideation Reduction Therapy] for Obsessive Compulsive Checkers: A comprehensive guide to treatment.* Bowen Hills, QLD: Australian Academic Press.

PANIC ATTACKS

Aisbett, B. (2000). *Living With It: A survivor's guide to panic attacks.* Sydney: HarperCollins Publishers.

Bassett, L. (1997). *From Panic to Power: Proven techniques to calm your anxieties, conquer your fears and put you in control of your life.* New York: Harper Perennial.

Page, A. C. (2002). *Don't Panic: Anxiety, phobias and tension.* Sydney: ACP & Media 21.

Silove, D. & Manicavasagar, V. (2009). *Overcoming Panic: A self-help guide using cognitive behavioral techniques.* London: Robinson.

PERFECTIONISM

Antony, M. & Swinson, R. (1998). *When Perfect Isn't Good Enough: Strategies for coping with perfectionism.* Oakland, CA: New Harbinger Publications.

Shafran, R., Egan, S. & Wade, T. (2010). *Overcoming Perfectionism: A self-help guide using cognitive behavioural techniques.* London: Constable & Robinson.

SELF-ESTEEM

Fennell, M. (2009). *Overcoming Low Self-esteem: A self-help guide using cognitive behavioral techniques.* London: Robinson.

McKay, M. & Fanning, P. (2000). *Self-Esteem.* Oakland, CA: New Harbinger Publications.

McKay, M. & Fanning, P. (2005). *The Self-Esteem Companion.* Oakland, CA: New Harbinger Publications.

Schiraldi, G. R. (2001). *The Self-Esteem Workbook.* Oakland, CA: New Harbinger Publications.

SOCIAL PHOBIA

Antony, M. & Swinson, R. (2008). *The Shyness and Social Anxiety Workbook: Proven techniques for overcoming your fears.* Oakland, CA: New Harbinger Publications.

Butler, G. (2008). *Overcoming Social Anxiety and Shyness: A self-help guide using cognitive behavioral techniques.* New York: Basic Books.

Hope, D., Heimberg, R. G., Juster, H. R. & Turk, C. L. (2010). *Managing Social Anxiety: A cognitive behavioral therapy approach*. New York: Oxford University Press.

Rapee, R. M. (2004). *Overcoming Shyness and Social Phobia: A step-by-step guide*. Lanham, MD: Rowman & Littlefield.

TRAUMA

Cori, J. L. (2007). *Healing from Trauma: A survivor's guide to understanding your symptoms and reclaiming your life*. Cambridge: Marlowe & Company.

Schiraldi, G. (2009). *The Post-Traumatic Stress Disorder Source Book*. Chicago: McGraw-Hill/Lowell House.

Williams, M. B., Poijula, S. (2002). *The PTSD Workbook: Simple, effective techniques for overcoming traumatic stress symptoms*. Oakland, CA: New Harbinger Publications.

GUIDED RELAXATION AND MEDITATION CDS BY THE AUTHOR

Letting Go
Letting Go of Anxiety
Moments of Stillness
Sleep Soundly
Mindfulness Meditation

RECOMMENDED AUSTRALIAN CBT SELF-HELP WEBSITES

Anxiety Online: *www.anxietyonline.org.au*
Source: Swinburne University
Self-help treatments for Generalised Anxiety Disorder, Panic Disorder, Post Traumatic Stress Disorder, Obsessive Compulsive Disorder and Social Anxiety Disorder

Black Dog Institute: *www.blackdoginstitute.org.au*
Large number of professional and consumer resources for managing depression and bipolar disorder.

E-couch: *www.ecouch.anu.edu.au*
Source: Australian National University
Interactive self-help program with modules for depression, generalised
    anxiety disorder, social anxiety, relationship breakdown, and loss
    and grief.

MoodGYM: *www.moodgym.anu.edu.au*
Source: Australian National University
Interactive online CBT program for depression.

MoodSwings: *www.moodswings.net.au*
Source: University of Melbourne
Self-help program for adults with bipolar disorder.

OnTrack: *www.ontrack.org.au*
Source: Queensland University of Technology
Programs include treatment for depression, alcohol plus depression,
    psychotic episodes and support of relatives and friends of people with
    psychological problems.

This Way Up: *www.thiswayup.org.au*
Source: St Vincent's Anxiety Disorders Unit
Self-help programs for depression, generalised anxiety disorder (GAD),
    mixed depression and GAD, panic/agoraphobia, social phobia.
    Referral needs to be made by a clinician (GP, psychologist or allied
    mental-health professional).

References

Csikszentmihalyi, M. (1990). *Flow: The psychology of optimal experience*. New York: HarperCollins.

Gibran, K. (1980). *The Prophet*. London: William Heinemann Ltd.

Greiger, R. M. & Woods, P. J. (1993). *The Rational-Emotive Therapy Companion: Clear, concise, and complete guide to being an RET client*. New York: Scholars Press.

Horney, K. (1950). *Neurosis and Human Growth*. New York: WW Norton & Co Inc.

Jansen, D. & Newman, M. (1989). *Really Relating: How to build an enduring relationship*. Sydney: Random House.

Kabat-Zinn, J. (1990). *Full Catastrophe Living*. New York: Bantam Dell.

Matthews, A. (1988). *Being Happy: A handbook to greater confidence and security*. Singapore: Media Masters.

Matthews, A. (1990). *Making Friends: A guide to getting along with people*. Singapore: Media Masters.

McKay, M., Davis, M. & Fanning, P. (1995). *Messages*. Oakland, CA: New Harbinger Publications.

McKay, M. & Fanning, P. (2000). *Self-Esteem*. Oakland, CA: New Harbinger Publications.

Millman, D. (1992). *No Ordinary Moments: A peaceful warrior's guide to daily life*. Tiburon, CA: H J Kramer Inc.

Montgomery, B. (1995). *The Truth about Success and Motivation: Plain advice on how to be one of life's real winners*. Melbourne: Lothian Publishing.

Montgomery, B. (1983). *Living and Loving Together: A practical manual for better relationships*. Melbourne: Nelson.

Peck, M. S. (1978). *The Road Less Traveled*. London: Rider Books.

Peck, M. S. (1994). *Further Along the Road Less Traveled*. New York: Touchstone.

Russianoff, P. (1988). *When Am I Going to be Happy?: How to break the emotional bad habits that make you miserable*. New York: Bantam Books.

Tanner, S. & Ball, J. (2012). *Beating the Blues*. Sydney: NewSouth Books.

Index